THE BANBURY & CHELTENHAM DIRECT RAILWAY

Frozen water tank, Bourton-on-the-Water, circa 1910.
Michael Mitchell collection

Looking northwards across the Vale of Bourton towards the Slaughters in the mid 1930s. The railway runs across the middle of the photograph, coming down from Notgrove, off to the left, and passing behind the houses of Lansdown on a long embankment. It then executes a gentle curve to pass under Station Road and into Bourton-on-the-Water station, which is obscured by the clump of trees, before heading off north-east towards Stow-on-the-Wold. *Bob Brown collection*

THE BANBURY & CHELTENHAM DIRECT RAILWAY

STANLEY C. JENKINS,
BOB BROWN & NEIL PARKHOUSE

Lightmoor Press

Station Road, Stow-on-the-Wold, circa 1900. The station, however, lay a mile away to the south of this point, at the bottom of a long steep hill. The road was also part of one of the old Roman routes, the 'Fosse Way' ; today, this is the busy A46.
Neil Parkhouse collection

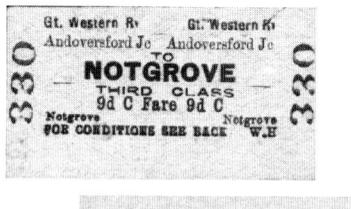

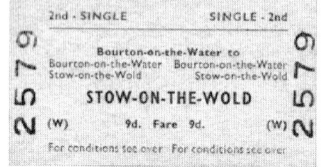

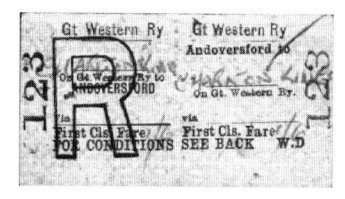

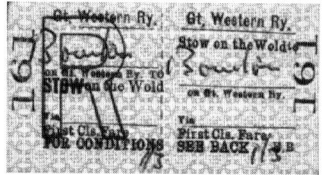

A selection of tickets from the western end of the line. *Paul Strong collection*

Copyright
Lightmoor Press, Stanley C. Jenkins, Bob Brown and Neil Parkhouse
2004
Designed by Neil Parkhouse

British Library Cataloguing-in-Publication Data. A catalogue
record for this book is available from the British Library
ISBN 1 899889 15 9

All rights reserved. No part of this publication may be reproduced, stored in a retrieval system or transmitted in any form or by any means, electronic, mechanical, photocopying, recording or otherwise, without the written permission of the publisher.

LIGHTMOOR PRESS
Unit 144B, Lydney Trading Estate, Harbour Road, Lydney Gloucestershire GL15 4EJ
www.lightmoor.co.uk
Lightmoor Press is an imprint of Black Dwarf Lightmoor

Printed by Cromwell Press, Trowbridge

CONTENTS

Introduction & Acknowledgements .... page 7
Preamble .... page 9

Chapter One .... page 11
ORIGINS OF THE LINE
The Historical Background ✣ Early Railway Development around Cheltenham ✣ The Oxford, Worcester & Wolverhampton Railway ✣ Origins of the Chipping Norton Railway ✣ Opening of the Chipping Norton Railway ✣ Some Details of the Chipping Norton Line ✣ The Bourton-on-the-Water Railway ✣ A Note on Early Locomotives

Chapter Two .... page 27
THE EAST GLOUCESTERSHIRE RAILWAY AND OTHER ABORTIVE SCHEMES
Some Abortive Railway Mania Schemes ✣ Formation of the Witney Railway ✣ The First East Gloucestershire Proposals ✣ The Second East Gloucestershire Proposal ✣ The Northampton & Banbury Junction Railway ✣ The Midland Counties & South Wales Railway ✣ Some Other Abortive Schemes

Chapter Three .... page 37
THE BANBURY & CHELTENHAM DIRECT RAILWAY
Formation of the Banbury & Cheltenham Direct Railway ✣ Construction Begins ✣ Completion Between Cheltenham and Bourton-on-the-Water ✣ Completion Between Chipping Norton and King's Sutton ✣ Opening Between Chipping Norton and King's Sutton ✣ Some Details of the Line ✣ The Cost of the Line ✣ The Midland & South Western Junction Railway ✣ The Andoversford & Stratford-upon-Avon Railway ✣ The Great Central Reaches Banbury ✣ Improvements to the Banbury & Cheltenham Direct Railway ✣ The Witney, Burford & Andoversford Light Railway

Chapter Four .... page 69
THE RAILWAY IN OPERATION
Passenger Train Services in the GWR Era ✣ The 'Ports-to-Ports' Express and Through Services ✣ Freight Trains and Traffic ✣ GWR Tank Engines on the Banbury to Cheltenham Line ✣ Tender Locomotives on the B&CDR Line ✣ Great Western Motor Bus Services ✣ Rural Delivery Services ✣ Other Developments in the 1920s & 1930s ✣ World War Two

Chapter Five .... page 119
THE ROUTE FROM CHELTENHAM TO BOURTON-ON-THE-WATER
Cheltenham Spa St James ✣ Cheltenham Malvern Road ✣ Lansdown Junction ✣ Cheltenham South & Leckhampton ✣ Charlton Kings ✣ The Leckhampton Quarries Branch ✣ Dowdeswell Viaduct ✣ Andoversford ✣ Syreford ✣ Notgrove ✣ Bourton-on-the-Water ✣ Stow-on-the-Wold

Chapter Six .... page 207
KINGHAM AND THE CHIPPING NORTON BRANCH
Kingham ✣ Churchill Crossing ✣ Sarsden Halt ✣ Chipping Norton ✣ The Bliss Mills ✣ William Bliss & His Family

Chapter Seven .... page 267
THE ROUTE FROM CHIPPING NORTON TO BANBURY
Rollright Halt ✣ Hook Norton Tunnel ✣ The Earl of Dudley's Siding ✣ The Hook Norton Viaducts ✣ Hook Norton ✣ The Hook Norton Ironstone Partnership ✣ The Brymbo Ironstone Works ✣ Bloxham ✣ Bloxham Ironstone Quarries (Clay Cross Company) ✣ Bloxham Quarries (Bloxham Ironstone Company) ✣ Milton Halt ✣ Adderbury ✣ Adderbury & Sydenham Ironstone Quarries ✣ King's Sutton ✣ Banbury

Chapter Eight .... page 337
THE FINAL YEARS
Locomotives & Train Services in the BR Era ✣ Closure Between King's Sutton & Chipping Norton ✣ Closure of the Cheltenham to Kingham Line ✣ Closure of the Chipping Norton Branch ✣ Some Post Closure Developments on the B&CDR Line ✣ The Railway Today

BIBLIOGRAPHY & FURTHER READING .... page 365
INDEX .... page 366

In a classic sunlit scene, which captures all that was so attractive about this Great Western branch line, '45xx' Class small prairie No. 4573 waits at Chipping Norton with a Kingham-bound service in the early summer of 1960. By this date, the station was once again the terminus of services from Kingham, passenger trains over the section between Chipping Norton and Banbury having been withdrawn in the summer of 1951. However, the occasional goods train still wandered through the tunnel to serve Rollright Siding. This section of the Banbury & Cheltenham Direct Railway was destined to last another two years when this photograph was taken, passenger and goods services east of Kingham being withdrawn completely on 3rd December 1962. The tree-lined station approach road can be seen to the right of the water tower. No. 4573 carries an 85A Worcester shed plate on its smokebox door and the engine was also nearing the end of its working life. Built at Swindon in November 1924, it was withdrawn from service just over a year after this picture was taken, in August 1961.

Photo D. Johnson, courtesy Millbrook House Ltd

Introduction & Acknowledgments

Stanley C. Jenkins, Bob Brown & Neil Parkhouse
August 2004

The Banbury & Cheltenham Direct Railway was one of those long, meandering, cross-country routes which the latter half of the 20th century had no need for. It grew piecemeal, through the second half of the 19th century, when the country was teeming with grandiose plans for railways hither and thither, and any town of any size fought to be connected to the network. For a while it became an important route for heavy ironstone trains and it also carried the 'Ports to ports' express across the lower spine of England, on its way between Newcastle and Swansea. Essentially, however, it was a country branch line, traversing glorious Cotswold territory, the nature of the terrain being one of the reasons so many people have fallen in love with it. As such, the age of the internal combustion engine brought about its demise, a protracted affair which began in 1951 and only finally ended in 1969. Today, reminders of its existence are not easy to find.

All three authors confess to a long and abiding interest in the Banbury & Cheltenham Direct Railway, for various diverse reasons because none of us ever travelled over any part of the route or, indeed, saw it in operation. Stanley's interest stemmed from a lifelong study of railway history and a particular interest in the local history of Oxfordshire. Many years ago, he had completed detailed manuscript histories of the Witney Railway and the Oxford, Worcester & Wolverhampton Railway (abbreviated versions of which were published by The Oakwood Press). Moreover, his MA dissertation on local railway history contained many references to the troubled history of the East Gloucestershire Railway and these inter-related studies have formed the basic narrative of the present book, albeit in greatly enlarged form.

Bob, who can just about recall steam at Cheltenham St. James station in 1966 at the tender age of three, had his interest stimulated by his passion for model railways and a desire to one day model one of the stations on the route. To this end, he amassed a collection of over 500 photographs of the line, which have formed the pictorial backbone of the book. He has also lived alongside the trackbed of the line near Hatherley all his life and has walked much of the entire route over the years. He was told that the crane used on the track-lifting operations frightened him as an infant, when its jib peered over the hedge at the bottom of the garden! His late father also dug up clay pipes left behind by the navvies who had built the bridge by their house. Quite naturally the trackbed and a nearby bridge were an unofficial playground for the children of the area and Bob and his brother were no exception. They even walked parts of the route as children but only as far as Leckhampton station, where the platforms and signal box remained. Alas he did not have a camera until a few years later but, by then, the main line trains at Cheltenham Lansdown station beckoned and, by the time he returned to the Kingham line a few years later, all that was left were the many bridges *en route*. It wasn't until he got his first car that he ventured further afield, to Notgrove and Bourton.

Neil had collected much historical material on the line, a legacy of 25 years dealing in old postcards and photographs. A wealth of historical pictorial material has passed through his hands, much of which has been copied or scanned. With the text having been largely the work of Stanley, to Bob and Neil fell the task of writing the captions for this huge collection of material.

It has proved a long job getting all of this material together and it was therefore to our great consternation that we found out another history of the line was in preparation by another publisher and a second set of authors. However, as we were already so far advanced in our endeavours, we decided to continue. What we hope to have achieved here is a well rounded, overall history of the line, throughout its existence, presented in a single volume, backed up with a plethora of maps, plans and photographs, which will furnish both local people and railway historians with a good picture of what the line was like. For those who want every last sleeper, detail and reminiscence, no doubt they will find much to please them in both histories.

The authors would like to express their thanks for general assistance and for help with locating photographs, maps and plans of the line, over a number of years and in no particular order, to the following: Roger Carpenter, without whom most prospective authors would find locating photographs much more difficult; the late John Smith (Lens of Sutton), sadly missed; Kate Robinson, for the use of photographs from the Nash Collection; Mike Barnsley, an unfailingly generous source of information on the Cheltenham end of the line; and to John Alsop, R.K. Blencowe, Alan Brain, Barry Davies, Mrs Freda Gittos, Michael Hale, Paul Laming, Julian Lane, Neil Lover, Michael Mitchell, Nigel Oram, John Strange, Paul Strong, Jane Cavell and Chris Turner.

We should also like to pay tribute to the staff at the various public bodies and institutions visited, for their courteous assistance with our many inquiries and searches. Again in no particular order, we should mention the Public Record Office at Kew, Kidderminster Railway Museum, the National Railway Museum at York, Cheltenham Museum, the Witney & District Museum, the House of Lords Record Office, the University of Leicester Library, Witney Library, Chipping Norton Library and finally the Oxfordshire County Council Photographic Archive at Oxford Westgate Library, the repository of the magnificent Packer Collection.

Special thanks go to Ross Lewis for the use of his wonderful photographs concentrating on the Cheltenham end of the line; to Barry Davies for the loan of some stunning early postcard views without which the coverage of the eastern section of the route would have been so much the poorer; and finally to Ian Pope for many hours spent drawing up maps and track plans, and also for providing much additional background information on coal merchants and other wagon owners connected with the line.

Finally, Bob would like to thank his brother Richard for his endless encouragement and for accompanying him on his many expeditions along the route of the Banbury & Cheltenham Direct Railway, and to record his appreciation to his mother, Sheila, and late father, for nurturing an interest in railways which has never diminished. Neil could not have brought this project to fruition without the support of his wife Heather, particularly in carrying out the thousand and one little tasks that need doing around a family household whilst he is buried in his office on the computer.

It is interesting to speculate if the B&CDR could have played any sort of role in the modern world. One can certainly see benefits in the tourist centres of Bourton-on-the-Water and Chipping Norton still being rail connected, as well as the southern outskirts of Cheltenham, which have expanded beyond all recognition. As for the rest ... well just maybe history was right.

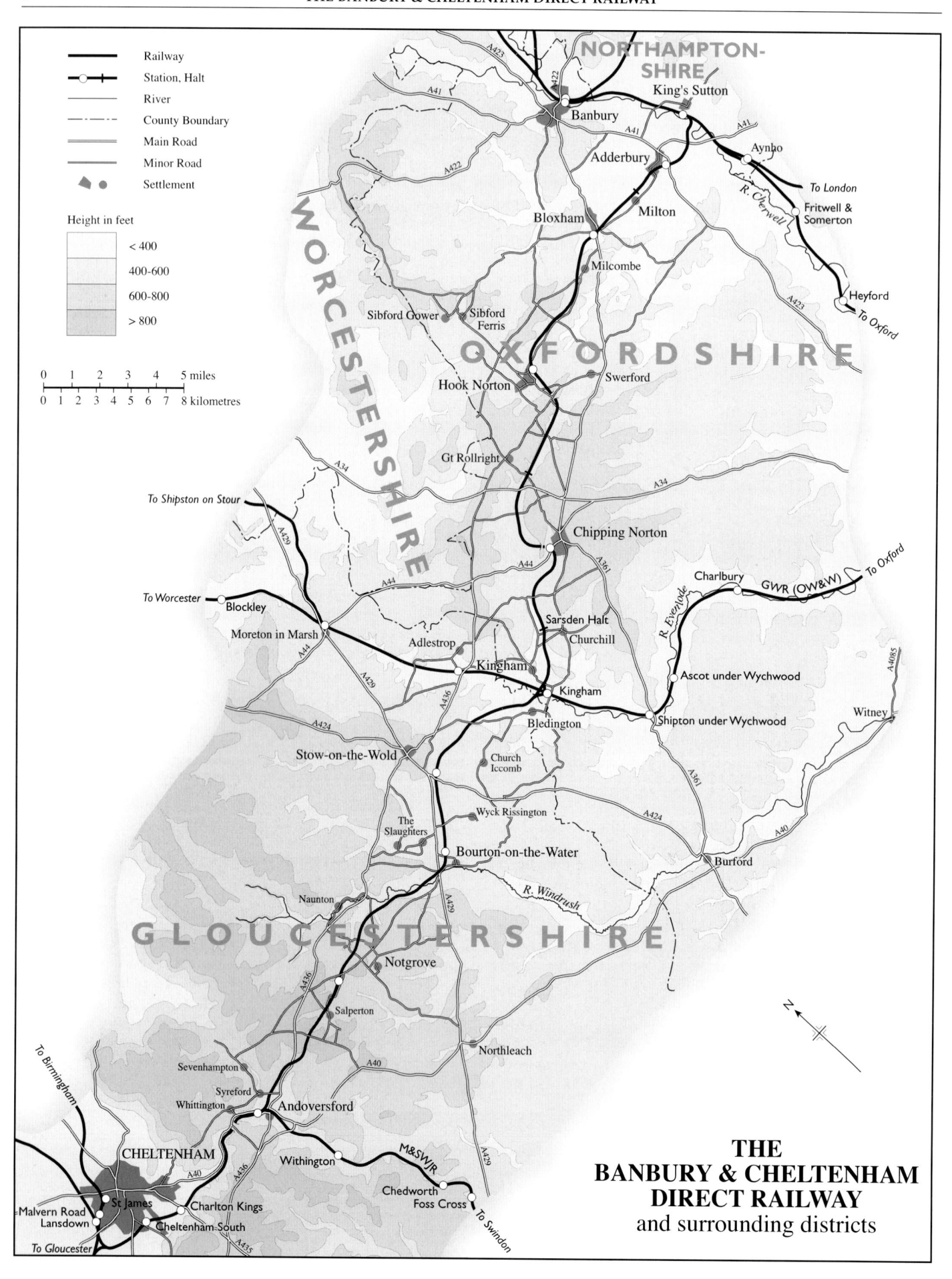

THE BANBURY & CHELTENHAM DIRECT RAILWAY and surrounding districts

Preamble

The Cotswolds are a distinctive region on the periphery of the West Country, with many attractive towns and villages. This area of Oolitic limestone is situated mainly in Gloucestershire, although the Cotswold Hills also extend into the neighbouring counties of Wiltshire and Oxfordshire. Prior to rationalisation, the Cotswold railway system incorporated many picturesque branch lines and cross-country routes. Most of these lines followed convenient river valleys, though one line – the lengthy cross-country route between Banbury and Cheltenham – ran more or less over the top of the hills.

This Great Western Railway line has a complex and interesting history. It involves the Oxford, Worcester & Wolverhampton Railway, and the nominally independent Chipping Norton and Bourton-on-the-Water Railways, as well as the GWR itself, which eventually absorbed all three companies. Later, an undertaking known as The Banbury & Cheltenham Direct Railway was formed, with the intention of linking the Chipping Norton and Bourton-on-the-Water branch lines, and integrating them into a new cross-country route between Banbury, Chipping Norton, Bourton-on-the-Water and Cheltenham. Although initially an independent concern, the B&CDR eventually passed into Great Western control.

The story of the Banbury & Cheltenham Direct line is made even more complicated by a lengthy and tortuous pre-history, involving unsuccessful, or partially successful lines, such as The East Gloucestershire Railway and the Northampton & Banbury Junction Railway. For example, the East Gloucestershire company obtained Parliamentary consent for a line from Cheltenham to Bourton-on-the-Water as long ago as the 1860s and managed to construct part of the route before abandoning its original scheme; the unfinished earthworks later became part of the Banbury & Cheltenham line.

This contorted history falls naturally into several distinct episodes and these, in turn, have formed an obvious basis for the following chapters. Chapter One deals with the early history of rail transport in the Cotswold area, and the construction and opening of the Chipping Norton and Bourton-on-the-Water Railways. Chapter Two outlines the unhappy history of the East Gloucestershire Railway and other abortive east-to-west cross country schemes, while Chapter Three covers the successful promotion of the Banbury & Cheltenham Direct Railway.

The strictly chronological sequence is interrupted by Chapter Four, which deals with operational details, and by chapters five, six and seven, which describe the stations and infrastructure of the Cheltenham to Banbury route in considerable detail. Finally, Chapter Eight covers the British Railways period, and the ultimate run-down and closure of the former Banbury & Cheltenham Direct Railway.

DISTANCES

The milepost distances between Kingham and Cheltenham Spa St James were calculated from Paddington, Kingham station being 84 miles 59 chains from London whereas Cheltenham St James was 121 miles from the Capital. Confusingly, the mileposts on the western section of the Banbury & Cheltenham Direct Line continued westwards from Kingham to Hatherley Junction – the latter point being 107 miles 78 chains from Paddington.

In the opposite direction, the official GWR distances ran eastwards, from 84 miles 59 chains at Kingham station to 89 miles 21 chains at or near the mid-point of the platforms at Chipping Norton new station. Thereafter, the official distances descended from 97 miles 75 chains at Chipping Norton to 82 miles 55 chains at King's Sutton station. This anomaly can be explained insofar as 82 miles 55 chains is the distance from Paddington to King's Sutton via Oxford and Heyford; Chipping Norton passenger station was thus 89 miles 21 chains from London via Kingham and 97 miles 75 chains from London via King's Sutton.

For the purposes of this present study, the datum point for the calculation of distances in chapters five, six and seven will be Cheltenham St James station. Moving eastwards in the Up direction, Kingham was 24 miles 17 chains from Cheltenham, while Chipping Norton was 28 miles 59 chains via Kingham station, and King's Sutton 43 miles 79 chains. Banbury, some 3 miles 41 chains to the north of King's Sutton, was thus 47 miles 40 chains from Cheltenham. This latter figure, therefore, was the total distance travelled by a passenger on his or her journey over the Banbury & Cheltenham Direct route, via Bourton-on-the-Water, Chipping Norton and King's Sutton, and inclusive of the necessary reversal at Kingham station.

Bourton-on-the-Water around a hundred years ago, before the age of the motor car and the advent of mass tourism. In this evocative scene, two little girls with a shopping basket between them pose shyly for the photographer as he captures the village centre on a warm summer's afternoon. An unidentified dray stands outside Fosters' grocers on the right, a box of Huntley & Palmers biscuits waiting to be carried inside the store. These will have arrived at Bourton goods shed for onward delivery. On the left, the white horse is attached to an unseen cart in the entrance to Bourton Mill, another local industry which made use of the railway. The sparkling River Windrush flows silently past in the foreground.
Neil Parkhouse collection

Chapter One

ORIGINS OF THE LINE

The remote, limestone uplands which form the Cotswold Hills are popularly associated with Gloucestershire, although in reality 'Cotswold' type scenery can also be found in other counties to the south-west and north-east. North-west Oxfordshire is geologically identical to the Gloucestershire Cotswolds but, as one travels east towards Banbury, the Oolitic limestone is replaced by underlying beds of Middle Lias or Marlstone – producing both building stone and deposits of ironstone. Visually though, the great swathe of countryside which was traversed by the Banbury & Cheltenham Direct Railway has an obvious unity and the term 'Cotswold' will therefore be applied indiscriminately.

The Oolitic uplands, which give the Cotswold area its distinctive character, reach a maximum elevation of 1,130 feet at Cleeve Hill near Cheltenham, though the hills fall gradually towards the south-east, where they eventually meet the Thames valley and the Oxford claylands. The principal rivers of the Cotswolds are the Thames, Windrush, Evenlode, Cherwell and Chelt, and some of the most attractive scenery is found along these river valleys. Although the appearance of the Cotswolds is determined by its geology, history has also helped to define the character of the region, and it would therefore be useful to fill-in a few brief details of the area in pre-railway times.

THE HISTORICAL BACKGROUND

In Roman times, the indigenous Celtic and pre-Celtic people of the district were known as the *Dobunni*, while their neighbours around the Thames valley area were the *Atrebates*. These early Britons were primarily farmers and traders, the *Dobunni* being a relatively advanced people who had issued their own coinage before the Roman invasion. The Romans, who occupied southern Britain in 43AD, commenced a long process whereby colonisation was extended into the less civilised tribal areas of the north and west but the *Dobunni* willingly accepted Roman rule and their territory was soon transformed into one of the most prosperous areas of the new province of Britannia.

The period of Roman occupation was significant in that it saw the construction of Akeman Street and the Fosse Way, as major arteries of communication which cut through the Cotswolds from east to west and from north-east to south-west respectively. In addition to these main roads, a network of subsidiary tracks enabled the rich agricultural lands of the Dubunnic areas to be fully exploited, with an emphasis on corn production in the valleys and sheep rearing on the higher land.

As far as can be ascertained, there were three large towns in the Cotswold area during the Roman period; *Glevum* (Gloucester), *Corinium* (Cirencester) and *Aquae Sulis* (Bath) to the south. The Roman countryside was covered by a patchwork of country estates, each of which had a large house or villa at its centre. These villas were typically situated in proximity to one of the Roman roads, good communications being an essential prerequisite for large scale commercial agriculture. One of the best-known villas was that at Chedworth, to the south of Andoversford, but others were scattered around the prosperous Cotswold area.

The official end of Roman rule in 410AD was followed by a period of social and political turmoil, known as the Dark Ages. In those years, urban life was abandoned, while the luxurious villas, such as that at Chedworth, became total ruins. The countryside was colonised by invaders from across the North Sea, including the Angles and the Saxons, who attacked the Britons and settled among them, imposing their Germanic language, laws and customs but never entirely eradicating the earlier Celtic population. The Romano-British city of *Glevum* was occupied by the Anglo-Saxons in 577 and, under its new name of *Glevumcaestre*, it subsequently became a county town and an important ecclesiastical centre.

The development of the Cotswold area was disrupted by a conflict between Wessex and Mercia, the likelihood being that these Oolitic uplands formed a natural barrier between the rival English kingdoms. The Kingdom of Mercia was at its peak during the 8th Century and much of the Cotswold area was under Mercian control by that time. In the event, the power of Mercia was soon destroyed by an invasion of Danish Vikings, who plundered and burned their way across England. The story of King Alfred's eventual victory over the Danes is well known; suffice to say, Wessex forces moved north into what was left of Mercia, making it a client state of Wessex and putting the Cotswolds under English control.

There had, meanwhile, been a significant development in that, for administrative purposes, England had been sub-divided into a system of shires. This system originated in Wessex, and it was gradually extended into Mercia and other parts of the country as Alfred and his descendants consolidated their control over the rest of England. The County of Oxford was in existence by the 10th Century, Oxford itself being laid out as one of the fortified 'burghs' which the West Saxons employed in their campaign against the Danes, while the surrounding territory became the newly created county of Oxfordshire. A similar situation pertained in the case of Gloucester, which become the county town of Gloucestershire.

Late Saxon England was undoubtedly one of the richest countries in Europe, and it was perhaps for this reason that it fell victim to William the Conqueror and his followers from Normandy. However, William had at least some claim to the throne, and he was clever enough to adapt the existing laws and institutions of England to his own needs. For this reason, the Norman Conquest did not mark any great break with the past, and the English system of manors, parishes and shires was retained as the basis of Anglo-Norman rule.

Over the next few centuries, the Cotswolds developed into one of the most prosperous parts of England, with a rural economy based firmly on agriculture and wool production. By 1334, Oxford was the eighth richest town in England in terms of its tax quota, while Gloucester was the sixteenth richest town in the country. This enviable wealth was based mainly on agriculture and especially wool production, which was already becoming a major activity throughout the Cotswold region.

Large scale sheep farming was particularly important by the end of the Medieval period, especially in the Cotswolds, and this in turn prepared the way for the creation of an important textile industry in the years to come. At the same time, as people moved from farming villages to urban settlements, such as Stow-on-the-Wold and Chipping Norton, these towns began to flourish as regional marketing and trading centres. Meanwhile, a growing 'middling class' of wool merchants and yeomen were quietly, yet inexorably, building up the nation's wealth, this new prosperity being underlined by a wave of church rebuilding throughout the Cotswold woollen region.

Church building seems to have ended at the Reformation, possibly because gothic architecture had became associated with the unpopular and discredited Roman Catholic church. The money and effort that had earlier been directed towards the beautification of religious buildings was then expended on secular architecture and, from about 1530 onwards, towns and villages such as Stow and Chipping Norton were extensively rebuilt in Cotswold stone. Their two, or even three storey buildings were in a cohesive architectural style, which derived visual unity from the employment of local building materials.

The Cotswolds had reached the peak of their prosperity by the early 17th century but the region suffered as a result of the Civil War, when towns such as Gloucester and Banbury sustained major damage. In 1646, for example, a petition to the House of Lords suggests that Banbury had been severely damaged, *'one halfe of the Towne'* having been *'burned down'*. Indeed, it could be argued that parts of the Cotswolds never fully recovered from the trauma of the Civil War.

By the following century the area was in decline. Little new building took place after 1700, and many of the remote Cotswold towns and villages entered a period of picturesque decay which would last until the 20th century. The Industrial Revolution led to the mechanisation of the textile industry, with the result that production became centralised in distinct areas such as Lancashire and the West Riding of Yorkshire. The West of England textile industry itself became concentrated in a handful of minor industrial towns, such as Witney and Stroud, while the surrounding Cotswold villages experienced economic distress and a loss of population as unemployed labourers left the area in search of work.

Relative decline continued into the 19th Century and, by the start of the Victorian period, the Cotswolds had become something of a backwater. There were, nevertheless, several towns of varying importance, notably the fashionable spa town of Cheltenham, and small market towns such as Witney and Chipping Norton, several of which had managed to retain their links with the traditional Cotswold woollen industry. Such towns would, in the next few years, play a major part in the creation of the local railway network, although in the short term Cheltenham was a more obvious target for early railway promoters.

EARLY RAILWAY DEVELOPMENT AROUND CHELTENHAM

The first railway in the Cheltenham area was the Gloucester & Cheltenham Tramroad, authorised in 1809, with powers for the construction of a line from the Gloucester & Berkeley Canal basin at Gloucester to Knapp Toll Gate in Cheltenham. This pioneering, horse-worked line was opened in 1811, and it was soon carrying coal and building materials to the flourishing and fashionable town of Cheltenham. Lines of this type were essentially products of the canal age, which functioned as extensions of the waterway system. They were rapidly superseded following the development of efficient steam locomotives during the 1820s and 1830s.

Railways were then a new and revolutionary form of transport but the obvious success of the Liverpool & Manchester Railway seemed to guarantee that this new system was safe and efficient. Inevitably, there were demands for new railways in the Gloucestershire area, one of the earliest lines being the Birmingham & Gloucester Railway, which was incorporated by Act of Parliament on 22nd April 1836. It was opened between Gloucester and Bromsgrove on 24th June 1840 and was completed throughout to Birmingham (Camp Hill) on 17th December 1840. The line was engineered by Captain William Scarth Moorsom (1804-63) and constructed to the standard gauge of 4 ft 8^1/$_2$ ins.

Another scheme promoted at this time was the Cheltenham & Great Western Union Railway, which, as its name suggests, was intended to form a connecting link between the town of Cheltenham, the city of Gloucester, and the Great Western main line at Swindon. The project was supported by the GWR and, with Isambard Kingdom Brunel (1806-59) as its Engineer, the railway was projected as a 7 foot broad gauge route. The Cheltenham & Great Western Railway Bill received the Royal Assent on 21st June 1836 and the resulting Act provided consent for railways from Cheltenham to *'the east side of the new cattle market'* at Gloucester, and from Gloucester to a junction with the Great Western Railway near Swindon.

As the proposed line between Cheltenham and Gloucester would otherwise have been parallel to the Birmingham & Gloucester Railway, Parliament decided that this part of the line would be shared between the two companies. To facilitate this plan, the existing Gloucester & Cheltenham

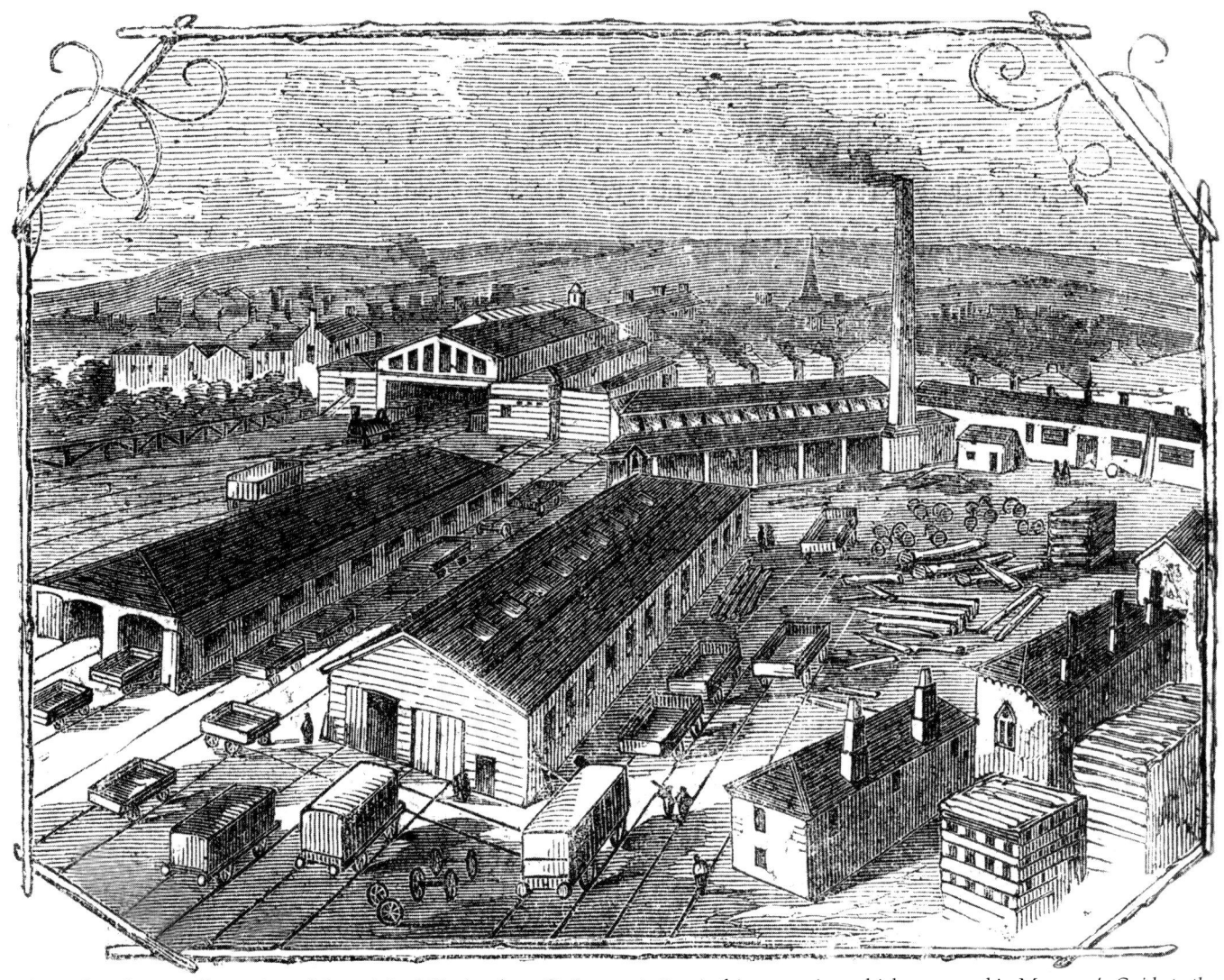

The earliest known illustration of the original Cheltenham St. James station is this engraving which appeared in Measom's *Guide to the Great Western Railway*, published in 1856. It shows the station, with its wooden buildings and overall roof, in broad gauge days. In the foreground is Mr Shackleford's Railway Carriage & Wagon Works, which was an important supplier of wagons and carriages at this time, in broad and standard gauges. The company relocated to Swansea a few years later. *Neil Parkhouse collection*

Tramroad would be purchased for £35,000 and part of its route would then be incorporated into the new railway. Meanwhile, further to the south of the county, an entirely separate company, known as the Bristol & Gloucestershire Railway, had succeeded in obtaining an Act for construction of a 10-mile line from Bristol Harbour to collieries near Coalpit Heath.

When opened on 6th August 1835, this single track line was worked by horses, an attempt to introduce steam traction having ended in total failure when an experimental 'steam carriage' blew up during a trial run. Undeterred by this setback, the proprietors of the Bristol & Gloucestershire line envisaged that their route might one day be continued towards Gloucester and on 1st July 1839 they obtained another Act, providing Parliamentary consent for a 22-mile extension to a point later known as Standish Junction, on the Cheltenham & Great Western Union line. By this same Act, the B&G company became known as the Bristol & Gloucester Railway.

At this stage, the Bristol & Gloucester Railway was still an independent concern but logic dictated that the B&GR should move towards closer association with the C&GWUR. As the Cheltenham company was itself an ally of the GWR (it was purchased outright in 1843), the Bristol & Gloucester Railway was brought firmly into the Great Western sphere of influence. Brunel had already been appointed engineer to the B&GR company and it was agreed that the line would be built as a broad gauge route, in conjunction with the Cheltenham & Great Western Union Railway.

The B&GR line was ceremonially opened between Bristol and Gloucester on 6th July 1844 and public services began two days later, a temporary station at Gloucester having been erected alongside the terminus of the standard gauge Birmingham & Gloucester line. The Cheltenham line was not yet complete, although a 7 mile 30 chain section of it between Standish Junction and Gloucester had been constructed and opened in connection with the B&GR, by arrangement between the two companies.

The Cheltenham & Great Western Union Railway was opened between Swindon and Kemble on 31st May 1841, and extended from Kemble to Standish Junction on 12th May 1845. Great Western services began running north-eastwards into Cheltenham on 23rd October 1847, broad gauge rails having been installed on the existing Birmingham & Gloucester line.

In the interim, there had been an important development; in 1845, the Birmingham & Gloucester Railway had been amalgamated with the Bristol & Gloucester company to form the Bristol & Birmingham Railway. Parliament refused to sanction this amalgamation but, in 1846, the two Gloucester companies were absorbed by the Midland Railway – itself the result of an amalgamation in 1844 between the Birmingham & Derby Junction, the Midland Counties and the North Midland railway companies. The Midland began working the Bristol & Birmingham line on 7th May 1845 and this arrangement was formalised by Act of Parliament on 3rd August 1846.

As a result of these complex developments, Cheltenham gained two main line stations, the Midland station being a through station on the Bristol to Birmingham line, whereas the Great Western station at St James was a terminus to the east of the Midland line. The rival lines merged at Lansdown Junction and then continued as a mixed gauge route towards Gloucester. Confusingly, the Gloucester to Cheltenham section was not a 'joint' railway in the accepted sense, because the southern end of the line was regarded as part of the Midland Railway, whereas the northern half was wholly-owned by the Great Western company.

THE OXFORD, WORCESTER & WOLVERHAMPTON RAILWAY

The first line to penetrate the Cotswold area had been the Great Western Railway, which was opened throughout its length from London to Bristol by 1841. The GWR management was soon planning extensions to the north and west of the original main line, one of these being the C&GWUR, which, as already noted, was completed throughout to Cheltenham in October 1847. Meanwhile, other GWR-backed lines were being planned elsewhere in the Cotswold area, an important first step in the northwards advance towards Worcester and Birmingham being the Oxford Railway, which was sanctioned by Parliament on 11th April 1843.

The Great Western opened its branch from Didcot to Oxford on 12th June 1844 and, in the following year, Bills were sent up to Parliament seeking consent for two northwards extensions from it, one of which would run north-westwards towards Worcester and Wolverhampton, while the other would extend boldly northwards along the Cherwell Valley, in the direction of Rugby. These two related schemes were entitled the Oxford, Worcester & Wolverhampton Railway, and the Oxford & Rugby Railway. Both projects would ultimately be of great importance in relation to the future Banbury & Cheltenham Direct line, though in the 1840s and 1850s the OW&WR scheme was of immeasurably greater significance.

The Oxford, Worcester & Wolverhampton Railway had been promoted by Black Country industrialists and coal owners, hoping to build a main line from Oxford, through Moreton-in-Marsh and Worcester, to Wolverhampton. The OW&WR was initially seen as a full member of the Great Western 'family' and with Brunel as its Engineer, this new main line through the Cotswolds was planned as an important broad gauge route.

At a public meeting held in the Guildhall at Worcester, Francis Rufford, a Stourbridge banker who was to become chairman of the OW&WR, declared that by adopting the Great Western broad gauge, the Worcester line would gain untold advantages, not only because of the increased speeds made possible by the wider gauge but also because of the bigger loads that could be carried in broad gauge vehicles. He went on to say that, although they were independent of the GWR, *'they had, in their dealings with that company, received from them the most courteous treatment; and in future proceedings should act only in connection with them, and in confirmation with their advice and recommendations.'*

With enthusiastic support from West Midlands manufacturers and the backing of the Great Western Railway, the Oxford, Worcester & Wolverhampton Bill was presented to Parliament in the early months of 1845, together with a related Bill for a northwards extension of the broad gauge from Oxford to Rugby. Both lines would diverge from the existing Great Western railhead at Oxford, the OW&WR line heading north west to Worcester via the Evenlode Valley, while the Oxford & Rugby Railway would strike due north along the Cherwell valley towards Banbury.

Although at first glance the idea of two broad gauge main lines to the north may have been somewhat extravagant, the Great Western plans were quite logical. The Worcester line, intended to connect with the Grand Junction Railway at Wolverhampton, would enable goods and passengers from the GWR to reach the west coast main line to Scotland, whereas the O&RR would provide a useful connection with the Midland Counties system at Rugby.

The two Great Western Bills passed through Parliament at a time in which there was immense concern over the evils of the 'break of gauge'. Indeed, certain radical politicians were known to favour state intervention to ensure eventual uniformity of gauge. The Bills were, as a result, subjected to unprecedented scrutiny but, in spite of bitter opposition from the London & Birmingham and Midland railways, as well as individual politicians such as Richard Cobden, the Oxford & Rugby and Oxford, Worcester & Wolverhampton Bills both received the Royal Assent on 4th August 1845.

The Oxford, Worcester & Wolverhampton Railway Act (*8 & 9 Vic.cap.184*) provided consent for the construction of a railway from the Oxford branch of the GWR, through Evesham and Worcester, to the Grand Junction Railway station at Wolverhampton, with branches to the River Severn at Diglis Basin, to the Birmingham & Gloucester Railway at Stoke Prior, from Amblecote to Stourbridge, and from Brettel Lane to Kingswinford.

The Act stipulated that the OW&WR was to be *'constructed and completed in all respects to the satisfaction of the engineer for the time being to the Great Western Railway'*, and be *'formed of such a gauge, and according to such mode of construction as will admit of the same being worked continuously with the said Great Western Railway'*. The Great Western was empowered to complete the 89-mile line, should the OW&WR fail to do so, and six of the sixteen directors of the new company were to be Great Western nominees.

Construction was soon under way on the new main line

An early view of the original OW&WR station at Moreton-in-Marsh, some 6 miles to the north of Chipping Norton Junction. The station buildings seen here were quite different in appearance to those at Chipping Norton Junction, which had a 'cottage' style main building and a much larger canopied roof to its wooden island platform building. This photograph dates from circa 1860, in which year the OW&WR became a constituent of the newly formed West Midland Railway. *Neil Parkhouse collection*

but wet weather and a series of failed harvests in 1845, 1846 and 1848 brought an abrupt end to the railway building boom. At a time when most of the nation's surplus capital was tied up in new railway schemes, the Victorian stock market collapsed and in these melancholy circumstances many of the grandiose projects promoted during the Railway Mania failed in their entirety, while other projects were severely impeded as their hapless promoters struggled to raise sufficient capital. By 1848, there was revolution in Europe and mass starvation in Ireland.

The OW&WR main line was still, as yet, unfinished, although in September 1849 the long-suffering shareholders were told that from Tipton to Dudley the line was *'practically completed and ready to receive the permanent way'*. From Dudley to Stourbridge, a distance of about 4 miles, very little had been accomplished but south of Stourbridge, the sections of line between Droitwich and Worcester, Droitwich and Stoke Prior, and from Worcester to Pershore were *'nearly ready to receive the permanent way'*.

From Pershore towards Shipton-under-Wychwood the works were in a forward state but the southernmost extremity of the line was the least advanced. On 5th October 1850, a single line between Abbots Wood Junction on the Midland line and a temporary station at Shrub Hill was brought into use. However, with Campden Tunnel, to the north of Moreton-in-Marsh, still unfinished there seemed little possibility of an early opening of the main line to Oxford. The OW&WR directors had appealed to the GWR for help but the latter company was itself suffering during the prevailing trade depression and could do little to assist its former protégé.

However, the Great Western seemed to be hurrying on with the completion of the rival Oxford & Rugby main line between Banbury, Birmingham and Wolverhampton. The OW&WR directors, viewing this as a monstrous breach of faith, broke away from their former GWR allegiance and formed a new alliance with the rival London & North Western Railway. An agreement signed on 21st February 1851 opened the way for completion of the OW&WR as a standard gauge line, worked with the aid of L&NWR locomotives and rolling stock.

The Oxford & Rugby Railway was opened between Oxford and Banbury on 2nd September 1850 and, on 1st October 1852, a further extension enabled GWR trains to run to and from Birmingham. Meanwhile, after many vicissitudes, the OW&WR was being built in stages and, on 1st May 1852, a major portion of the line, between Stourbridge and Evesham, was ceremonially opened. A further ceremony took place on 2nd April 1853, when the OW&WR directors decided to open the line between Evesham and Oxford. Public services finally began on Saturday 4th June 1853, when the southern portion of the Oxford, Worcester & Wolverhampton main line was completed throughout to Oxford.

The new main line was a mixed gauge route, although it never carried broad gauge traffic. Intermediate stations were provided on the Oxford to Worcester section at Handborough, Charlbury, Ascott, Shipton, Adlestrop, Moreton, Blockley, Campden, Honeybourne, Evesham, Fladbury and Pershore. These wayside stopping places immediately became railheads for the surrounding Cotswold area and in some places the OW&WR engaged local carriers to provide road feeder services to nearby towns such as Witney and Winchcombe.

ORIGINS OF THE CHIPPING NORTON RAILWAY

The first railways in the Cotswold area were essentially main line routes connecting major centres of population, such as London, Worcester and Birmingham. Although they also served numerous towns and villages *en route*, there was still a demand for short distance branch lines which would provide useful rail links for communities that had been by-passed by the main line routes. Accordingly, a variety of local branch lines were constructed as feeders for the main

This lovely panoramic study of Chipping Norton, taken from the Churchill Road sometime in the 1930s, shows William Bliss's beautifully proportioned mill building nestling in the valley below. The view was taken by Frank Packer, the Chipping Norton photographer, whose work is extensively featured in these pages. *Oxfordshire County Council Photographic Archive*

line system. One of these was the Chipping Norton Railway, a company formed in 1853 to construct a branch line between the OW&WR main line and the Oxfordshire market town of Chipping Norton, some $4^1/_2$ miles to the east.

The promoters of the Chipping Norton scheme included local mill owner William Bliss (1810-1883) and William Simkins Hitchman (1799-1881), the proprietor of Hitchman's Brewery. William Bliss, who had inherited a thriving textile firm from his father, had already introduced steam power into his mills but the construction of a railway would enable him to obtain ample supplies of coal fuel at a much lower cost. Similarly, W.S. Hitchman was a leading member of the local trading community, who had an obvious interest in the provision of improved transport links in this hitherto remote part of the Oxfordshire Cotswolds.

There was support, too, from farmers and landowners, who would be able to use the suggested railway to send their cattle, milk and other products to markets in distant places such as London and the Midlands. In this context, the backing of James Haughton Langston MP, who resided at neighbouring Sarsden House, was of particular importance. J.H. Langston was a major landowner and as he owned most of the land upon which the railway would be built, his approval was essential.

The promoters also approached Samuel Morton Peto MP (1809-1889), a major supporter of the Oxford, Worcester & Wolverhampton Railway, who agreed that the OW&WR would work the proposed branch line as an integral part of its own system. Peto – who would shortly be created a baronet – also agreed to become a major investor in the Chipping Norton Railway scheme and he was thereby able to exert considerable influence over the entire project.

As a contractor (rather than a financier or engineer), Peto had already earned enough money to set himself up as a country gentleman at Somerleyton Hall, near Lowestoft in Suffolk. Born in Woking in 1809, S. Morton Peto (who rarely used his first name) had started work for his uncle's contracting company and in 1830 he inherited half the firm in conjunction with his cousin, Thomas Grissell. By the end of the 1840s, Peto had already constructed numerous railways, invariably in partnership with Edward Ladd Betts (1815-1872). He had also secured major interests in many companies, including the Eastern Counties, East Suffolk and Oxford, Worcester & Wolverhampton railways.

Like James Langston, Peto was an influential figure and his involvement was an incalculable advantage. Moreover, Peto was a dominant force within the OW&WR company, and

Sir Samuel Morton Peto. *S.C. Jenkins collection*

their support was thereby assured. Accordingly, on 31st July 1854, the Oxford, Worcester & Wolverhampton Railway (Chipping Norton Branch) Act received the Royal Assent.

The Chipping Norton Branch Act provided consent for a railway commencing by a junction with the OW&WR main line *'situated midway between Shipton and Adlestrop stations, where a house has been erected for the issue of tickets'* and terminating in Chipping Norton. The proposed line would be 4 miles 42 chains long and to pay for its construction, the promoters were authorised to raise the sum of £26,000; £14,000 was provided by Sir Morton Peto, while the remaining £12,000 was subscribed by William Bliss, W.S. Hitchman and other local investors.

The chosen route ran generally north-eastwards from 'Chipping Norton Junction' to the proposed terminus at Chipping Norton, the valley of the River Swale being followed for a distance of over 3 miles. Construction began in August 1854, under the overall direction of John Fowler (1817-1898), who, in 1852, had replaced Brunel as Engineer-in-Chief to the OW&WR. Perhaps inevitably, the main contract was awarded to Messrs Peto & Betts, this being S.M. Peto's own firm.

Cynics might wonder how Morton Peto could have awarded such a contract to his own firm without attracting a barrage of criticism. On the other hand, as he had clearly invested a large amount of his own money in the scheme, the great contractor was probably regarded as something of a public benefactor. In practice, Sir Morton Peto liked to play a leading role in as many railway projects as could – yet there seems little doubt that his energy and vision was an immense advantage as far as the Chipping Norton line was concerned. Most of Peto's railway contracts were pressed forward at a furious rate and the Chipping Norton Railway was to be no exception.

In fact, the rate of progress was phenomenal and the railway was virtually completed within a period of about nine months. Unfortunately, problems arose when the Board of Trade Inspector objected to a level crossing that Morton Peto, in conjunction with John Fowler, had built near the village of Cornwell. Having obtained much of his experience of railway construction in the relatively flat areas of East Anglia, Peto saw nothing inherently wrong with the idea of railways crossing public roads on the level and, in accordance with his usual practice, he had laid out the Chipping Norton line with a number of public and private level crossings.

The Board of Trade tended to regard level crossings as sources of danger, particularly during the earliest days of railway construction, when road users were sometimes unable to estimate the speed of approaching trains. In the case of the Chipping Norton line, there was disagreement in respect of a level crossing that had been installed in lieu of an overbridge, about 1½ miles to the south of Chipping Norton. The controversial crossing carried a minor road across the railway, the route in question being used as a short cut between Chipping Norton and the OW&WR station at Adlestrop.

The railway company pointed out that this traffic would cease when the new branch line was open, because goods and passengers that had formerly travelled via Adlestrop would immediately start travelling to and from the new station at Chipping Norton. This perfectly logical argument failed to convince the Board of Trade inspector, who refused to 'pass' the Chipping Norton Railway as safe for the carriage of passengers until the offending level crossing had been replaced. It was, in consequence, agreed that the railway would be opened for goods traffic but not for passengers and, on Saturday 2nd June 1855, the *Oxford Chronicle & Berks & Bucks Gazette* printed the following brief report:

'BRANCH RAILWAY - The opening of this line for goods traffic is expected to take place in a few days, a further postponement of the opening for the conveyance of passengers being unavoidable.

The Board of Trade seeming inclined to insist on a bridge being erected in place of a level crossing, as at present, near Swalesford Bridge, a necessity for which exists only in their imagination, the average number of vehicles being very few per day, and more than half of those which now cross it being destined to Adlestrop Station for coal, etc, all of which traffic will cease as soon as the line is opened.

A large majority of our townsmen have petitioned against the bridge as unnecessary, and far less safe than the crossing, and at a little distance further up the line, when a bridge is erected, the residents near would be only too glad to have it exchanged for a level crossing'.

The railway was, accordingly, opened for goods traffic, apparently without ceremony. In a subsequent report, on Saturday 9th June, the *Oxford Chronicle* stated that *'the branch from the Oxford, Worcester & Wolverhampton Railway to Chipping Norton was opened on Friday last for goods and cattle traffic'*. It is unclear if the opening had taken place on the previous day (i.e. Friday 8th June), or in the preceding week (1st June). There is, moreover, confusion in that, in its report of the opening for passenger traffic on 18th August 1855, the same newspaper reported that goods traffic had commenced *'on Whit Monday'*.

These conflicting dates suggest that the railway may have opened for business on a Friday, whereas the first incoming goods train may have arrived in the terminus on the following Monday. Despite this confusion, it was reported on 9th June that *'considerable quantities of merchandise'* had already been received and despatched from the new station, while the inhabitants of Chipping Norton and the surrounding district were already able to *'procure coal at a reduced rate'*. Coal traffic, in fact, was an important source of revenue from the very start and, in this context, William Bliss had earlier estimated that his mills required 3,800 tons per annum.

The first weeks of operation did not pass without incident and, on Thursday 5th July 1855, the newly-opened terminus was the setting for an alarming accident that could easily have proved fatal. On the day in question, the diminutive OW&WR tank locomotive which had been allocated to Chipping Norton as the designated branch engine, failed to stop when approaching the terminus at the head of an incoming goods train, due at 11.00 am. Mr Wheeler, Chipping Norton's first station master, was on the footplate at the time and when he realised that the train was not going to stop, he attempted to jump onto the platform.

The train was moving relatively slowly and the station master may have hoped to pin down some of the wagon brakes to avert a greater disaster. Unfortunately, he slipped on landing and fell against the train, breaking his leg below the ankle and suffering cuts and abrasions. The runaway train, meanwhile, continued through the platform and finally crashed violently into two cattle wagons and one coal wagon that had been left against the stop blocks at the very end of the line.

The ensuing impact pushed the three goods wagons into the buffer stops, the coal wagon being *'driven into the bank'*. As the speed of the train was presumably very low at the time of the collision, the engine sustained little damage *'other than one buffer'*. Mr Wheeler was less fortunate; in its account of the accident, published on 7th July 1855, the *Oxford Chronicle* reported that he was recovering from his injuries but was still weak from loss of blood.

On a happier note, the railway was ceremonially opened for the carriage of passenger traffic on Friday 10th August, a compromise agreement having been made with the Board of Trade concerning the level crossing dispute. In the meantime, the BoT's Inspecting Officer, Lieutenant-Colonel Yolland, had submitted the following report, dated 26th July 1855, on the new railway:

REPORT ON INSPECTION OF CHIPPING NORTON RAILWAY
Sir,
In compliance with the instructions contained in your letter of the 19th instant, I yesterday inspected the Chipping Norton Branch of the Oxford, Worcester & Wolverhampton Railway, and I have the honour to report, for the information of the Lords of the Committee of Privy Council for Trade, that this branch line is of 4½ miles in length and extends from the junction with the main line of the Oxford, Worcester & Wolverhampton Railway, situated midway between Shipton and Adlestrop stations, to the town of Chipping Norton. It is laid with a single line of rails throughout with sidings at the junction, at Chipping Norton and at Churchill.

The land has been purchased and the works constructed with a view to making a double line hereafter.

The width of the line at formation level is 19 feet, the gauge 4ft 8½in; the rails are double flanged edge rails in lengths of 21 and 24 feet, averaging 60 Lbs weight per linear yard: the chairs are of cast iron, weighing 30 Lbs at the joints and 20 Lbs for the intermediate chairs and they are fixed to the sleepers with 2 wrought iron spikes ⅞ inch in diameter. The rails are secured to the chair by compressed elm keys. The sleepers are of larch, the scantling being mostly 8ft 6in x 9in x 4in placed transversely at the average distance of 3 feet apart: the ballast is of gravel 20 inches in depth.

There is, at the present time only one bridge (over) on the line, and it appears to be substantially constructed.

The embankments and cuttings are very light and the line is throughout in good order. There are no viaducts, and no turntables have been constructed, as it is intended to work the line with a single tank engine.

There is only one station on the line, viz: that at Chipping Norton, but a house has been erected at the junction for the issue of tickets to passengers.

Two public level crossings now exist on the line, both are provided with gates which close the road but not the rails, and a lodge has been erected at one and the foundations built for another. The Company's Act 17 & 18 Vic.C.209 sec X authorises both of these level crossings, but under the powers contained in Sec XII of the same act, the Board of Trade made an order dated 11th May last that a bridge should be substituted for one of these level crossings, that numbered 5 on the deposited plans of the Parish of Churchill, and in

The only known representation of the terminus at Chipping Norton is on this engraving of Bliss's mills, from a company letterhead. It shows the rebuilt lower mill of 1875, on the right but this may have been superimposed on an earlier engraving; the locomotives depicted in the station look more circa 1860. The view has also been 'manipulated' to fit everything in – the Bliss family residence on the left, the upper mill and the lower mill, leaving the latter apparently on the wrong side of the railway line. The location of the two storey station building is correct, although there is no sign of the train shed, whilst the goods shed appears rather on the large size. The suggested layout equates with the early track plan, opposite, including the weighbridge in the foreground. It would have been highly unlikely, however, to have seen two locomotives here at the same time. *Oxfordshire County Council Photographic Archive*

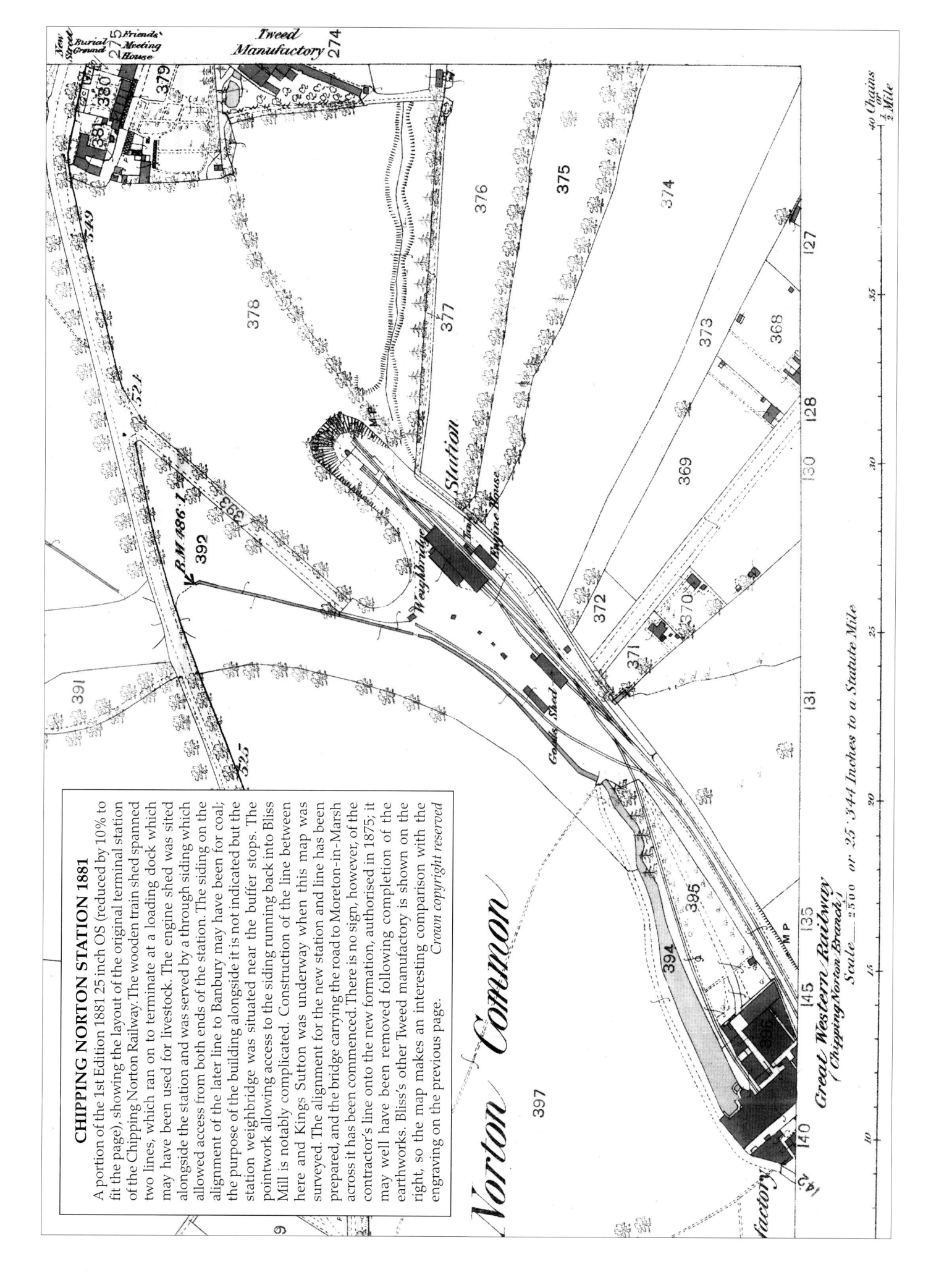

CHIPPING NORTON STATION 1881

A portion of the 1st Edition 1881 25 inch OS (reduced by 10% to fit the page), showing the layout of the original terminal station of the Chipping Norton Railway. The wooden train shed spanned two lines, which ran on to terminate at a loading dock which may have been used for livestock. The engine shed was sited alongside the station and was served by a through siding which allowed access from both ends of the station. The siding on the alignment of the later line to Banbury may have been for coal; the purpose of the building alongside it is not indicated but the station weighbridge was situated near the buffer stops. The pointwork allowing access to the siding running back into Bliss Mill is notably complicated. Construction of the line between here and Kings Sutton was underway when this map was surveyed. The alignment for the new station and line has been prepared, and the bridge carrying the road to Moreton-in-Marsh across it has been commenced. There is no sign, however, of the contractor's line onto the new formation, authorised in 1875; it may well have been removed following completion of the earthworks. Bliss's other Tweed manufactory is shown on the right, so the map makes an interesting comparison with the engraving on the previous page.   *Crown copyright reserved*

consequence the erection of the second lodge was suspended, but no steps have yet been taken towards the erection of a bridge; and as the promoters of this branch line did not on the receipt of your letter of the 11th January addressed to the secretary of the Oxford, Worcester & Wolverhampton Railway, lower out this part of the line to the limits sanctioned by the acts for the regulation of railways, this bridge when it is constructed will now present an unnecessary obstruction to the road traffic of the district.

I enclose a document numerously signed by some of the principal inhabitants of Chipping Norton and promoters of and interested in the Chipping Norton Branch Railway, in which they send their firm and unaltered opinion that a bridge is not required over this road.

I informed the gentlemen Messrs Wilkins & Rolls from whom I received the paper, that if I was furnished with a proper document guaranteeing the construction of the bridge, I would submit it for your Lordships favourable consideration, so that no unnecessary delay should take place in the opening of the line; but I am of opinion that until this requirement shall have been met, or be guaranteed to be met, in consequence of the incompleteness of the works, the opening of the Chipping Norton Branch of the Oxford, Worcester & Wolverhampton Railway for traffic, cannot be sanctioned without danger to the public using the same.

I have the honour sir to be your obedient servant,
W. Yolland
Lt. Col., Royal Engineers

OPENING OF THE CHIPPING NORTON RAILWAY

As usual on such occasions, the first day was celebrated in considerable style, the first train being welcomed by the ringing of church bells and a brass band from nearby Blockley. The streets of Chipping Norton were decorated with flags and bunting, and a banner bearing the word 'SUCCESS' was displayed above the track. With the Crimean War still in progress, the decorations were of an inevitably patriotic nature, the flags of Britain, France and Turkey (the three wartime allies) being prominently displayed

The official 'first train', headed by a locomotive that had temporarily been named *Eugenie* in honour of the Empress of France, left the new main line station at Chipping Norton Junction shortly after 12 o'clock. On arrival at Chipping Norton it was met by an official reception party and a band playing '*See the Conquering Hero Comes*'.

The celebrations continued with a public dinner held in the town hall, after which the usual speeches were made. A full report of the First Day celebrations was published in the *Oxford Chronicle* on Saturday 18th August 1855 and some of this interesting account may be worth quoting in full:

'The formal opening of the Chipping Norton branch of the Oxford, Worcester & Wolverhampton Railway took place on Friday the 10th instant, and the event was celebrated by the inhabitants of the locality in a manner which shows how highly they appreciate the importance of the railway, and the benefits it is calculated to confer upon the district generally.

The railway is four and a half miles in length, and consists of a single line of rails, the gradients throughout being easy. It commences at the junction with the main line situate in the Parish of Churchill, about three quarters of a mile below the Shipton station. The question of forming a line of railway to this small borough town had been for several years imagined, but little progress was made towards a practical realisation of the wishes of the whole of the inhabitants until the present Mayor of Chipping Norton (W.Bliss, Esq.) took the matter energetically in hand.

The Act was obtained last session of Parliament, and in August of the year 1854 the works were commenced by the well-known firm of Peto & Betts. It is gratifying to add that the landowners on the line offered no opposition to the scheme, but on the contrary consented to dispose of their land at a fair, remunerative price, without imposing any of those conditions which so often cause useless expense to the shareholders without any corresponding advantage to the public.

Three fourths of the land through which the railway line passes was the property or our respected city member J.H.Langdon, Esq., who not only cheerfully gave up his land to the purpose of the railway, but has also given his time and attention whenever they were required by the promoters of the scheme. The principals on which it has been constructed, and the low cost per mile, merit special notice. The cost of the line, which does not present any engineering difficulty, has been £26,000, including stations. Of this commendably small sum (for a railway constructed at a cost of only £6,000 per mile is of very rare occurrence in this country), £14,000 has been contributed by Sir S.M. Peto.

The line was completed within the original estimate, and was opened for goods traffic on Whit Monday in the present year. The opening of the line for passenger traffic has been delayed up to the present time, in consequence of difficulties that have been thrown in the way of the directors with reference to the erection of bridges in lieu of level crossings. The Board of Trade has at length, however, given the Company permission to open the railway for general traffic, on the Company giving a guarantee to erect bridges when required to do so.

The Oxford, Worcester & Wolverhampton Company has undertaken to work the line, taking fifty per cent of the revenue, the remainder being appropriated to the payment of dividend to the shareholders, so that of every shilling the Company take, the shareholders will receive sixpence. The Company also engage to keep the line in thorough repair, to purchase the plant and working materials, and to pay to the Chipping Norton shareholders a fair proportion of the profits brought by means of the branch to the main line.

A clause is inserted in the Act enabling the Oxford, Worcester & Wolverhampton company to purchase the shares at par, paying fair interest to the shareholders for their capital, so there is a great probability that in a few years hence the borough will enjoy the immense advantages of a direct railway communication to London and the north-west without incurring any of the risk arising from the fluctuations which occasionally deteriorate railway investments.

Shortly after twelve o'clock on Friday, Sir S.M. Peto, Bart., accompanied by Lady Peto, Miss Peto, Mrs Kemp, Miss Broadbent, Noel T. Smith, Esq., (Secretary of the Oxford, Worcester & Wolverhampton Railway), John Parson, Esq., (Deputy Chairman of the Oxford, Worcester & Wolverhampton Railway), John Fowler, Esq., (the Engineer of the line), and Mr Johnson, Esq., a Director of the Company, arrived by special train at the Chipping Norton Junction, the band playing 'See the Conquering Hero Comes'. They were met at the station by W. Bliss, Esq., Mayor of Chipping Norton, Alderman Lewis (of Worcester), and G.H.Busby, also Directors of the Company.

A considerable number of the respectable inhabitants of the locality were congregated at the station, which was decorated with evergreens and banners, besides other indications of pleasure appropriate to the occasion. A few yards from the platform was erected a triumphal arch, in evergreens and flowers, surmounted with the arms of England, France and Turkey, indicative of the firm alliance that now subsists

Photographer Frank Packer was given access to the Bliss Mill for this panoramic view of the old Chipping Norton Railway terminus site in the early years of the 20th century. An unidentified '517' Class 0-4-2T is shunting the sidings, which are on the alignment of the old Chipping Norton Railway terminus, the engine shed and water tower from which can be seen beyond the right-hand end of the later GWR goods shed. This occupied a broadly similar location to the original goods shed, whilst the site of the terminal building and train shed had been behind the goods shed seen here, alongside the engine shed. The coaches for the next service to Chipping Norton Junction can be seen behind the tree in the centre and a wagon laden with coal has been positioned just inside the gated entrance to the mill siding; presumably it will be horse-hauled to the mill boiler house when its contents are required. The stable block seen on the far left of this view was the last railway building to survive after closure of the line and clearance of the entire station site.

The Lens of Sutton Collection

between these countries.

A small locomotive, named 'Eugenie' in honour of the French Empress, and gaily decorated with banners, conveyed the train to Chipping Norton, where it arrived shortly before one o'clock amid the cheers of a large assemblage of the inhabitants. The station house and its vicinity presented a very gay and animated appearance.

The feeling of the whole town was of a very enthusiastic character. The whole of the shops were closed; flags were pendant from various parts of the borough; the church bells rang a merry peal; a really very good brass band from Blockley played some inspiriting march or national melody during the day; and, altogether, the example set by this 'independent' little place is one that not only does it infinite credit, but will, we trust be followed by hundreds of towns situated within short distances from through lines of railway.

On leaving the station, the visitors proceeded to the residence of the Mayor, where a party numbering between twenty and thirty partook of an elegant luncheon, and afterwards proceeded to Mr Bliss's new factory in course of erection near the railway station, where about one hundred and fifty men, women and children in his employ were provided by him with a substantial dinner, furnished by Mrs Bishop of the Crown & Cushion Inn. The health of Sir S.M.Peto and Lady Peto were drunk in a most enthusiastic manner, and the former responded to the compliment in a very appropriate address.

He took the opportunity of adverting to the delightful state of feeling which appeared to subsist between the employer and the employed in Chipping Norton. He had been told that the operatives of Chipping Norton presented a striking and favourable contrast to the factory operatives in the north of England, and that, as regarding healthiness and appearance and general character they could not be surpassed. That high and gratifying estimation was fully borne out by what he had witnessed with his own eyes on that occasion, for he had never seen a number of persons employed daily in that particular calling who presented such a healthy, smiling and good humoured appearance as those operatives he thus had the pleasure of seeing before him. He was glad to see such a kind feeling appeared to exist between them and their employer, which was creditable to both parties, and he (Sir S.M. Peto) would be rejoiced to see such a feeling universally extended. He congratulated them on the event of the day, in the opening of a line of railway into their town, and expressed a hope and confident belief that all classes, from the lowest, would be benefited by it, either in a greater or lesser degree.

The worthy baronet was heartily cheered on the conclusion of his address. Several other toasts were proposed, and on leaving, the Mayor expressed a hope that they would enjoy themselves during the afternoon, and complimented them upon the manner in which they had conducted themselves, which was equally creditable to them as it was gratifying to him. The visitors were loudly cheered on leaving the factory.'

The initial timetable provided three up and three down workings between Chipping Norton and Chipping Norton Junction. As a general rule, the line was worked as a simple, dead-end branch, with one locomotive and set of coaches running to and from the junction. There were, on the other hand, a limited number of through services and in the 1860s it became the practice for the first morning Up train to run through to Handborough, in order to make its connection with an express service to Oxford and Paddington. All train services were worked by the Oxford, Worcester & Wolverhampton Railway, which had agreed to work the branch in return for fifty per cent of the receipts.

SOME DETAILS OF THE CHIPPING NORTON LINE

The newly-opened branch line was single track throughout, with no intermediate stations. At Chipping Norton, it ended with some formality in a terminus with extensive, two-storey station buildings. Contemporary prints depict a gable-roofed train shed, together with an adjoining structure which is assumed to have been an engine shed. These assumptions are confirmed by the 1881 Ordnance Survey map, which reveals that the station incorporated a single platform on the west side, with a run-round loop to the east. Both of these lines were covered by the overall roof, which also protected much of the platform.

Train sheds were rarely provided at smaller stations in the Oxfordshire area and in this respect the original terminus at Chipping Norton was somewhat unusual. On the other hand, many of the lines promoted and built by Morton Peto in East Anglia featured stations with large two-storey buildings – the East Suffolk route being a typical example. Branch line termini such as Aldeburgh and Wells-next-the-Sea also boasted gable roofed train sheds, and so it was that Chipping Norton's first railway station was remarkably similar to stations built by Morton Peto in Norfolk and Suffolk.

Two loop sidings passed around the east side of the train shed and one of these served a single road engine shed. The running line continued north-eastwards beyond the platform to reach a loading dock, although the main goods yard was sited to the south of the platform on the west side. This contained a loop siding serving a goods shed and a longer, dead end siding that appears to have been the coal road; the latter siding was entered via a connection from the running line. In its report dated 9th June 1855, the *Oxford Chronicle* opined that the passenger and goods stations were *'commodious, and replete with every convenience'*.

Two additional sidings extended south-westwards to reach the nearby Bliss Lower Mill and both of these crossed the aforementioned coal siding by means of 'diamond' crossings. One of the mill sidings was intended for use as a coal siding, while the other evidently served a loading bay. The mill had itself been extensively reconstructed in connection with the new rail link, so that by 1855-56 it consisted of a five-storey main block, with an attached engine and boiler house. The main block was built across the mill race in the usual way, while the boiler room was conveniently sited at the end of the railway siding.

The permanent way was laid in conventional fashion, with double-headed rails weighing 65lbs per linear yard, supported on cross sleepers by ordinary chairs. When opened in 1855, it was one of the first parts of the OW&WR system to be laid on cross sleepers, the permanent way on the company's main line being formed entirely of bridge rails on longitudinal timber sleepers.

THE BOURTON-ON-THE-WATER RAILWAY

In 1859, a separate group of promoters decided to seek Parliamentary consent for a second branch line from Chipping Norton Junction, which would run westwards for a distance of 6 miles 47 chains to reach Bourton-on-the-Water. The necessary private Bill was sent up to Parliament in time for the 1860 session and, after an easy passage, the Bill for construction of a railway from Chipping Norton

This photograph, the earliest known view of the station at Stow-on-the-Wold, provides us with a tiny glimpse of the Bourton-on-the-Water Railway, albeit taken some time after this small company had been absorbed by the GWR in 1874. The similar architectural style employed both here and at Bourton – timber-framed construction, with decorative barge boards, patterned tiled roofs and very tall chimneys – marked both stations out as being conspicuously different to those found on the rest of the B&CDR route and indeed, the rest of the GWR system. Interestingly, Col. Rich's report indicates that the line was opened before they were built, wooden ticket huts being provided on the platforms initially. What must be the entire staff are posed on the platform, and the uniforms and dress of those featuring in the picture also date it to circa 1890. There is an air of newness to the whole scene but the station has obviously been open for business for a while; the flower bed is flourishing and the chimney pots are soot blackened. However, just edging into the photograph on the right – and standing on the running line – is a GWR 2-plank wagon loaded with bricks, whilst closer study of the view shows building work in progress in the left background, in the area of the small goods yard. Note the piles of crates and other goods on the platform around the station building; a small goods shed was later built on the platform on the far side of the building from here. The platform face looks quite fresh, suggesting that work on raising it up to standard height had just been completed, whilst the running line has also been reballasted. There is also no sign of the signal box on the platform. An extension to the platform was authorised in 1892, along with the provision of a signal box and signalling, the latter completed in 1893. It is likely therefore that this photograph dates from 1892, with the platform finished but prior to construction of the signal box and it thus captures the station at Stow-on-the-Wold at an interesting stage of its development. The painted nameboard is worthy of note, whilst the poster on the station building advertises the removals and storage business of the Cheltenham-based Barnby Bendall company. *Bob Brown collection*

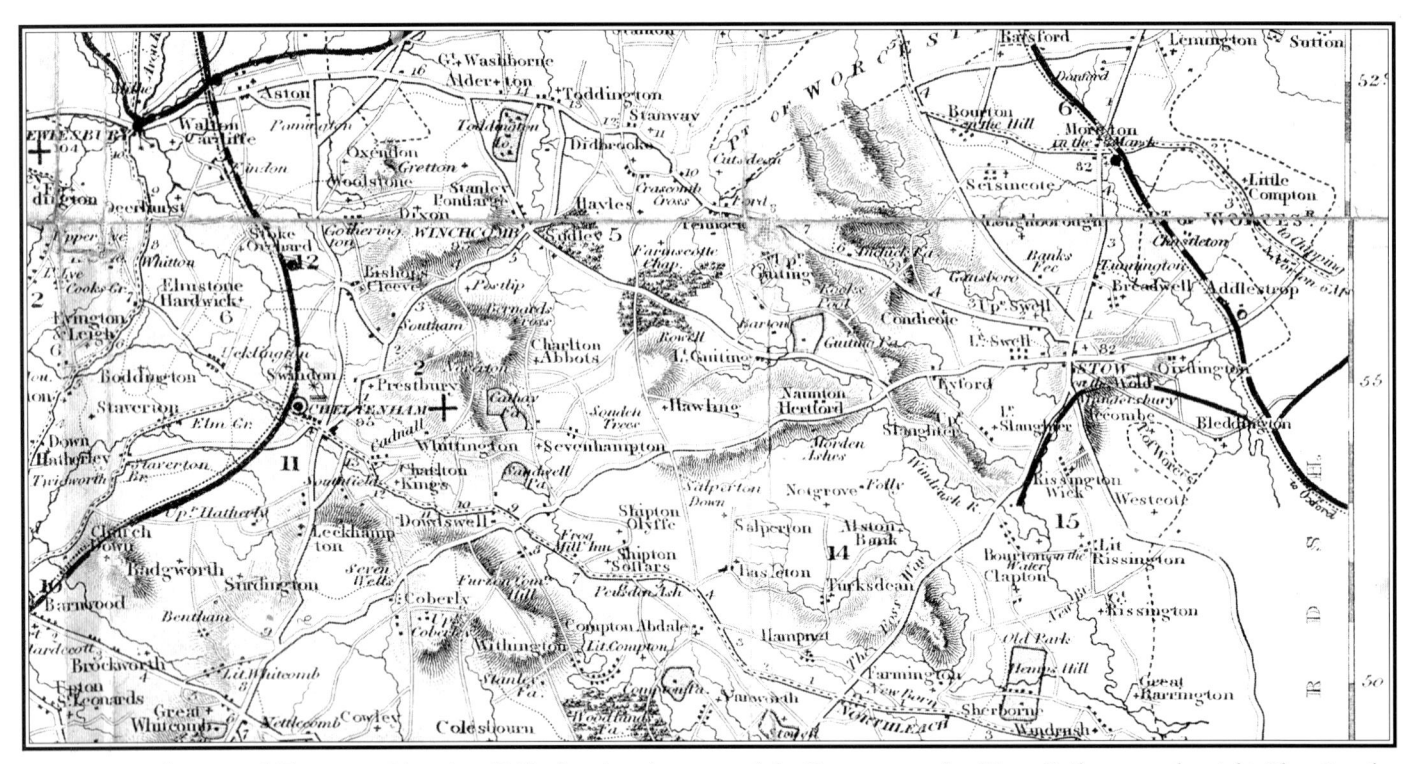

A portion of a map of Gloucestershire circa 1865, showing the route of the Bourton-on-the-Water Railway, on the right. The site of Chipping Norton Junction is hidden beneath the word 'Bleddington' and the Chipping Norton Railway is also marked heading off east from the OW&WR line. On the left, the Birmingham & Gloucester Railway heads north past Cheltenham. The GWR line running into St. James station is not indicated, although it had been in existence for nearly 20 years by this date. *Michael Mitchell collection*

Junction to the town of Bourton-on-the-Water received the Royal Assent on 14th June 1860.

The proposed line would run generally west-north-westwards from Chipping Norton Junction to Stow-on-the-Wold and then south-westwards through hillier terrain to its destination at Bourton-on-the-Water. Unlike Chipping Norton, which was at that time a textile manufacturing centre of some importance, Bourton-on-the-Water offered little scope for the development of either passenger or freight traffic. It remains a matter of conjecture why a railway should have been needed at such a place, the likeliest explanation being that its promoters regarded the line as a convenient starting point for further extensions towards Cheltenham.

At this juncture, external events intervened before the Bourton-on-the-Water scheme could be put into effect. As mentioned above, the OW&WR had originated as a close ally of the GWR but, as a result of serious disagreements between the two companies, had broken away from its parent company and formed new alliances with other concerns. In pursuance of this policy, the OW&WR initially moved closer to the L&NWR, although it was also willing to enter into joint ventures with smaller companies. One such company was a Welsh border line known as the Newport, Abergavenny & Hereford Railway.

The NA&HR's line had originally been worked by the L&NWR but its operating agreement with that company was terminated following a disagreement about through traffic. Having broken away from its former allegiances, the Abergavenny company had to find a new eastern outlet for its South Wales coal traffic and in 1858 it joined forces with the OW&WR, in order to complete the Worcester & Hereford Railway. The latter company had been authorised in 1853, as a link between Worcester, Great Malvern and Hereford, but little progress was made until 1856, when the NA&HR injected new life and money into the scheme.

Although the NA&HR was prepared to support the Worcester & Hereford scheme, the Abergavenny company was a struggling local railway with few capital resources. The OW&WR, on the other hand, was comparatively well-off by the late 1850s and the new partnership between the two geographically disparate companies was in effect an OW&WR takeover of the NA&HR. It was agreed that the two railways would be merged into a new undertaking, to be known as the West Midland Railway, which would also include the Worcester & Hereford Railway. These arrangements were formalised by the provisions of an Act of Parliament, obtained on 1st July 1860.

By this Act, the NA&HR and the W&HR companies were dissolved and merged with the OW&WR under its new name. Sixteen OW&WR directors were joined by five from the NA&HR and two from the W&HR to form an enlarged board, based at Worcester. The then Chairman of the OW&WR, William Fenton, became Chairman of the West Midland Railway, while W.P. Price, the former Chairman of the NA&HR, became Deputy Chairman of the West Midland Railway.

A few months later, in the early part of 1861, it was decided that the West Midland company would be leased to the parent Great Western, while the WMR would be granted running powers over the GWR system. Two years later, in 1863, the West Midland and Great Western companies were fully amalgamated, and the branch lines to Chipping Norton and Bourton-on-the-Water thereby passed into GWR control.

The formation of the WMR was a development of considerable significance for local companies such as the Bourton-on-the-Water Railway. The creation of this enlarged undertaking offered greater opportunities for traffic development and future investment, and with West Midland support the Bourton-on-the-Water scheme was rapidly put into effect. The single track branch was completed by the beginning of 1862 and, having passed its Board of Trade inspection in February, the railway was opened for passenger traffic on 1st March 1862.

Colonel F. Rich's inspection report is the best description we have of the Bourton-on-the-Water Railway, giving a good idea of the somewhat rudimentary nature of its construction. Indeed, it was admitted at the time that the line had been built as cheaply as possible, which, whilst understandable in many respects, is also slightly surprising because, even then, the intention to extend the line further at some stage was quite clear. This is mentioned in the Colonel's report which, for its great interest, is worth reproducing in full:

15th Feb 1862
Sir,
I have the honour to report for the information of the Lords of the Committee of Privy Council for trade, that in accordance with your minute of the 8th, I yesterday inspected that portion of the Bourton on the Water Railway, which extends from Chipping Norton Junction to Bourton on the Water.

The said piece of railway is 6 miles and 53½ chains long, single throughout with sidings at Stow station and at Bourton. The land has been purchased and the overbridges have been constructed for a double line.

The width of the line at formation level is 18 feet, the gauge is 4ft 8½ inches. The interval between the two lines of rails where there are sidings is 6 feet.

The rail used is double headed in lengths of 27 feet and weighs 65 lbs per yard. The joints are fished, the chairs weigh 23 lbs each. They are spiked to larch sleepers, laid at 3 foot intervals. The sleepers are semi-circular, 9 feet 9 inches long.

The flat side is laid on ballast, which is gravel 12 inches thick under the sleepers.

There are three overbridges, two with masonry piers and brick arches, the third has wrought iron girders.

There is one underbridge which has wrought iron girders and masonry abutments, besides several culverts conveying small brooks under the railway, two of these are of timber with brick piers.

The whole of the above are well built and of sufficient strength.

There are no level crossings and no engine turntables.

It is anticipated to extend the line.

I beg to forward herewith, an undertaking as to the method proposed for working the line which appears satisfactory, and likewise to erect turntables at the terminal stations of the line, until which time nothing except tank engines are to be used.

The general state of the line is good, but two of the approaches of the overbridges are not yet completed. The company undertakes to keep a man at the gates till they are completed, which will probably be in a week or ten days.

The stations at Stow and Bourton are not yet built, but there are

A busy moment at Bourton-on-the-Water station circa 1905, viewed from the road overbridge which crossed the line at the western end of the station. A 'Metro' 2-4-0 tank engine waits with a train for Cheltenham St. James, which is crossing a Kingham-bound service standing at the Up platform. The station's rural location on the outskirts of the village is emphasised by this view. This was the terminus of the line from 1862 to 1881 and it was presumably sited here to allow for a future extension westwards without interfering with the village. The Up platform was provided when the Cheltenham extension was built but, apart from that, the station would probably have looked pretty much like this in Bourton-on-the-Water Railway days. The original track layout is not known but it is assumed not to have altered much apart, probably, from the loop having been lengthened to allow for passing trains. *Bob Brown collection*

good platforms provided with semaphore distant signals, and a wooden ticket box.

The new line is carried outside the Parliamentary limits for a few chains at 2 miles 8 chains from Chipping Junction [sic]. The curves are somewhat increased, it is stated to have been done at the request of the landowners. The gradients are somewhat improved.

I beg therefore to report that I consider that the portion of the Bourton on the Water Railway between Chipping Norton and Bourton may be opened for passenger traffic without danger to the public using the line.

I have the honour to be sir, your obedient servant,
F.H. Rich, R.E.

The new branch commenced on the down side of the OW&WR main line at Chipping Norton Junction and terminated on the north side of Bourton-on-the-Water. There was just one intermediate station, at Stow-on-the-Wold, probably built with the siding accommodation which it retained throughout its life, although it appears from an early photograph of the station that the GWR improved the yard facilities shortly after absorbing the line. Indeed, the general approach to building the railway was to do it as cheaply as possible, the only significant engineering works being some embankments and a cutting in the vicinity of Stow. As the report notes, there were three road overbridges, one road underbridge and a number of crossings over minor lanes. Further bridges carried the single line across the rivers Evenlode, Dikler and Eye. Even the station buildings were completed a while later, simple wooden huts from which tickets were sold sufficing to begin with.

The report also mentions the signalling arrangements, referring to wooden distant signals on the platforms. This would indicate that the branch was intended to be worked on the one engine in steam principle, with fixed distant signals provided to warn train crews of the whereabouts of the stations; without proper station buildings, it may have been felt that the platforms were not sufficiently visible to an approaching train. There is no mention of signal boxes and it is quite likely that full signalling was not provided until the Cheltenham extension was completed.

The train service of four trains in each direction between Bourton-on-the-Water and Chipping Norton Junction was provided by the WMR, which undertook to work and maintain the line as part of its system. However, this arrangement lasted for only a few months and in 1863 the working of the branch passed into Great Western hands, following the GWR-WMR amalgamation. The GWR continued to work the Bourton-on-the-Water Railway until 1874, when the local company was fully and finally absorbed by its mighty neighbour.

No photographs are known to exist of the two WMR tank engines, Nos. 52 (*Ben Jonson*) and 53, which spent much of their working lives on the Chipping Norton and Bourton-on-the-Water branches but this drawing of the former as GWR No. 223 by E.L. Ahrons appeared in *The Locomotive Magazine* in 1915. It would seem the GWR could do little to disguise the engine's somewhat eccentric appearance. A rough scale can be taken off the 5ft. 6ins. centre driving wheel.

A NOTE ON EARLY LOCOMOTIVES

The West Midland Railway worked its own system with a fleet of 131 locomotives until 1860, when the operation of it was taken over by the GWR. Many former West Midland locomotives continued to work on their own system and, in this context, it is known that the WMR branch lines to Chipping Norton and Bourton-on-the-Water were operated by two small 2-2-2 tank engines, which had been built by Robert Stephenson & Co in 1859. One of these engines, OW&WR No. 52, was named *Ben Jonson* and, in the way of the world, its un-named sister, No. 53, thus became known locally as 'Mrs Jonson'!

These two tank locomotives had 12-inch by 18-inch outside cylinders, 5 foot 6 inch driving wheels and large American type cabs; they became GWR Nos. 223 and 224, and were scrapped in 1878 and 1877 respectively. Like most mid-Victorian locomotives, Nos. 52 and 53 were painted dark green with reddish-brown frames; OW&WR green was said to have had a blueish tint, a similar shade of green being employed by the Great Western after the 1860 takeover.

A problem of interpretation arises insofar as Nos. 52 and 53 were not delivered until 1859, whereas the Chipping Norton branch had been in operation since 1855. It is unlikely that the line would have been worked by tender locomotives on a regular basis, because there were at that time no turntables at Chipping Norton or Chipping Norton Junction stations. For this reason, it is likely that the line would have originally been worked by OW&WR 0-4-2Ts Nos. 35 and 36, which were the only tank locomotives that the company possessed prior to the arrival of 'Mr and Mrs Jonson'. Nos. 35 and 36 were built in 1853 by E.B. Wilson & Co of the Railway Foundry, Leeds; they became GWR Nos. 221 and 222 respectively.

Chapter Two

THE EAST GLOUCESTERSHIRE RAILWAY AND OTHER ABORTIVE SCHEMES

The very first attempt to build an east-to-west cross-country line across the Cotswolds in opposition to the Great Western Railway came as early as 1836, with the promotion of the 'Cheltenham, Oxford, London & Birmingham Union Railway'. The proposed line would have been a standard gauge route, commencing at Tring by a junction with the London & Birmingham Railway, then running through Oxford and Witney to Cheltenham. This line, which would have followed the route of the present A40 between Oxford and Cheltenham, had been rejected by Parliament on the grounds that the GWR's Cheltenham & Great Western Union Railway would furnish a better route for Cheltenham traffic.

SOME ABORTIVE RAILWAY MANIA SCHEMES
A spate of similar schemes came ten years later, starting in 1845 with the Oxford, Witney, Cheltenham & Gloucester Independent Railway, which hoped to build a main line, running via Witney, Burford and Andoversford, to Cheltenham, with a possible eastwards extension to High Wycombe. At about the same time, the Oxford, Worcester & Wolverhampton Railway included a branch to Witney as a sort of afterthought to its major scheme for a main line from Oxford to Wolverhampton.

Before construction could start on either of these lines, the London & Birmingham Railway launched a frontal attack on the Great Western with a revival of the earlier Tring scheme, while the GWR immediately parried with a line of its own – the Cheltenham, Oxford & London Junction Railway being suggested as a link between Oxford, Witney and Cheltenham. Faced with opposition from the main line companies, the supporters of the Oxford, Witney, Cheltenham & Gloucester Independent Railway were forced to admit defeat, and they accepted the Great Western's offer to purchase their shares.

The standard gauge scheme for a line from Tring to Oxford, Witney and Cheltenham was resurrected in 1846, and the Great Western again put forward a counter proposal for a broad gauge line between Oxford and Cheltenham. On this occasion they actually obtained Parliamentary consent but when it became clear that the rival proposals had been thwarted, the Great Western allowed its powers to lapse. In the meantime, the shifting sands of railway politics were changing the overall balance of power; the Midland and London & North Western railway companies were both formed by amalgamation in 1846, while the Oxford, Worcester & Wolverhampton Railway was consolidating its position in the Cotswold area.

The strained relations that existed between the GWR and the OW&WR during the 1850s have already been alluded to. As a concomitant of this bitter quarrel between two former allies, the OW&WR directors dreamed of building a new trunk line between London, Oxford and Cheltenham that would be entirely independent of the GWR and, in 1852, they sought Parliamentary consent for the so-called Oxford & Brentford Railway. The immediate result was hostility from the L&NWR, which revived its old stand-by scheme for a line from Tring to Cheltenham as a counter-measure.

If implemented in its entirety, the Oxford & Brentford scheme would have provided a 50-mile main line between Oxford, Princes Risborough, High Wycombe and a junction with the London & South Western Railway at Brentford. However, Parliament made short work of the Oxford & Brentford Bill and it was thrown out after just fifteen days.

Undeterred, the OW&WR revived its grand design in 1853 – this time under the appropriate title The London & Mid-Western Railway. The deposited plans of the 1853 extension scheme show that the main line would have started at Wolvercote, to the north of Oxford, and run parallel with the Great Western main line into Oxford. At this point, the OW&WR line would have turned sharply eastwards on a 40 chain curve, to cross the Great Western to the north of the present Oxford station. Continuing first east and then south-eastwards, the line would have run via Headington, Tiddington, Thame, Princes Risborough and High Wycombe, the chosen route being very similar to the later Great Western & Great Central Joint line.

In connection with the Mid-Western extension scheme, and indeed an integral part of it, the OW&WR also proposed a western extension from Wolvercote to Cheltenham. From Wolvercote, the Cheltenham & Oxford Union Railway would have followed the usual route via Witney, Burford, Northleach and Andoversford, while at Cheltenham it was envisaged that OW&WR trains would run into and out of the Midland Railway station. Much of the capital needed to float these ambitious schemes was subscribed by Sir Morton Peto and his associates, and with a certain amount of support from towns and villages along the route of the proposed lines, the OW&WR extension schemes might have enjoyed a modest success.

In the event, opposition from the Great Western Railway and other established main line companies was sufficient to defeat both the London & Mid-Western and Cheltenham & Oxford Union schemes, and the Bills for these lines were thrown out at committee stage. There were, thereafter, further suggestions that a line might be built from Oxford to London via Princes Risborough and High Wycombe but little more was heard of the proposed direct line from Oxford to Cheltenham. Instead, the supporters of new rail links in the area between Oxford, Witney, Andoversford and Cheltenham pinned their hopes on less ambitious proposals for the construction of short branch lines.

FORMATION OF THE WITNEY RAILWAY

The Chipping Norton and Bourton-on-the-Water lines were originally conceived as local branch lines but, once they were opened, they began to feature in a number of extension schemes which would have transformed them into cross-country routes. The Bourton-on-the-Water Railway, in particular, became the focus of considerable attention as early as the 1860s, when a company known as the East Gloucestershire Railway was promoted with the aim of constructing one or more routes to Cheltenham in competition with the GWR. The Witney Railway, just ten miles further south, also featured prominently in a number of abortive Cheltenham extension schemes.

The idea of an east-to-west cross-country railway linking Oxford, Witney, Cheltenham and South Wales was first mooted during the 1830s, and the idea was raised at intervals during the Railway Mania years of the middle 1840s, when various schemes were put forward. As recounted above, these early projects were all failures, though in the late 1850s a local company was formed to build a modest branch line between Yarnton Junction on the Oxford, Worcester & Wolverhampton line and Witney, in Oxfordshire.

The Witney Railway was essentially a localised venture which, with strong support from the Witney district, was incorporated by Act of Parliament on 1st August 1859 (22 & 23 Vic. cap. 46) with powers for the construction of a line from Yarnton, on the OW&WR, to Witney, a distance of 8 miles 14 chains. Supporters of the scheme included landowners such as Walter Strickland of Cokethorpe Park and Henry Akers of Black Bourton, together with traders, bankers and industrialists such as John Clinch, Charles Early (1824-1912) and Malachi Bartlett (1802-1875).

Construction started at Eynsham in May 1860 and the railway was opened on Wednesday 13th November 1861, little more than eighteen months having elapsed since the cutting of the first sod. The line was engineered by Sir Charles Fox (1810-1874), of Crystal Palace fame, at a cost of £41,531 for the works and £7,000 for land – the total expenditure being just £48,531.

The Witney branch was initially worked by the West Midland Railway as part of an 11 mile 55 chain route from Oxford. However, the successful promotion of this modest

If the East Gloucestershire Railway scheme had come to fruition, this Fairford-bound train at Witney would actually have been heading to Cheltenham. The train is composed of a milk siphon and four bogie clerestory carriages, in the charge of an unidentified 'Metro' 2-4-0T, while a large number of very well-dressed passengers have got off. This station was opened in 1873 when the line was extended to Lechlade and it consisted simply of the passing loop, two platforms, a carriage dock, a water tower and associated buildings. The original Witney Railway terminus of 1861 (to the north of this station) became a goods station and almost all the buildings survived remarkably intact well into the 1990s. Regrettably, they have since been demolished to make way for a new industrial estate. Nigel Oram collection

scheme was an obvious source of encouragement for people living in the area between Witney and Cheltenham, who viewed the line from Yarnton as a viable starting point for further extensions towards the west. Moreover, the Witney Railway proprietors were understandably keen to see their line up-graded to main line status and, with this ultimate aim in mind, the railway had been made wide enough to accommodate a second line of rails, in case traffic should ever become heavy enough to justify the provision of a double track.

There were, from time to time, suggestions that the Witney Railway could be extended as far west as Lechlade, at which point the line would have made a connection with a new main line that had been proposed between Cheltenham and Faringdon. The suggested extension would have run via Bampton and Alvescot, while at Witney it would have diverged from the original Witney branch at a junction sited some 20 chains to the south of the Witney Railway terminus.

In the event, it was decided that the proposed branch from Lechlade to Witney would be built, not by the Witney Railway but by a new, Cheltenham based company. The latter company was first mooted in 1860 but the scheme began to assume a more tangible form in the following year, when a number of promotional meetings were held to raise support for what was, by this time, being called The East Gloucestershire Railway.

THE FIRST EAST GLOUCESTERSHIRE PROPOSALS

The East Gloucestershire Railway was born at a meeting held at Hatherop Castle in 1861. This meeting was attended by the squires and landowners of East Gloucestershire and West Oxfordshire and '*the whole gentry of the county ... who had for many years been trying to get the railway*'. Those present included Lord Sherbourne, Sir Michael Hicks Beach MP, the Honourable Ashley Ponsonby, the Honourable and Reverend G.G.C. Taylor of Withington, and Mr J.R. Raymond Barker of Fairford Park. Together, these gentlemen decided that a provisional committee would be appointed, with the aim of raising support for a new rail link between Cheltenham and London.

The railway concerned was to run from Cheltenham, along the Chelt Valley through Charlton Kings to Andoversford, and thence along the Coln Valley to Fairford and Lechlade. Here the line would divide, with one arm heading east to join the Witney Railway, while the other would ran southwards via Chedworth to form a junction with the Faringdon Railway. This ambitious scheme would thereby provide two routes to London, the Faringdon route being a 7 foot broad gauge line, while the proposed branch to Witney would enable standard gauge trains to proceed eastwards onto the Oxford, Worcester & Wolverhampton main line via Witney and Yarnton Junction.

The Great Western Railway was in favour of the suggested broad gauge line to Faringdon but the GWR directors objected to the proposed line through Witney, which could have allowed the rival London & North Western Railway to obtain an interest in the area by means of its connecting line from Bletchley to Yarnton. The Great Western therefore offered a cash inducement to the East Gloucestershire promoters if they would drop the Witney branch and build one to Bourton-on-the-Water instead. The EGR company accepted the Great Western's offer of friendship and the East Gloucestershire scheme was submitted to Parliament as a purely GWR project, the final route being decided by John Fowler, the GWR Engineer.

The routes of the proposed new railways were prepared by the engineers John Fowler, Edward Wilson and James Burke, and the deposited plans reveal that a whole system of lines was envisaged. For convenience, the proposed routes were treated as several distinct lines. 'Railway One' would commence at Cheltenham and terminate in a field known as Sandford Mead, while 'Railway Three' would form a continuation from Sandford Mead to Andoversford. 'Railway Five' would run eastwards from Andoversford to Bourton-on-the-Water, and 'Railway Four' would extend southwards to Faringdon. 'Railway Two' would be merely a short spur from 'Railway One' to the Great Western station at Cheltenham.

In spite of some initial opposition from certain property owners in Cheltenham, who feared that the railway would damage their houses and disturb their quiet terraces, the EGR seemed destined for immediate success. The *Railway Times* was highly supportive and, on 19th October 1861, the paper printed a glowing report that would have been read by a large proportion of the Victorian investing public. The editorial opined that:

> This project, embracing a line from Faringdon on the Great Western to Cheltenham, with connecting links to the West Midland, is now fairly before the public ... The natural advantages of the route are considerably strengthened by the alliance effected by the united companies, which provides that the line, when constructed, shall be officially worked by the Great Western, a minimum number of daily trains already being arranged.

Elsewhere in the same issue, the paper reported that meetings in support of the lines from Cheltenham to Bourton-on-the-Water and from Andoversford to Faringdon had been held in 'several parts of the district', and a provisional committee had already been appointed.

The East Gloucestershire scheme was sanctioned by Parliament on 7th August 1862, and the resulting Act (*25 & 26 Vic. cap. 10*) provided consent for the construction of a railway commencing at Cheltenham, in the County of Gloucestershire, and terminating in 't*he Parish of Faringdon in the County of Berkshire by a junction with the authorised line of the Faringdon branch*'. The Act provided that the intended railways would be constructed '*with a double line of rails, on the mixed gauge*', while further provisions dealt with easements and other matters of concern to the Faringdon and Bourton-on-the-Water railways. As far as the junctions were concerned, the Act provided that:

> The several junctions of the Railway with the authorised Faringdon Railway, and the authorised Bourton-on-the-Water Railway, respectively, shall be effected by means of junction rails and points, with proper signals in connection therewith, of the construction most approved, and in every case to the reasonable satisfaction of the Engineer of the respective company with whose railway the junction is made; or, in the case of differences, as shall be settled by arbitration

under the Railway Companies Act 1859, by a single arbitrator to be, in the case of difference, appointed by the Board of Trade.

Unfortunately, before construction could begin, a group of Great Western shareholders suddenly decided that the EGR scheme was an unnecessary and risky proposition. One of these dissidents, Mr Thomas C. Brown of Cirencester, commenced an intensive campaign of letters to the press, in which he argued that the existing line from Cheltenham to Swindon was better than the proposed East Gloucestershire route – which would in any case be impracticable because of the steep gradients that would be necessary between Cheltenham and Andoversford. In one of his letters, published in the *Railway Times* on 22nd March 1862, the troublesome Mr Brown argued that:

> If Cheltenham, an important town, had no railway to London ... I should admit the necessity of adopting it; but having already a better and safer line, the roundabout of twenty miles, to a population whose business is to kill time, seems to me to be not worth a moment's consideration.

He went on to add that, as Cheltenham was situated under hills 1,000 feet high, the GWR would lose £25,000 a year operating the steeply-graded East Gloucestershire line. Eventually, so many shareholders joined the anti-East Gloucestershire campaign that the Great Western was obliged to withdraw its support.

THE SECOND EAST GLOUCESTERSHIRE PROPOSAL

It seemed that the EGR project would be abandoned but, at this point, the colourful figure of Sir William Russell appeared on the scene, to rally the supporters of the proposed railway. Sir William, the second baronet of Charlton Park, appears to have been the driving force behind the East Gloucestershire scheme after its initial failure. An energetic and fairly young man, he had seen active service with the 7th Hussars during the Indian Mutiny but having been placed on half pay in 1864, he probably found civilian life intolerably dull.

Although Sir William managed to get himself elected as Liberal MP for Norwich, he doubtless found even the cut-and-thrust of Parliamentary debate boring after his adventures during the siege of Lucknow. What better then, than to lead a small and embattled railway company into action against the Great Western Railway; the life of a would-be business buccaneer might not have been quite the same as that of a Victorian cavalry officer but it was perhaps a step in the right direction.

The East Gloucestershire Railway Bill was sent up to Parliament for the second time in 1864, albeit in a slightly different form. The branch from Andoversford to Bourton-on-the-Water was dropped and in its place the original plans for a line to Witney were resurrected. The route, surveyed by Charles Liddell, would run from Cheltenham to Andoversford via Leckhampton and Dowdeswell, and then south to Faringdon. From Lechlade, the proposed Witney branch would head eastwards, through Bampton, to converge with the Witney Railway at a junction to the south-east of the original Witney Railway terminus.

At Yarnton, a loop was proposed to allow trains from Cheltenham to pass onto the L&NWR without coming into physical contact with the rival GWR, while at Cheltenham a loop line would enable East Gloucestershire traffic to gain access to the Midland Railway.

Petitions in favour of the Bill were received from many towns and villages along the projected route, including Cheltenham, Leckhampton, Badgworth, Charlton Kings, Withington, Bibury, Fairford, Lechlade, Bampton, Witney, Faringdon and Oxford, while the Witney Railway promoted a Bill to raise capital in order to double its own line between Yarnton and Witney. The Midland Railway was known to be in favour of a line which might one day link its own lines in the Cheltenham area with some future main line to London. On the other hand, the Great Western was bitterly opposed to the East Gloucestershire scheme in view of the very real threat posed by the Midland's involvement.

It should, perhaps, be explained that there were fundamental differences between the Midland Railway and its supporters, and the Great Western Railway. Moreover, these differences were very deeply ingrained. The Midland Railway and its original constituents had been founded by Quakers and other Nonconformists, whereas the patrician Great Western Railway was dominated by landowning interests. In the context of Victorian politics, these factors more or less guaranteed that the Nonconformist Midland proprietors would tend to be Liberal voters, while the rival Great Western supporters would tend to be both Anglican and Tory in their political and religious affiliations.

In view of the Midland's involvement, the Bill was examined at great length by a Select Committee of the House of Commons, which subjected Sir William to a rigorous cross-examination, and at still greater length by a Lords Committee. Several other witnesses were called to give evidence, including Walter Strickland, Charles Early and Henry Akers from the Witney Railway Company. Mr Strickland, the Witney Railway Chairman, declared that the Witney line had always been considered '*the first link in a railway to Cheltenham*' but plans for an extension to Lechlade had been abandoned following the failure of the 1862 East Gloucestershire proposals.

Charles Early, a well-known blanket manufacture and mill owner in Witney, stated that the Witney Railway had been an '*immense advantage to Witney as a manufacturing town*'. His mills and workshops consumed considerable amounts of wool, oil and coal, although very little coal came from South Wales because of the lack of a suitable rail link between West Oxfordshire and the Welsh coal fields; however, he thought that this situation would change if the EGR line was built. He added that several carriers' carts ran to and from Witney station each day but the stage coaches that had once provided a service between London, Witney and Cheltenham had all been '*taken off the road*'.

Henry Akers, who farmed 600 acres at Black Bourton, said that, in his opinion, the Witney to Lechlade section of the EGR would serve '*fertile arable land*', whereas the higher, Cotswold districts beyond Fairford were given over to sheep farming. The sheep farmers would, he suggested, '*require to send their stock by train*'. Mr Akers also explained that many local people were interested only in a link to Witney; '*In the small town of Bampton'*, he added, *'there were more than fifty subscribers'*, whilst in the town of Fairford there were *'considerably more than fifty'*. Other witnesses included Malachi Bartlett, a Witney building contractor, and Mr J.R. Raymond Barker, the Squire of Fairford.

The Committee eventually decided in favour of the Bill, having accepted Sir William's assurance that *'there was no agreement with the Midland'*. The Bill was finally passed by Parliament on 29th July 1864, when the revised East Gloucestershire scheme received the Royal Assent (*27 & 28 Vic. cap. 285*).

The East Gloucestershire Railway Company was thereby empowered to build a 50-mile railway, commencing in Cheltenham and terminating *'in the Parish of Great Faringdon in the County of Berks at or near the Faringdon Station of the Faringdon Railway'*. The Witney branch, defined as *'Railway No. Four'* in the 1864 East Gloucestershire Railway Act, would commence at Lechlade and terminate *'in the Parish of Cogges, in the County of Oxford, by a junction with the Witney Railway, at or near a point thereon about three furlongs from, and on the south-east side of, the centre of the platform of Witney Station'*.

In addition to the main lines between Cheltenham, Witney and Faringdon, the 1864 Act provided consent for the construction of a circuitous loop line around the eastern side of Cheltenham, by means of which EGR trains would be able to gain direct access to the Midland Railway system. This interesting line, which would have been about three miles in length, was designated *'Railway No. Three'*, and it was described as:

> A Railway, also in Gloucestershire, commencing in the Parish of Swindon by a junction with the Midland Railway on the north side of the bridge whereby the said railway is carried over the road leading to Swindon, by Hide Farm, into the turnpike road from Cheltenham to Bishop's Cleeve, passing through Prestbury, and terminating in the Parish of Cheltenham by a junction with the Bristol and Birmingham Railway, north of the point where the rails of that railway are joined by the Cheltenham Branch of the Great Western Railway.

To pay for this ambitious scheme, the East Gloucestershire promoters were empowered to raise the not inconsiderable sum of £600,000 in £10 shares, with a further £200,000 by loans. The number of directors was fixed at eight, the qualification for directorship being £2,000.

The first meeting of the independent, reconstituted EGR was held at Cheltenham on 22nd August 1864 and Sir William was obviously in a jubilant mood; he congratulated the shareholders, now that they were:

> 'A company constituted, possessed of its Bill [sic] and about to carry out the same purposes and intentions as before, but modified so as to suit the views of some who they hoped would now be the supporters of a scheme which must of necessity prove an advantage to the town of Cheltenham.
> Since obtaining the Bill we have had communications with the Midland, they met us most frankly, and they agreed, if we chose to accent the terms ... to work us at the rate of fifty per cent of the gross rates, they to pay all expenses, they are to find all carriages, working stock and engines, and to maintain the line, to do every single thing, to undertake every shilling of cost in every form!'

It is difficult to see what the Midland directors hoped to achieve by this working agreement and one must conclude that the Midland, knowing the Great Western would never agree to any working arrangement between Derby and the East Gloucestershire Railway, went ahead with the plan merely to antagonise its enemies at Paddington.

It was widely felt at the time that the East Gloucestershire Railway had become nothing more than a pawn, being used by the Midland to annoy the rival GWR; the Editor of the *Railway Times* was certainly of this opinion and on 1st October 1864 he wrote:

> The Midland Railway is simply pursuing the ordinary course of railway tactics in endeavouring to play off the East Gloucestershire against the Cheltenham interests of its friends at Paddington. What will become of the East Gloucestershire – of its Chairman, Directors and contractors – should the two companies make up their differences in the meantime?

Nevertheless, if the Midland had offered help to the East Gloucestershire Railway in an attempt to antagonise the Great Western, that attempt was highly successful, at least

The earthworks at the Cheltenham end of the East Gloucestershire Railway, looking up the hill towards Andoversford. The photograph was taken circa 1935 and the noted railway historian D.S. Barrie is seen standing on the uncompleted embankment. The works remain in substantially similar condition today and are clearly visible from the A40 Cheltenham to Oxford road, seen here on the right, which is now widened to three lanes at this point. John Alsop collection

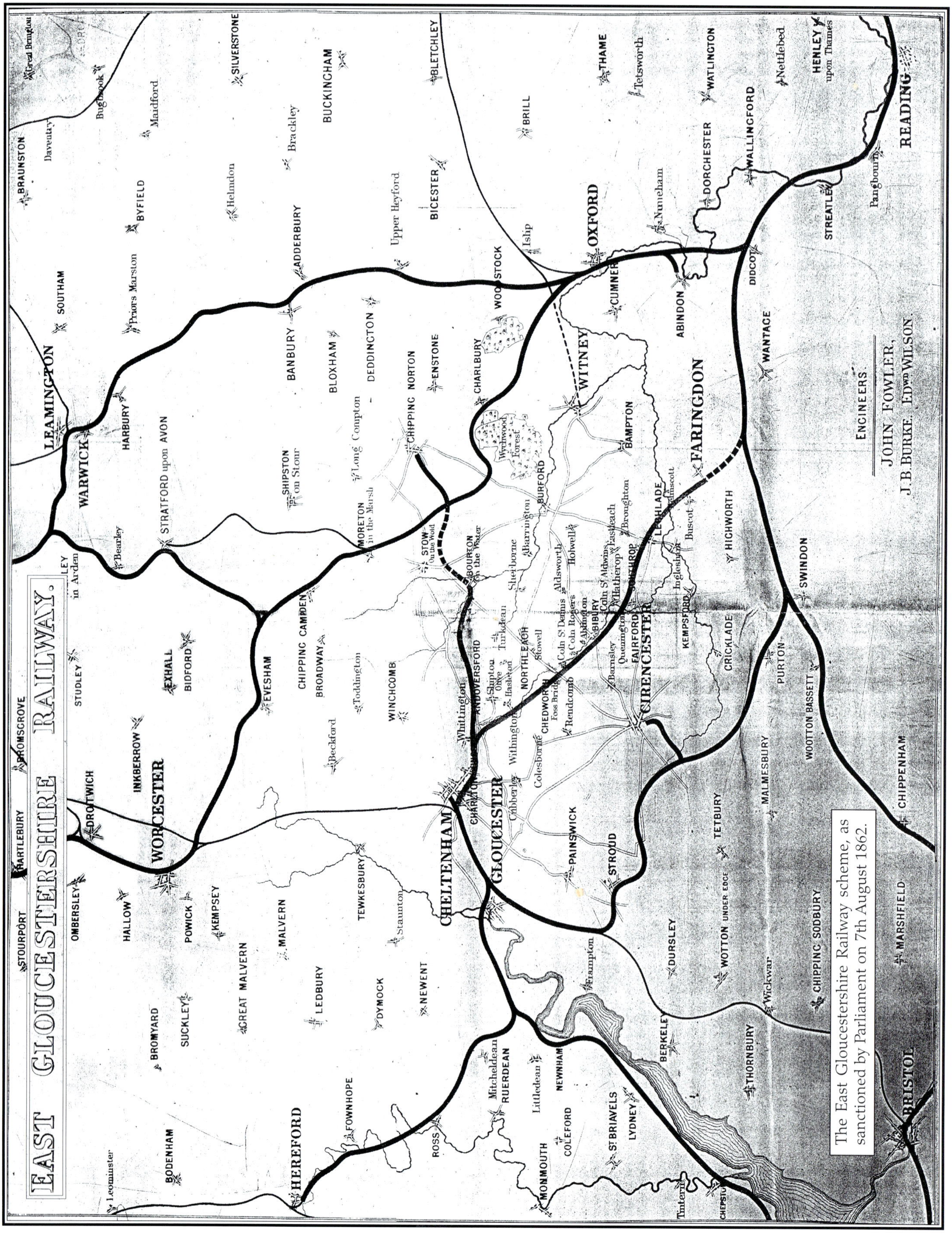

The East Gloucestershire Railway scheme, as sanctioned by Parliament on 7th August 1862.

THE BANBURY & CHELTENHAM DIRECT RAILWAY

Two further views of the East Gloucestershire Railway earthworks near Cheltenham circa 1935. The picture left is looking towards Andoversford and Sandywell Tunnel, whilst the view on the right is in the opposite direction. *Both John Alsop collection*

in the first instance. The GWR, remembering when the Oxford, Worcester & Wolverhampton Railway had run its narrow gauge trains to London over the Yarnton Loop, had nightmare visions of the Midland doing likewise. Fortunately, the Great Western could find an easy way out.

The EGR company had only obtained Parliamentary consent for its scheme on the clear understanding that it would be an entirely independent concern; the Great Western could therefore object most strongly to the proposed agreement with the Midland Railway. Moreover, a clause in the Act of Amalgamation passed when the Great Western absorbed the West Midland Railway had provided that the GWR and the Midland Railway should *'agree as to subscribing to any new lines in the districts in which the companies are directly interested'*.

Since the two companies were clearly not in agreement over the East Gloucestershire line, the Great Western was able to prevent the Midland company from engaging in any lasting involvement with the EGR scheme. The Midland's position was clearly untenable and when, in May 1865, Parliament ruled that the MR should give no financial help to the East Gloucestershire company, it seemed that the whole scheme was doomed to failure.

However, the Midland then mischievously announced that it still intended to work the East Gloucestershire line and Captain Galton of the Board of Trade was called in to arbitrate. He finally ruled that, although the Midland might work a local service in the Cheltenham area, it would not be allowed to work the EGR main line, as this would be contrary to the existing agreement with the Great Western. After one final attempt to obtain direct Parliamentary sanction in 1866, the Midland Railway abandoned the cause of the East Gloucestershire and retired from the scene.

Meanwhile, the authorised route of the EGR line had been staked out for most of its 50 mile length and construction had actually been started at the Cheltenham end of the route. Charles Liddell, the company's engineer, had recommended the difficult Sandywell Tunnel contract should be started first and, by the autumn of 1865, the tunnel and its associated earthworks were taking shape in the Cotswold countryside,

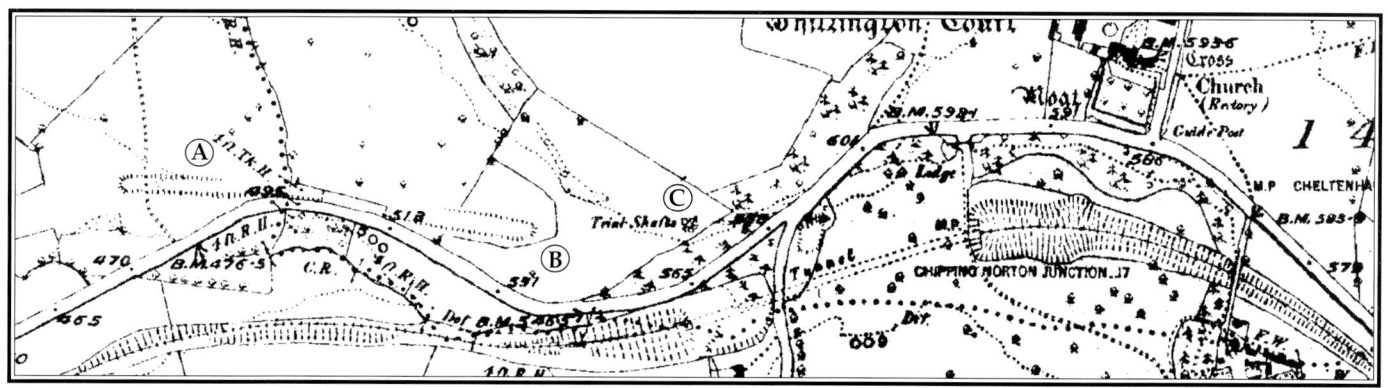

A portion of the 1885 6 inch OS showing the tunnel and cuttings by which means the B&CDR made its way through the Sandywell Estate at Andoversford. However, what this map also proves is that, contrary to popular belief, the Banbury & Cheltenham company's tunnel did not follow the course of the East Gloucestershire Railway's tunnel. Indeed, it is doubtful if anything of the latter was built. The course of the abandoned earthworks is clearly shown on the left of the map, marked 'A', just north of the Cheltenham to Oxford coach road (now the A40). 'B' marks the intended site of the western portal of the tunnel. Just to the right of there, marked 'C', the annotation 'Trial Shafts' indicates that exploratory borings for the tunnel were commenced. The B&CDR used the EGR earthworks from Andoversford station, which began on an embankment and then went into cutting to reach the eastern portal of the tunnel. What is obvious from the map is that although the eastern portal would have been in the same place, the route of the B&CDR tunnel then deviated substantially from the intended route of the EGR one. The latter line was heading north of Cheltenham, whilst the B&CDR was built to the south. The mileage is measured from Chipping Norton Junction. *Courtesy Cheltenham Library, Crown copyright reserved*

alongside the once-busy coach road to Oxford and London.

It was reported that half of the land required for the railway had been purchased and *'a responsible contractor'* had been found. The contract included the main line from Cheltenham to Witney, the avoiding line at Yarnton, the branch to Faringdon, the Cheltenham loop and *'the line into the town of Cheltenham'*. Unfortunately, the EGR was faced with serious financial and other problems, following the failure of bankers Overend, Gurney & Co in May 1866. The results were catastrophic and with the bank rate standing at ten per cent, small companies such as the EGR were unable to raise their authorised capital.

Although *'considerable progress'* had been made at the Cheltenham end of the East Gloucestershire route, it soon became obvious that the EGR company would not be able to finance its entire scheme and it was decided that the works at Andoversford would be abandoned. Instead, the EGR directors would concentrate their efforts on the completion of a 14-mile branch between Witney and Fairford. This small section of the original EGR scheme had the advantage of cheapness of construction and, as it would traverse an almost dead level tract of countryside, there would be no tunnels, few real cuttings and only one modest embankment at Curbridge.

Against this, the directors must have realised that, as their line would end virtually in the middle of nowhere and serve no settlements of real importance, its traffic would be almost nil. Yet it would be wrong to criticise the supporters of the railway – men who, living in an an age of material progress, sincerely believed that their own small corner of the world could share in that progress once its branch line was built. Significantly, the directors themselves were by this time local men; apart from J.R. Raymond Barker, they now included Walter Strictland and Henry Akers – all of whom lived on or near the route of the truncated East Gloucestershire line.

The company obtained an extension of time to complete the works in 1867 and in 1869 construction resumed on the Fairford to Witney section. The line was ceremonially opened on 14th January 1873, when what must have been the first Down train arrived at Fairford as an empty stock working. Otherwise, the main celebrations took place on Wednesday 15th January (the date usually given for opening), in connection with the start of public services. Thus, after many vicissitudes, the East Gloucestershire Railway was finally opened to the public as a 14 mile 10 chain branch from Witney to Fairford. All thoughts of completing the scheme in its entirety, as a main line to Cheltenham, had long been abandoned.

THE NORTHAMPTON & BANBURY JUNCTION RAILWAY

On 28th July 1863, a company known as the Northampton & Banbury Junction Railway had obtained an Act (*26 & 27 Vic. cap. 220*), the authorised capital for which was £140,000 in shares and £48,300 by loan, for the construction of an 18-mile line, commencing:

> 'In the parish of Blisworth by a junction with the siding on the west side of the London & North Western Railway, at or near the Blisworth Station of that Railway, and terminating in the parish of Gretworth,

otherwise Greatworth, by a junction with the Banbury Extension of the Buckinghamshire Railway about forty yards eastward of the bridge which carries the public road from Marston St Lawrence to Farthinghoe over the said Banbury Extension Railway in the County of Northamptonshire'.

The Act named Dr. Alexander Beattie, Cooke Baines, William Gregory, Robert Stanton Wise and George Eady as the first directors, while other leading supporters included C.J. Tahourdin and Jasper W. Wood. As far as can be acertained, none of the promoters were local people, and this underlines a significant point about the Northampton & Banbury Junction Railway. The new company was a purely speculative venture and its promoters had little or no interest in the transport needs of the immediate locality; instead, they hoped to grow rich by carrying long distance coal and iron ore traffic over a new main line between the East Midlands and South Wales.

Many of the directors had investments in other railway companies. Alexander Beattie, for example, was involved with several other railways, including the Carnarvon & Llanberis Railway and the South Eastern Railway. His address was given in *Bradshaw's Shareholders Manual & Guide* as 45 Porchester Terrace, Hyde Park, London but he also resided at *'Summerhill'*, Chiselhurst, Kent. George Eady was similarly involved with other railways besides the Northampton & Banbury Junction line and it is interesting to find that he was also solicitor to the Carnarvon & Llanberis Railway in North Wales.

It appears, from this evidence, that Messrs Beattie, Eady and their co-directors viewed the Northampton & Banbury Junction Railway as merely one of a diverse number of investments. Such men were clearly willing to risk their own (or their clients') money when the economic climate was favourable but in times of financial stringency, speculative investors normally lacked the personal commitment needed to see projects through to a successful conclusion. For this reason, the N&BJR scheme would soon find itself in serious financial trouble – though in the short term the project seemed destined for early success and, having obtained their Act, the promoters were eager to begin construction.

The Northampton & Banbury Junction promoters were not content with running a useful but minor cross-country branch. In the ensuing months, they initiated a series of grandiose projects which, if successfully completed, would have transformed the original Blisworth to Banbury line into an integral part of a major trunk route between the Northamptonshire and Oxfordshire iron producing areas and South Wales. Such a line, when completed, would enable good quality iron ore to reach the Welsh coalfields, where it could be profitably smelted prior to export overseas.

In February 1865, the Northampton & Banbury Junction Railway applied to Parliament for powers to deviate a small portion of the 1863 line *'and extend it to the town of Banbury'*. The new Bill was read for the first time on 21st February 1865 and ordered to be read a second time. In connection with this scheme, the company also sought powers to construct extensions to Chipping Norton and Blockley, and the Northampton & Banbury Junction (Extension) Bill received its first reading on 22nd February 1865. Both of the

1865 Bills were ultimately successful and, as a result of their latest application to Parliament, the N&BJR promoters obtained wide-ranging additional powers.

The Northampton & Banbury Railway (Branch) Act (28 & 29 Vic. cap. 361) authorised the construction of a branch connecting the original N&BJR line to the Northampton & Peterborough line of the London & North Western Railway. To pay for this and other works, the company was empowered to raise additional share capital of £145,000 '*by preference shares or otherwise*', while borrowing on mortgage a further sum of £48,300. Three years were allowed for the compulsory purchase of land and the time limit set for completion of the works was five years.

An agreement between the Northampton & Banbury Junction and North Western companies was scheduled to the Act, and this agreement clarified the position regarding running powers over a section of the L&NWR between Cockley Brake Junction and Banbury; a further provision provided for N&BJR trains to use the North Western and Great Western stations at Banbury.

The Northampton & Banbury Railway (Extension) Act (28 & 29 Vic. cap. 362) provided consent for the construction of lines from Banbury to Blockley and Chipping Norton. For convenience, these new lines were treated as four railways: '*Railway No. One*' would be the Chipping Norton branch, while '*Railway No. Two*', '*Railway No. Three*' and '*Railway No. Four*' would together constitute the main line to Blockley. To finance this ambitious scheme, the company was empowered to raise a further £500,000 by preference or other shares and to borrow an additional £166,600; the time limit for completion of the works was again five years.

The extension from Banbury to Chipping Norton was, like the ill-fated East Gloucestershire line further to the west, an immediate predecessor of the Banbury & Cheltenham Direct Railway. As far as the N&BJR scheme was concerned, the proposed line would have passed through or near Tadmarton and then run further north than the later B&CDR route, although the suggested junction at Chipping Norton would have resulted in the creation of a very similar link between Banbury and the OW&WR main line.

The proposed lines between Banbury, Blockey and Chipping Norton had been surveyed by Charles Liddell and John Collister. Liddell, of 24 Abingdon Street, Westminster, was a well-established railway engineer who had already carried out much work on other lines. He is unlikely to have spent much time on a comparatively minor project such as the N&BJR survey and it is therefore likely that most of the work was carried out by John Collister, at one time joint Engineer of the Northampton & Banbury Junction Railway. At a later stage, Collister was replaced as Resident Engineer by Edward Richards, who was apparently an associate of Charles Liddell and shared his office at 24 Abingdon Street.

It is both interesting and significant to find that Edward Richards and Charles Liddell were also responsible for the second East Gloucestershire Railway scheme, which was promoted at the same time as the Northampton & Banbury Junction line. This suggests at least tacit collusion between the promoters of these schemes, although there were no formal links between the East Gloucestershire and Northampton & Banbury Junction companies.

THE MIDLAND COUNTIES & SOUTH WALES RAILWAY

The Northampton & Banbury Junction supporters were now playing for high stakes and if their schemes were completed as planned, the company would be a force to be reckoned with in the railway world. A project of such magnitude attracted considerable attention from publications such as the *Railway Times* and, on 12th August 1865, this influential investors' journal printed a very full report of an N&BJR meeting that had been held at the company's London office on the previous Saturday. The meeting was chaired by Dr Beattie, and the first item of business was the directors report:

> The report stated that the works were progressing satisfactorily, and there was reason to believe that the railway would be opened for traffic by the time originally contemplated. An Act was obtained in the last session for making an extension line from Chipping Norton to Banbury, and running powers were secured over the London & North Western, by which they would be enabled to convey iron ore from Northamptonshire to South Wales.
>
> Running powers were confirmed by Parliament, and also the making of a half mile branch of the Northampton & Peterborough at Northampton. The whole length of the line would be fifty one and a half miles. They would ask the proprietors for power to raise capital on five per cent preference shares authorised by the company's Branch Act, 1865, and also by their Extension Act, 1865. The report of Mr Collister, the engineer, stated that the entire line would be completed by the Autumn of 1866.

In moving the adoption of the report, Dr Beattie warmly congratulated the directors on:

> ... the success of their exertions in obtaining the extension from Banbury to Blockley, which would have the effect of conferring great local benefit upon the district through which it would pass, and ultimately be of great advantage to the through traffic in coal and cattle from South Wales to Northampton and Banbury, while it would afford the means of transporting a great deal of iron ore to South Wales.

The other extension, from Banbury to Chipping Norton, would, suggested Dr Beattie, be of similar importance in that it would produce '*the shortest possible route to South Wales, Cheltenham and Gloucester*'.

The Chairman then referred to the Severn Junction Railway which – when completed – would provide a useful link with Monmouthshire. The report of the Engineer was, he thought, '*satisfactory*', and it was hoped that the railway would be completed '*within the period originally anticipated*'. Having passed these observations, Dr Beattie added that some of his colleagues resided on the spot and were more conversant with the '*advantages that would, accrue, both locally and generally, from the construction of the proposed works*'.

The next speaker was Mr H.J. Sheldon, of Brailes House, Shipston-on-Stour, who had recently been elected to the N&BJR Board of Directors. Living as he did, within the area which would be served by the new railways, he was:

> Well acquainted with the wants of the locality, and could bear evidence to the great requirement there had been, ever since he could remember,

for additional means of communication throughout the district. It was a thickly populated agricultural country and a large grazing district, from which many thousand head of cattle might be conveyed to the metropolis if proper communication were afforded.

The line would also be a great benefit to the inhabitants of the district, by giving them coal at a much less cost, which, under the present disadvantages of carriage – it having to be carted a distance of ten miles – raised the price to a frightful extent, and which indeed, almost precluded the use of it to the poorer classes. He was sure the projected line would secure not only a great local, but a great through traffic.

William Banks – another new director – agreed with Dr. Sheldon that there was a pressing need for improved communications in the districts which would be served by the projected lines. He had himself resided all his life in the neighbourhood of Hereford and no one could *'speak more feelingly than he of the want of communication between Hereford and Northampton'*. He knew that *'enormous quantities of coal were sent by the most circuitous routes to the Northamptonshire district'* but when the new lines were open to traffic there would be a much shorter route for both coal and iron ore, resulting in *'a vast saving of expense'*.

The meeting ended in an atmosphere of unbounded optimism and, having concluded their ordinary business, the proprietors held a special meeting to discuss the creation of new five per cent debenture shares as authorised by the 1865 Acts. Although their original line between Blisworth and Banbury was not yet open, the N&BJR directors had no intention of finishing the line at Blockley; indeed, the Blockley extension was merely the starting point for further lines and in 1866, the company deposited another Bill, with the intention of completing a rail link between Blockley and Ross-on-Wye.

This grandiose scheme received the Royal Assent in 1866. The resulting Act (*29 & 30 Vic. cap. 310*) provided consent for a 34-mile railway between Blockley and Ross-on-Wye, which would form an integral part of a 96-mile main line between Ross-on-Wye and Northamptonshire. The 1866 Act granted running powers over the Ross & Monmouth Railway and other lines while, in view of the magnitude of their projected scheme, the Northampton & Banbury Junction promoters were permitted to change the name of their undertaking – The Midland Counties & South Wales Railway was deemed a suitably expansive title for the enlarged concern!

With Northampton & Banbury Junction ambitions now directed firmly on South Wales, there was little incentive for the company to pay much attention to its original line between Blisworth and Banbury. Five miles of line between Blisworth and Towcester were nevertheless complete and the railway was opened to traffic on 30th April 1866. Unfortunately, what should have been a happy event was overshadowed when, less than two weeks later, on 10th May, the great banking firm of Overend, Gurney & Co ceased trading.

The Victorian banking system was plunged into chaos and speculative companies such as the East Gloucestershire Railway and the Midland Counties & South Wales Railway were unable to raise their authorised capital. In these circumstances, the proposed South Wales trunk route was confined to just four miles of branch line route between Blisworth and Towcester.

At length, a gradual improvement of the underlying economic situation enabled the supporters of the MC&SWR to make limited progress, and the company eventually managed to complete its line between Towcester and Cockley Brake Junction on 1st June 1872. Having resumed its former identity as the Northampton & Banbury Junction Railway, this Northamptonshire line settled down to eke out an impecunious existence as a humble branch line.

SOME OTHER ABORTIVE SCHEMES

The East Gloucestershire and Northampton & Banbury Junction schemes were both speculative ventures which, if implemented in their entirety, would have competed vigorously with the GWR. For this reason, the Great Western opposed both projects – the East Gloucestershire scheme being reduced to branch line status and eventually brought under Great Western control, whereas the Northampton & Banbury Junction Railway was subsequently merged into the Stratford-upon-Avon & Midland Junction Railway. Arguably, the EGR had posed the greatest threat to Great Western interests and for this reason the GWR devoted much attention to defeating this threat to its interests at Cheltenham.

At the same time, the Great Western was forced to pay at least some attention to the threat posed by the N&BJR on its eastern flank and thus, as a precautionary measure, John Fowler and Edward Wilson surveyed a Bourton, Chipping Norton & Banbury Railway. This scheme envisaged the construction of a cross-country line from Chipping Norton to Banbury, with a triangular junction at the Banbury end, and a system of connections at Chipping Norton Junction to permit through running between Banbury, Chipping Norton, Bourton-on-the-Water and Cheltenham.

Although the Bourton, Chipping Norton and Banbury Railway had originated merely as a defensive measure against rival projects, it can be seen as the immediate predecessor of the Banbury & Cheltenham Direct Railway.

Chapter Three

THE BANBURY & CHELTENHAM DIRECT RAILWAY

The more or less total failure of the East Gloucestershire Railway meant that a large swathe of the Gloucestershire Cotswold area remained cut off from the national railway system. There were, in consequence, very real fears that the towns and villages in this isolated rural region would be unable to share the benefits of progress and industrialisation. In the event, the abortive East Gloucestershire route from Cheltenham to Bourton-on-the-Water was revived in the early 1870s by a new company, entitled the Banbury & Cheltenham Direct Railway.

FORMATION OF THE BANBURY & CHELTENHAM DIRECT RAILWAY

The new scheme was, in many ways, similar to the original EGR proposal, in that its promoters envisaged the construction of an east-to-west cross-country line between Bourton-on-the-Water and Cheltenham. However, instead of the southern line from Andoversford to Faringdon, it was suggested that a new eastwards link might be provided between Chipping Norton and a junction with the GWR Oxford to Birmingham line at King's Sutton, to the south of Banbury. In this way, the existing Bourton-on-the-Water and Chipping Norton branch lines would be conveniently utilised as part of a new, direct route between Banbury in the east and Cheltenham in the west.

The promoters of this new concern thereby envisaged the construction of two separate lines, one of which would commence at Bourton-on-the-Water, by a junction with the existing GWR branch from Chipping Norton Junction, and terminate at Cheltenham. The other line would begin by a junction with the Chipping Norton branch and extend north-eastwards across north Oxfordshire, to join the GWR Oxford to Birmingham main line at King's Sutton. In effect, the eastern part of the suggested B&CDR line would be a revival of the Bourton, Chipping Norton & Banbury Railway, which had first been put forward in response to the Northampton & Banbury Junction extension scheme.

This early 20th century postcard view of Cheltenham is looking in a north-easterly direction towards Cleeve Hill. St. James station can be seen in the centre behind St. George's Road, which runs from left to right across the picture. The station buildings and platform awnings are largely hidden behind the bulk of the massive goods shed the GWR provided here. This picture emphasises how well placed the station was in relation to the town centre. Prominent, too, are the spires of St. Gregory's Catholic church, centre, and St. Matthew's Anglican church, to its right.

Bob Brown collection

It was anticipated that the completed line would place the North Oxfordshire iron ore producing district in direct communication with the South Wales Coalfield, thereby facilitating the growth of lucrative mineral traffic. The company's aims, as set out in its prospectus, included the creation of a line which would connect London and the Midlands and Eastern districts *'by a shorter and more direct route with the South Wales Coalfield and the West of England'*. One firm alone would require 1,000 tons of ironstone per day to be sent from the north Oxfordshire area to Wales, while it was confidently expected that around 12,000 tons of minerals would be conveyed over the line each day.

The ultimate success of the B&CDR scheme would be entirely dependent upon Great Western co-operation, while it would also be necessary for the Banbury & Cheltenham Direct Railway to reach an agreement with the East Gloucestershire company concerning the use of EGR land and works between Cheltenham and Andoversford which would be needed by the B&CDR. Great Western acquiescence was secured at an early stage and, after detailed negotiations had taken place, it was agreed that the GWR would work the Banbury & Cheltenham line in perpetuity.

Plans and sections of the proposed B&CDR were deposited with the Clerks of the Peace for the counties of Oxfordshire and Gloucestershire in the latter part of 1872, the intention being that the necessary private Bill would be submitted to Parliament for the 1873 session.

Having passed successfully through all stages of the complex Parliamentary process, the Banbury & Cheltenham Direct Railway was incorporated by Act of Parliament on 21st July 1873, with powers for the construction of lines between Banbury and Cheltenham, in connection with the existing Great Western branches to Chipping Norton and Bourton-on-the-Water. In addition to the two main sections of line between Cheltenham and Bourton-on-the-Water, and from Chipping Norton to King's Sutton, the 1873 Act also provided for the construction of an-east-to-south curve at King's Sutton, an avoiding line at Kingham and an east-to-west curve at Hatherley, to the south-east of Cheltenham.

The 1873 Act authorised the construction of $34^{1}/_{4}$ miles of line and, to pay for their scheme, the promoters were authorised to raise the sum of £600,000 by way of 30,000 £20 shares, with a further £200,000 by loan. The first Banbury & Cheltenham directors included George D. Reed, Walter Howell and Octavius Ommanney, and the Company's Engineer was Edward Wilson – a pupil of Brunel and formerly Engineer to the West Midland Railway Company.

CONSTRUCTION BEGINS

Having obtained Parliamentary consent for their scheme, the promoters were eager to begin construction and, in the closing weeks of 1874, Edward Wilson was asked to commence work on the Banbury & Cheltenham Direct line. In engineering terms, the proposed route between Cheltenham and Banbury presented many problems. The railway would cut across the grain of the country, rising from an elevation of about 150 feet at the Cheltenham end, to a height of a little under 800 feet above mean sea level in the Cotswold uplands near Notgrove.

The Chelt Valley would provide a convenient route into the Cotswolds, albeit with a viaduct and other major engineering works in the vicinity of Dowdeswell, while on the eastern side of the summit, the Windrush Valley furnished a corresponding route towards Bourton-on-the-Water. Thereafter, the Bourton-on-the-Water branch could be utilised, with very little modification, for the eastwards link towards the Oxford, Worcester & Wolverhampton main line at Chipping Norton Junction.

From Chipping Norton Junction to Chipping Norton, the existing OW&WR branch would be used, though the position of Chipping Norton station in relation to the surrounding hills meant that a new passenger station would have to be constructed to the north of the original terminus. There would, on the other hand, be no requirement for a new goods station, as the existing Great Western facilities were considered to be adequate for that purpose.

Eastwards of Chipping Norton, the proposed line would have to surmount an intervening ridge of higher land, necessitating a tunnel at Chipping Norton and a 600 foot summit near Great Rollright. Beyond there, the line would descend towards the Cherwell Valley via Hook Norton, Bloxham and Adderbury, major earthworks being required in the vicinity of Hook Norton. At the eastern end of the route, the terrain would be much more favourable, notwithstanding the need to construct bridges across the Sor Brook, the Oxford Canal and the River Cherwell – the Cherwell being so close to the canal that the resulting bridge would, in effect, form one long, low structure.

In an atmosphere of growing enthusiasm, it was reported that stations would be constructed at Adderbury, Bloxham, Hook Norton, Chipping Norton, Bourton-on-the-Water, Salperton, Andoversford and Cheltenham, £35,000 having been granted for that purpose. In December 1874, it was decided that the proposed station at Salperton would be sited slightly further to the east at Ayslworth Down, near Westfield, although the Banbury & Cheltenham directors were unable to reach a firm decision about the need for a station at Adderbury, the junction station at King's Sutton being barely two miles from the village.

Regarding the arrangements at Chipping Norton Junction, the B&CDR directors were informed that the GWR was willing to let the Banbury & Cheltenham company use the station. Encouraged, perhaps, by the Great Western's helpful attitude, it was also suggested that the proposed Banbury & Cheltenham Direct Railway station at Cheltenham (Leckhampton Road) might be developed as the town's main station in preference to the terminal station at St James.

At this stage also, serious consideration was given to making all bridges and tunnels to double track width from the outset, to allow for future doubling should traffic warrant it. A log of events kept by the company records that the Engineer and Secretary were due to see the contractors about this on 4th February 1875. By the time this date arrived, a decision had been taken not to go ahead with widening the bridges but to still consider the doubling of the tunnels. By 13th of May that year, however, it had been decreed on cost grounds that the tunnels (with the exception of Sandywell Park near Andoversford, which was built to double line specifications) should also be constructed to single line width.

Steady progress was made throughout 1875, particularly on the western section between Bourton-on-the-Water and Cheltenham. In that year, petitions were received from local residents, requesting the provision of stations at Charlton Kings and Great Rollright. It was eventually decided that a station would be constructed at Charlton Kings, although the Banbury & Cheltenham directors rejected the idea of a stopping place at Great Rollright. They did, however, agree that a station would, after all, be needed at Adderbury, where several ironstone quarries were already in operation.

With lucrative ironstone traffic in mind, the directors also decided that crossing loops with a length of at least 800 feet would be provided at each station, together with sidings of a similar length. Meanwhile, the railway was taking shape in the remote Cotswold countryside. Generally speaking, construction proceeded without serious incident between Bourton-on-the-Water and Cheltenham but there were various problems on the more difficult eastern section between Chipping Norton and King's Sutton.

Perhaps coincidentally, this part of the line cut through some important ironstone deposits and this factor may well have influenced the final choice of route. In the event, it was decided that the railway would be constructed somewhat nearer Hook Norton village than had originally been proposed, despite the delays involved in obtaining Parliamentary consent for a deviation of the authorised route. At the same time, the altered route would necessitate the construction of a tunnel and viaduct in place of an open cutting, at an estimated additional cost of £25,000.

There had, in the interim, been some major boardroom changes. In 1876, the B&CDR directors included Lieutenant-Colonel J. Wilkinson, Lord Alexander Gordon Lennox, Seymour Clarke, Hew Dalrymple, the Earl of Devon and Octavious Ommanney.

These gentleman were, collectively, the representatives of various interests, although most of them appear to have been landed proprietors. Edward Baldwin Courtney (1836-1891), of Powderham Castle, near Exeter, the 12th Earl of Devon, was a director of several other small companies in which the Great Western was interested, while Hew Dalrymple and Lord Lennox were both members of well-known Scottish landed families. Octavius Ommanney, a 59-year old gentleman living quietly with his family and two servants at Bloxham, had a more obvious interest in the provision of improved transport facilities in North Oxfordshire; his address was listed in *Bradshaw's Shareholders' Manual* as *'Bloxham and Great Westminster Street'*.

The most interesting of them all was probably Seymour Clarke. It is believed that this was the well-known individual who commenced his railway career as Chief Clerk to Isambard Kingdom Brunel during the construction of the GWR main line and later became the first Traffic Superintendent at the London end of the route. In 1850, he became General manager of the Great Northern Railway, retiring eventually after a long and distinguished career in 1870. It appears that he became associated with the Banbury & Cheltenham Railway towards the end of his life, possibly as a sort of 'retirement job' in his old age.

On 23rd July 1877, the B&CDR Company obtained a new Act of Parliament authorising the issue of £400,000 in debentures, respecting which the Great Western Railway would pay an agreed proportion of the gross receipts payable to the company, or so much as would be sufficient to cover the interest for the preceding half year on the debenture stock created and issued under the provisions of the Act. A little under one year later, an Act obtained on 8th August 1878 permitted the holders of 1877 debenture stock to vote and otherwise have the same rights as ordinary B&CDR shareholders, holdings of £20 worth of debentures being regarded as the equivalent of one ordinary Banbury & Cheltenham Direct share.

These complicated provisions masked the fact that, despite GWR support, the B&CDR was in financial trouble and had been unable to raise its authorised share capital. The situation became so serious that, in 1878, all construction work was suspended. After a hiatus of several months, work was resumed towards the latter part of 1879. In the meantime, the directors had agreed that priority would be given to finishing the western section of the route, between Cheltenham Lansdown Junction and Bourton-on-the-Water, as the works on this section had been substantially completed.

It was reported that, with the exception of Notgrove, all of the stations had been completed, while over 12 miles of track had been laid. The company's finances were, nevertheless, still in a critical state and, on 11th August 1879, a further Act of Parliament authorised the creation of £60,000 worth of debenture stock, specifically for the purpose of completing the Bourton-on-the-Water to Cheltenham line. This new stock would pay interest at five per cent per annum and it would be a first charge upon the sum payable in respect of debenture interest by the GWR under the 1873 Act of Incorporation.

There had, meanwhile, been minor problems with the Great Western over the arrangements at Cheltenham and with the East Gloucestershire Railway concerning the EGR lands at Andoversford. As far as the Great Western was concerned, the outstanding difficulties were resolved under the provisions of an Act obtained on 6th August 1880, which authorised a junction at Cheltenham and provided for a settlement of all other disputes between the Great Western and Banbury & Cheltenham Direct companies.

At this juncture, it is also apposite to look at the history of the short section of railway at Cheltenham leading from the B&CDR and heading towards Gloucester – the third arm of the triangular junction which for many years existed here. This connection was known as the Hatherley Loop and it has previously been reported in the railway press and histories of the line as having been installed for either the ironstone traffic from the Oxfordshire field heading for the South Wales steel industry or the so-called 'Ports-to-Ports express'. Whilst this is true when explaining why the section was actually *opened* it does not take into account the fact that the earthworks for it were built many years earlier, or explain why they lay abandoned for over 20 years.

The loop was included in the Banbury & Cheltenham Direct Railway Act of 1873 as Railway No. 5. The earthworks are known to have been constructed at the same time as the main Cheltenham-bound curve, as they feature in the numerous reports detailing the progress of the works. At some stage prior to opening, however, the GWR objected to the B&CDR's requirement for the curve and the latter sought adjudication on the matter under the Railway Companies' Arbitration Act 1859.

A Mr Cawkwell was appointed as arbitrator and duly notified both parties on 26th September 1881 that the B&CDR should pay the GWR a 'one off' sum, amounting to £15,000, for running rights over their line from Railway No.5 and that *'the GWR should not (upon payment being made) hinder the B&CDR in any way.'*

No record has been found of the course of events following this but a remarkable record of the earthworks can be found on the First Edition 50 inch OS for Cheltenham. They remained without track until the early years of the 20th century, which would suggest that the B&CDR decided that £15,000 for the privilege of working direct to Gloucester did not represent value for money. The 1882 6 inch Ordnance Survey map of the area also shows it as *'Course of old railway'*.

Regarding the East Gloucestershire company, the problems appeared to be more persistent. In theory, the unfinished East Gloucestershire earthworks in and around Andoversford should have expedited the work of construction and, in this context, it is interesting to note that the EGR company had tried to sell its unwanted land to the B&CDR. Perversely, the latter Company attempted to deviate its own route in order to avoid the cost of purchase but the East Gloucestershire Railway successfully opposed the B&CDR deviation Bill, with the result that the Banbury & Cheltenham Railway company had to pay rent to the East Gloucestershire company for the use of its land and embankments at Andoversford.

It was eventually agreed that the Banbury & Cheltenham Direct line would run along an existing East Gloucestershire embankment from a point near Andoversford station. This left a substantial section of embankment isolated in a field to the south of the Banbury & Cheltenham Direct route, which remains to this day as a memorial to the East Gloucestershire Railway's unrealised dreams of reaching Cheltenham.

COMPLETION BETWEEN CHELTENHAM AND BOURTON-ON-THE-WATER

Although horses, mechanical excavators and other mechanical aids were used during the construction of the Banbury & Cheltenham Direct line, much of the work relied on human muscle-power, and for this purpose the contractors employed up to 400 navvies at various times. Many of these construction workers lived in hutted encampments beside the unfinished railway, one such shanty town being established in the vicinity of Dowdeswell and Andoversford, where the nature of the work required a large number of labourers, together with a range of specialist workers such as bricklayers, who would obviously have been needed in connection with the building of Dowdeswell Viaduct.

Generally speaking, standards of accommodation, behaviour and cleanliness appear to have been commendably high, possibly because many of the navvies were married men who lived with their wives and children in the construction camps. Many of the navvy huts were presided over by a resident 'landlord' or 'landlady', who ensured that the buildings were regularly cleaned, supervised laundry duties, and arranged regular food and cooked meals for the occupants. The 'landlady' was sometimes the wife of a ganger or other senior navvy, although other wives, mothers or daughters would also have been available to carry out cooking, cleaning, ironing or other routine domestic chores.

The 1881 Census provides an insight into the organisation

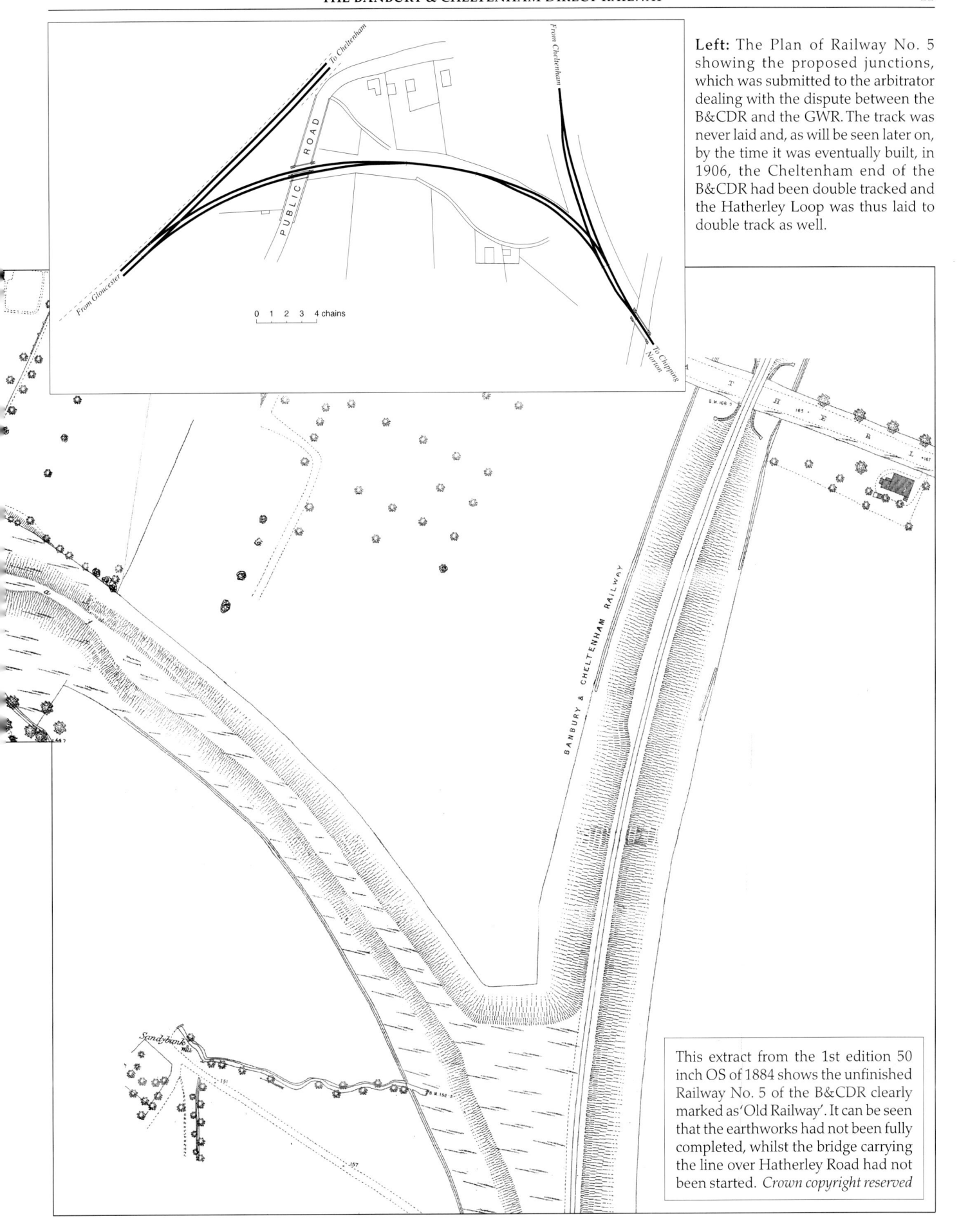

Left: The Plan of Railway No. 5 showing the proposed junctions, which was submitted to the arbitrator dealing with the dispute between the B&CDR and the GWR. The track was never laid and, as will be seen later on, by the time it was eventually built, in 1906, the Cheltenham end of the B&CDR had been double tracked and the Hatherley Loop was thus laid to double track as well.

This extract from the 1st edition 50 inch OS of 1884 shows the unfinished Railway No. 5 of the B&CDR clearly marked as 'Old Railway'. It can be seen that the earthworks had not been fully completed, whilst the bridge carrying the line over Hatherley Road had not been started. *Crown copyright reserved*

of the navvy camps in and around Andoversford. The census returns indicate that many of the men lived in a number of so-called 'temporary buildings', most of which were said to have been at Dowdeswell. Each hut typically housed eight or ten men, plus their wives and children, around 100 people being accommodated in this one navvy encampment. Interestingly, the census refers to 'hutkeepers', such as Ann Dennies and Mercy Kibblewhite, who no doubt carried out the various domestic functions outlined above. The occupants of the Dowdeswell navvy camp at the time of the census are shown in the table reproduced below.

In addition to the navvies, bricklayers and other workers housed in the 'temporary buildings', many other railway navvies were living in local inns and alehouses at the time of the 1881 census. Yet others were indigenous labourers, who lived in their own cottages, and would have walked to and from work at the beginning and end of each day. The census shows that these 'railway labourers' were distributed along the western section of the B&CDR line between Bourton-on-the-Water and Cheltenham, suggesting that work was being pressed forward on this part of the route in order that it could be opened first; there was no

NAME	STATUS / AGE	PLACE OF BIRTH	RELATIONSHIP	OCCUPATION
DWELLING 1: Lower Dowdeswell, Temporary Building				
William ATKIN	M / 44	Gedburgh, Roxburgh, Scotland	Head	Horsekeeper
Mary ATKIN	M / 38	Crossmichael, Kirkcudbright, Scotland	Wife	Horsekeeper's Wife
Annie ATKIN	U / 13	Newell, Derby, England	Daughter	Scholar
William ATKIN	U / 11	Mansfield, Nottingham, England	Son	Scholar
Elizabeth Jane ATKIN	U / 9	Ellesbridge, York, England	Daughter	Scholar
Isabella ATKIN	U / 6	Ellesbridge, York, England	Daughter	Scholar
Andrew ATKIN	U / 2	Dowdeswell, Gloucester, England	Son	
John ATKIN	U / 8mths	Dowdeswell, Gloucester, England	Son	
Isabella THOMASON	M / 58	Kirkcudbright, Scotland	Mother-in-law	Housekeeper (Dom)
Richard DENMAN	M / 58	North Cadbury, Somerset, England	Boarder	Rly. Platelayer
William DENMAN	U / 16	Harwich, Essex, England	Boarder	Rly. Labourer
David GREGORY	U / 22	Badgworth, Gloucester, England	Boarder	Rly. Labourer
Joseph BARNES	U / 20	Shepton Mallett, Somerset, England	Boarder	Rly. Labourer
James WOOLLEY	U / 22	Fairford, Gloucester, England	Boarder	Rly. Labourer
DWELLING 2: Dowdeswell, Temporary Building				
Alfred TURNEY	M / 32	Slapton, Bedford, England	Head	Blacksmith
Clara TURNEY	M / 37	Islington, Middlesex, England	Wife	Blacksmith's Wife
Alfred TURNEY	U / 11	Islington, Middlesex, England	Son	Scholar
Richard TURNEY	U / 9	Settle, York, England	Son	Scholar
Emmaline TURNEY	U / 7	Settle, York, England	Daughter	Scholar
Thomas TURNEY	U / 1	Cheltenham, Gloucester, England	Son	
DWELLING 3: Dowdeswell, Temporary Building				
Mercy KIBBLEWHITE	M / 40	Elton, Kent, England	Head	Hutkeeper (Dom)
DWELLING 4: Dowdeswell, Temporary Building				
John HOLTHAM	M / 44	Cheltenham, Gloucester, England	Head	Brickmaker
Mary Ellen HOLTHAM	M / 34	Cheltenham, Gloucester, England	Wife	Brickmaker's Wife
Albert HOLTHAM	U / 11	Cheltenham, Gloucester, England	Son	Scholar
Emma HOLTHAM	U / 9	Cheltenham, Gloucester, England	Daughter	Scholar
Florence Ada HOLTHAM	U / 5	Cheltenham, Gloucester, England	Daughter	Scholar
Walter Thomas HOLTHAM	U / 4	Cheltenham, Gloucester, England	Son	
Charles Ernest HOLTHAM	U / 10mths	Dowdeswell, Gloucester, England	Son	
Charles LEVER	U / 45		Boarder	Rly. Labourer
Charles AUSTIN	U / 34	Diddeford[1]	Boarder	Rly. Labourer
DWELLING 5: Dowdeswell, Temporary Building				
Ann DENNIES	W / 77	Ipstock,[2] Leicester, England	Head	Hutkeeper (Dom)
Phillis Ann EYRE	U / 17	London, Middlesex, England	Granddaughter	Needlewoman
Tom Dennies EYRE	U / 13	Braday, York, England	Grandson	Rly. Labourer
George TINGLE	U / 5	Ripley, Derby, England	Grandson	Scholar
John FOSTER	M / 33	North Mail[3]	Boarder	Rly. Labourer
William WEBB	U / 32	Corse[4]	Boarder	Rly. Labourer
Adam LANE	U / 20	Redmarley, Worcester	Boarder	Rly. Labourer
George HOLDER	U / 19	Staunton[5]	Boarder	Rly. Labourer

DWELLING 6: Dowdeswell, Temporary Building				
Richard FOSTER	M / 59	Sutton Coldfield, Warwick, England	Head	Rly. Labourer
Jane FOSTER	M / 49	Rochdale, Lancashire, England	Wife	Rly. Labourer's Wife
May LOWDEN	U / 18	Rochdale, Lancashire, England	Granddaughter	Housekeeper (Dom)
Eliza Jane FOSTER	U / 16	Hyde, Cheshire, England	Daughter	
Ellen FOSTER	U / 7	Sheffield, York, England	Daughter	Scholar
William Henry LOWDEN	U / 5	Withington, Gloucester, England	Grandson	
Elizabeth Ann FOSTER	U / 12	Sheffield, York, England	Daughter	Scholar
Stephen MINCHIN	U / 22	Stow-on-the-Wold, Gloucester	Boarder	Rly. Labourer
Henry TAYLOR	U / 23	Salsford,[6] Warwick, England	Boarder	Rly. Labourer
Samuel HOLBROOKE	M / 55	Stanton Drew, Somerset, England	Boarder	Rly. Labourer

DWELLING 7: Dowdeswell, Temporary Building				
Charles FOSTER	M / 60	Whittinton,[7] Somerset, England	Head	Rly. Labourer
Mary Ann FOSTER	M / 60	Whittinton, Somerset, England	Wife	Rly. Labourer's Wife
Charles FOSTER	U / 9	Whittinton, Somerset, England	Grandson	Scholar

DWELLING 8: Dowdeswell, Temporary Building				
James BISHOP	M / 46	Yatton, Somerset, England	Head	Rly. Ganger
Mary Ann BISHOP	M / 41	Yatton, Somerset, England	Wife	Rly. Ganger's Wife
George BISHOP	U / 9	Kirkswold,[8] Cumberland, England	Son	Scholar
Agnes BISHOP	U / 7	Jericho, York, England	Daughter	Scholar
Jane BISHOP	U / 3	Manchester, Lancashire, England	Daughter	
Ann HAWKINS	W / 61	Yatton, Somerset, England	Mother-in-Law	Housekeeper (Dom.)
Thomas MORGAN	U / 36	Bromley, Kent, England	Boarder	Rly. Labourer
William BROWN	U / 61	Bledlow, Buckingham, England	Boarder	Rly. Labourer
George SMITH	U / 21	Stow-on-the-Wold, Gloucester	Boarder	Rly. Labourer
Adam WILLIAMS	U / 24	Dean Forest, Gloucester, England	Boarder	Rly. Labourer
George MEMBERS	U / 28	Stow-on-the-Wold, Gloucester	Boarder	Rly. Labourer
George WILLIAMS	U / 38	New Passage, Gloucester, England	Boarder	Rly. Labourer
Leonard SMITH	U / 37	Wells, Somerset, England	Boarder	Rly. Labourer

KEY: M = Married   U = Unmarried   W = Widow or Widower   Dom= Domestic

NOTES:
1. No place known of this name. Might refer to Bideford?
2. No place known of this name. Almost certainly refers to Ibstock, Leics.
3. No place known of this name.
4. Corse is in north Glos., near Newent and Redmarley.
5. Most likely the Worcs. Staunton, also near Newent and Redmarley. These 3 men possibly already knew each other.
6. No place known of this name. Probably Salford Priors, near Alcester.
7. No place known of this name
8. Actually Kirkoswald

There are a number of other suspect place names such as Newell and Ellesbridge. Much of this may be down to vagueries of spelling and the poor education of some of those recording the information.

evidence of any comparable work taking place at the eastern end of the line. However, there were several empty huts noted, indicating that much of the work was completed and construction of this section drawing to a close at the time the census was carried out.

A further point to be made concerns the birth places of the navvies engaged on the B&CDR line, most of whom were local men. This was the usual pattern on railway construction projects in the agricultural areas of southern England, which were invariably built by farm workers or other labourers who would otherwise have been unemployed. The census lists one or two Scotsmen and several northern Englishmen but there were few (if any) Irishmen at work on the line in 1881 – Irish navvies were found more frequently in the industrial areas of the North and Midlands.

An inspection of the new railway was carried out on 28th March 1881, which indicated that a number of alterations were required, as well as minor works finished, before the line could be sanctioned for the use of passengers:

The Secretary
Railway Department
Board of Trade   28th March 1881
Sir
I have the honour to report for the information of the Board of Trade in compliance with your instructions contained in your Minute of the 17th instant that I have inspected the Banbury and Cheltenham Railway from the Lansdown Junction with the Great Western Railway near Cheltenham to Bourton on Water station of the same Railway.

The new line is about 16 miles 47 chains long. It is single throughout with sidings and looplines at the Junctions and at Andoversford Station which is the only place fitted as a passing place for trains.

Land has been enclosed for a second line of rails and the overbridges and the tunnel have been constructed for a double line. The ruling gradient is 1 in 60 and the sharpest curve except on crossings has a radius of 20 chains.

The Permanent way consists of a double headed iron rail that weighs 80 lbs per linear yard. It is fished and fixed with wooden keys in cast iron chairs that weigh 36 lbs each. The chairs are fastened with screw bolts to transverse wooden sleepers. There are eight sleepers to every 23 feet rail. The sleepers are 9 feet long 10 in. x 5 in. The line is well ballasted and well fenced.

The works are very numerous and consist of 33 under and 30 over bridges. Six under and seven over bridges have wrought iron girders on brick abutments and one footover bridge is constructed of timber. All the other bridges are built of brick and stone. The widest span is 43 feet. The Dowdeswell Viaduct which is built of brick consists of 12 openings of 40 feet span and there is a tunnel 385 yards long at the summit of the line.

These works appear to be substantially constructed and sufficiently strong. The iron girders gave very moderate deflections and are very strong according to calculation.

The wooden footbridge and the wooden staircase at Charlton Kings Station require to be strengthened.

The bricks are in many cases defective and disfigure the work.

The abutments at 16 miles 28 chains show signs of having settled and the abutments of the bridge at 15 miles 70 chains overhang 6 inches at one side and 4 inches at the other side. I do not think they will yield any more but these as well as the very numerous and very large slips along the Railway will require careful watching.

The stations are Notgrove, Andoversford, Charlton Kings and Leckhampton in addition to the terminal stations at Cheltenham and Bourton on the Water.

The following works are required:

Lansdowne [sic] Junction Cabin, separate distant signals instead of slotting the home signals are required for the line from Bourton and for the Midland Railway from Cheltenham to Gloucester and from Cheltenham to Bourton.

A safety point is required on the loop line from Cheltenham to Bourton.

The gauge rods to the stock rails and the connecting rods between the points require to be completed.

The curves require to be taken out of the line at Charlton Kings Station.

The platform fencing requires to be completed at Andoversford Station.

At Bourton Station the distant signal from Stowe [sic] requires to be placed at least 650 yards from the home signal.

Clocks are required at all the stations and in all the signal cabins.

Gauge rods are required for the stock rails in many cases near the facing points.

The rivulet culverts require to be protected by gridirons to prevent timber and grass from choking them.

The platforms are in many cases too far from the rails. They should be so arranged that the steps of the coaches should come within 2 inches of the edge.

In addition to the above there are heavy slips at each side of the tunnel which will require to be drained by cuttings and pipes at the top of the banks so as to prevent all water percolating through from the adjacent lands to the faces of the cutting and the slopes of the cutting will require to be regulated and dressed with stone and supported at the bottom by stone walls to prevent the water tables being choked.

The rock cuttings require to be completed so as to secure the Railway from falling stone.

The means of watering and turning the engines are also required.

I enclose an undertaking as to the proposed mode of working which is satisfactory if the train staff system can be carried out on so great a length of Railway with only one passing place.

I submit that the Banbury & Cheltenham Railway cannot be opened for passenger traffic without danger to the public using the same by reason of the incomplete state of some of the works.

Col. F.H. Rich, R.E.

The comment about the tunnel being at the summit of the line is odd because it was nowhere near; the summit was at Notgrove, about 5 miles further on and another 200 feet higher. The reference to Bourton-on-the-Water as a terminal station was purely in regard to the new works; it did not indicate any intention to terminate trains there. It would also seem likely that the restrictions imposed by the Inspecting Officer's *'proposed mode of working'* to allow for the use of the train staff system made it unacceptable to the directors of the new line. By the time services commenced just over two months later, passing places had also been provided at Charlton Kings and Notgrove, as well as Andoversford and Bourton-on-the-Water.

The line between Lansdown Junction and Bourton-on-the-Water was opened on 1st June 1881. The following report of the opening appeared in the *Cheltenham Examiner* for Wednesday, 8th June 1881:

BANBURY & CHELTENHAM DIRECT RAILWAY
Opening of the Cheltenham to Bourton section

The completed section of the Banbury and Cheltenham Railway, between Cheltenham and Bourton on the Water, was opened for traffic on Wednesday last, the first of June.

There was no formality at the opening. Indeed, the absence of ceremonial of any kind was one of the most remarkable features of a day which might fairly claim to be a 'red letter' one in the railway calendar of the locality.

It is thirty-four years since the opening of a railway of direct importance to Cheltenham took place, and then the completion of the Great Western branch from Swindon to Cheltenham was celebrated by fete trains and banquets and such like evidences of public rejoicing. In the interval there has been an almost perennial effort on the part of the district to obtain further accommodation in the direction which the Banbury and Cheltenham Railway will serve, but after so many years' waiting and disappointment the line on Wednesday was opened without any attempt at official celebration, and as though the occasion were anything rather than a day of rejoicing to those having control of the undertaking. The people of the locality did show their interest in the occasion by the simple process of patronising the trains run during the day, but never was a line opened, we would think, with a greater appearance of desire on the part of the controlling power to check inconvenient enthusiasm and to make the opening as matter-of-fact and prosaic as possible. The new line, by its alliance with the Great Western Company, is under that Company's absolute direction, the Banbury and Cheltenham Company merely receiving a moiety of the traffic receipts from their undertaking, and the credit or otherwise of the opening arrangements rests therefore entirely with the Great Western Company. Notwithstanding all the delay that has taken place in the use of the line by the public, less than a week's official notice of the date of opening was given, and so little effort was made to make the traffic arrangements known, that on the day before the opening there were not half a dozen time-bills in the town, and the public were chiefly dependant on the publication of the time-tables in the columns of the Press, on the evening prior to and on the day of opening, for any information on the subject. But for the energy of the Deputy-Chairman of the Banbury and Cheltenham Company (Mr Allen), who with the Secretary (Mr Looker), was in town on the day before the opening, the publicity given to the arrangements would have been less even than it was. If any overture had been made to the Corporation with that view, we believe that the Mayor of Cheltenham would have been pleased to take part in a formal opening of the undertaking, and it is to be regretted that some such inauguration of it was not provided for.

The first train left the St. James's Square station at 6.30 in the morning. It consisted of eleven carriages well filled with passengers, chiefly booked for Leckhampton and Charlton Kings, people determined to have a first ride on the new line. Among the passengers booked through were Mr Allen, the deputy chairman of the Banbury and Cheltenham Company, Mr J.S. McIntyre (a member of the firm of Messrs. E. Wilson & Co., the engineers of the line), Mr Looker, the Secretary, and two or three representatives of the local press, among whom one gentleman had chosen to reach Epsom for the Derby. As the train passed out of the station it fired its own salute of honour in the shape of a number of fog signals which had been placed along the rails.

There was little in the way of incident to report *en route*. People had gathered on the bridges and at the stations to watch the train go by, and by these it was occasionally cheered, but it was not until nearing Bourton that any other demonstration was made. Some of the houses near to the line there had flags displayed, and at a prettily situated little seat on the left hand side of the way, before reaching Bourton, there were some effective decorations, including a pretty floral arch, standing in the park-like field in front of the house, with the word 'Success' emblazoned upon it. At Bourton station there was a crowd of the people of the little town, by whom the train was lustily cheered as it approached. The station offices had been tastefully decorated with flowers by the daughters of the host of the neighbouring hotel (Mr Stokes) who had placed along the waiting shed on the up platform the legend 'Long life to Lovatt', Mr Lovatt being, we need hardly add, the contractor of the line, – and over the booking office on the down side the words 'Success to our New line'. The majority of the passengers left the train at Bourton and enjoyed a stroll through the quiet town and along the banks of the lovely stream which is the attraction of the place, but others, after a late breakfast at Mr Stokes' comfortable hostelry, travelled on over the old line, by Chipping Norton junction, to Oxford, and spent the remainder of the day in the University city. Two or three went on to London, two of these, on their way to the Derby, gaining half an hour

A Banbury & Cheltenham-line train waiting to leave Cheltenham St. James around 1908. The formation is fairly typical of passenger trains over the route from its opening until the early years of the 20th century, with the exception of the clerestory bogie coach at the rear. This was most probably a through coach for London, which would have been detached at Chipping Norton Junction for connection to a London-bound service. The locomotive is 'Metro' 2-4-0 tank No. 4 from the '455' series. The name derived from the fact that the early members of the class worked over Metropolitan Railway metals in the capital. No. 4 was in fact one of the early builds, to Lot 18 in 1869; these 20 engines formed a sub-class as noted above but were also referred to as 'Small Metros' due to their shorter coupled wheelbase. As built, No. 4 was also fitted with condensing apparatus for working on the Met. but when seen here, it was probably allocated to Gloucester and sub-shedded at Cheltenham. They were very useful engines with a noted turn of speed and many examples lasted well into the 1930s. No. 4 was not so lucky, however, being withdrawn in 1913.   *John Alsop collection*

Prior to the opening of the GWR's new route to Birmingham, via Honeybourne and Stratford on Avon, in 1907, trains leaving St. James station ran under St. George's Road Bridge and past the original Cheltenham engine shed, which dated from the opening of the line in 1847. It was on a restricted site, tucked into the west bank of the cutting between St. George's Road and Malvern Road bridges. The shed was a two-road affair, built mainly of wood but with the far side, which butted against the cutting bank, constructed of stone. It was 161 feet long and had a slate roof, with hipped ends and a central louvre vent which ran almost the entire length of the building. There had been a 40 foot diameter turntable in front of the shed (with three short stabling stubs running off it, as well as the two shed roads) but this was removed in 1895. The simplified layout then consisted of the two shed roads and a stabling siding running back towards Malvern Road. It was demolished in 1906 to make way for the junction with the Honeybourne line, being replaced by a new facility at Malvern Road. This turn of the century view shows an express leaving St. James in the charge of an unidentified 4-4-0. *Ian Pope collection*

as compared with those, on a similar errant bent, who chose the first train by the Swindon route for their journey.

The later trains in the day carried large freights, and the excitement at the stations along the route became greater as the day wore on. There was, however, no incident calling for record. The weather was warm and fine, and the change of temperature from the valley to the high ground at Andoversford and Notgrove was pleasant, but the heat made the atmosphere very hazy, and the lovely view to be obtained on a clear day from the Dowdeswell valley was scarcely seen at its best. The travelling arrangements were well carried out, and we should not be doing justice if we did not acknowledge the courtesy and good temper with which Mr Cooke, the station master, and the officials at St. James's Square station, discharged the extra and somewhat trying duties which the opening of the new line, and the general ignorance of its fares and arrangements on the part of the passengers, threw upon them.

We have very recently given particulars of the route of the new line, in connection with the Government inspection, and the report we then published has been generally adopted by our contemporaries. For the information of those, however, who may wish to read it in connection with the opening of the line we may here repeat that the new line, after travelling over the Great Western branch to the main Midland and Great Western line at Lansdown, passes for a short distance over the joint track before branching off through Hatherley towards Leckhampton. Originally the junction was intended to be made by two branches, like the arms of the letter Y, one (that already made) diverging towards Cheltenham, and the other sweeping towards Gloucester, along which through fast trains were intended to pass, without the delay of running into and backing out of the St. James's Square station. The second branch is only partly formed, and work has long been discontinued upon it, but the piers of the girder bridge, by which it will be carried over the Hatherley Road, are standing, and its completion would be comparatively a light work at any time.

Whether or not it will be completed will depend probably on the future alliance of the line. As originally planned too, the arm towards Cheltenham joined the Great Western line on the Cheltenham side of the Lansdown junction so as to touch the Great Western branch alone, but during its estrangement from the Great Western the new company got the arm shortened so as to join the joint track of the Midland and Great Western companies. Thus nothing but the sanction of Parliament is required to make a connection with the Midland system. The two arms of the Y will converge near the Alma Road, on the late Mr. Winterbotham's property. The completed branch crosses the Hatherley Road to this point by a girder bridge, and similar bridges span the

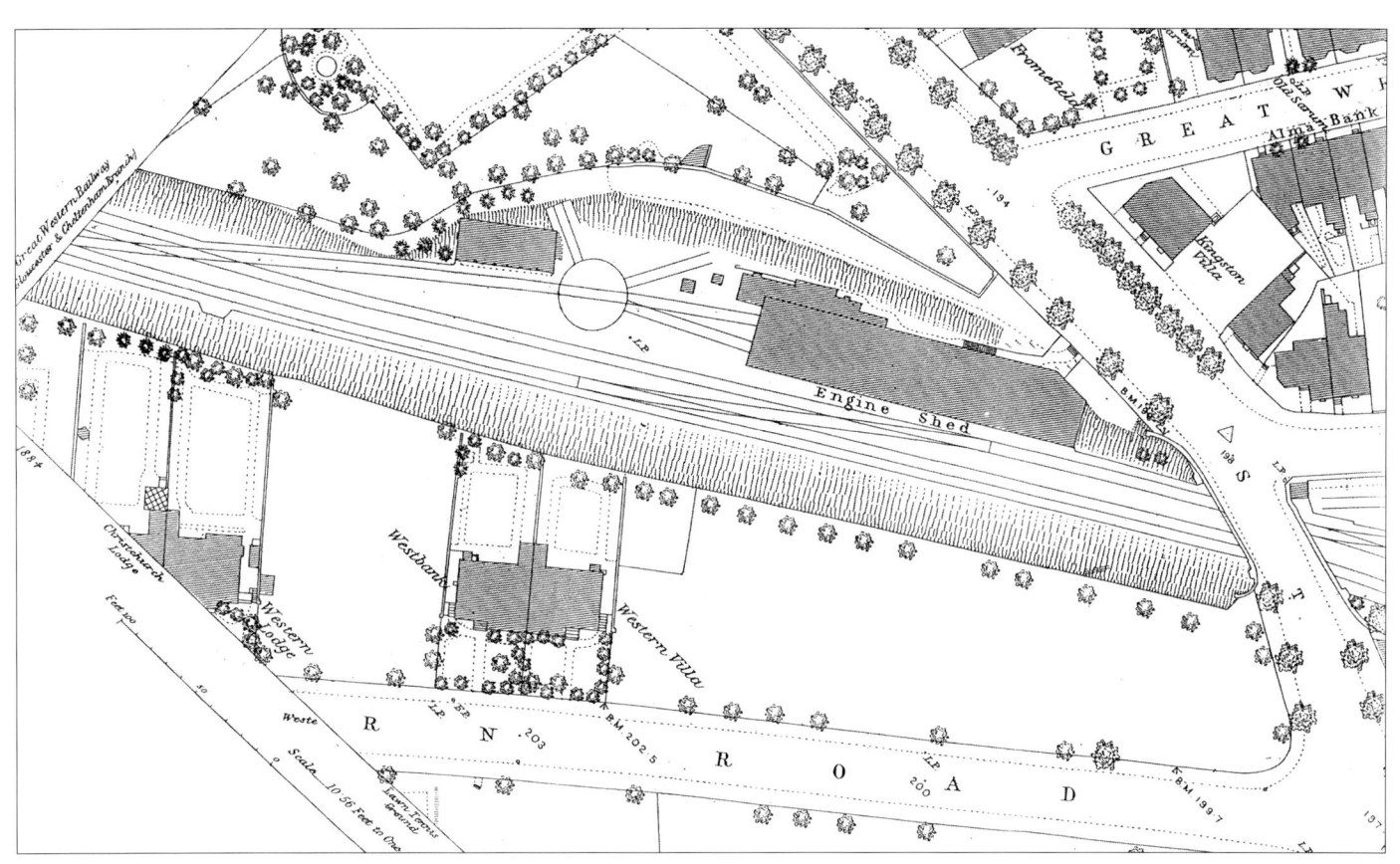

A section from the 1884 50 inch Ordnance Survey showing Cheltenham engine shed. St. James station is to the right. The map has been reduced by approximately two thirds but the scale has been included bottom left. The 40 foot diameter turntable is shown but with only two stabling stubs running off it. The coaling platform is to the left of the turntable. *Crown copyright reserved*

Alma Road and one or two other roads on the Hatherley estate before the line passes by cutting under the road from Cheltenham to Shurdington, the Moorend Park, and the Leckhampton roads. Upon this latter road is the Leckhampton station. The platform is about 300 feet in length. On the side nearer the town there is the usual station accommodation, and there is on the same side some provision for wharfage, though it is scarcely equal to what we believe will be the need as the traffic with the hills is developed. Still chiefly in cutting, but with glimpses of pretty scenery around, the line proceeds towards Charlton Kings station, the first passing station on the line, placed at the point where the Cirencester Road crosses the track, and not far from the foot of the hill. Thence the line passes in cutting above the village of Charlton Kings. It then rises by gradients of about 1 in 70, cutting through outlying ridges of the hill and passing over the intervening ravines, necessitating a succession of heavy work in cuttings and embankment, which the nature of the soil, a treacherous, heavy clay, has made the more difficult to contractors. At the back of Whithorne, the pretty residence of Col. Holmes, the work has been very heavy, through the subsidence from time to time of the high embankment, but the soil has now settled, it is believed, at its natural angle, and no further difficulty is apprehended. The effect has been to spread the base of the embankment a long way towards the London Road, which here runs parallel with the line. The long slope is planted with shrubs, the roots of which will be useful in binding the soil, while their appearance will be pretty. The view from the line at this point is very fine. Facing up the line, the wooded top of Dowdeswell, with its pretty Church and Court among the trees, can be seen, and the first glimpse is here obtained of the intervening viaduct. On the left one looks down on Col. Holmes's gable-ended house, with its well kept lawns; beyond this is the London road, its white surface dotted with passing traffic; and still beyond, rise the hills on the other side of the Chelt valley. On the right is a wooded gorge, with its watercourse. Turning toward the town, a good view of the open valley of the Severn is gained, anf of the suburbs of Cheltenham. There is constant variation as the line still rises up the valley of the Chelt stream. At other places similar engineering difficulties have been met with to those at Col. Holmes's, a more serious one being at Woodbank, just before the viaduct is reached. The subsidence of the embankment here has carried out the base some 200 feet or so towards the road, but this also has now been conquered, and no further settlement is feared. The embankment at Woodbank terminates in the viaduct, which carries the line over the Dowdeswell Hill road and the ravine down which the main stream of the Chelt runs. Originally it was intended to cross the London road on a high embankment, some way nearer Cheltenham than Woodbank, as proposed by the old East Gloucestershire scheme, and to ascend the Dowdeswell valley on the left hand side of the road. But by the course adopted, the London road is not interfered with, and the line crosses from Woodbank to the high ground on the opposite side of the ravine on a viaduct running parallel with the road. This viaduct is the most interesting work on this section of the line. From below it is of light appearance, but closer acquaintance satisfies one that this appearance is due to the proportions of the design and not to any lack of solidity. As a fact, it is particularly strong. The bricks were all made upon the line, and are laid in mortar largely compounded of blue clay and ballast. This has set like iron. The viaduct, with its abutments, is about 548 feet long. It has twelve openings, each of 40 feet span, and the highest arch, from the bed of the brook running below, to the crown, is 70 feet in

Cheltenham Lansdown Junction, looking north towards St. James station around 1890, with the Midland line to Birmingham curving off to the left. The magnificent signal box, a Gloucester RC&W Company product, was provided for the opening of the Banbury & Cheltenham line, the extra height being necessary to allow sight of the new junction over the adjacent Lansdown Road bridge, on which the photographer was standing. Note that also for sighting purposes, the bracket signal for GWR trains approaching Lansdown Junction is high up on the right hand bank, allowing locomotive crews a view of it from beyond the road bridge in the distance. This box was closed in May 1914 and replaced by a standard GWR hipped-roof, brick-built cabin, which was sited in the recess in the bank visible to the right of the actual junction. *Gloucester Graphic, courtesy Gloucester Public Library, Local Studies Collection*

height. About a million-and-a-half of bricks have been used in the construction of the viaduct. Beyond the viaduct the line again emerges on an embankment, soon, however, again to pass into a cutting, which ends with a tunnel under Sandywell Park, at the top of Dowdeswell Hill. This tunnel is 385 yards long, bricked throughout, and has taken about $3^{3}/_{4}$ millions of bricks in its construction. A little distance from the outlet of the tunnel the line again reaches the open country, and Andoversford station, a few hundred yards from the Andoversford inn, is on an embankment. This is also a passing station, the rails here being double. Between the stations the line is a single one, though the overhead bridges and tunnel have been made for a double line, and sufficient land acquired for that purpose. The works on the section of the line beyond Andoversford are heavy, though very different to those on the earlier section of the line. Up the Dowdeswell Valley the difficulty was found in the peculiar soapy clay of the district. When excavated it is almost as hard as stone, but when exposed to the air and damp it slakes like lime, and becomes of the consistency of soap. But beyond Andoversford the excavations are almost all through rock, in some places so hard that every yard of it had to be blasted. Here was no danger of shifting of cuttings or embankments.

Two and a half miles or so beyond Andoversford. Notgrove (Westfield as it was first named) station is reached. The work about here is very heavy. At the top of Hampen Hill the line reaches its highest point, 634 feet above the junction at Lansdown.

It crosses the summit in a cutting of an extreme depth of 62 feet through the solid oolite; the sides are a mass of rugged stone which seems almost to overhang the way, and is suggestive of rich store for geologists. This Hampen Hill cutting is the deepest cutting along the line; it is three quarters of a mile long, and for a good portion of its length 54 feet deep. The embankment which grows out of it towards Notgrove is also the highest on the section. From the summit of Hampen Hill there is a steady decline to Bourton, which is still 288 feet above the level of the Lansdown junction. At Bourton the new line finds its continuation in the line from Bourton to Chipping Norton Junction, and the only work here done by the new company has been in the enlargement of the station, and adapting it for through service. To complete the project of the Banbury and Cheltenham Company, the section between Chipping Norton and Banbury has yet to be

The first two stations out from St. James on the new line were both still within the environs of Cheltenham. **Above**, a service from Kingham, hauled by one of the ubiquitous 'Metro' tanks which seemed to be synonymous with passenger services on the route at this period, calls at Leckhampton *en route* to St. James around 1905, again with a bogie clerestory coach in the formation. The enamel advertising signs on the station building include one for Daleforty Pianos of Cheltenham, as well as the more common ones for Sutton's Seeds and Van Houten's Cocoa. **Below**, an unidentified 0-6-0 saddle tank pauses at Charlton Kings with a Kingham to Cheltenham St. James service around 1906, making a change from the 'Metro' tanks that were more usually photographed with the local passenger trains at this time. The station always had two platforms, being one of the crossing places for trains when the line was first opened. However, when this section was doubled, the platforms were lengthened and the extensions are quite evident, with bricks being used instead of the original stone and the new sections being slightly higher. *Top: John Alsop collection; bottom: Michael Mitchell collection*

The long climb from Charlton Kings to the line's summit near Notgrove was broken about midway by the station at Andoversford. This circa 1910 view is looking west towards Sandywell Tunnel and Cheltenham, along the section of line which utilised the earthworks of the abortive East Gloucestershire Railway. For the first 10 years of its existence, Andoversford was a simple country station and a passing place on the route between Cheltenham and Kingham. However, from 1891, it became a junction where the cross-country Midland & South Western Junction Railway route met the B&CDR to share its metals into Cheltenham. However, the interloper then ran into a bay at Cheltenham Lansdown station, rather than using the GWR facilities at St. James. *Michael Mitchell collection*

Another 'Metro' tank at Notgrove station around 1905, with a train of 6-wheeled passenger stock plus a milk van at the rear. This posed view was taken from the steps of the signal box and the signalman can be seen standing on the platform holding the single line train staff. In the background is the 62 foot deep cutting referred to in the newspaper report, spanned by the triple-arched bridge carrying the Andoversford to Bourton road. *Bob Brown collection*

The Bourton-on-the-Water Railway station at Bourton is shown here again, in an early 20th century scene taken from the inclined approach to the road bridge. The similarity of the main station building to that at Stow-on-the-Wold is clearly shown. Whilst both were undoubtedly attractive buildings, the mock Elizabethan features owed little to local architectural practice. The fact that both stations were replaced with plainer buildings of local stone in the 1930s would suggest perhaps that the various rather fussy features incorporated in the original designs did not wear well over the years. This view gives a useful glimpse of the rear of the wooden shelter on the Up platform, as well as the original signal box, in the left distance. This was replaced by a standard GW brick-built example in 1912. The conifers on the platform are probably a GWR addition dating from when the Cheltenham extension opened.
Neil Parkhouse collection

The Railway Hotel at Bourton, Alex A. Stokey, proprietor, on a picture postcard of around 1903. The card was published by Taunt & Co., the company established by the noted Oxfordshire photographer Henry Taunt. Behind the hotel on the right is the bridge which carried Station Road across the line. The signal visible is the Up Home. Besides its proximity to the station at Bourton-on-the-Water, the Railway Hotel is also of importance in the history of the B&CDR as it was used as a meeting place by the promoters of the line in the 1870s. *Neil Parkhouse collection*

completed. Considerable progress has been made with it, and the Company have a bill in Parliament authorising the raising of the capital to complete this portion. Though not perhaps as heavy throughout, some portions of the line are even heavier than any this side of Bourton, and the cutting and embankment at Hook Norton are among the heaviest works of their kind in England. When this section is completed a new country will be opened up and a direct access be given to the eastern counties.

The following are the fares for the single journey:

From Cheltenham to:	1st class s. d.	2nd class s. d.	3rd class s. d.
Leckhampton	0 8	0 5	0 3½
Charlton	1 0	0 8	0 5
Andoversford	1 8	1 1	0 9½
Notgrove	2 8	1 10	1 3½
Bourton-on-the-Water	3 9	2 7	1 9½
Stow	4 4	3 0	2 1½
Chipping Norton Junc	6 2	4 3	2 6½

To Oxford the fares by way of Didcot are – 1st, 12s. 6d.; 2nd, 9s 9d.; 3rd, 5s. 11½ d. By the new route they will be – 1st, 9s. 11d; 2nd, 7s 3d.; 3rd, 4s. 9½ d.

These fares, we believe, are all above the ordinary fares for the mileage covered, and probably one of the first efforts to make the new line really what it should be, will be a struggle with the Great Western over the charges it makes over the line it has adopted.

The report makes interesting reading although, with its decidedly critical stance, not for the GWR. It alludes to the fact the new line had taken an unconscionably long time to complete, whilst recognising there had been some severe problems encountered during the construction. The fact the line was opened with none of the usual fanfare and with little advance publicity also comes in for strong comment, quite unusual in a paper of the period. Perhaps the lack of advertising placed in the local press had left noses out of joint in the area. The strongest comment, however, is reserved for the fares, which were deemed far too high for the line to be a success, although it was pointed out the new route provided a quicker means of reaching the capital.

The new section of line was a 16 mile 38 chain single track route, with intermediate stations at Leckhampton, Charlton Kings, Andoversford and Notgrove. The line was, from its inception, worked by the Great Western, as an extension of the original branch from Chipping Norton Junction to Bourton-on-the-Water, with trains running through from Chipping Norton Junction to Cheltenham St James, a distance of 24 miles 17 chains.

Trains travelling eastwards from Cheltenham to Bourton-on-the-Water were designated Up workings, while those proceeding in the opposite direction were regarded as Down services. Crossing loops were provided at Charlton Kings, Andoversford, Notgrove and Bourton-on-the-Water, but Leckhampton, a single platform station, was not a block post or crossing station. Similarly, Stow-on-the-Wold, on the original Bourton-on-the-Water Railway, remained a simple, single platform stopping place, with just one platform and no provision for crossing passenger or freight trains.

It is likely that all of the signal cabins originally provided for the opening of the line came from the Gloucester Railway Carriage & Wagon Company. Those at Charlton Kings and Notgrove seem to have been something of an afterthought, prompted by Col. Rich's misgivings regarding the operating of this single track route by the train staff system with only one passing place, at Andoversford. A plan showing Notgrove as a single line halt in 1880 certainly exists but when the line opened it had a passing loop and signal box. Charlton Kings had also become a passing place complete with cabin by the time of opening. The wooden station buildings and platform shelters at Charlton Kings, Andoversford (platform shelter only) and Notgrove are also likely to have come from Gloucester. They have the look of William Eassie & Company designs. This concern, which specialised in standard designs of wooden buildings, was used as a sub-contractor by the GRC&W Company for much of their joinery work. In late 1875, they took over Eassie's and in February 1876, a contract was signed with the newly enlarged company for joinery work on the Banbury & Cheltenham Direct Railway. The station buildings at Andoversford and Leckhampton, plus the platform shelter at the latter, were built of brick.

The principal engineering features included a twelve arch brick viaduct at Dowdeswell and the 381 yard Sandywell Park Tunnel, which utilised at least part of the earlier East

Stow-on-the-Wold was the only station between Cheltenham and Kingham at which passenger trains could not cross. This circa 1930 view is taken from the bridge carrying the A424 Stow to Burford road across the railway and it shows the original station building shortly before it was replaced by the GWR. The signal box on the platform, just visible at the far end of the station, was provided in 1892. The platform canopy was also a later addition, whilst the foliage has matured over the years. *Bob Brown collection*

Gloucestershire approach works at its eastern end. Incidentally, the length of the tunnel would appear to be a matter of slight conjecture. Most sources seem to give it as 384 yards, whilst Col. Rich's report of 28th March 1881 says 385 yards. The 381 yards figure, however, is taken from the MT6 plan, surely the most reliable source. The steepest gradients included long stretches of 1 in 60 on either side of the 784 foot summit at Salperton, near Notgrove.

Early timetables reveal that the Kingham to Cheltenham line was worked by train staff and ticket, the single line sections being: Chipping Norton Junction to Bourton-on-the-Water; Bourton-on-the-Water to Notgrove; Notgrove to Andoversford; Andoversford to Charlton Kings; and Charlton Kings to Lansdown Junction. The train staff and ticket system employed was a form of 'divisible staff', the train staffs being fitted with a detachable 'ticket', so that a series of Up or Down trains could follow each other in succession through a single line section, the actual train staff being carried by the last train of an Up or Down series.

COMPLETION BETWEEN CHIPPING NORTON & KING'S SUTTON

Having opened their line between Chipping Norton Junction and Cheltenham, the B&CDR directors were able to devote their full attention to the unfinished eastern portion of line, between Chipping Norton and King's Sutton. About 9 miles of this 15¾ mile section had been finished by 1880, although major civil engineering works, such as the tunnel at Chipping Norton, had not yet been commenced. As mentioned earlier, it had been agreed that a tunnel and viaducts would be built at Hook Norton, instead of an open cutting.

Parliamentary consent for the proposed deviation and an alteration of levels was obtained by an Act passed on 11th August 1881. The Act also allowed the creation of £250,000 in debentures, paying five per cent, and ranking after the 1873 and 1879 stock but in priority to the 1877 debentures. The 1881 Act enabled interest on the company's debenture debt which, under the provisions of the 1873 Act, had been paid by the GWR direct to the debenture holders, to be paid to the B&CDR company for distribution among the debenture holders. This same Act also allowed the period for completion of the unfinished portion of the line to be extended to July 1884.

The company was, by this time, making fitful progress on the difficult section of line in and around Hook Norton, where, at one stage, over 200 men and 120 horses were engaged on the excavation of a 76 foot deep cutting on the approaches to Hook Norton Tunnel. It is interesting to discover that, in addition to horses and human muscle power, the railway builders were assisted by traction engines, steam navvies and other mechanical appliances. Indeed, the *Banbury Guardian* reported that some of the local roads were being '*badly cut up by the railway traction engines*'.

In the early months of 1883, similar complaints about contractors' traction engines damaging the local roads were reported in the *Witney Gazette*. However, at the same time, the newspapers were able to print some more optimistic reports. On 24th February 1883, the *Witney Gazette* contained the following note referring to the transfer of some of the contractor's plant from the western portion of the route to the eastern half, beyond Chipping Norton:

CHIPPING NORTON – BANBURY & CHELTENHAM RAILWAY

Preparations for pushing forward the work at this end of the line are daily being made, and on Sunday, what is believed to be the first Sunday train to run on the Chipping Norton Branch, brought between twenty and thirty truck loads of tip wagons from Bourton, Notgrove, etc.

As the massive earthworks began to take tangible shape along the route between King's Sutton and the authorised junction at Chipping Norton, a number of archaeological discoveries were made, including part of *'a Roman burial urn'*, which was found in a cutting at Duck Pool Farm, near Hook Norton. The fragment was said to have been *'about as large as a threepenny piece, with a notched edge, and the figure of a Roman soldier on the side'*. In her book *A History of Hook Norton*, published over forty years later, Margaret Dickens referred to the many problems and delays that had beset the railway builders in the vicinity of the village:

The part through Hook Norton presented so many difficulties that the project was abandoned more than once. In 1884, the 250 navvies working on the line were entertained to tea in Hook Norton ... soon after, the work was stopped for a time; but in August 1885 the Company advertised that they had made arrangements to complete the railway, and had taken on a number of hands.

Further east, better progress was made on the 4 mile 53 chain section between King's Sutton Junction and Bloxham, and this part of the Banbury & Cheltenham line passed its Board of Trade inspection on 25th August 1884. There was, however, no attempt to open the completed section for public traffic, because the two viaducts at Hook Norton were still far from complete. In fact, work on the viaducts was in progress for about four years, having commenced in February 1883 and with completion not taking place until the early months of 1887.

Interestingly, the two viaducts needed at Hook Norton to carry the railway across the valley of the River Swere were unlike the other large B&CDR viaduct at Dowdeswell, their design and construction being entirely different. Instead of the arched brick spans at Dowdeswell, the Hook Norton viaducts incorporated horizontal iron girders and stone piers. On 3rd December 1885, the viaducts were the scene of an unfortunate accident, when some timber supports near the top of one of the piers collapsed, throwing two men to their deaths in the valley below.

A rare view of one of the two viaducts at Hook Norton under construction around 1885. One of the massive stone blocks used in the building of the piers is being lifted by a steam powered tripod crane. Note that the entire work force has stopped to pose for the photographer, necessary with the long time exposures required with early cameras. Although the difficulties the viaduct builders faced are alluded to in many published accounts, the actual nature of the problems encountered are not refered to, barring one small collapse in late 1885. However, the fact work was stopped for several months in 1884 and 1885 would seem to indicate that financial difficulties most likely caused at least some of the delay.
Courtesy Kidderminster Railway Museum

On 1st September 1884, the *Banbury Guardian* carried a report detailing Colonel Rich's official inspection of the first part of the new works, from King's Sutton to Bloxham, on behalf of the Board of Trade:

We last week gave a short notice of this line which runs from King's Sutton to Chipping Norton, completing the whole system of the Banbury & Cheltenham Direct Railway. Colonel Rich arrived at King's Sutton station at 8.36am on Thursday morning, the 25th ult., and was met by the Engineer, Mr William Wilson ...; Mr R.B. Looker, the Secretary of the Banbury & Cheltenham Direct Railway; Mr Charles Eckersley Daniel, the Contractor ...; Mr Robotham, Mr Burlinson, Mr Cleasly and Mr Gibbs of the several departments of the Great Western Railway Company, and Mr Low, agent for the contractor, and immediately commenced to inspect the signal boxes at that station and at the junction. He then proceeded with a saloon carriage and a couple of heavy Great Western tank locomotives, weighing 43 tons each, to inspect the lines and the different bridges, over and under, each bridge and culvert was separately and individually inspected and tested. The next station arrived at was Adderbury. Here Colonel Rich examined the signals, platforms and station buildings, and passing on to the individual bridges up the line to the next station, which is Bloxham. This forms the first portion of the present section. Colonel Rich asked for some small alterations with regard to the signalling and has sent in a certificate to the Board of Trade sanctioning the opening of the line for passenger traffic on condition that these small requirements were made at once ... The line from Bloxham up to Hook Norton road is also complete with all the bridges over and under, leaving only the small embankment to be

From the end of the 19th century, the village and its viaducts also became the site of two separate ironstone undertakings. The larger operation was owned by the Brymbo Steel Company, who were supplying their steelworks at Wrexham with ore mined and calcined at Hook Norton. The second workings were owned by the Earl of Dudley and were situated almost underneath Hook Norton No. 2 Viaduct. This view across the valley of the River Swere shows No. 2 Viaduct on the left and the Earl of Dudley's kiln in the valley bottom, the finished product being despatched by rail to his lordship's Round Oak Steelworks at Wolverhampton. No. 1 Viaduct is in the middle distance and Hook Norton station in the right background beyond. The photograph also well illustrates the difficulties faced by the builders of the 3&CDR in crossing this piece of terrain, via a mixture of high embankments and lofty viaducts. This 1920s postcard view is the work of Chipping Norton photographer Frank Packer, who made countless forays with his camera equipment into the Cotswolds, on the Oxfordshire side in particular. He was succeeded by his son, 'young Frank' (who was stilled referred to as such well into his seventies) and the business later took over the photographic collection of their friendly rival Percy Simms. Their legacy is a marvellous record of the social, rural and industrial life of this most picturesque part of the English countryside from around 1905 to the 1940s, and the massive collection of glass plate negatives is now in the care of Oxfordshire Libraries & Museums. The many postcards produced, such as the example here, are today much sought after by collectors.   *Bob Brown collection*

made at Hook Norton which joins the fine and massive stone viaducts which are just upon completion, and beyond this up to Chipping Norton the line is also ready for inspection. With regard to the viaduct, a good many of the girders are fixed and the remainder are on the ground close to the piers and are being lifted with all possible speed. This work we specially referred to in our last week's report as being peculiarly successful.

At Bloxham and also at Hook Norton there is a very rich bed of iron ore, which has been purchased by the Oxfordshire Ironstone Company, and a very large income is expected to be derived from this source over the Banbury & Cheltenham Direct Railway.

The Great Western Railway Company have already made large additions at Banbury Station for the traffic of the Banbury & Cheltenham Railway, also at Chipping Norton there are new goods sheds and various other improvements, together with sidings, etc., and indeed at Chipping Norton Junction it seems more to resemble Clapham Junction, than the old station at Chipping Norton Junction, evidently showing the opinion that is formed of the traffic to be expected in this long looked for line. The opening of this portion is the first grand step towards the full advantage which the line will obtain by the direct route to the Eastern counties from the Western, and *vice versa*, and as the whole line is practically complete, we may look forward at a very early date to the opening of the same …we sincerely congratulate all on the succes of an undertaking which, almost at one time seemed as though the difficulties attending it were insurmountable.

This report is interesting for a number of reasons; to begin with, it indicates that sanction for opening the line between Chipping Norton and King's Sutton was given piecemeal. However, although Colonel Rich had given his permission for passenger services to begin on the section from King's Sutton to Bloxham, there is no evidence – and indeed it is highly unlikely – that they ever did. The report also indicates that work and new buildings at both ends of the new line, including at Banbury, had been finished for some while, and that it was just the viaducts at Hook Norton which were holding up completion. There is also a hint as to the rudimentary nature of the original facilities provided at Chipping Norton Junction, although no actual description of them, unfortunately. Finally, on a whimsical note, as most railway enthusiasts will have used the expression "Its like Clapham Junction round here!", it is interesting to note how far back in railway history this simile can be traced!

OPENING BETWEEN CHIPPING NORTON & KING'S SUTTON

With the viaducts and other major civil engineering works in the vicinity of Hook Norton ready for opening, the eastern section of the Banbury & Cheltenham Direct line was finally completed by the early months of 1887 and, after years of effort, the supporters of the scheme could at last look forward to the inauguration of through traffic over the entire length of the route between Banbury and Cheltenham. On Thursday 10th March 1887, the following brief report was printed in the pages of the *Witney Express*:

BANBURY & CHELTENHAM DIRECT RAILWAY

This undertaking, which has severely taxed the patience of all associated with it, whether as engineers, contractors or shareholders, has at last been brought to the point of completion. In April it will probably be opened for traffic throughout, and the long suffering shareholders may look forward to a substantial advance in the value of their property. Part of the debenture interest is in arrears, but that will no doubt be earned at an early date, leaving a margin for the preference, and, as the ironstone traffic develops, something for the ordinary shareholders.

The eastern section of the B&CDR line was opened between Chipping Norton and King's Sutton on 6th April 1887, although little notice seems to have been given. On the following day, the *Banbury Guardian* reported that the new railway had been '*fairly well patronised*', although the news that the line would be opened for public traffic had only been publicly announced on the previous Tuesday. More people would have turned up, commented the paper, '*if longer notice of the opening of the line had been given*'.

A slightly more detailed account of the opening appeared in the *Oxford Chronicle*, on Saturday 16th April 1887. The following quotation makes no mention of any form of celebration, the assumption being that the first day of operation was a somewhat low-key affair:

OPENING OF THE BANBURY & CHELTENHAM RAILWAY

This branch was opened for passenger traffic last week. The line begins with a junction at King's Sutton, and the distance to Chipping Norton is nearly sixteen miles. The next stations are Adderbury, Bloxham and Hook Norton. The deep valley beyond Hook Norton is spanned by a viaduct of five spans of one hundred feet each, formed of massive stone piers 73 feet high and iron girders.

The line then crosses a bank, succeeded by another viaduct of eight one hundred feet spans, consisting of stone piers 90 feet high with iron girders. There is no station between Hook Norton and Chipping Norton, but efforts are on foot to induce the company to plant a station at Great Rollright. Just before entering Chipping Norton, there is a tunnel half a mile long under part of the Common. When Chipping Norton is reached, a junction is formed with the branch of the Great Western Railway, and the Banbury & Cheltenham line proper commences again at a junction with the Bourton-on-the-Water branch of the Great Western, and runs thence to Cheltenham.

The distance between Banbury and Cheltenham is fifty one miles, shorter by this than by the existing route, and there is a saving of forty one miles between Banbury and Gloucester. Mr William Wilson, of Dean's Yard, Westminster, was the Engineer of the line, which will be worked by the Great Western Company.

The completed B&CDR route was worked as two distinct branch lines, with separate train services between Cheltenham and Chipping Norton Junction, and between Chipping Norton Junction and Banbury. All train services were worked by the Great Western in return for 45 per cent of the gross receipts but if the receipts exceeded £25 per mile per week, the operating agreement provided that the working expenses would rise to 50 per cent.

SOME DETAILS OF THE LINE

The newly-opened section of line between King's Sutton Junction and Chipping Norton was 15 miles 34 chains in length and single track throughout, with intermediate stations at Adderbury, Bloxham and Hook Norton. All three

Chipping Norton station in its Edwardian heyday, circa 1908. On the platform, two small boys in sailor suits look up in wonder at the footplate crew of '517' Class 0-4-2T No. 563, which has just drawn into the station with a service from Chipping Norton Junction. The fact that the train consists only of two short-wheelbase carriages would suggest that this is one of the Chipping Norton Junction to Chipping Norton services, of which there were six, with corresponding return workings, each day. It is likely that this is either the 1.10 pm or 3.55 pm working from the Junction, as both of these trains had a near 2 hour stopover at Chipping Norton. It is probably the latter, as there are a number of passengers waiting on the Down platform and it can be seen the signals are off for an approaching train. This would be the 3.25 pm from Banbury, due into Chipping Norton at around 4.25 pm, about 10 minutes after the train seen here had arrived. Once the train from Banbury had departed, the '517' would uncouple and draw forward clear of the loop, before reversing back through the station on the Down line. Crossing back over to the Up line, it would couple up to the other end of the carriages and draw them back out of the station, shunting them onto a siding alongside the goods shed. The locomotive would then head off to the shed for water and coal, in readiness for the next service to Chipping Norton Junction at 6.10 pm. No. 563 was a long-lived locomotive, having been built as a saddle tank at Wolverhampton in 1869. It was withdrawn just a few months short of its sixtieth birthday in 1929. The wrought iron lattice footbridge, with its ornate gas lamps on the balustrade at either side, is another Victorian gem. *Nigel Oram collection*

Hook Norton station, looking east towards King's Sutton and Cheltenham in another Packer view taken around 1910, with the station staff proudly posing for the camera. A couple of these men probably worked in the goods yard, which would have been busy handling the produce of the local ironstone workings. The station was built on an artificial embankment, supported by a framework of girders which can be seen at the bottom of the platform to the left. Phil Coutanche, who was in charge of dismantling the line in the 1960s, recalls that when the station was being demolished, one of his gang's tasks was to remove the station safe. However, the floor in the station building was rotten and it was decided it was too dangerous to retrieve the heavy metal safe. The solution was to collapse the building, complete with the safe, into the 20-foot deep cellar below where, presumably, it remains to this day. *John Alsop collection*

stations were passing places, with up and down platforms for passenger traffic, and adequate provision for goods traffic. Station buildings and goods sheds of a standardised design were provided at all three locations, and also at Chipping Norton, where a new through station had been erected to the north of the 1855 terminus.

The principal engineering works included the two viaducts at Hook Norton, the bridges across the River Cherwell and the Oxford Canal near King's Sutton, and tunnels at Hook Norton and Chipping Norton. Elsewhere, there were numerous over or underbridges, some of these structures having single-span, brick arches, while the remainder consisted of metal girders on brick abutments.

The eastern part of the Banbury & Cheltenham line was, from its inception, intimately connected with the transport needs of the local ironstone industry. At first, the newly-excavated ironstone was taken by carts or wagons to the goods yards at Bloxham, Hook Norton or Adderbury but plans were soon being made for the installation of private sidings to facilitate the transshipment of ironstone. The first ironstone siding was provided at Hook Norton station in 1889, to serve the Hook Norton Ironstone Partnership Ltd. This firm had been formed by a small group of entrepreneurs, most of whom seem to have been connected with the B&CDR in one way or another.

As previously mentioned, the B&CDR route passed through an area that was thought to be replete with mineral resources and, as early as 1884, land on both sides of the authorised line had been conveyed to a partnership consisting of Henry Lovatt, John Wilson and Richard B. Looker. On 21st April 1888, the land was conveyed to the Hook Norton Ironstone Partnership, the first Manager being Richard Looker, who was later succeeded by C.H. Looker – presumably his son, or some other close relative.

In view of these transactions, it is instructive to consider the composition of the B&CDR board of directors at the time of the line's opening. The Chairman was General Sir Michael Kennedy, of 102 Gloucester Terrace, Hyde Park, while the Deputy-Chairman was Colonel J. Wilkinson of Southampton Lodge, Highgate. The other directors were: Charles Kemp Dyer of St Albans; John Wilson of Stoke Works, Astwood, near Worcester; and Henry Lovatt of Wolverhampton. The officers of the company included Secretary Richard B. Looker and Engineer William Wilson. The B&CDR company offices were at 43 Finsbury Square, London EC.

THE COST OF THE LINE

Although the Banbury & Cheltenham Direct line was now open throughout its length, the company's financial situation remained precarious and it was perhaps fortunate for all concerned that the Great Western Railway was willing to support the smaller company in a number of ways. In particular, the GWR guaranteed interest payments on the B&CDR debentures, thereby ensuring a financial safety net for the long-suffering Banbury & Cheltenham proprietors.

Under the provisions of a further Act of Parliament,

Above: Bloxham, as viewed around 1910 from the road (later the A361) which crossed over the line just to the east of the station, boasted some impressive gardens by the early part of the 20th century, courtesy of the station staff. Palmers were one of the local coal merchants and their nameboard can be seen above their office behind the main building. **Below**: Adderbury station is seen here circa 1920, looking east from the road bridge carrying what is now the A423. The design of the station buildings and goods sheds provided at these two stations, and also at Hook Norton, was almost identical. Note the row of ironstone wagons in the siding on the left, belonging to Cochrane & Co., operators of the West Adderbury Quarries at this time. The connection to the quarries was to the right, behind the signal box. Cochrane's operation here ceased in 1922. *Above: Bob Brown collection; below: John Alsop collection*

A rare glimpse of the Cheltenham to Andoversford section of the B&CDR in single line days in the late 1890s. A Kingham-bound pick-up goods train is seen entering the western portal of Andoversford Tunnel. That the tunnel and the formation was built originally to take double track is clearly evident from this view.
M.P. Barnsley collection

obtained on 8th August 1887, the B&CDR was empowered to abandon certain works authorised in 1873 and 1877, and confirm the existing agreement with the Great Western Railway. The 1887 Act also authorised the creation of another £1,000,000 in debentures. The company's accounts reveal that £1,646,429 had been expended by 30th June 1887, while income had amounted to £1,618,239, leaving a balance against the company of £28,190. The capital structure, at the time of opening, was as follows:

Ordinary shares	£ 35,400
Ordinary stock	£ 18,836
Preferred stock (6 per cent)	£ 272,882
Deferred stock	£ 272,882
Preference stock	£ 23,546
Debentures	£ 985,349
Rent-charge	£ 9,344

These published figures suggest that the Banbury & Cheltenham line had cost the not inconsiderable sum of £1,646,429. At the time if its completion, the B&CDR route consisted of the Lansdown Junction to Bourton-on-the-Water section (16 miles 38 chains) and the Chipping Norton to King's Sutton section (15 miles 34 chains), a total length of 31 miles 72 chains. Based on expenditure to 30th June 1887, this system of a little under 32 route miles had cost around £51,000 per mile.

The Banbury & Cheltenham Direct Railway remained a legally separate undertaking, with its own chairman and board of directors, until the 1890s, when it was fully and finally absorbed by the GWR under the provisions of a Great Western General Powers Act obtained on 1st July 1897.

The junction between the B&CDR, on the left, and the M&SWJR, on the right, is seen here in the mid 1950s. The main A40 London road passed under the railway at the east end of the station and the girders of the bridge are seen here, together with the starting signals for both routes. Andoversford Junction Signal Box can be glimpsed in the distance, to the left of the Kingham line. Latter day road improvements have swept away this bridge and the site of the junction.
Photo J.H. Russell

A Midland & South Western Junction passenger train heads westwards across Dowdeswell Viaduct towards Cheltenham around 1910; the M&SWJR company excerised running powers over this section of the B&CDR line. *Michael Mitchell collection*

THE MIDLAND & SOUTH WESTERN JUNCTION RAILWAY

The promoters of the East Gloucestershire Railway had always intended to build two cross-country routes from Cheltenham, one of which would run eastwards to join the Oxford, Worcester & Wolverhampton line, while the other would head south-eastwards from Andoversford, via Chedworth and Fairford. Although the EGR scheme was a more or less total failure, the Banbury & Cheltenham Direct line eventually fulfilled the need for an east-to-west route from Cheltenham to the OW&WR and beyond. The B&CDR promoters had no intention of building southwards from Andoversford but other interests were eager to create such a route and, in the event, a railway was eventually built between Andoversford, Cirencester, Swindon and Andover.

This line, known as the Midland & South Western Junction Railway, originated in the early 1870s, when a small group of landowners, businessmen and other interested parties called a meeting in the Forest Hotel, Savernake, with the aim of promoting a 12-mile line between Marlborough and Swindon. At its southern end, the proposed line would form a connection with an existing GWR branch from Savernake to Marlborough and it was suggested that a further line might be constructed between Savernake and the Hampshire coast – the result being a useful cross-country route connecting the Midlands with new port developments on the Channel coast.

This new scheme was eagerly taken up by local investors and the Swindon, Marlborough & Andover Railway received the Royal Assent on 21st July 1873 (*36 & 37 Vic. cap. 194*). The railway would be built in two stages, the northern section running between the Great Western station at Swindon and an end-on junction with the Marlborough Railway, while the southern portion would extend from Wolfhall Junction, near Savernake, to the London & South Western Railway near Andover. To pay for their project, the promoters were authorised to raise £375,000 in shares and a further £125,000 by loan, the total capital being half a million pounds.

The first section of the Swindon, Marlborough & Andover Railway was opened on 26th July 1881, and trains started to operate between Swindon and Marlborough. The southern portion of the SM&AR line was brought into use on 1st May 1882 but through running over the intervening Marlborough branch did not commence until 5th February 1883. In the meantime, a separate undertaking, known as the Swindon & Cheltenham Extension Railway, had been incorporated on 18th July 1881, with powers for the construction of a northwards link between Rushey Platt, near Swindon, and the Banbury & Cheltenham Direct Railway at Andoversford.

The Swindon & Cheltenham Extension line was opened as far north as Cirencester on 18th December 1883, all train services being worked by the Swindon, Marlborough & Andover company. In 1884, the SM&AR and the S&CER companies were combined to form a new undertaking, the Midland & South Western Junction Railway, the amalgamation being effected under the provisions of an Act of Parliament obtained in that same year. Unfortunately, the newly-formed M&SWJR company was in serious financial difficulties from the very start and its line to Cheltenham was still far from complete.

A little construction work had been carried out on the extension to the north of Cirencester, where deviations from the original plans had been authorised in 1883 and 1884. However, a major crisis was close at hand, as funds ran out and creditors became more pressing. The contractors,

Messrs Watson, Smith & Watson, were released from their contract in November 1884 and, in the following month, the company was placed in receivership, following a petition from the M&SWJ's own Engineer.

Work was restarted north of Cirencester in May 1889, under a contract let to Charles Braddock, a Wigan-based contractor. Proceeding simultaneously from several different places, Mr Braddock made commendable progress on what was, after all, a comparatively difficult contract. The greatest obstacle between Cirencester and Andoversford was the 494-yards long Chedworth Tunnel but there were, in addition, several large embankments and deep cuttings – including 60 foot embankments near Foss Cross and through Chedworth Woods.

The Cheltenham extension was more or less complete by the summer of 1890 but when the railway was nearly ready for opening in June 1890, a portion of Chedworth Tunnel fell in, bringing down about 60 foot depth of earth and leading to an inevitable dispute over responsibility. The tunnel collapse was soon rectified but further problems ensued when an underline bridge to the north of Chedworth failed in February 1891. Moreover, the completion of the junction at Andoversford was held up by delays in agreeing terms with the Great Western Railway for the use of the line between Andoversford and Lansdown Junction, over which the M&SWJR had secured running powers.

A further problem arose because accommodation was not yet available for M&SWJR traffic at the Midland station in Cheltenham. Goods traffic nevertheless commenced running as far as Dowdeswell on 16th March 1891, mainly as a sop to impatient creditors. The full opening was delayed until 1st August 1891, when M&SWJR passenger trains started to run through from Cirencester to Cheltenham (Midland). A few weeks previously, on 30th June 1891, what was apparently the very first through passenger train had traversed the line, carrying over four hundred excursionists on a trip from Marlborough to Birmingham.

The line from Cirencester to Andoversford was a little under 14 miles in length, with intermediate stations at Foss Cross, Withington and Dowdeswell; a station was opened at Chedworth in 1892. Chedworth Tunnel and the bridges were built to double-line width but the engineering works as a whole were kept to a bare minimum to save cost. Accommodation for Midland & South Western Junction traffic at Cheltenham was secured by enlarging the Midland station at Lansdown for passenger trains, and by acquiring land at Alstone for sidings and a goods yard, adjacent to the High Street (Midland) goods station.

THE ANDOVERSFORD & STRATFORD-UPON-AVON RAILWAY

The opening of the Midland & South Western Junction line brought additional traffic to the 6 miles 60 chain single line section between Andoversford Junction and Lansdown Junction. Delays inevitably resulted, and the M&SWJR directors began to suspect that their own services were being deliberately obstructed. To overcome this difficulty, they prepared a Bill for the construction of an independent M&SWJR line between Dowdeswell and Stratford-upon-Avon, where connection would be made with the Birmingham, North Warwickshire & Stratford-upon-Avon Railway. The proposed line from Andoversford to Stratford would be 25 miles 70 chains in length and it would run via Winchcombe and Broadway.

The Andoversford & Stratford-upon-Avon Railway Bill was sent up to Parliament in the 1898 session but the scheme was rejected after the GWR agreed to build an alternative line from Cheltenham to a junction with the former OW&WR branch to Stratford-upon-Avon at Honeybourne.

The M&SWJR made another attempt to extend its route northwards in 1899, when powers were sought for a northern extension from Andoversford to Ashchurch, where a junction would have been made with the Midland Railway. These attempts to secure an independent route to the Midlands led to negotiations between the M&SWJR, Midland and Great Western companies, as a result of which relations between the M&SWJR and its neighbours were finally settled. As far as the GWR was concerned, the M&SWJR agreed that the Northern Extension Bill would be withdrawn, while the Great Western undertook to double the line between Andoversford and Lansdown Junction.

An agreement made between the two companies, on 14th March 1899, also gave the M&SWJR the freedom to fix rates and fares in respect of through traffic carried over the line between Andoversford and Lansdown Junction, without interference from the GWR. A second agreement, made between the M&SWJR and the Midland Railway on 10th April 1899, formalised the alliance between the two companies, and enabled the Midland to lend £200,000 to the M&SWJR, so that the smaller undertaking would be able to improve and partially double its line. The Midland was also granted running powers over the M&SWJR system.

With a system of just 63 route miles, the M&SWJR was one of the smaller pre-Grouping companies but the agreements with the GWR and Midland companies enabled it to develop as an efficient undertaking, with a guaranteed flow of regular through traffic between the Midlands and Southampton. As far as the B&CDR was concerned, the arrival of the Midland & South Western Junction line brought additional traffic to the western extremity of the route, and compelled the GWR to double the line between Andoversford and Lansdown Junction.

In the longer term, however, developments in the Banbury area were destined to play an even more significant role in the story of the Banbury & Cheltenham Direct line.

THE GREAT CENTRAL RAILWAY REACHES BANBURY

The Great Central Railway was originally a purely northern line, its heartlands being firmly established in and around the bleak Pennine hills. The line had a long pre-history, commencing with the formation of a Sheffield & Manchester Railway Company in 1831. Unfortunately, the promoters of this early scheme were unable to raise the necessary capital but six years later, on 5th May 1837, a new but substantially similar Sheffield, Ashton-under-Lyne & Manchester Railway obtained Parliamentary consent for a trans-Pennine line; this ran from Sheffield to Manchester via Penistone, Woodhead and Dinting, with a major tunnel through the Pennines at Woodhead.

An early 20th century view of Banbury Great Western station, looking south towards King's Sutton. Standing in the bay is a Great Central service bound, via the GC's recently opened Banbury branch, for Woodford & Hinton, on the company's main line to London. The three 6-wheel coaches which comprise the train are in the charge of an ex-MS&LR Class '12A' 2-4-0 locomotive of 1875 vintage.
Neil Parkhouse collection

The first sod was cut at Woodhead by Lord Wharncliffe on 1st October 1838, and with Charles Blacker Vignoles (1793-1874) and Joseph Locke (1805-1860) as engineers, major construction work was soon under way. The first section of the line was opened between Manchester (Travis Street) and Godley on 17th November 1841, and this initial section was extended to Dinting (then called Glossop) by 24th December 1842. On 7th August 1844, the line was extended eastwards as far as Woodhead, and the railway was ceremonially opened throughout between Manchester and Sheffield on 22nd December 1845.

The original Manchester to Sheffield line was soon extended to serve other destinations in the north of England. In 1844, for example, the Great Grimsby & Sheffield Junction Railway was empowered to construct 36 miles of railway from Gainsborough to Great Grimsby, with branches to New Holland and Market Rasen. The latter route was opened between Grimsby and Habrough on 1st March 1848, and from Habrough to Market Rasen and Brigg on 1st November 1848.

These diverse lines had, by that time, been merged with the Sheffield to Manchester route, to form the Manchester Sheffield & Lincolnshire Railway. The MS&LR system continued to expand until, by the 1870s, it extended from Grimsby on the east coast to Liverpool and Chester in the west – the latter two cities being reached via the jointly-owned Cheshire Lines Committee.

Manchester Sheffield & Lincolnshire trains served huge conurbations and booming industrial areas in the north of England but the company's dynamic Chairman, Sir Edward Watkin (1819-1901), was determined to transform the undertaking into a great trunk line. In order to achieve this aim, he embarked upon a grandiose extension scheme, involving the construction of over 90 miles of new railway between Annesley and London. When completed, the 'London Extension' would transform the entire system into a major trunk route between Marylebone and the north of England, and to underline this change of status, the more expansive title of Great Central Railway was adopted by the MS&LR company in 1897.

Contracts for construction of the GCR London Extension line were let in September 1894 and this important scheme was virtually complete by 1898. Coal trains began running over the new main line in July 1898 and the route was ceremonially opened on 9th March 1899. Public services commenced six days later, on 15th March, the first express working over the Great Central main line to the North being the 5.15 Down service from Marylebone, which left London with only four passengers aboard.

The Great Central main line ran northwards from London, via Aylesbury, Rugby, Leicester and Nottingham. It passed to the east of Banbury, the nearest GCR main line stations being at Brackley, Helmdon, Culworth and Woodford & Hinton. There was not, at first, any particular intention of serving Banbury and indeed, the GCR Banbury branch was something of an afterthought. Its origins can be traced back to 1895, when the MS&L, Midland and L&NW railways had proposed an ambitious scheme known as the London & South Wales Railway.

If successful, the London & South Wales proposal would have resulted in the creation of a new trunk route from the capital to South Wales, via Beaconsfield, Oxford and the Upper Thames Valley. The suggested main line would have run more or less parallel to the long-established GWR route but, understandably, they were bitterly opposed to the whole idea. In the event, the Great Western was able to 'buy off' the MS&LR and so abort the London & South Wales scheme in its entirety. However, one result of these complex behind-the-scenes negotiations was the construction of what later became the Banbury branch of the Great Central Railway.

The proposed branch would form a useful cross-country link between the GCR and the neighbouring GWR system, while at the same time it would furnish the ambitious Great Central company with a suitable outlet to the south and south-west of England, and South Wales. It was built by the GCR at Great Western expense, under an agreement between the two companies, and opened for goods traffic on 1st June 1900 and for the carriage of passengers on 13th August. All train services were provided by the Great Central company, although trains ran over the GWR for a distance of 1 mile 14 chains in order to use the Great Western station at Banbury.

The branch, which was double track throughout, left the

The first underline bridge from Lansdown Junction on the B&CDR route carried the railway over what later became Hatherley Lane when this official photograph was taken in 1901, to show the bridge as it had been rebuilt following the doubling of the line to Andoversford. The bridge had a single wrought iron span resting on brick abutments and the rather limited headroom will be noted. In later years, this became a busy urban route, the roadway having to be lowered for higher vehicles. This area today is heavily built up and all trace of the line where it crossed Hatherley Road has been virtually obliterated but the dip in the road where the bridge used to be is still evident.

M.P. Barnsley collection

The next bridge spanned a track to Green Farm, which later became Alma Road with the post-war development of this area. Gloucester Loop Junction Signal Box was situated just out of sight to the left of this official view, **above**, of the newly rebuilt bridge following the doubling of the line. It was constructed entirely of brick and on a slight skew, as the photograph **below**, taken from the opposite side, shows. It was a masterpiece of bridge building, the height of the embankment at this point necessitating quite substantial abutments and retaining walls. All trace of this structure, too, has been removed since the line's closure. The cottage beyond the bridge was the residence of the Gloucester Loop Junction signalman. The hay cart, above, provides a nice period touch.   *Both M.P. Barnsley collection*

Whilst we are obviously not going to cover every bridge *en route* to Banbury, it was thought that this particular collection was too good to omit. The final view in the sequence shows the next bridge out from Lansdown Junction. It spanned a rough track leading to Warden Hill Farm, which became Warden Hill Road in the 1950s. For anyone who knows the area, this is looking away from Cheltenham and the present-day Winchester Way would be on the left, halfway along the visible part of the lane beyond the bridge.   *M.P. Barnsley collection*

Great Central London Extension at Culworth Junction, to the south of Woodford & Hinton station, and then ran south-westwards across the high wolds of Northamptonshire and Oxfordshire for a distance of 8 miles 18 chains, before converging with the GWR at Banbury Junction. The total distance from Woodford to Banbury was 11 miles 1 chain. In connection with this new line, extensive marshalling yards were opened at Banbury, together with a much enlarged engine shed and other improved facilities.

The Woodford to Banbury line transformed Banbury into an important junction and a major interchange point between the Great Western and Great Central systems. The new Great Central link was of equal importance to the Banbury & Cheltenham Direct line, which formed a natural westwards continuation for traffic flowing southwards from the Midlands and North towards South Wales. In the reverse direction, it formed a similar cross-country route for coal traffic heading northwards to great industrial cities such as Leicester, Nottingham and Sheffield.

IMPROVEMENTS TO THE BANBURY & CHELTENHAM DIRECT RAILWAY

For the reasons given above, it could be said that the opening of the Great Central main line enabled the Banbury & Cheltenham Direct line to function in the way that its promoters had intended – as a direct link between the industrial areas of the Midlands and South Wales. As a heavily-graded single track route, the B&CDR was not entirely suitable as a path for long distance freight traffic and, as a consequence, the Great Western made considerable efforts to up-grade the line during the early 1900s. The improvement programme entailed the installation of double track on two sections of the line, new avoiding lines at Kingham and Cheltenham, and other works at many of the intermediate stations.

At the western end of the line, the double track section between Charlton Kings and Andoversford Junction was ready by 9th February 1902, while the remaining section between Charlton Kings and Lansdown Junction was completed on 28th September 1902. Four years later, in 1906, a double track curve was opened between Gloucester Loop Junction, on the B&DCR route, and Hatherley Junction, on the former Cheltenham & Great Western Union line, so that through workings would be able to run between Banbury, Kingham and Gloucester without reversing at Cheltenham.

Apart from plans of the stations as originally built, which will appear in a later chapter, little has been discovered on the western end of the line in its single track days. To date, no photographs have been unearthed of Leckhampton or Charlton Kings stations before they were rebuilt, or of Dowdeswell viaduct before it was widened. Similarly, no photographs and very few details of the work itself have been discovered. The sole exception is a number of official photographs of the new bridges carrying the line around the southern outskirts of Cheltenham and of the newly widened viaduct at Dowdeswell. Cheltenham residents who live in the suburban sprawl which now covers most of this area will probably struggle to recognise many of these outlying roads and their rural surrounds, as they appeared in the early years of the 20th century.

At the eastern end of the route, the 1 mile 56 chain section from King's Sutton Junction to Adderbury was converted to double track, which was brought into operation on 8th January 1906. Just one week previously, on 1st January, the

An official view of Dowdeswell Viaduct, taken just after it had been widened in connection with the doubling of the line in 1901, the contrast between the old and new brickwork on the piers being only too clear. This 190-yard long structure consisted of 12 arches each of 40 foot span with a maximum height of 69 feet. After doubling, it measured 25 feet 6 inches in width between the parapets. The lime mortar bonding caused problems when demolition was attempted in 1967, as it had reputedly set harder than the bricks themselves; a second attempt later the same year was more effective, however, and all trace of this fine structure has now been removed. *M.P. Barnsley collection*

The avoiding line bridge at Kingham, photographed in 1913. It had a 60 foot span, crossed six tracks and was formed of wrought iron girders resting on brick abutments. The ironwork appears to be painted in GWR light and dark stone colours. The imposing wooden-posted bracket signal is the Up Home. *Courtesy National Railway Museum*

Kingham Avoiding Line had been brought into use. This was quite a major construction, requiring the provision of two new junctions, Kingham East and Kingham West, although only East had a signal box, and a bridge over the Oxford-Worcester main line. The new line was double track, feeding into a single line junction at Kingham West.

Other improvements carried out between 1902 and 1907 included the provision of extended crossing loops at Notgrove, Bourton-on-the-Water, Hook Norton and Bloxham, the opportunity being taken to add new signal boxes, of standard Great Western design, in place of the wooden contractors' boxes that had originally been installed by the Banbury & Cheltenham Direct company.

As a result of these early-20th century improvements, the Banbury & Cheltenham line enjoyed an enhanced status as a through route for passenger and freight traffic, its new role being underlined by the introduction of the 'Ports-to-Ports' express between Newcastle and South Wales, which will be described in greater detail in the following chapter.

THE WITNEY, BURFORD & ANDOVERSFORD LIGHT RAILWAY

Mention of the London & South Wales proposal serves as a reminder that the idea of a new main line to South Wales remained strangely persistent. On a less ambitious level, there was also much talk of an eastwards extension from Cirencester or Andoversford to form a connection with the Fairford branch. One of these schemes was the Witney, Burford & Andoversford Light Railway proposal of 1899. Curiously, this modest scheme came very near to success. The 1896 Light Railways Act enabled local and national government assistance to be made available to the promoters of cheaply-constructed light railways and there was in consequence a minor boom in light railway schemes.

The idea of a railway between Witney, Andoversford and Cheltenham had never been entirely abandoned and in the late 1890s a possible standard gauge line was surveyed by Sir J. Szlumper. Leaving the Fairford branch near Witney station, it would have run via Curbridge, Burford and Northleach to Andoversford. With Oxfordshire and Gloucestershire County Councils offering cheap loans of £15,000, and the GWR willing to work the line, it seemed that a Witney to Andoversford railway would, at long last, actually be built.

A public enquiry was held in Witney in March 1900, and the scheme was enthusiastically supported by several local landowners and business leaders, including Lord Sherbourne, R. Hurst of Barrington Grove, E. Rhys Wingfield of Barrington Park, W. Fox of Bradwell Grove, Major-General Waller of Farmington Lodge and James Vanner Early (1853-1920) of Witney. Sadly, the government refused to support the project and when all efforts to find alternative sources of capital had failed, the Witney, Burford & Andoversford Light Railway scheme was abandoned.

Further extension plans were suggested in the 1920s, although these final efforts were centred on Cirencester rather than Andoversford. In the interim, the Great Western Railway had become heavily-involved with the provision of road motor services, and it is perhaps no coincidence that one such service was eventually arranged along the old coach road between Cheltenham, Andoversford, Burford, Witney and Oxford. Thus, after many years of wasted effort, the hoped-for public transport link between Cheltenham and Oxford finally materialised in the form of a Great Western Railway motor bus service.

Chapter Four

THE RAILWAY IN OPERATION

The Banbury to Cheltenham Direct line served a largely rural area that offered very few opportunities for large scale traffic development. In these circumstances, the route was unable to rise above local branch line status and its passenger train services were modest in the extreme. There were no more than five or six passenger workings per day each way during the Great Western era – although the presence of extensive ironstone deposits at the eastern end of the line, between Hook Norton and King's Sutton, ensured that the railway could rely on at least one source of bulk freight traffic.

PASSENGER TRAIN SERVICES IN THE GWR ERA

At the western end of the line, trains ran through to the GWR terminus at Cheltenham St. James, whereas Banbury remained the terminus for local workings on the eastern section of the B&CDR line. The two portions of the route were, in general, treated as two distinct branch lines and there was little attempt to work the Banbury & Cheltenham Direct line as a through route. Cheltenham travellers hoping to reach Chipping Norton or other destinations on the Banbury line therefore had to change en route at Chipping Norton Junction, where cross-platform interchange facilities were available. Conversely, in the westbound direction, travellers from Banbury were faced with a similar intermediate change.

The train service provided on the western section of the line, between Cheltenham and Kingham, typically consisted of about five daily workings in each direction, and this pattern of operation remained constant for many years. In the early 1880s, for example, there were five trains each way, with Up workings from Cheltenham to Chipping Norton Junction at 6.50 am, 10.00 am, 11.20 am, 3.15 pm and 6.50 pm, and balancing Down workings from Chipping Norton Junction to Cheltenham at 8.50 am, 9.42 am, 1.00 pm, 5.24 pm and 8.58 pm. The usual journey times were 1 hour 5 minutes in the Up direction and 1 hour 15 minutes for Down services.

There were no advertised Sunday services and, indeed, regular Sunday services never became an established feature of operations on the Banbury & Cheltenham Direct line. On the other hand, excursion trains were sometimes arranged

This circa 1905 view over the wall by St. George's Road is looking towards St. James station, with an array of mainly clerestory roofed coaching stock on view. The 4-4-0 locomotive in the centre of the picture has probably brought in the train standing at No. 1 platform (far left) and has just been turned on the station turntable, which was tucked into a corner behind the large buildings to the left of St. Gregory's church. However, the driver will have to wait for the carriages to be shunted up to the stop blocks before he can reverse back onto the train. The sidings fanning out to the left of the engine served New Street coal yard. *Neil Parkhouse collection*

A busy moment at Notgrove station captured in a commercial postcard view of circa 1907. Another unidentified but smart looking 'Metro' tank waits in the Down platform with a Cheltenham-bound train, composed of a mixture of 4- and 6-wheeled stock and with possibly a milk van or horse box at the rear. An assortment of well-dressed folk bustle around the train, suggesting possibly a market day service. The station staff on view are all watching the photographer; the head porter, holding the shunter's pole, would appear to have taken a few moments off from dealing with the goods train on the other line, no doubt with the full permission of the Notgrove station master standing alongside him. Just behind them, the junior porter holds open one of the carriage doors. The goods train is in the process of being shunted, the brake van having been dropped off just behind the photographer and the train drawing forward to the position seen here. It will then shunt back into the small yard to deposit the empty large cattle wagon and possibly one or two other wagons as well. Note the milepost on the right, denoting the 96½ miles from Paddington. In early 1906, the GWR made slight modifications to the yard layout at Notgrove and in conjunction with this work, a new brick-built signal box was provided, which opened on 24th May 1906. The old Gloucester RC&W cabin was dismantled, its timber-built top section being sold for use as a summer house. It only moved a short distance, however, and can be seen at the top of the cutting in the centre background, still complete with finials and decorative barge-boarding. It is thought that the station building and platform shelter were most likely Gloucester RC&W structures, provided shortly after the company had taken over the timber buildings business of William Eassie & Co. *Bob Brown collection*

Another early postcard view, this time showing two passenger trains crossing at Bourton-on-the-Water, with a GWR saddle tank hauling the Down service. This will be a late afternoon view, taken just after 4 o'clock, when the 3.40 pm from Kingham, due at Bourton at 3.58 pm, crossed the 3.10 pm Up train from Cheltenham, due in at 4.00 pm. It was the only time that local passenger services crossed each day on the western section of the line.
The Lens of Sutton Collection

to selected destinations, such as London, Weston-super-Mare or other seaside resorts.

The eastern section of the route was not as busy in terms of passenger traffic as the Cheltenham to Kingham line, although additional local workings were maintained on the former Chipping Norton Railway, and for this reason there was an enhanced service between Chipping Norton Junction and Chipping Norton. In the early 20th Century, for instance, there were ten trains each way on the Chipping Norton section, including one or two 'mixed' workings which conveyed both passenger vehicles and goods rolling stock.

The January 1902 GWR timetable provides a useful glimpse of the railway in operation in the halcyon years before World War One. There were, at that time, five trains each way between Cheltenham St. James and Chipping Norton Junction, and four workings in each direction between Chipping Norton Junction and Banbury. In the Up direction, eastbound workings departed from Cheltenham at 6.50 am, 10.20 am, 11.40 am, 3.10 pm and 7.05 pm, arriving at Chipping Norton Junction at 7.50 am, 11.22 am, 12.27 pm, 4.14 pm and 8.05 pm respectively. The 11.40 am service was a limited stop working that called only at Bourton-on-the-Water, whereas the other services called at all of the intermediate stations.

In the reverse direction, the balancing Down workings left Chipping Norton Junction at 8.58 am, 1.05 pm, 3.40 pm, 5.00 pm and 9.40 pm, arriving at Cheltenham at 9.57 am, 2.17 pm, 4.30 pm, 6.05 pm and 10.40 pm respectively. The 3.40 pm afternoon service was another limited stop working, although it will be noted that its overall time of one hour

A view of Bloxham station circa 1910, with a motor train service *en route* to Banbury, in the charge of an 0-4-2T, waiting at the station. The view is looking west towards Kingham. A pony and trap waits patiently on the station forecourt; one of the local farmers, perhaps, dropping his wife off to catch the train. This rural station was always well known for the high standard of its gardens and successive station masters left their mark with various improvements. The first man in the post grew strawberries on the embankments for his wife's jam making.
Bob Brown collection

This Edwardian scene, dated 19th September 1909, shows army volunteers disembarking at Charlton Kings having returned from their summer camp. This is almost certainly an M&SWJR train, running as a special from Tidworth or Ludgershall. The length of the train has left the front portion clear of the platform and it may have been the case that these carriages were emptied first, with the train then carefully drawing forward to allow the men in the rear coaches to be detrained. The vehicles nearest the camera appear to be horse boxes. *M.P. Barnsley collection*

for the 24-mile journey hardly placed it in the 'express' category; this service generally crossed the 3.10 pm up working in the loop at Bourton-on-the-Water.

At the eastern end of the Banbury & Cheltenham Direct line, Up workings left Chipping Norton Junction at 8.10 am, 12.00 pm, 4.49 pm and 8.35 pm, while Down services left Banbury at 7.00 am, 11.15 am, 3.25 pm and 7.15 pm. In addition, there were short distance local services from Chipping Norton Junction to Chipping Norton at 9.10 am, 10.20 am, 1.10 pm, 3.55 pm, 6.45 pm and 9.35 pm, and return workings from Chipping Norton at 8.30 am, 9.55 am, 11.25 am, 3.15 pm, 6.10 pm and 9.00 pm. The 11.25 am and 6.10 pm Up, and 9.10 am and 1.10 pm Down workings were 'mixed' passenger and goods services.

On a footnote, it should be mentioned that Chipping Norton Junction was renamed 'Kingham' on 1st May 1909, which name it has retained until the present day. Three years earlier, on 1st May 1906, Leckhampton had been officially renamed 'Cheltenham South & Leckhampton', although many people continued to refer to it simply as Leckhampton. There is also ample evidence to show that the full appellation 'Cheltenham South & Leckhampton' had been widely used in M&SWJR timetables and *Bradshaw's Guide* for several years before 1906.

The timetable in operation during the mid-1930s was substantially the same as that which had been in force during the pre-Grouping period, with Up trains from Cheltenham at 6.32 am, 10.35 pm, 12.10 pm, 3.16 pm and 7.05 pm, and Down workings from Kingham at 8.38 am, 1.20 pm, 2.22 pm, 5.10 pm and 8.55 pm. On the eastern section of line, the passenger service was worked by an auto-train, with four trips in each direction between Banbury and Kingham. These left Kingham at 7.47 am, 12.30 pm, 5.20 pm and 8.55 pm, while the corresponding Down services departed from Banbury at 6.22 pm, 10.30 am, 4.00 pm and 7.40 pm.

This basic timetable did not change in any appreciable way throughout the 1930s, apart from one or two minor alterations in times of arrival and departure. On the Cheltenham to Kingham line, for instance, the summer 1939 train service was generally similar to its 1934 predecessor, with five local trains in each direction on weekdays, together with one long distance through service. In the Up direction, eastbound trains left Cheltenham St. James at 6.32 am, 10.36 am, 12.10 pm, 3.20 pm and 7.05 pm, while the balancing Down services departed from Kingham at 8.36 am, 12.32 pm, 2.23 pm, 5.10 pm and 8.55 pm.

The westernmost extremity of the B&CDR route, the 6 mile 60 chain section of line between Landsdown Junction and Andoversford Junction, also carried M&SWJR trains travelling between Cheltenham (Midland) and Southampton. In pre-Grouping days, there were around half a dozen M&SWJR services each way; in 1913, for instance, there were six southbound services between Cheltenham and Andover, together with one short distance working that terminated at Swindon. In the northbound direction, the M&SWJR timetable provided seven through trains between Andover and Cheltenham.

These Midland & South Western Junction workings did not necessarily call *en route* at the GWR stations between Landsdown Junction and Andoversford, and their value to through travellers was, thus, somewhat limited. One or two M&SWJR services did, nevertheless, stop at Cheltenham South, Charlton Kings and Andoversford, while others called at one or more of the intermediate GWR stations. The M&SWJR company had its own station at Andoversford, and although a few of their trains also served the Great Western station, the inconvenient arrangements at this somewhat remote spot were hardly conducive to the development of through traffic between the two systems.

In truth, the Midland & South Western Junction and Great Western companies were rivals, and in these circumstances it is hardly surprising that little attempt was made to arrange connecting services. When, in the aftermath of World War One, the government decided that Britain's diverse railway companies would be 'grouped' into four larger, regionally-based undertakings, the M&SWJR resisted an amalgamation with the GWR. In the end, however, the smaller company was absorbed by its mighty neighbour with effect from 1st July 1923, and there was, thereafter, at least some attempt to integrate the two services between Cheltenham and Andoversford, the separate ex-M&SWJR station being closed in 1927.

'3521' Class 4-4-0 No. 3528 has just left Charlton Kings and is bound for Cheltenham St. James with the 3.12 pm stopping service from Kingham on 5th July 1924. At the rear of the train are three through coaches from Paddington, which have been slipped from a Worcester-bound express at Kingham. The accommodation bridge in the background marks the point where the short-lived branch to Leckhampton quarry diverged. The locomotive's history deserves special mention as it actually started life as a broad gauge 0-4-2 tank engine in 1887. After conversion to an 0-4-4 tank and later complete reversal to a 4-4-0 tender locomotive in June 1900, it was rebuilt with a long-cone superheated taper boiler in May 1912, final withdrawal coming in July 1927.
Humphrey Household collection, courtesy National Railway Museum

A wonderful archive of railway photographs which has recently come to light is the Nash Collection. William Nash was a career railwayman, who began photographing trains in 1922 at the age of 13 and who rose through the ranks of the LMS Railway after starting as a signalman in Cumbria. By 1952 he was working in the LMR headquarters at Euston, when he was tragically killed in the appalling disaster at Harrow & Wealdstone station. Two volumes of his work have been published by The Oakwood Press, covering a whole panorama of railway subjects and locations. Nash had family connections in Cheltenham so, fortuitously for us, a number of his early photographs are of this area. Here, 4-4-0 No. 3555, another '3521' Class engine with a similar history of rebuilding as its classmate above, brings a Kingham to Cheltenham service past the Gloucester Loop Junction bracket signal in 1926. Nash had noted this as a working from Paddington; this again refers to the last two coaches, which would have been slipped from a north-bound express passing Kingham. In the background, the line curves to the left to pass under Shurdington Road bridge and one of the authors lives in a bungalow whose garden butts up to the course of the line on the right. The occupation bridge from which the picture was taken carried a lane to Bourneside Farm.
William Nash collection, courtesy Kate Robinson

A recently discovered archive of photographs documents the Banbury to Chipping Norton Junction auto trains and the locomotives involved in some detail. They originally belonged to one of the old drivers on the eastern section of the line, Ted Parry, and all seem to date from the period 1909-18. In this first view, Ted Parry poses for photographer Frank Packer on his trusty steed for the day, '517' Class 0-4-2T No. 218, alongside the platform used by B&CDR trains at Chipping Norton Junction. Built at Wolverhampton in 1876, No. 218 is seen here with small capacity (620 gallon) tanks and an open cab, with the weather sheet rolled and tied on the cab roof. Larger 900 gallon tanks were fitted in the late 1920s, by which time the engine had also gained an enclosed cab. This view also indicates that No. 218 was fitted with auto apparatus from quite an early date; it is not noted in RCTS *Locomotives of the GWR Part 6* as being one of those so equipped. Auto coach No. 11, with 'Banbury' destination boards mounted at either end, was a 70 foot trailer built in late 1905 to Diagram 'E'. No. 11 was photographed at Banbury in the 1940s, so may have spent much of its life in the area. It was condemned in 1954.

Barry Davis collection

One of the later '517s', No. 1470 of 1883, is seen at Chipping Norton, **above**, with an auto service *en route* from Banbury to Kingham around 1908, with Ted Parry on the footplate on the right, with carnation buttonhole. No. 1470 is fitted with a Churchward enclosed cab and is fully lined out and polished up.
It may be that this photograph in fact shows one of the inaugural auto trains on this section of the B&CDR. In the circa 1918 view at Kingham, **below**, driver Ted Parry is seen standing with a wartime volunteer lady porter on his left, plus a regular porter and guard, alongside a recently arrived service from Banbury. The auto coach, in crimson lake livery, has been supplemented by the addition of a clerestory carriage. No. 558 is another of the '517' Class tank engines, built in 1869. This view also provides a tantalising glimpse of the kiosk that was set up beneath the footbridge steps around the time of the First World War. *Both Barry Davis collection*

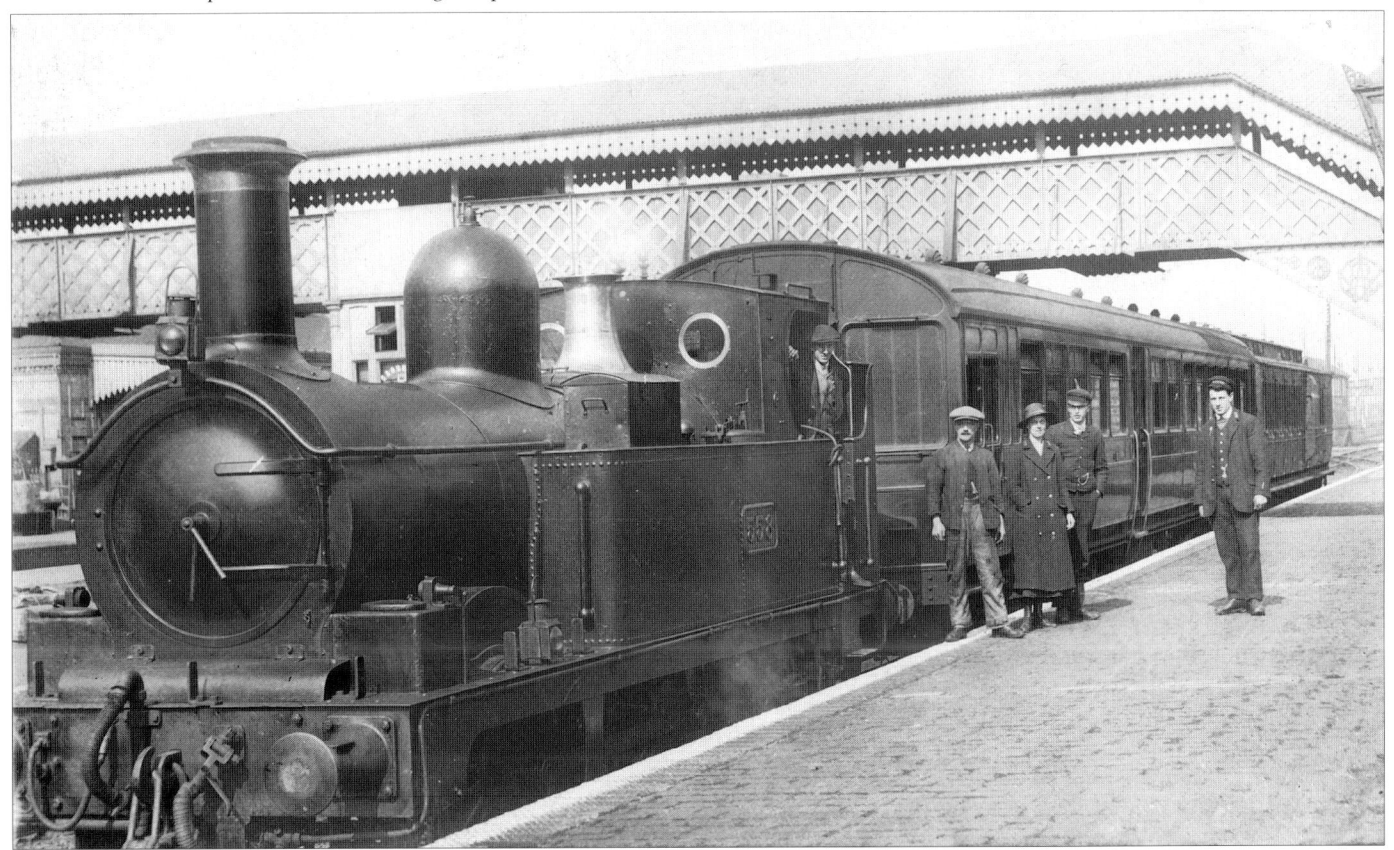

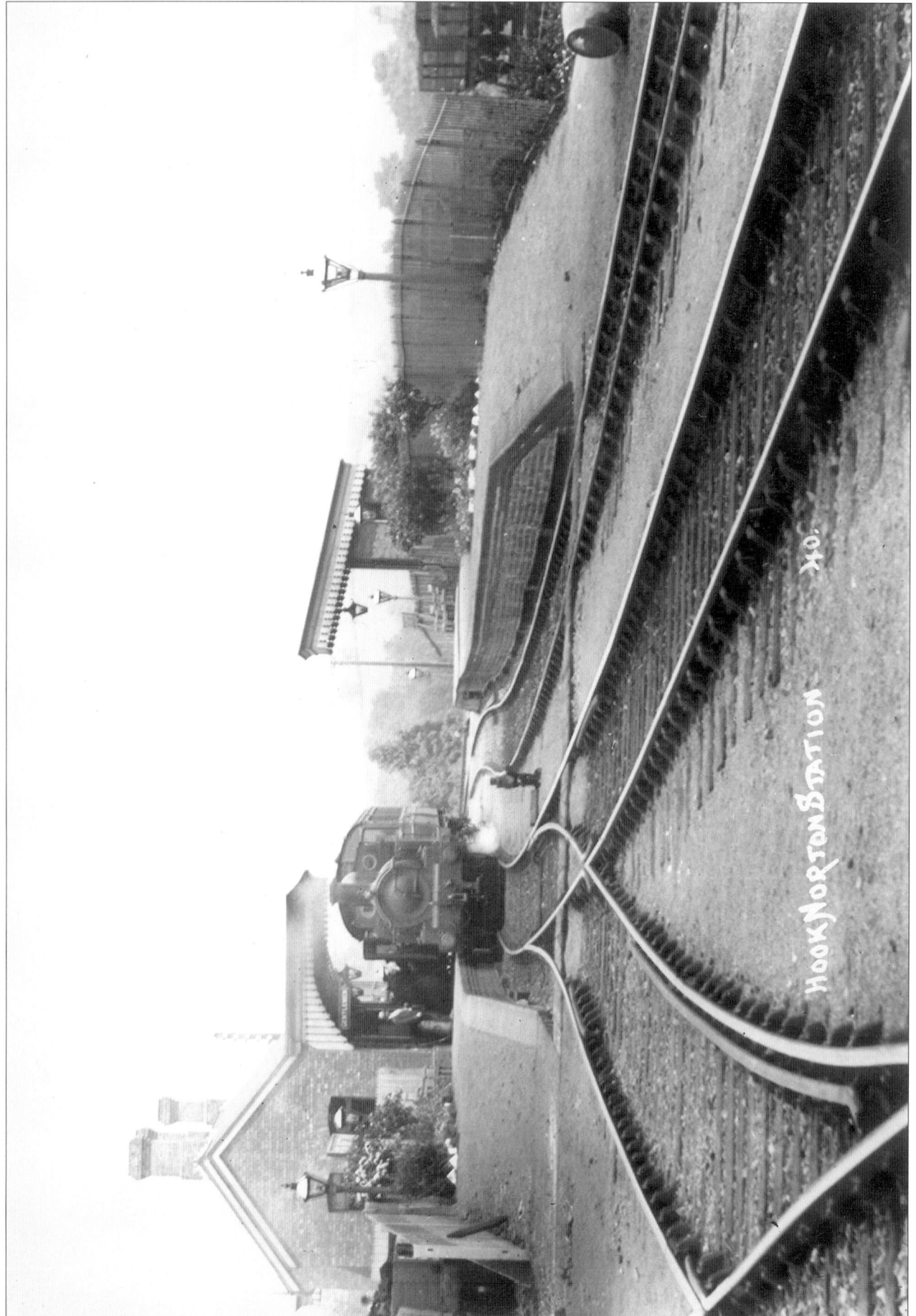

A '517' Class 0-4-2 tank pauses at Hook Norton station with an auto service bound for Kingham some time after the First World War. The auto coach sports chocolate and cream livery, so the photograph probably dates from the mid 1920s, while the station boasts a fine array of flowering shrubs. *Oxfordshire County Council Photographic Archive*

Another of the ubiquitous 'Metro' tanks, No. 628, is seen here near Charlton Kings with the 10.35 am Cheltenham to Kingham local service on 5th April 1924. It has just passed under the bridge carrying Sandy Lane over the railway. The first vehicle is a short wheelbase bogie parcels brake, while the rest of the train is a mix of 4- and 6-wheeled coaches. All appear to be in the brown livery adopted in 1908, which began to be discontinued from 1922. The locomotive was from the second batch of 'Metro' 2-4-0Ts, one of 20 built in 1871. It was withdrawn in March 1930, eighteen months short of its 60th birthday.
Humphrey Household collection, courtesy National Railway Museum

This superb circa 1907 study of Sarsden Halt is once again the work of Frank Packer, who, if not having a direct interest in railways, certainly recognised the social role that they played in the community and did much to record this over the years. An unidentified '517' Class 0-4-2T pauses at this rural stopping place, on its way to Chipping Norton and Banbury, and the throng on the platform shows how well used these services were in the years before the First World War. The '517's were regulars on the line in the early years. The presence of the wheelbarrow in the foreground suggests that the porter has temporarily broken off from tending his cabbages to look after the passengers, whilst the driver is more interested in the photographer.
Bob Brown collection

In its heyday, the B&CDR line was vey much a part of the community through which it ran and the pictures on these two pages illustrate that fact. **Above**, Car No. 15 of the Cheltenham & District Light Railway ambles down Leckhampton Road on a sunny day around 1907. It is just about to cross the bridge by Cheltenham South & Leckhampton station and thus was a direct connection provided to or from most parts of the town for passengers. **Below**, this view of Chipping Norton market dates from around 1930. Market days were always busy on the line in the decades leading up to the Second World War. *Top: Michael Mitchell collection; bottom: Neil Parkhouse collection*

Above, a travelling fair set up in the centre of Bourton on another golden summer's day in the Edwardian era. Whilst, unlike the regular market days, an event like this would maybe only happen two or three times a year, it would nevertheless bring extra passengers to the line whilst it was on. The village's attraction for tourists goes back a long way and the well-heeled traveller did not expect to walk to his hotel from the station. The best establishments, such as the New Inn (J. Clarke, Prop.), **below**, had their own transport ready to meet the latest arrivals from London, as well as offering trips around the locality during their stay. *Both Michael Mitchell collection*

The 'Ports-to-Ports Express' at Cheltenham South and Leckhampton, probably in 1907. This appears to be a posed view as the train is stationary but has pulled clear of the platform for the benefit of the photographer. The service was worked by two sets of coaches, one each from the GWR and the Great Central Railway. It is the latter set which is seen in use on this occasion, hauled by 'Bulldog' Class 4-4-0 No. 3708. Also of interest in this view is the coal delivery wagon visible in the right background in the station yard; it belonged to local coal merchant Alfred G. Stockwell, who was based at No. 17 Upper Bath Road, Cheltenham. He is known to have been in business from 1889 and possibly earlier, trading up until the outbreak of the First World War at least. It is not known if he ever owned any railway wagons. By 1923, the business was trading as Stockwell & Son but it does not feature in the *Kelly's Directory* for 1927.

Phil Coutanche collection

At first sight, this appears to have been taken on the same day as the previous picture, with the same locomotive and crew; however, the coaches are not the same and there is no roofboard on the second vehicle. It was probably taken a day or so earlier and No. 3708 is seen here a little sooner in its journey, at Gloucester. Built in June 1906, 'Bulldog No. 3708 became GWR No. 3418 as part of the great renumbering scheme carried out in 1912 and, as such, it was named *Sir Arthur Yorke* in March 1916. *Phil Coutanche collection*

THE 'PORTS-TO-PORTS EXPRESS' & OTHER THROUGH SERVICES

The Cheltenham to Banbury Direct line was served by just one long distance working, which was first introduced in May 1906 as a link between South Wales and the north-eastern ports. The train originally ran between Newcastle and Barry, to facilitate the transfer of merchant ships' crews between Tyneside and South Wales. In pre-Grouping days, it was a joint venture between the North Eastern, Great Central, Great Western and Barry Railway companies, North Eastern locomotives being used between Newcastle and York, while GCR engines were employed between York and Banbury. The Great Western was responsible for operation over the Banbury to Cardiff section, and Barry Railway motive power was used between Cardiff and Barry.

This ambitious cross-country express service, which ran each day in both directions, started its journey at Newcastle and ran along the East Coast main line to York, from where it used the Swinton & Knottingley Joint Railway in order to reach the Great Central main line. The train then ran southwards to Banbury via the GCR, after which the B&CDR line provided a convenient cross country route to Gloucester and South Wales. The train was not officially named, although it became widely-known as the 'Ports-to-Ports Express'. An alternative appellation, used along parts of the route, was 'The Central' or 'The Great Central' train.

The service was worked by two train sets, the Great Western providing a six-coach set, while the Great Central train was composed of five vehicles. The two trains made one northbound and one southbound journey each day, so uninitiated travellers gained the impression that the 'Ports-to-Ports' service was worked by GWR and GCR stock on alternate days. When first introduced, the GCR vehicles had sported an attractive chocolate and cream livery but in 1910 the company adopted a varnished teak finish for its coaches; in 1908, the GWR had changed its coaching stock livery from chocolate and cream to all-over brown, though in 1912 the brown was replaced by a crimson lake livery which remained in use until the post-Grouping period.

The Great Western vehicles were normally clerestory-roofed 'Milford Haven Boat Train' stock, whereas the Great Central provided a very smart train of elliptical-roofed coaches. After World War One, the service was extended from Barry to Swansea, and in later years a through coach was introduced to and from Hull. In the early post-Grouping period, the formation normally comprised five corridor vehicles, plus a restaurant car and the Hull through coach.

In the 1920s, the 'Ports-to-Ports Express' left Newcastle at 9.30 am and, after a fast run on the Great Central line, it arrived at Banbury at 3.21 pm. After an engine change, the train left Banbury behind a Great Western locomotive,

The running of an express service over such an unlikely route as the B&CDR line obviously fascinated the local postcard photographers of the time and several views of the train at various stations on the line have been found. Here, it is seen approaching Andoversford Junction station around 1910. The big moment of the day for the station staff, however, is undoubtedly the chance to have their photograph taken and scant notice is being paid to the on-coming express. The obligatory GWR 'Bulldog' Class 4-4-0 is again hauling a train of GCR stock, although this time it can be seen that all of the carriages have roofboards. Note that the waiting shelter on the Up platform has a stove-pipe chimney which does not show up in any of the later views, indicating that originally a stove was installed inside – perhaps at the request of the local gentry?

Bob Brown collection

What a stirring sight this must have been on an otherwise sleepy cross-country route. A 'Bulldog' Class 4-4-0 swings through Hook Norton station with the eastbound 'Port to Ports Express' around 1907/8. The train again consists of the Great Central Railway set of carriages. The Great Western appeared to make more use of roofboards than the GCR. *John Alsop collection*

The 'Ports to Ports Express' was the only regular train to traverse the direct line at Kingham, apart from the ironstone trains, so views of it in use are rare. Here, on 6th September 1922, an unidentified '43XX' Class 2-6-0 brings the express off the bridge over the Oxford-Worcester line and past Kingham East Junction box. The clerestory roofed stock is in crimson lake livery. The Churchward '43XX' Class moguls were more powerful than the four-coupled 'Bulldog's but, as they were not named, they lacked the glamour of their 4-4-0 counterparts. *Humphrey Household collection, courtesy National Railway Museum*

Another gem from the William Nash archive! A double-header on the 'Ports to Ports' as it storms through Charlton Kings to attack the long climb up to Andoversford. A short piece of level running through the station there will then be followed by an even stiffer climb up to the summit near Notgrove. By the summer of 1926, when this view was taken, the Grouping three years previously had seen the demise of the Great Central Company, swallowed up in the new London & North Eastern Railway, so Nash noted this train as comprising L&NER stock. Little can be seen of the coaches, so it is not possible to determine their ancestry but they are likely to be a pre-Group set, probably either GCR or North Eastern Railway. Unusually, perhaps, 'Bird series 'Bulldog' No. 3449 *Nightingale*, which might be considered the train engine, is piloting '43XX' Class 2-6-0 No. 5310. The 'Birds' were a small sub-class of the 'Bulldogs', comprising fifteen locomotives built in 1909-10. They had deeper frames than their earlier compatriots, plus larger sandboxes and longer smokeboxes, which all contributed to their overall weight being increased by some 4½ tons. Although, by the time they were built, the 'Star' and 'Saint' Class 4-6-0s were taking over, the 'Bulldogs' found much work on secondary routes like the B&CDR, the Didcot, Newbury & Southampton route and the Cambrian main line until the Second World War. No. 3449 was one of the last of the class in service when withdrawn in June 1951. As well as providing a tantalising glimpse of the entrance to the tiny goods yard at Charlton Kings, this photograph also documents the Leckhampton Quarry sidings in use on the left. These new sidings were laid in 1923 and into use the following year but the quarry went into liquidation and closed down in late 1926. The private branch line curving off to the quarry can just be seen in the left background. The sidings were lifted in 1932.

William Nash collection, courtesy Kate Robinson

Just to give an idea of how the motive power on the 'Ports-to-Ports' changed in the course of its run and also of the route it traversed, this view shows the train in the early stages of its journey from Newcastle. In September 1932, 'A1' pacific No. 2569 *Gladiateur* powers past Eryholme, 4 miles south of Darlington, with the southbound leg of the express, composed of L&NER stock. It is unlikely the 'A1' worked all the way through to Banbury, an engine change most likely being effected at Leicester. *William Nash collection, courtesy Kate Robinson*

arriving in Cardiff by 6.40 pm. It then continued along the Taff Vale coastal route via Penarth, arriving in Barry at 7.19 pm and Swansea at 8.45 pm. In the reverse direction, the northbound working left Swansea at 7.30 am and reached Newcastle by 6.15 pm. In 1939, the service was re-routed via the Great Western main line between Cardiff and Bridgend, and the departure time for the northbound working was then changed to 8.30 am.

The train normally ran non-stop between Banbury and Cheltenham, this being the only passenger service to use the east-to-west Avoiding Line at Kingham. There was a scheduled stop at Cheltenham South, while, in the pre-Grouping period, the southbound service called at Stow-on-the-Wold or Bourton-on-the-Water to set down on notice being given to the guard. A similar situation pertained in the northbound direction, in that the train called at those two stations to pick-up only. However, these arrangements applied only to long distance travellers with tickets to or from Leicester or stations further north.

In the later Great Western period, the 'Ports-to-Ports Express' left Banbury at 3.31 pm, and called at Cheltenham South & Leckhampton at 4.53 pm, having run non-stop over the B&CDR line. The eastbound working left Cheltenham South at 11.16 am and reached Banbury at 12.39 pm. As the 'Ports-to-Ports' service did not cater for local travellers from

Another '43XX' 2-6-0, No. 6346, passes Churchdown, near Gloucester, with the eastbound 'Ports-to-Ports Express' on 1st May 1937. The train is composed mainly of L&NER stock, although the first vehicle is Great Western. *Humphrey Household collection, courtesy National Railway Museum*

Some of the Chipping Norton Junction station staff pose for the camera around 1907, accompanied by a couple of members of the local gentry and with the imposing station footbridge dominating the background. Of particular interest here are the carriages on the right, which carry Cheltenham destination boards. These have been slipped from the 12.42 pm Paddington–Worcester express, GWR regulations permitting up to four 8-wheeled coaches to be slipped at once, although two or three seems to have been the norm for this service. They will be attached to the next train to Cheltenham, the 1.05 pm departure, stopping all stations *en route* and taking around an hour and ten minutes for the journey, despite which this still offered a faster connection with the capital than via Swindon and Gloucester. Note, also, the Down Main starting signals on Platform One in the left distance; these were later replaced with an underslung bracket, to aid sighting for locomotive crews beneath the footbridge. Some cattle wagons can be seen in the yard behind Platform One and in the far distance, the newly built bridge carrying the avoiding line can also be made out. *Neil Parkhouse collection*

the intermediate stations, it was of little use for people wishing to travel between Paddington and the Cotswolds. The Great Western did, however, make some attempt to provide a fast service to and from London by providing a limited number of through coaches between Cheltenham St. James, Kingham and Paddington.

For many years the through portion was provided by slip coaches. This service seems to have commenced around 1905, with normally two or three coaches being 'slipped' from the 12.42 pm Paddington to Worcester express on the approaches to Kingham, the Cheltenham coaches being brought to a stand in the station under the control of the guard's brake. Passengers for Chipping Norton would get off and catch the 1.10 pm departure, whilst those for Cheltenham remained on board while the coaches were attached to the 1.05 pm train for Cheltenham, which arrived there at 2.17 pm. This service ceased following the introduction of a Kingham stop for the 12.45 pm Paddington to Hereford express.

In the 1930s, the service was provided by through coaches which were attached to the early afternoon train from Cheltenham and taken along the branch to Kingham, at which point they were attached to a Worcester to Paddington express for a fast run to London. In the reverse direction, a through portion was detached at Kingham from the 12.45 pm from Paddington and taken forward to Cheltenham by the 2.22 pm branch train.

With an overall journey time of less than three hours, this was at one time the fastest service available between Paddington and Cheltenham, although the Great Western generally did little to exploit the Banbury & Cheltenham route. It was never regarded as a serious alternative to the GWR main line through Stroud and Swindon.

FREIGHT TRAINS & TRAFFIC

Goods traffic was important on the Cheltenham to Kingham line, although such traffic was never particularly heavy. Like other rural lines, the railway carried coal and general merchandise inwards, and agricultural traffic outwards. Important customers on the Kingham to Banbury line included Bliss's Tweed Mill at Chipping Norton, and Chipping Norton Gas Works, both of these lineside industrial concerns being served by private sidings.

Further private sidings made connections on the section of line between Chipping Norton and King's Sutton, these being associated mainly with ironstone traffic. In the early 1900s, the sidings concerned included the Earl of Dudley's

Views of The Leys at Chipping Norton were a favourite of the Packers, father and son, over the years; no doubt the cards sold well to those living in the houses featured. Fortuitously for the railway enthusiast, they also include a section of the goods sidings and thus document a fair selection of the wagons using the yard, from around 1908 up to the early 1950s. This circa 1912 view is typical. No less than five of Bliss's wagons feature here, sporting two different liveries, as well as two from the Chipping Norton Co-Operative Society, whilst in the background can just be seen a wagon belonging to H. Burlingham of Evesham. The passenger stock for the next service to Kingham is also stabled in the yard, two 6-wheel coaches looking very smart in crimson lake livery. *M.P. Barnsley collection*

A goods working is seen alongside the eastbound platform at Charlton Kings, probably circa 1938 judging by the two styles of wagon lettering on view. The train has probably paused for some of the wagon brakes to be pinned down in preparation for the long climb up to Andoversford. The style of tender without the rearmost steps would suggest the locomotive is one of the 10 Beyer-Peacock 0-6-0s inherited from the M&SWJR, which were 'Swindonised' but kept their old tenders. These were modified by replacing the coal rails with the normal GWR fenders. It is likely therefore, that the train is bound for the ex-M&SWJR line at Andoversford Junction.
The Lens of Sutton Collection

and the Hook Norton Ironstone Partnerships' sidings at Hook Norton, the Brymbo Steel Company's Siding at Council Hill, additional Hook Norton Ironstone Partnership sidings at Bloxham and Adderbury, and Alfred Hickman's siding at Sydenham, as well as other sidings on the Oxford & Rugby main line in the vicinity of King's Sutton.

There was normally just one local goods train in each direction on the Cheltenham to Kingham and Banbury to Kingham sections. In the early 1880s, a daily goods train left Chipping Norton Junction at 9.00 pm, and arrived at Cheltenham at 1.05 pm. In the up direction, a balancing eastbound service departed from Cheltenham at 2.05 pm, and reached Chipping Norton Junction by 5.23 pm. There was, in addition, a short distance goods service from Bourton-on-the-Water at 7.45 am, and a return working from Chipping Norton Junction at 6.40 pm.

An unidentified 'Bulldog' 4-4-0 drifts down the bank from Dowdeswell towards Charlton Kings on a short goods from Kingham, late one summer's afternoon in 1944. Thirty-five years earlier, this engine may have hauled the 'Ports-to-Ports Express' along this same route. By this date, however, the remaining members of this fondly remembered class were eking out their twilight years on more mundane duties as seen here. On a lighter note, the taking of such pictures in wartime, when film was almost impossible to get and photography was frowned on due to fears of spying, was a somewhat hazardous occupation. Years later, photographer Bill Potter recalled he would take just the one shot and then run for his bicycle and pedal off home as fast as he could in case the engine crew were not 'friendly'! The line curves to the left in the centre distance, to cross Dowdeswell Viaduct.
Photo W. Potter

One of the earliest known photographs of the station at Bourton-on-the-Water is this view showing the road entrance to the goods yard, which, from the costumes, must date from around 1890. The premises of two coal merchants feature prominently on the right; Geo. Clifford and Henry Burlingham & Co., whose headquarters were in Evesham. The latter also had an office at Notgrove station on the B&CDR line and the delivery wagon standing on the weighbridge belongs to him. Both merchants were in business by 1868 at least but Clifford disappears from the coal merchant listings in trade directories just before the First World War. The company were mainly builders, however, and still appeared under that heading in later directories. I is likely they continued to supply coal locally and, indeed, their coal business is noted as having been bought by Pratt & Haynes of Shipton-under-Wychwood in 1935. Burlingham & Co. are listed in local directories as coal merchants up until the early 1930s. Note the coal stacked up neatly behind the wooden offices, whilst several other delivery carts are also on view. The array of cattle vans and sheeted wagons in the sidings provide further evidence of Bourton's importance as a railhead for the surrounding rural community. The coach and horse outside the station on the left will be waiting to meet someone off the next train from Kingham, a client for one of the local hotels most probably.

Neil Parkhouse collection

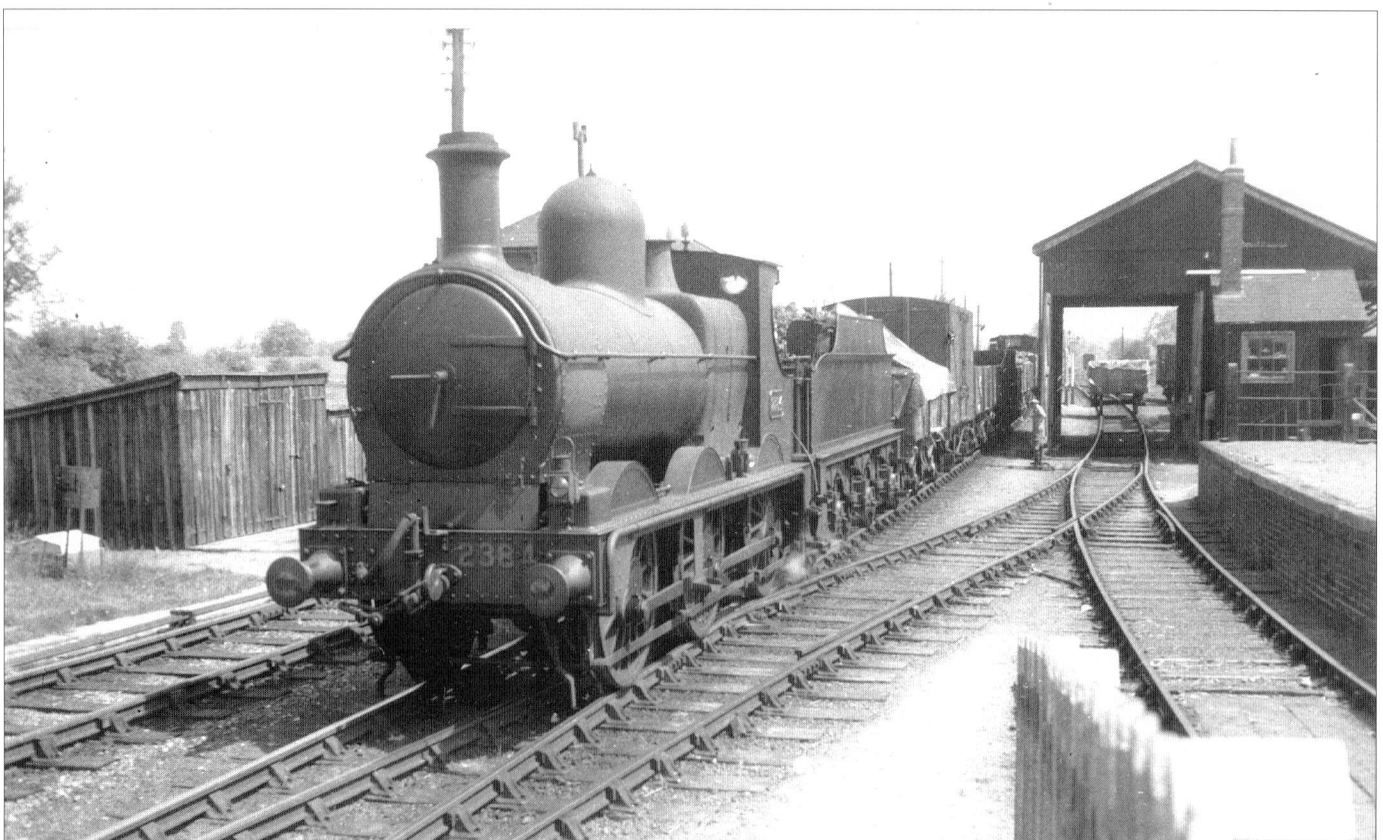

A busy scene at Bourton-on-the-Water station probably shortly before the First World War – the replacement signal box of 1912 can just be seen on the left and the 4-wheel stock appears to be in the all-over chocolate or the slightly later lake livery. The locomotive of the pick-up goods has most probably run round to detach some wagons from the rear of the train and is shunting them in the yard, out of sight of the camera. *The Lens of Sutton Collection*

GWR 'Dean Goods' 0-6-0 No. 2384 arrives at Bourton-on-the-Water in the late 1930s with a Kingham to Cheltenham pick-up goods, drawing to a halt beside the wooden goods shed. Again the locomotive will run round its train before detaching wagons destined for the sidings here from the rear of the train and possibly then adding one or two as well. No. 2384 was one of a batch of 20 'Dean Goods' built in 1890 and was nearing the end of its career when this picture was taken, being withdrawn in December 1938. The sleeper-built PW sheds on the left provided secure accommodation for the ganger's inspection trolley and trailer. *Roger Carpenter collection*

The final offering from the Nash collection is this superb study of the Cheltenham to Kingham pick-up goods passing Cheltenham South & Leckhampton station on another gloriously sunny day in 1926. The locomotive, Dean outside-framed '2361' Class 0-6-0 No. 2376, is hauling an assortment of vans and (mostly sheeted) open wagons. Another sheeted open can be seen in the siding behind the platform on the right and the photograph also provides a view of the entrance into the station from the Leckhampton Road. Note the tall Home signal visible just beyond the overbridge; the extra height enabled it to be seen by the Leckhampton signalman. No. 2376 was one of a small class of twenty locomotives built in 1885-6 which, although numbered within the 'Dean Goods' number series, differed quite radically from them. The class were part of an interesting experiment in standardisation carried out by William Dean during the period 1884-7. Four new classes of locomotive – passenger tender/tank and goods tender/tank – were built, with identical cylinders and motion, the same size coupled wheels with springs hung under the axles and double frames. The boilers, however, showed variations between the goods and passenger types. As can be seen, the result was an attractively proportioned engine and they were quite successful, most of the class leading fairly long lives. No. 2376 was withdrawn in December 1938. It is likely that a few members of the class worked over the B&CDR line for a period, although many spent their time allocated to the London and Wolverhampton Divisions. In 1926, No. 2376 may have been shedded at Honeybourne (No. 2375 was allocated there a few years later) and working a round trip via Cheltenham, Kingham and then back via the Oxford & Worcester line.

William Nash collection, courtesy Kate Robinson

TROUBLE AT 'T MILL!

As an important customer of the railway at Chipping Norton, events at Bliss's Mill obviously had an effect on the day to day fortunes of the line. Coal arrived in wagons for the mill boilers and finished Tweed products were despatched by rail. By and large it was an uneventful and harmonious existence. However, in the winter of 1913-4, a strike occurred here which ran on for several weeks and became as bitter as any which took place in the more industrialised areas generally associated with such activity.

William Bliss had been a popular employer but when the Bliss family lost control of the mill industrial relations began to deteriorate. A.H. Dunston, the manager of the mill in 1913, was hated by the workforce and this may have prompted an attempt to form a branch of the Workers' Union. In retaliation, the management formed a so-called 'Employees' Association' and three union activists were dismissed. This resulted in the outbreak of the Great Strike on 18th December 1913, when 125 women and 112 men withdrew their labour, leaving only 130 non-strikers to carry on the work of the mill. The strike soon became a *cause célèbre* and, with sympathetic support from a range of well-wishers, including radical Oxford students and the Anglican Church, the strikers held out until June 1914. In the meantime, the management had employed strike-breakers and various other tactics to defeat the strikers. In the event, about 160 workers lost their jobs and the legacy of ill-feeling lasted for many years.

Frank Packer covered the events in detail with his camera – the series number 96 will be noted on one of these cards. The top view shows Chipping Norton West Box in the left background. The police, seen here guarding the mill, its entrance and siding, as well as a group of non-unionists leaving work, were not local, being brought in from another force, a normal occurrence with disputes such as this. When things got a bit nasty, it did not do to have the local police and population falling out with each other.

Oxfordshire County Council Photographic Archive

Hook Norton is still justifiably famous for its family brewery, the history of which stretches back 150 years. The remarkable building seen here dates from 1900 and reflects a vogue for 'Bavarian' architecture then in force for breweries, probably as a result of the rise in the popularity of Continental beers, as more well-off folk undertook various tours courtesy of Thomas Cook. Today, Hook Norton Brewery still employs steam power in the production of its beers and they remain some of the finest 'real' ales the connoisseur can imbibe. The railway was used for transporting its products but they had to be taken there by road as the brewery was too far from the station for a private siding to be laid in.
Oxfordshire County Council Photographic Archive

The Chipping Norton branch was, at that time, served by seven mixed trains in each direction. Mixed trains remained a feature of operations on the Chipping Norton branch for many years, although a daily goods working was introduced when the B&CDR route was completed throughout between Chipping Norton and Banbury. In the 1920s, this service generally left Banbury around mid-day and arrived in Chipping Norton by 2.42 pm. The engine then spent the rest of the afternoon engaged in shunting work, before continuing its journey to Kingham at around 5.30 pm. In the opposite direction, the returning up service left Kingham at 6.50 pm.

A similar pattern of local goods operation pertained for many years. In the late 1930s, a daily pick-up service left Banbury at 10.40 am, returning from Kingham at 6.40 pm, while the Kingham to Cheltenham line was served by an Up working from Cheltenham at 10.46 am and a Down service from Kingham at 10.15 am. In addition to these local goods workings, the B&DCR route carried variable amounts of long distance goods traffic in the form of coal and iron ore.

As previously mentioned, the B&CDR line was built as a direct link for heavy freight traffic between the South Midlands and South Wales, and at various times in its history it did indeed carry large amounts of coal and iron ore – although such traffic was subject to severe fluctuations. In pre-Grouping days, for example, there had been a large amount of coal traffic between South Wales and the London & North Western system, this major traffic flow being routed via Kingham, Yarnton Junction and the Oxford, Worcester & Wolverhampton line. In the westbound direction, there was a corresponding flow of empty wagons, which were also routed via Yarnton, Kingham and the B&CDR route to Cheltenham.

Long distance coal traffic suffered a severe decline during the 1920s and 30s, as the coal industry itself contracted in the face of foreign imports and competition from other forms of fuel. In 1929, Lord Churchill, the Great Western Chairman, reported that coal and coke shipments had fallen from 36,500,000 tons in 1923 to 26,500,000 tons in 1928; he added that no less than 117 Welsh coal mines had been closed since 1923. The Great Depression resulted in a further loss of coal traffic during the early 1930s and, by the end of that decade, long distance coal traffic had virtually ceased on the Banbury & Cheltenham Direct line.

The iron and steel industry experienced a similar decline during the same period, although in this case the reduction

GWR '28XX' Class 2-8-0 No. 2872 is seen stopped at the signals outside Charlton Kings station on 7th June 1923, with a long train of private owner wagons belonging to Baldwins Ltd. They were a major ironstone mining company, who operated quarries in the Wroxton area as the Oxfordshire Ironstone Co. Ltd. From somewhat inauspicious beginnings in 1917-8, this grew to be one of the largest and most successful ironstone mining operations in the area, with its own standard gauge railway system of equally sizeable proportions. The train seen here will be bound for the steelworks of South Wales. *Humphrey Household collection, courtesy National Railway Museum*

in activity was not quite as severe. Some of the local ironstone quarries were abandoned but others were retained by their operators in anticipation of a trade revival and for this reason, a certain amount of ironstone traffic continued to flow over the B&CDR route during the 1930s. At the end of the decade, ironstone was normally being conveyed by the 2.30 pm working from Banbury to Margam and the 5.10 pm service from Banbury to Cardiff.

The goods rolling stock used on the line reflected the types of traffic carried, with wooden open wagons being used for many years for both coal and general merchandise traffic. As usual on the Great Western system, domestic coal was normally carried in privately-owned coal merchants' or colliery wagons, the GWR itself having very few coal or mineral-carrying vehicles in its own wagon fleet. Various private owner wagons appeared on the line over the years, among them vehicles belonging to local coal merchants such as Bernard T. Frost of Witney, Colletts of Bourton-on-the-Water and the Chipping Norton Co-operative Society. The various concerns which owned wagons and based them at regularly used stations along the route will be looked at in more detail in following chapters.

Open wagons were employed for timber, sacked goods or other commodities, sheets being used to protect vulnerable consignments. Later, covered vans began to appear in increasing numbers for a range of goods including general merchandise and fertilizers, together with specialised vehicles for meat, bananas or other perishables. Contemporary photographs suggest that local Great Western vehicles were predominant, though Midland Railway (later LMS) rolling stock was also very common.

Other specialised Great Western vehicles which would have been seen on the line included standard 'Mex' cattle wagons and characteristic 'Siphons' for the carriage of milk churns by passenger or parcels trains. Consignments of felled timber or other long thin loads were conveyed on 'Macaw' bolster wagons, while machinery or other heavy consignments would have brought 'Loriat' low loading vehicles onto the branch. In the latter context, most of the B&CDR stations were equipped with end loading docks for agricultural machinery, portable engines or road vehicles.

The various ironstone sidings at the eastern end of the B&CDR route brought many other privately-owned iron ore vehicles onto the line. In pre-Grouping days, iron ore was normally conveyed in wooden open wagons but larger organisations, such as the Brymbo Steel Company, were already extensive users of steel hopper wagons. They had obtained twenty such wagons by the 1920s and these were used to carry a regular supply of calcinated ore to their Brymbo Steel Works. The vehicles in question were of 20

The postcard photographers of the Edwardian era were often quick off the mark when it came to recording local events and Frank Packer was no exception, as this view shows. On 23rd May 1907, '517' Class 0-4-2T No. 546 came to grief at the end of the headshunt immediately adjacent to Chipping Norton West Box, shunting a brake van through the buffers and demolishing the cabin steps. As a result, the signalman's only means of egress was via the ladder propped against the front window but this slight nuisance would no doubt have been tempered by the recognition of his lucky escape from more serious injury; the box could easily have been more badly damaged. The steam hissing gently from No. 546 and small crowd of interested onlookers watching the railwaymen set about their task of re-railing engine and brake van, gives an indication of how promptly the photographer had arrived on the spot with all his cumbersome gear. No. 546 was built at Wolverhampton in 1869 as a short wheelbase saddle tank. It was rebuilt with a longer wheelbase and side tanks, as seen here, in 1878. Later, under Churchward's tenure, it was rebuilt again with a longer wheelbase still, new frames and outside bearings, and an enclosed cab. It was also one of the class to be fitted with auto apparatus and painted for a few years in lake livery, to match the carriage stock. No. 546, which looks in very tidy condition here, survived this minor mishap and completed another twenty-one years of service before withdrawal in 1928. The 'TOAD' Goods Brake Van No. 56124 was built circa 1895 to Diagram AA3 and carries an unusual cast iron plate proclaiming its home base to be Wolverhampton. *John Alsop collection*

tons capacity and had been supplied by the Birmingham Carriage & Wagon Company.

Photographic evidence, personal recollections and incidental references suggest that wagons from firms such as the Shelton Iron, Steel & Coal Company of Etruria, and the Robert Heath & Low Moor Company of Stoke-on-Trent, were among those seen on the line during the 1920s and 30s. These vehicles were used to carry ironstone to steel works in Stoke-on-Trent, Sheltons being an important customer for the quarries, together with other non-Brymbo steelworks in South Wales.

GWR TANK ENGINES ON THE BANBURY TO CHELTENHAM LINE

Local passenger services on the Banbury & Cheltenham Direct route were, for many years, worked by 4- or 6-coupled tank locomotives. The indigenous Oxford, Worcester & Wolverhampton and West Midland tank engines were all withdrawn during the Victorian period and, in view of this, it is likely that George Armstrong's 0-4-2 saddle tanks appeared on the B&CDR at a comparatively early date, together with the visually-similar 'Metro' Class 2-4-0Ts.

Introduced in 1866, the Armstrong 0-4-2STs had 15 inch by 24 inch inside cylinders, and 5 foot coupled wheels. The initial batch of fifty locomotives had very short coupled wheelbases and this gave them an ungainly appearance. They were, nevertheless, highly efficient machines, with a commendably small coal consumption. From 1879 onwards, the engines were rebuilt as side tanks and given an extended wheelbase. As such, they became the first members of the famous '517' Class – large in number, they were seen all over the GWR system. In later years, the '517' Class engines were given 16 inch by 24 inch cylinders and 5 foot 2 inch coupled wheels.

Numerous '517' Class engines appeared on the Banbury & Cheltenham route at different times. In 1918, Banbury's allocation included Nos. 218, 558, 574 and 1486, while in 1921 the local allocations comprised No. 1160 at Cheltenham, No. 535 at Chipping Norton and Nos. 547, 572 and 1486 at Banbury. Other '517' Class locomotives recorded on the Banbury & Cheltenham route included Nos. 546, 549, 826, 835 and 1470. Although these versatile engines appeared on both sections of the line, they enjoyed a particularly long association with the Banbury to Kingham section, which was normally worked by a push-pull fitted 0-4-2T hauling a single auto-trailer.

The Collett '48XX' (later '14XX') Class 0-4-2Ts were introduced in 1932, as replacements for the '517's and other elderly GWR tank classes. The new locomotives soon appeared in the Banbury area, Nos. 4830, 4858 and 4873 having been allocated to Banbury shed by 1938 for employment on local passenger services to Kingham and Princes Risborough.

At the other end of the B&CDR, Cheltenham had a number

This view of the original Cheltenham engine shed shows it in the process of being dismantled in 1906, despite which it was still in use for stabling locomotives. The collection of 'Metro' tanks revealed within is apposite, for all of them would undoubtedly have worked mixed and local passenger services over the Cheltenham to Kingham section of the B&CDR at some stage. *Ian Pope collection*

'Metro' Class 2-4-0 tank No. 1464 outside Cheltenham shed circa 1904. This engine is mentioned in the text as having been delayed at Bourton in 1906. It was the final locomotive of the fifth batch of 'Metro' tanks, built in 1881/2. These were the first of the class to be built with cabs and this batch also were originally fitted with domeless boilers, which meant they appeared quite different from other 'Metro's. It was rebuilt as seen here with a domed S4-type boiler in 1896. In 1928, No. 1464 was one of a number of the class fitted with auto working apparatus, as other older auto-fitted engines were withdrawn. The engine finished its service in January 1936. *Ian Pope collection*

of 'Metro' Class 2-4-0Ts for use on local passenger services. Introduced in 1869, these attractive 2-4-0 tank locomotives had, at one time, worked on the sub-surface Metropolitan line, for which purpose many of them were originally fitted with condensing apparatus. Later, many of them gravitated away from the London area and lost their condensing apparatus as a result. Photographs of the B&CDR route taken in the first decade of the 20th century show that their use on passenger services in particular was widespread. Cheltenham shed's locomotive allocation on 1st January 1901 comprised Nos. 627, 1448, 1462, 1491, 1497 and 1500, all 'Metro' tanks, and one solitary 0-6-ST, No. 1078. By 1921, the allocation comprised Nos. 458, 464, 628, 1449 and 1497, although by now housed in the new shed at Malvern Road, in service on local passenger routes. Another 'Metro' tank used on the Cheltenham to Kingham line was No. 1464 which, on 29th January 1906, was delayed for 46 minutes at Bourton-on-the-Water while working the 1.00pm Up service from Chipping Norton Junction to Cheltenham, the problem being attributed to a *'pre-existent flaw in the little end strap'*.

The 'Metro' Class 2-4-0Ts worked on the Cheltenham to Kingham line for many years, their duties sometimes taking them eastwards onto the Chipping Norton branch. They remained regular performers during the early 1920s but by the mid 1930s they had almost all been withdrawn and replaced by the '14XX' Class 0-4-2Ts. However, on the

The end of an era! Another of the 'Metro' tanks, No. 457, waits at Chipping Norton with a morning service for Kingham on 4th August 1934, the final year that this type saw service on the line. The 'Metro's suffered wholesale withdrawals in the early 1930s, as the new '14XX' Class 0-4-2Ts were introduced. No. 457, another of the early members of the class dating from 1869, was just over three months away from its last day of service. It was allocated to Oxford shed during its final year.
Photo H.B. Priestley, courtesy Milepost 92½

A lovely view looking north-west across the southern end of the platforms at Chipping Norton Junction, towards Stow-on-the-Wold, with Driver Parry filling the tanks of '517' Class 0-4-2T No. 218 from the column on the platform. The fireman's 'ghost' can be seen near the bunker, which looks rather empty so a visit to the coaling stage may have been next on the agenda. The view dates from before the station was renamed in May 1909 and it may well have been taken on the same day as the picture on page 74. The auto coach for the return service to Banbury can be seen standing in Platform 3.
Barry Davis collection

Three more photographs of Driver Ted Parry posing with various colleagues and different locomotives at Chipping Norton. In this first view, **right**, Ted stands on the left, with grease gun in hand, in front of 1873-built '517' Class No. 826. The fireman stands on the right, whilst the engine is posed in front of the goods shed, so the other two men may well be goods yard staff. No. 826 was obviously one of the earlier fittings of this class with auto apparatus and has also been given an enclosed cab. Note that the coal bunker has been built up level at the top; when the cabs were fitted, the old Swindon bunkers with the drop front were originally left as they were, leaving a gap at either side.

These views were actually produced as postcards and the last two Ted Parry sent to friends, so they carry a postmark date giving us an idea when they were taken; this one, **left**, was posted on 16th September 1912. Standing in the yard at Chipping Norton, 0-4-2T No. 220 demonstrates the large range of variations to be encountered in the '517' Class. The locomotive was built at Wolverhampton in 1876 and carries a flared top bunker typical of the Works. Driver Parry again stands on the left, with fireman to the right, whilst the gentleman in between is probably either a goods guard or yard shunter.

All Barry Davis collection

The final view, **right**, is most interesting, with the only named Class '517' seen paying an historic visit to Chipping Norton station. Although shedded at Oxford, *Fair Rosamund* was mainly employed on the Woodstock branch, having been named in 1896 prior to working a Royal train over this line. The lady who gave her name to the engine was Rosamund Clifford, who lived at Woodstock and was a mistress of Henry II. The nameplates were retained for the rest of the engine's life, although the number plates were moved to the cab-side when No. 1476 was fitted with an enclosed cab. It is most likely in the charge of an Oxford crew here, with Ted Parry and some of the station staff posing between the tracks, suggesting this was indeed a rare visit by such a locally renowned engine. Built in 1883, *Fair Rosamund* led a relatively short life for a '517', being withdrawn in 1929.

The '45XX' Class 2-6-2Ts took over passenger services on the line during the 1930s and they remained at work on the B&CDR route until the BR era. No. 4564 of Gloucester (Horton Road) shed, is seen here in BR days, on 3rd June 1952, at Andoversford Junction station with a Kingham to Cheltenham service. The locomotive carries the early British Railways 'unicycling lion' emblem but is clearly devoid of its smokebox number plate and generally looks in rather grubby condition. The plume of steam visible in the left background suggests some shunting is in progress in the Up loop.
Bob Brown collection

B&CDR route itself, their duties were taken on by the more powerful '45XX' Class prairie tanks. At the beginning of 1934, there were two 'Metro' tanks at Oxford, one of which certainly visited the eastern section of the line.

In 1904, the Great Western had constructed a prototype 2-6-2 side tank locomotive with outside cylinders and 4 foot 10½ inch coupled wheels. Ten similar engines emerged from Wolverhampton Works in 1905 and these eleven locomotives – which subsequently became the '44XX' Class 'small prairies' – were later joined by the visually-similar '45XX' Class with 4 foot 7½ inch coupled wheels. The small prairies were intended for use on steeply-graded branch lines and secondary routes, their large boilers, short coupled wheelbases and small wheels being ideal for routes such as the Banbury & Cheltenham Direct line.

The '45XX' Class small prairies became well-established on the western section of the line during the 1930s, a number of them being based at Cheltenham Malvern Road. Several of these 2-6-2Ts appeared on the route at various times during the later Great Western and early British Railways periods, some random examples being Nos. 4535, 4564, 4567, 4571, 4573, 4578, 5514, 5515, 5538 and 5574. The engines employed on the route included the '45XX' series with 1,000 gallon tanks and the slightly-heavier '4575' sub-Class, with sloping-topped 1,300 gallon side tanks. Large 2-6-2 prairie tanks of the '51XX' Class appeared on the line during the British Railways era (see Chapter Eight).

TENDER LOCOMOTIVES ON THE B&CDR LINE

When first introduced in May 1906, the 'Ports-to-Ports Express' had been hauled by diminutive 2-4-0 tender locomotives of the 'Barnum' Class. In a letter to the *Railway Magazine*, published in November 1955, A.J. Pritchard stated that:

The first GWR engine to work this train from Cardiff to Banbury, and return the same day, was No. 3222, a 2-4-0 of the 'Barnum' Class, which was the largest that could be turned at Banbury. ... a pilot engine, usually a 'Grasshopper' 4-4-0, was provided between Gloucester and Notgrove, if the load exceeded the normal formation of six GWR or five GCR bogie coaches.

'Barnum' Class 2-4-0 No. 3225 looks very spruce in this circa 1900 view. Sister engine No. 3222 worked the first eastbound 'Ports-to-Ports' Express and members of the class were regular performers on the train in its first two years of operation. *Neil Parkhouse collection*

The twenty 'Barnum' Class locomotives introduced in 1889, were primarily intended for mixed traffic duties – for which purpose they combined high tractive effort with a wide route availability. They were among the very last GWR sandwich-framed locomotives, the idea being that they could easily have been adapted for 7 foot gauge operation, if traffic requirements should have called for additional 'convertible' locomotives during the final years of the Great Western broad gauge. In the event, their reign as 'express' engines on the Banbury & Cheltenham Direct line was cut short around September 1908, when a new locomotive shed, with a larger diameter turntable, was brought into use at Banbury.

The 'Barnums' were replaced by 'Bulldog' Class 4-4-0s. These double-framed locomotives were, in effect, an improved version of the 'Duke' Class, with larger boilers and a widened cab. They had 18 inch by 26 inch inside cylinders and 5 foot 8^1/$_2$ inch coupled wheels, their weight (with tender) being 88 tons 11 cwt. Several of them were stationed at Banbury or Cardiff at various times, including Nos. 3411 *Stanley Baldwin*, 3342 *Bonaventura*, 3345 *Smeaton*, 3375 *Sir Massey Lopes* (actually *Sir Watkin Wynn*), 3418 *Sir Arthur Yorke* and 3393 *Australia*.

Left: Neither the pilot, a 'Bulldog' 4-4-0, nor the train engine, a Class '43XX' 2-6-0, are identified here, as they head the Swansea-Newcastle 'Ports-to-Ports Express' through Charlton Kings station on 8th June 1922. In its earlier years of operation, the 4-4-0 would have been sufficient to work the train but, as loadings increased, double-heading on the Gloucester to Kingham section became more commonplace. The leading carriages are older GCR stock, dating from circa 1900. The goods wagons on the Down line would probably be part of a Cheltenham-bound goods, whose shunting was interrupted by the passage of this, the most prestigious working over the route.
Humphrey Household collection, courtesy National Railway Museum

Right: With a lighter loading of just six coaches, Great Western '43XX' Class mogul No. 6335 provides ample motive power on 3rd April 1924, as it heads out of Cheltenham with the eastbound 'Ports-to-Ports' service. The train departed Swansea at 7.30 am. This particular working is formed of the ex-Great Central rake and it is pictured here just after passing under Sandy Lane Bridge.
Humphrey Household collection, courtesy National Railway Museum

Left: Three months later, Humphrey Household photographed the corresponding westbound 'Ports-to-Ports' service, which had departed from Newcastle at 9.30 am. The train is seen here just after passing through Charlton Kings station on 8th July 1924, with 43XX mogul No. 6335 in charge. On this particular day it was the turn of the Great Western rake to form the westbound train, which would then be used on the next day's eastbound working.
Humphrey Household collection, courtesy National Railway Museum

As the first section of the B&CDR as far as Andoversford Junction was also used by M&SWJR trains, quite a number of photographs were taken featuring trains hauled by locomotives of that company, a situation which persisted for some years after the 1923 Grouping. Here, GWR 4-4-0 No. 1128 (former MS&WJR No. 31) is seen heading the 10.28 am Cheltenham to Andover train on 13th July 1925. No. 1128 was rebuilt by the Great Western and 'Swindonised' with a typical GW taper boiler and copper capped chimney. The photographer noted the train comprised an ex-Midland Railway/ex-M&SWJR bogie coach painted in GW chocolate and cream, two Dean clerestories and an ex-L&NWR passenger brake – quite an eclectic mix! This part of Cheltenham, then known as Shurdington Fields, was a popular destination for Sunday school outings but the whole area was changed in the late 1950s when the Warden Hill development was built. The fields beyond the train are now occupied by Bourneside school. *Humphrey Household collection, courtesy National Railway Museum*

The 'Aberdare' Class 2-6-0s were the first Great Western moguls, the prototype having appeared in 1900, while further batches were built between 1901 and 1907. These double-framed locomotives were designed for employment on long distance freight services, in which capacity they appeared on Hook Norton ironstone workings during the Edwardian period. At the other end of the B&CDR route, members of the 'Aberdare' Class subsequently worked on the Midland & South Western Junction line, these duties bringing them onto the Cheltenham to Andoversford Junction section on a regular basis during the 1930s.

In the longer term, the '43XX' 2-6-0s were destined to enjoy a much longer association with the B&CDR Line. Designed by Harry Holcroft, the '43XX' Class moguls were introduced in 1911 as general mixed traffic engines for use throughout the GWR system. Nos. 4302, 5308 and 5312 were among the first locomotives of this type to be stationed at Banbury, though by 1921 only No. 5308 was left. By the later 1930s, Banbury's allocation included eight '43XX' Class moguls and, as fast mixed traffic engines, they normally worked the 'Ports-to-Ports Express', as well as local and long distance freight services.

The '43XX' Class 2-6-0s became familiar sights on the Banbury & Cheltenham line, particularly on the eastern section of the route between Banbury and Kingham. Some further examples recorded on the line at various times included Nos. 5318, 5325, 5332, 5336, 5361, 5391, 6316, 6327, 6362, 6395, 6399, 7335, 8314 and 9300.

In the 1930s, 'Ports-to-Ports Express' typically consisted of seven or eight GWR or LNER bogie coaches, although its formation was sometimes increased to ten vehicles. Perhaps for this reason, the Great Western decided that the '43XX' moguls which had latterly been employed on the Newcastle to Swansea service, would be replaced by the very latest 'Manor' Class light 4-6-0s, which were introduced

An unidentified member of the 'Aberdare' Class, many of which worked heavier freight services over the B&CDR line in the pre-First World War period. *Neil Parkhouse collection*

In the twilight years of the 'Ports-to-Ports Express' on the line, two engines were regular performers on the Banbury-Swansea part of the journey. This is one of them, No. 7811 *Dunley Manor*, seen coasting down the hill from Notgrove towards Bourton in 1938. The service was curtailed by the Second World War and although it started up again afterwards, it was routed away from the Banbury & Cheltenham line. *Railways Pictorial*

in 1938 for use on express passenger and fast freight services. The new engines were designed for employment over secondary routes such as the Banbury & Cheltenham Direct line and the former Cambrian system, and for this reason they had a wide route availability.

In April 1938, the *Railway Magazine* reported that No. 7800 *Torquay Manor*, the first of the class, had been '*put into service in the middle of February*' on the Banbury to Swansea section of the through Newcastle to South Wales express working. The report pointed out that this duty involved '*running over the Banbury - Stow-on-the-Wold - Cheltenham branch, on which nothing larger than a 2-6-0 of the 4321 Class had previously been permitted to work.*'

No. 7800 was first used on the 'Ports-to-Ports Express' in February 1938 and, in the next few months, sister engines Nos. 7810 *Draycott Manor* and 7811 *Dunley Manor* arrived at Banbury for use over the Kingham branch. Nos. 7810 and 7811 soon became regular performers on the 161 mile run between Banbury and Swansea. They were used alternately in the Up and Down directions, each engine performing six runs per week.

Other tender locomotives appearing on Banbury & Cheltenham freight duties on a regular basis included the well-known 'Dean Goods' 0-6-0s. These ubiquitous GWR goods engines worked on the route for many years, some examples recorded on the line at different times being Nos. 2340, 2363, 2364, 2365, 2374, 2377, 2404, 2406, 2413, 2444, 2445, 2247, 2531, 2541, 2550 and 2564. The local allocation in March 1938 comprised Nos. 2349, 2350, 2398, 2402 and 2580 at Gloucester, and Nos. 2531 and 2550 at Banbury. Some of the Gloucester locomotives were normally out-stationed at Cheltenham Malvern Road or Kingham, both of these depots being sub-sheds of Gloucester.

Photographic evidence also indicates that two or three members of the visually similar '2361' Class 0-6-0s appeared on the line in the 1920s, probably quite regularly. No. 2376 was certainly one example. Above the footplate, these well-proportioned engines closely resembled a 'Dean Goods' and their number sequence fell within the long list of '2301' Class locomotives. However, below the footplate they were quite different, having double frames and underhung outside springs. They were part of an experiment in standardisation carried out by Dean in the mid 1880s.

Pick-up goods duties were latterly handled by Collett '2251' Class 0-6-0s. These sturdy-looking locomotives were introduced in 1930 and in its report on these new engines,

An unidentified 'Dean Goods' or Class '2301' 0-6-0 off the rails at the east end of Hook Norton station, sometime in the early years of the 20th century. It would appear that the locomotive has run through the catch point at the entrance to the passing loop and then keeled over the bank, which will have made the task of re-railing it all the more difficult. The driver, who most probably thought the engine was going to turn right over, must have had quite a fright.
Courtesy Kidderminster Railway Museum

THE ENGINE THAT CAME OFF THE LINE AT KINGHAM STATION Nr 1914

Another 'Dean Goods' in trouble! No. 2410 has come to grief on the curve between Kingham station and Kingham West Junction in 1914 and is being attended to by the engineers. It would appear that this engine has also run through the catch points and has sunk into the soft turf at the end of the line. The breakdown train can be seen in attendance behind, most probably called out from Oxford. No. 2410 is in the process of being re-railed using screw jacks and stout wooden packing pieces. The engine appears to have come to little harm and, with the tender already having been removed, the photograph provides a superb view of the cab interior. No. 2410 was just reaching middle age at the time of the mishap, having been built in 1891. After a long career with the GWR, the locomotive was amongst 100 'Dean Goods' Class called up for war service at the outbreak of the Second World War. After various modifications (No. 2410 was one of fourteen treated at Eastleigh rather than Swindon), many of them were shipped to France. They also acquired WD numbers, No. 2410 becoming WD 183. No. 2410 was listed in GWR records as having been withdrawn in November 1940 but this was actually the date many of these engines were written off and deemed as sold to the War Department, following the fall of France into the hands of the Germans. Many of these engines were subsequently used by the German occupation forces on the French railway system, WD 183 being one. It survived the war but was in such poor condition that, along with many of the other survivors, its return to these shores was solely to keep a date with the scrapman.

John Alsop collection

This Kingham-bound goods working has stopped just short of the platforms at Adderbury for an impromptu photo call on behalf of Frank Packer; such was the pace of life on the country railway. As well as the footplate crew, the station master and a few members of the station staff are assembled, along with the guard who is holding a shunting pole. The locomotive is another of the GWR's '2361' class 0-6-0s with double frames. Incidentally, standing on the left is 'young Frank' – Packer's son. He was always referred to as 'young Mr Packer' by townsfolk, even in the early 1980s, when he was in his late seventies and still running the photographic business that his late father had established at Chipping Norton. *Oxfordshire County Council Photographic Archive*

the *Railway Magazine* opined that the design was *'singularly neat and pleasing in appearance'*. The new mixed traffic engines were the first 0-6-0s to have been designed with coned domeless boilers and Belpaire fireboxes, and they retained the usual Great Western copper-capped chimneys and green livery. No. 2258 was soon sub-shedded at Kingham in order to work the 10.15 am down goods to Cheltenham. Other '2251' Class 0-6-0s seen on the line included Nos. 2254, 2256, 2299, 3204, 3205 and 3215.

The anomalous position of the Midland & South Western Junction Railway in relation to the B&CDR line has already been alluded to. As we have seen, M&SWJR and GWR services shared the line between Lansdown Junction and Andoversford Junction, and for this reason M&SWJR engines and rolling stock were regularly seen on the western end of the B&CDR route. As an independent company, the M&SWJR worked its system with a relatively small fleet of locomotives, many of which were Beyer Peacock or North British 4-4-0s or 0-6-0s. There were also three picturesque 2-4-0s, which had been supplied by Messrs Dübs & Co in 1894, together with a selection of 0-6-0, 0-4-4, 2-4-0 and 4-4-4 tank locomotives. In their crimson lake livery, based closely on Midland Red, they made a smart contrast to the GWR locomotives on this section of the line. They also brought a varied selection of traffic, with express trains to Southampton, through coaches of the L&NWR from Liverpool and horse boxes in connection with Cheltenham Races, as well as the usual run of goods and local passenger trains. Most of these workings carried on into the GWR era after the 1923 Grouping.

Many of the M&SWJR locomotives were scrapped after the Grouping, though others were retained for further use by the GWR, some of the absorbed engines being rebuilt with standard Great Western boilers and fittings. The Beyer Peacock 0-6-0s, for example, were all rebuilt with standard GWR tapered boilers and renumbered in sequence from 1003 to 1013. These attractive and unusual six-coupled locomotives were used on various parts of the Great Western system but a number remained at work in the Cheltenham area and, in the early 1930s, they were regularly employed on Cheltenham to Kingham goods workings.

The Cheltenham to Kingham line was regarded as a

An ex-M&SWJR Beyer Peacock 0-6-0, which the photographer thought was probably No. 21, at Charlton Kings on 7th June 1923. The train is likely to be a pick-up goods, destined for stations on the M&SWJR route between Andoversford Junction and Swindon. The engine was rebuilt by the GWR in 1925, acquiring a domeless taper boiler and shorter chimney, considerably altering its appearance. At the same time, it was renumbered into GWR stock as No. 1005. It was withdrawn in 1938. Note that despite the locomotive's recent change of ownership, it still sports the ornate intertwined MSWJR initials on the tender. *Humphrey Household collection, courtesy National Railway Museum*

The nearest the M&SWJR came to an express engine was a class of nine 4-4-0s built by the North British Locomotive Co. and numbered 1-8 and 31, which were introduced for faster passenger services from 1905. There was a slight compromise in the design, however, as they were given smaller driving wheels to cope with the climbs through the Cotswold Hills and so they could be used as mixed traffic engines as necessary. One of the class is seen here leaving Charlton Kings on 8th June 1922, under the watchful eye of the signalman, with the 8 am from Andover to Cheltenham. The first two vehicles consist of a Midland 6-wheeled brake van and a horse box.

Humphrey Household collection, courtesy National Railway Museum

THE BANBURY & CHELTENHAM DIRECT RAILWAY

M&SWJR 4-4-4 No. 17 departs from Charlton Kings for Cheltenham with the 2.40 pm from Andover on 13th June 1922. This was one of a pair of locomotives delivered in 1897 from the Glasgow firm of Sharp Stewart. They were not a resounding success however, having poor riding qualities and being prone to slipping. For all that, one cannot deny they were rather handsome machines. This view also provides another tantalising glimpse of the tiny goods yard at this station, photographs of which have proved particularly elusive.
Humphrey Household collection, courtesy National Railway Museum

'Dotted Red' route under the Great Western system of engine weight restrictions and this meant that it could be worked by the vast majority of GWR classes. In general, the '43XX' Class moguls and 'Manor' Class 4-6-0s were the largest, heaviest engines used on passenger services, although '72XX' Class 2-8-2Ts and '28XX' Class heavy freight locomotives worked over the route at the head of ironstone workings between Banbury and South Wales. Some of these workings were hauled by one locomotive, though many ironstone trains were banked by two eight-coupled engines on the approaches to Notgrove summit.

Branch passenger trains were, for many years, composed of five or six short-wheelbase vehicles. Photographic evidence suggests that the usual formation comprised four third class or composite coaches sandwiched between two passenger brake vans. The Great Western abolished short-wheelbase stock at a comparatively early date and, thereafter, trains on the Banbury to Kingham line were normally formed of a single auto-trailer. Contemporary photographs reveal that several different passenger vehicles were used, among them No. 34, a 70 foot trailer dating from 1906.

There is no evidence that Steam Rail Motors were ever used on the line – they would only have appeared on the Banbury to Kingham section in any case – but GWR diesel railcars are known to have worked some services for a number of years. Due to an increase in traffic over the railway network following the outbreak of the Second World War, many of the GWR's diesel railcars were temporarily withdrawn from service as having insufficient capacity to justify their line occupation. However, most were soon reinstated to work services on lines with lighter usage.

This rare view shows Oxford-based Railcar No. 10 calling at Sarsden on 20th June 1940. No. 10 was new into service in 1936, built for the GWR by AEC and with bodywork by the Gloucester RC&W Co. It had a seating capacity of 63, slightly less than some of the other cars because it was one of three – including Nos. 11 and 12 – fitted with lavatory compartments, which no doubt came in handy on the long run between Chipping Norton and Oxford. No. 10 was withdrawn in 1956. *M.P. Barnsley collection*

A railcar service from Oxford to Kingham operated three times a day and at least one of these workings was extended through to Chipping Norton. The service was still operating ten years later in 1950 but on Saturdays only. Diesel Railcars likely to have worked on the line in GWR days (i.e. those allocated to Oxford for any length of time) include Nos. 9, 10, 11 and 13.

The local trains themselves had more than one nickname. On the Banbury to Kingham line, for instance, the push-pull service provided in later years was generally known as 'The Hookey Flyer' – presumably an ironic reference to its slow speed. Alternatively, other local people called the train 'The Chippie Dick'.

GREAT WESTERN MOTOR BUS SERVICES

The GWR was a notable pioneer in the use of motorised road feeder services, the company's original 'road motor' route between Helston and Lizard Town being one of the very first rural bus services in the country. By 1910, the Great Western had introduced road motor services on a very large scale, Wales, the Welsh borders and the south-west peninsula being regarded as ideal areas for the deployment of these railway-owned motor buses. The Cotswolds were not, at first, served by many GWR bus services but there was nevertheless a very popular service between Oxford and Cheltenham.

By 1929, there were several Great Western motor bus routes within the area bounded by Cheltenham, Swindon, Oxford and Banbury. One of these routes ran from Cheltenham to Oxford via Andoversford, Northleach, Burford and Witney, while another long-distance route extended from Swindon to Banbury via Burford and Chipping Norton. A depot was opened at Chipping Norton, which became for a while a centre for several local feeder services. One linked Chipping Norton and Bledington via Kingham station, whilst another connected Banbury, Hook Norton, Chipping Norton and Bledington, commencing operation on 1st July 1929. A third service ran from Ilmington and Shipston-on-Stour to Great Wolford and Chipping Norton on Saturdays only but this only lasted for a few months in 1929-30, terminating shortly after the depot at Shipston-on-Stour was closed on 31st December 1930.

These extensive road services needed a relatively large allocation of motor vehicles, and those working in the Cheltenham and Chipping Norton areas during the late 1920s included Guy buses Nos. 1626, 1652 and 1658, Maudslay 'ML3' vehicle No. 1658, and Gilford coaches Nos. 1601, 1602, 1603 and 1604. These GWR 'road motors' carried an attractive version of the company's famous chocolate and cream passenger livery, and they worked in conjunction with the trains as useful feeders for the local railway system.

The Oxford buses, for example, started their journeys at Cheltenham St James station and on arrival at Oxford, they drew up alongside the Up side station buildings, so that through travellers could make their connections with Paddington trains. The Gilford vehicles used on these services boasted many refinements, including armchair seating, loose cushions, opening windows, curtains, hot-water heating and chocolate vending machines! The Cheltenham to Oxford buses were so successful that, in 1929, the GWR introduced a Sundays only service between Oxford, Witney and Burford.

By the later 1920s, the GWR was one of the largest bus operators in the country, and it seemed at the time that the company would continue to expand and develop its huge road motor fleet as an important adjunct to the rail network. Unfortunately, the undoubted success of the Great Western bus fleet led to complaints from the road transport industry to the effect that the GWR (and other railway companies) did not have Parliamentary consent to operate road services and for this reason railway bus routes were said to be illegal.

There was an element of truth in the allegation of illegality

GWR bus No. 1662, seen here at Chipping Norton station, was a 14 seater Morris 25 cwt vehicle with bodywork by Buckingham. The panel on the side indicates it was operating the route from Chipping Norton to Kingham via the delightful village of Bledington. As that route was only in operation under the GWR from 1st-20th February 1932, it neatly ties down the date of this view. As part of the disposal of bus operations, this route was taken over by the City of Oxford Motor Services. In the left background is another GWR bus, probably one of the Guy buses on the Chipping Norton-Hook Norton-Banbury service. In the early 1930s, when all these services were running from Chipping Norton, the station forecourt was busier with buses than the station was with trains!
Oxfordshire County Council Photographic Archive

This view is looking up towards the centre of Hook Norton village around 1930, with one of the GWR Guy buses visible at the end of the street, on its way from Chipping Norton to Banbury. *Neil Parkhouse collection*

The Swindon to Banbury bus service was taken on jointly by Bristol Tramways and Midland Red. Here, a BT vehicle, sporting a remarkably GWR-like livery, is seen picking up passengers in West Street, Chipping Norton around 1935. The town hall is on the right, just behind the 'Eldorado' ice cream seller's bicycle, and High Street is in the distance. *Oxfordshire County Council Photographic Archive*

A Midland Red service to Banbury via Deddington waits in the High Street at Chipping Norton, with the bulk of the town hall on the right. Frank Packer may have taken this snowy winter's day photograph in late February or early March 1932, shortly after Midland Red had taken over this service from the GWR. Note the ornate lettering on the radiator, denoting MIDLAND RED MOTOR SERVICE. It must have been an interesting drive to Banbury in these conditions. *Oxfordshire County Council Photographic Archive*

and to formalise the situation whereby the GWR could operate its road services, the company obtained new powers under the provisions of the Great Western (Road Transport) Act 1928. This new legislation enabled the GWR to own, work and use motor vehicles in its own right, and to enter into arrangements with other parties for the operation of road transport services. By virtue of these powers, the railway company at once entered into detailed negotiations with road transport companies and, by 1933, all of the GWR motor bus services had been handed over to 'associated' bus companies.

As a result of this agreement, the two main Cotswold motor bus services were passed to the Bristol Tramways & Carriage Company, on the understanding that the bus company would not compete with the railway. The local service between Chipping Norton and Bledington (which had only been in operation for three weeks) was transferred in February 1932 to The City of Oxford Motor Services, together with one small 14-seater Thornycroft bus. The Bristol and Oxford companies were both associated with the GWR, the railway company having acquired substantial interests in both undertakings. Bristol Tramways also bought quite a number of the GWR buses.

The Birmingham & Midland Motor Omnibus Company, otherwise known as Midland Red, took over many of the local routes around Chipping Norton , including the service to Banbury. They also shared the Swindon-Banbury route jointly with Bristol Tramways. The GWR had a 20 per cent interest in Midland Red too, purchased in 1930 at the same time as the LM&SR bought a 30 per cent stake, giving the two railway companies a half share in the business.

These arrangements were supposed to lead to greater co-ordination between road and rail transport but there is no doubt that, in many cases, the buses began to compete with the railway for what little traffic was available in rural areas. This was especially true in the case of the eastern section of the B&CDR line between Banbury and Kingham, which suffered severely from bus competition after the Great Western company relinquished full control of its road passenger services. It was, for example, possible to travel on a direct bus service between Chipping Norton and Witney, whereas a similar journey by GWR train services would have entailed intermediate changes at both Kingham and Yarnton Junction.

RURAL DELIVERY SERVICES

The years following the end of World War One saw a great upsurge in the road transport industry. The war itself had produced vast numbers of new and improved road vehicles, and large numbers of those were sold off to private owners in the 1920s. Many former servicemen used their gratuities to start small scale transport undertakings and, at a time when there were no restrictions or licensing controls on road goods vehicles, these 'cowboy' operators were able to undercut the railways in a relentless fight for traffic. In response to this situation, the railways themselves became large scale road transport operators.

Country stations, such as Chipping Norton and Bloxham, had traditionally been seen as railheads for the surrounding area, carriers or railway cartage agents being employed to run horse-drawn road feeder services to outlying farms and villages. In the 20th century, the Great Western started to take direct control of these local cartage services. Horse transport was used for many years but, in 1910, the Great Western introduced its first motor parcels van and, in the 1920s, it was decided that 'country lorry services' would be established at specially-selected railheads throughout the GWR system.

In February 1928, the *Railway Magazine* reported that arrangements had been made for *'about one hundred country lorry services'*, which would enable farmers, village store keepers and others to get their parcels and perishables to and from the railway, special low collection and delivery rates having been fixed for distances of up to ten miles. The GWR thereby became a large scale user of motorised road transport, with railway-owned lorries being employed for local cartage work in urban areas or as 'country lorries' for collection and delivery work in rural areas.

In the case of the Banbury & Cheltenham Direct line, Andoversford and Bourton-on-the-Water both became country lorry centres, with further such centres established at Banbury, Cheltenham St. James and at selected stations on the Oxford, Worcester & Wolverhampton main line. Inevitably, this process marked the commencement of a period of rationalisation, which would ultimately result in the run-down and closure of hundreds of local goods yards.

So long as the GWR and the other railway companies were allowed to maintain their own fleets of wholly-owned road vehicles, this did not greatly matter, as the companies concerned were able to use road transport to combat the challenge from road transport operators – the main point being that trunk hauls still took place by rail, while customers were offered a door-to-door transport service for their goods and parcels. Indeed, at a time when many road transport concerns were one-man bands using poorly-maintained vehicles, the efficient railway-owned road services were able to win back much traffic from rival operators.

The Great Western made use of its large fleet of motor vehicles in several ways. Most stations of moderate importance were served by cartage services within clearly defined geographical areas. In general, goods and parcels were collected or delivered free within these areas, though traders and residents on the outer fringes of urban areas were usually charged a small fee. In some instances, road vehicles were based at larger stations, such as Bourton-on-the-Water, but worked from small stations in the immediate vicinity; in this way, the GWR ensured that smaller stations such as Notgrove were also served by local cartage services.

Country lorry centres such as Andoversford and Bourton-on-the-Water soon acquired fleets of road delivery vehicles, the lorries in use being of various types, including vans for general parcels and cartage work, and flat-bed trucks for container traffic. Some of the vehicles employed were articulated, with three-wheel tractor portions capable of hauling a variety of two-wheel trailers. Others were fixed wheelbase vehicles, many of these being Thornycroft or

A GWR official photograph of a typical country lorry service in operation elsewhere in the Cotswolds. This 2-ton Thornycroft lorry was photographed at Lechlade in January 1935 and carries the 'GWR Country Lorry Service' advertising plate on the plaform sides. The sides were detachable, so the vehicle could also operate as a flatbed.
Neil Parkhouse collection

Morris 'half-tilt' vehicles, such as GWR lorry No. 3530, a 3-ton Thornycroft based at Bourton-on-the-Water.

The company's road delivery services were so successful that the railway was prepared to undertake the transport of non-railborne traffic, such as roadstone for local authorities, or feed stuffs for farmers and agricultural merchants. Household removals became a particular speciality, demountable road-rail containers being ideal for this class of traffic. Charges were based upon a fixed hourly rate for the lorry and driver, and the estimated time that would be needed to perform the whole removal operation. If necessary, expert packers could be supplied by the GWR in return for an extra charge, while for longer distances the containers could be forwarded by fast freight trains.

In order to assist railway staff in deciding on the best collection and delivery arrangements for specific consignments, the Great Western printed an 896-page guide entitled *Towns, Villages & Outlying Works Etc. Served by the Great Western Railway*, and this large green volume listed all places served by the company, together with the mode of conveyance from the nearest Great Western station. Goods and parcels for Chipping Norton, for example, were sent to Chipping Norton station, from where the company's road vehicles were used for the final free delivery.

Some sample information from this book is given in the following table, which provides a useful insight into the way in which the Great Western Railway provided a door-to-door service during the later 1930s. The table shows various villages and hamlets along the route of the B&CDR line, the name of each location being listed on the extreme left. The delivery arrangements for each village are shown to the right, together with the approximate distance from the relevant station. Places with their own station, such as Notgrove and Chipping Norton, are shown in capital letters; it will be noted that these were, in most cases, provided with free cartage services.

COLLECTION & DELIVERY ARRANGEMENTS CIRCA 1938

NAME OF PLACE	DELIVERY ARRANGEMENTS
ADDERBURY	Cartage service (parcels) or carrier (goods) or lorry service from Banbury
ANDOVERSFORD	Lorry service or railway porter
Adderbury East	Cartage service (parcels) or carrier (goods)
Adderbury West	Cartage service (parcels) or carrier (goods)
Akerton	6 miles from Banbury by lorry service or carrier
Alyworth	2 miles from Notgrove by lorry service
Ascott	6 miles from Chipping Norton or 10 miles from Banbury by carrier
Aston Blank	$2^1/_2$ miles from Bourton by lorry service
BANBURY	Free cartage service
BLOXHAM	Cartage service (parcels) or carrier (goods), or lorry service from Banbury
BOURTON-ON-THE-WATER	Free cartage service
Barford St John	2 miles from Bloxham by carrier or 2 miles from Banbury by lorry service
Barford St Michael	$2^1/_2$ miles from Bloxham by carrier or 5 miles from Banbury by lorry service
Barton	$4^1/_2$ miles from Notgrove by lorry service
Birdlip	6 miles from Cheltenham South & Leckhampton by lorry service
Bledington	1 mile from Kingham or 5 miles from Bourton by lorry service
Broadwell	$2^1/_2$ miles from Adlestrop or 5 miles from Bourton by lorry service
Brockhampton	$2^1/_2$ miles from Andoversford by lorry service
CHARLTON KINGS	Free cartage service
CHELTENHAM	Cartage service
CHIPPING NORTON	Free cartage service
Charlton Abbots	4 miles from Andoversford by lorry service
Church Enstone	$5^1/_2$ miles from Chipping Norton by lorry service
Church Westcote	3 miles from Stow-on-the-Wold or 4 miles from Bourton by lorry service
Churchill	8 miles from Bourton by lorry service
Clapton	$2^1/_2$ miles from Bourton by lorry service
Clapton-on-the-Hill	$2^1/_2$ miles from Bourton by lorry service
Coberley	2 miles from Charlton Kings by lorry service
Cold Aston	$2^1/_2$ miles from Bourton by lorry service
Colesbourne	5 miles from Charlton Kings by lorry service
Compton Abdale	$3^1/_2$ miles from Andoversford by lorry service
Condicote	$3^1/_2$ miles from Stow-on-the-Wold by lorry service
Cotswold Hunt Kennels	1 mile from Andoversford by lorry service
Cowley	3 miles from Charlton Kings by lorry service
Donnington	2 miles from Stow-on-the-Wold by lorry service
Duns Tew	3 miles from Fritwell & Somerton by carrier or 9 miles from Banbury by lorry service
Enstone	$5^1/_2$ miles from Chipping Norton or 4 miles from Charlbury but no delivery arrangements
Evenlode	6 miles from Bourton by lorry service
Farmington	5 miles from Bourton by lorry service
Foscot	1 mile from Kingham but no delivery arrangements

NAME OF PLACE	DELIVERY ARRANGEMENTS
Great Barrington	6 miles from Bourton or 7 miles from Shipton by lorry service
Great Rissington	4 miles from Bourton by lorry service
Great Rollright	$3^{1}/_{2}$ miles from Chipping Norton but no delivery arrangements
Great Shurdington	$2^{1}/_{2}$ miles from Cheltenham by lorry service
Great Tew	$6^{1}/_{2}$ miles from Bloxham by carrier or 9 miles from Banbury by lorry service
Guiting Power	$5^{1}/_{2}$ miles from Toddington by lorry service (later cartage service from Bourton)
HOOK NORTON	Free cartage service
Hampnett	$5^{1}/_{2}$ miles from Bourton by lorry service
Hawling	2 miles from Notgrove by lorry service
Hazleton	3 miles from Notgrove of 4 miles from Andoversford by lorry service
Icomb	2 miles from Stow-on-the-Wold by lorry service
Idbury	5 miles from Bourton by lorry service
KINGHAM	1 mile from station but no formal delivery arrangements
KINGS SUTTON	Free cartage service
Kilkenny	$1^{1}/_{2}$ miles from Andoversford by lorry service
Kineton	5 miles from Notgrove but no delivery arrangements
Kingham Hill	$4^{1}/_{2}$ miles from Chipping Norton but no formal delivery arrangements
LECKHAMPTON	Free cartage service
Little Barrington	7 miles from Bourton or $8^{1}/_{4}$ miles from Shipton by lorry service
Little Rissington	2 miles from Bourton by lorry service
Little Rollright	3 miles from Chipping Norton but no delivery arrangements
Little Shurdington	3 miles from Cheltenham by lorry service
Longborough	3 miles from Moreton-in-Marsh or 6 miles from Bourton by lorry service
Lower Astrop	1 mile from Kings Sutton by cartage service or carrier
Lower Slaughter	2 miles from Bourton by lorry service
Lower Swell	2 miles from Stow-on-the-Wold by lorry service
Lower Tadmarton	$2^{1}/_{4}$ miles from Bloxham by carrier or 6 miles from Banbury by lorry service
Maughersbury	$1^{1}/_{4}$ miles from Stow-on-the-Wold by cartage service
Milton	$1^{1}/_{2}$ miles from Bloxham by carrier or $4^{1}/_{2}$ miles from Banbury by lorry service
NOTGROVE	2 miles from station by lorry service or $^{1}/_{4}$ miles by porter
Naunton	4 miles from Notgrove by lorry service
Northleach	$5^{1}/_{2}$ miles from Bourton by lorry service
Over Norton	$1^{1}/_{2}$ miles from Chipping Norton but no delivery arrangements
Rockcliffe	4 miles from Bourton by lorry service
Roel	4 miles from Notgrove by lorry service
STOW-ON-THE-WOLD	$1^{1}/_{4}$ miles from station by cartage service or lorry service
Salford	2 miles from Chipping Norton by lorry service
Salperton	2 miles from Notgrove by lorry service
Sandywell Park	$0^{1}/_{2}$ miles from Andoversford by lorry service
Sarsden	Sarsden Siding (goods) or lorry service from Shipston
Seven Springs	$1^{3}/_{4}$ miles from Charlton Kings by cartage service
Sevenhampton	$1^{1}/_{2}$ miles from Andoversford by lorry service
Sherborne	5 miles from Bourton by lorry service
Shipton Olliffe	2 miles from Andoversford by lorry service
Shipton Sollars	$1^{1}/_{2}$ miles from Andoversford by lorry service
Sibford Ferris	7 miles from Banbury by carrier
Sibford Gower	7 miles from Banbury by carrier
South Newington	2 miles from Bloxham by carrier or 5 miles from Banbury by lorry service
Swerford	3 miles from Hook Norton by carrier or 7 miles from Banbury by lorry service
Syreford	1 mile from Andoversford by lorry service
Taddington	$3^{1}/_{2}$ miles from Toddington or 9 miles from Bourton by lorry service
Tadmarton	5 miles from Banbury by lorry service
Temple Guiting	5 miles from Bourton or 5 miles from Toddington by lorry service
Turkdean	3 miles from Notgrove by lorry service
Upper Astrop	$1^{1}/_{4}$ miles from Kings Sutton by cartage service or carrier
Upper Slaughter	2 miles from Bourton by lorry service
Upper Swell	2 miles from Stow-on-the-Wold by cartage or lorry service
Upper Tadmarton	$2^{1}/_{4}$ miles from Bloxham by carrier or 6 miles from Banbury by lorry service
Whittington	1 mile from Andoversford by lorry service
Wick Rissington	2 miles from Bourton by lorry service
Wigginton	2 miles from Hook Norton by carrier or 6 miles from Banbury by lorry service

Study of the table will underline the extent to which stations such as Bourton-on-the-Water functioned as railheads for the surrounding district – most villages or hamlets between Cheltenham and Kingham being served by GWR cartage or lorry services. Conversely, the railway company seems to have shown less interest in developing local freight traffic on the eastern section of line between Chipping Norton and King's Sutton. Few of the villages around Bloxham or Hook Norton were served by Great Western road vehicles, most of the collection and delivery services in that area being provided by private carriers.

OTHER DEVELOPMENTS IN THE 1920s & 1930s

The gradual introduction of holidays with pay inevitably resulted in an increase in the numbers of working class visitors to the area and although it would clearly be absurd to suggest that the Cotswolds ever became a mass tourist destination such as Blackpool or Southend, there is no doubt that the various scenic and historic attractions in and around the district between Banbury and Cheltenham had started to become very popular by the 1930s. The Great Western Railway was only too glad for this development to take place, as it brought extra income to the company in the form of increased leisure travel.

In 1926, for instance, the company published a well-researched academic book entitled *Castles*, which described all of the major castles within the area served by the GWR. The author was Sir Charles Oman, of the University of Oxford, and this impressive volume was illustrated by line drawings, photographs, maps, plans and two full colour plates. A folding map at the back of the book showed the position of each monument in relation to the GWR network, and *'visitors contemplating a tour of the Cathedrals, Abbeys and Castles within the sphere of the Great Western Railway'* were invited to write to the Superintendent of the Line for details of the relevant train services.

Companion volumes on *Cathedrals* (1923) and *Abbeys* (1925) were written by Martin Briggs and M.R. James respectively, while the railway company also published a wide range of county guide books and an annual holiday guide entitled *Holiday Haunts*. These publications were available at Great Western stations, in book shops or direct (post free) from The Stationary Superintendent at 66, Porchester Road, Paddington.

Further publicity was obtained from the company's policy of naming its largest 4-6-0 passenger locomotives after castles, halls and other stately homes on the Great Western system. Local castles were represented by No. 5033 *Broughton Castle*, built during the 1930s, and No. 7011 *Banbury Castle* which was added during the British Railways era. The theme was continued by Nos. 5939 *Tangley Hall*, 6870 *Bodicote Grange*, 7815 *Fritwell Manor*, 7822 *Foxcote Manor*, 5931 *Hatherley Hall*, 5945 *Leckhampton Hall* and 7823 *Hook Norton Manor* – all of which derived their names from country houses in the areas of Oxfordshire and Gloucestershire served by the B&CDR.

The 1930s saw an upsurge in the growth of 'low cost' holidays such as hiking, camping and youth hostelling. In an inspired attempt to attract this new type of holidaymaker, the London & North Eastern Railway converted some of its obsolete short-wheelbase coaches into holiday camping coaches. The first LNER camping coaches were in service by 1933 and the concept was so successful that the Great Western immediately copied this novel idea.

In March 1934, the *Railway Magazine* reported that the GWR had *'decided to provide twenty old coaches specially adapted for use at certain selected camping sites'*. These vehicles would be let at a weekly rental and it was suggested that they would *'prove to be very popular with the ever-increasing number of camping holidaymakers'*. In a further report, in May 1934, the same magazine stated that nineteen Great Western camping coaches had been brought into use, at sites in Devon, Somerset, Cornwall and Wales. Elderly four and six-wheeled rolling stock was thereby *'diverted into a profitable old age as holiday caravans for the holiday camper'*.

The GWR camping coaches were as successful as their LNER counterparts and the company was encouraged to place further vehicles into use at a range of new locations. By 1935, Bourton-on-the-Water had joined the list of GWR camping coach sites, a suitable reconditioned six-wheeler being advertised for rent in that year. This vehicle followed the usual pattern for camping coaches, two of its five compartments being gutted to form a combined living and dining room, while the remaining compartments became three bedrooms sleeping up to six people.

Bourton-on-the-Water did not feature on the list of Great Western camping coach sites for the next two years, possibly because the station was the being reconstructed, but the 1938 and 1939 *Holiday Haunts* reveal that a camping coach was available at Bourton during the last years of peace.

This extremely cruel enlargement from the photograph on page 90, looking through the goods shed at Bourton, is believed to show the only known glimpse, in the distance, of the camp coach which was stationed here in 1935. *Courtesy Roger Carpenter*

On the B&CDR, the route was split up into four sections for the motor trolley system of maintenance, each having its own allotted gang. Gang No. 85 was based at Notgrove and covered the line between there and Andoversford. The gang are seen here circa 1935, on their trolley No. B-7. They are, from left to right, K. Parsons, A. Stratford and G. Fletcher, and the photograph was taken by the Notgrove signalman, Bill Keddle. *Courtesy John & Val Bland*

Until World War One, railway companies such as the GWR had enjoyed a virtual monopoly of land transport and, in these circumstances, they were able to operate a large number of rural branch lines that were never more than marginally profitable. Some lines may have even lost money but this situation was tolerated because of the 'system effect', whereby short, local lines could feed profitable traffic onto the main line network. In the changing economic conditions after World War One, the growth of road transport, rising wage bills and other factors made it increasingly difficult for lightly-used branch lines to survive and the GWR was obliged to seek a number of economies.

In the mid 1920s, the company carried out a thorough review of its entire branch line operations and, as a result, a programme of economies was put into effect. In a very few cases, it was reluctantly agreed that line closures would have to take place but in general, the Great Western branch line review led to the introduction of economy measures, such as track rationalisation or staff cuts. The introduction of country lorry centres, for instance, enabled the company to down-grade scores of local stations which would no longer have to handle sundries traffic, while many smaller stopping places lost their station masters, the stations concerned being placed under the control of neighbouring station masters.

In another attempt to introduce more efficient methods of operation on the Banbury & Cheltenham Direct line, the GWR introduced mechanised methods of line maintenance, with reduced numbers of permanent way men using PW trolleys for inspection and maintenance work. In earlier days, work of this kind had been carried out by gangers who patrolled their sections of line on foot but the introduction of manual or petrol-driven PW vehicles enabled each permanent way gang to cover a much greater length of track than had hitherto been possible.

To facilitate this mode of operation, the single line sections between Adderbury and Kingham, and Kingham and Andoversford were equipped with a Gangers' Occupation Key system, so that permanent way gangs could have complete possession of the single line sections upon which they were working. This system necessitated a degree of technical sophistication. In order that the petrol-engined motor trolley could safely work on the single line, the ganger responsible for the branch was furnished with an Occupation Key, which worked in conjunction with the normal single line signalling system. When a key was withdrawn from its instrument, the PW gang gained occupation of the single line and no trains could then enter the section of line concerned. As an aid to efficient operation, small 'Key Boxes' were installed at regular intervals along the line, each box being equipped with its own instrument and telephone link to the appropriate signal box.

The branch permanent way gang were able to travel to the place at which their work would be taking place on the motorised trolley which, if necessary, was able to tow a small trailer. In addition, the ganger was required to carry out regular inspections of the line in a small inspection car.

WORLD WAR TWO

Less than twenty years after the end of the Great War, England was plunged into World War Two, the declaration of war against Nazi Germany being broadcast live on the BBC by Prime Minister Nevile Chamberlain at lunchtime on Sunday 3rd September 1939. With horrific memories of the 1914-18 conflict still fresh in many minds, there were those who expected that the United Kingdom would soon be devastated by fleets of massed Nazi bombers. Nervous individuals were hardly reassured when, shortly after the declaration of war, air raid sirens wailed out across many parts of the country – though in reality this initial scare was merely a false alarm.

Government 'experts' had initially predicted that the enemy would launch a series of so-called 'knock-out blows' against British cities. High explosive and poison gas attacks were thought to be imminent, the expected targets being London and other major centres of population. Britain had in fact been preparing for war for several weeks and, on 1st September 1939, the government had taken control of the Big Four railway companies, together with London Transport, under the provisions of the Emergency Powers (Defence) Act 1939.

A nightly 'blackout' was imposed as an air raid precaution measure while, in an attempt to confuse Nazi parachutists or 'fifth columnists', station nameboards were removed or obscured in the summer of 1940. Although the war resulted in a diminution in the number of tourists and leisure travellers, petrol rationing and the restrictions placed on road transport ensured that rail traffic increased considerably and, like most parts of the British railway system, the Banbury & Cheltenham Direct line was soon

As part of the mass evacuation of children from London at the outbreak of World War Two, the intake from three schools were sent to Chipping Norton on 1st September 1939. Frank Packer was once again present to record the scene as the long train disgorged its bewildered occupants into a rural environment far removed from their native West Ham. Many would be put onto buses for dispersal to outlying areas but would soon return to London once the expected bombing failed to materialise. History would soon deal a cruel blow however, because once the blitz commenced in 1940, many would be hastily evacuated again. It would be interesting to know the route this special train took; its position in this platform strongly suggests it had arrived from the Banbury direction. The length of the train – twelve carriages – also means that unloading of the children had to be accomplished in two batches. *Neil Parkhouse collection*

playing a full part in the national war effort.

The Oxford area was though to be relatively safe from German bombing and for this reason large numbers of children were evacuated from London at the very start of the conflict, special trains of twelve packed GWR coaches being sent to Chipping Norton and other designated dispersal centres. Most of the children evacuated to the Chipping Norton and Witney areas were from West Ham, Canning Town and other parts of the East End, and although many of the evacuees subsequently returned to London, others remained with their 'host' families for the duration of the war.

Happily, pre-war fears of a 'knock-out blow' involving poison gas, fire bombs and high explosives had been wildly exaggerated, and in retrospect it is now thought unlikely that Adolf Hitler ever seriously intended to invade Britain. Although military action was taking place at sea and in other theatres of war, the Home Front was so quiet that people spoke derisively of a 'Phoney War'.

On 10th May 1940, the German forces finally struck in Western Europe and the massive French army collapsed within a matter of days. By June 1940, the British army had been evacuated from the beaches of Dunkirk, and Britain itself began to prepare for an enemy invasion. Perhaps surprisingly, the thought that Britain might actually lose the war does not seem to have arisen, and although the whole power of the Luftwaffe was soon being directed against industrial cities such as Liverpool and Birmingham, the British government was already preparing the first tentative plans for a cross-Channel counter-attack that would eventually lead to the liberation of occupied Europe.

The most obvious effect of the war was the creation of numerous RAF airfields, many of which were Bomber Command training stations. New aerodromes were established at various places, including Chipping Norton, Barford St John, Little Rissington, Moreton-in-Marsh, Edgehill and elsewhere. Meanwhile, former World War One airfields such as Witney were brought back into military use, while a number of well-equipped aerodromes had been opened before the war as part of an RAF 'Expansion Plan' that had been prompted by fears of German aggression. By the end of the war, there were no less than 40 aerodromes in Oxfordshire and the neighbouring counties.

Many of these wartime aerodromes were sited in conveniently close proximity to the Banbury & Cheltenham Direct line or other GWR routes, so that the railway system could be used for the movement of men, spare parts, fuel, ordnance or other vital equipment. As far as the B&CDR line was concerned, the most important wartime airfields were those at Little Rissington, Chipping Norton, Enstone and Barford St John. Most of these RAF stations were associated with flying training. By June 1944, for example, RAF Little Rissington was the home of No. 6 (Pilot) Advanced Flying Unit and No. 1523 Beam Approach Training Flight, the principal aircraft types seen at this location being Airspeed Oxford trainers.

Situated high on the remote, windswept uplands to the south-east of the town, Chipping Norton airfield was used as a Relief Landing Ground by Airspeed Oxfords from No. 6 (Pilot) Advanced Flying Unit, based at Little Rissington. In the earlier part of the war, the station had also accommodated part of No. 15 Service Flying Training School, equipped with both Harvards and Oxfords. This unit had the airfield from its opening in July 1940 until the end of 1940, when No. 15 SFTS completed its move to RAF Kidlington. Thereafter, Chipping Norton continued to serve as Relief Landing Ground for Little Rissington.

Neighbouring Enstone airfield was a satellite of No. 21 Operational Training Unit (Moreton-in-Marsh) and, as such, it was used by large aircraft such as Wellingtons, together with other types such as Tomahawks of 1682(B) DT Flight. The airfield featured three runways, a complex perimeter track, one 'T2' hangar and one 'B1' maintenance hanger. The aerodrome was sited about three miles to the east of RAF Chipping Norton. Barford St. John airfield was, similarly, used mainly for training purposes and, by June 1944, it had become the home of No. 16 Operational Training Unit, flying Wellingtons, Martinets and Hawker Hurricanes.

The exigencies of total war called for a massive increase in steel production and this, in turn, led to a revival of the local ironstone industry. It was anticipated that the war effort would require around 20,000,000 tons of home produced ore per annum and in these circumstances, the Oxfordshire ironstone field was expected to play an important role. Three of the quarries served by the B&CDR route were still operative at the start of the war but it was decided that extraction would be concentrated in the Brymbo quarries at Hook Norton and at the Oxfordshire Ironstone Company site at Wroxham, the smaller Clay Cross and Duffield Iron Corporation quarries being closed.

It was clear that huge amounts of armaments and other vital equipment would be necessary before the Liberation of Europe could take place, and Britain was soon producing enormous quantities of bombs, shells, aircraft and military vehicles. Civilian factories were adapted for wartime production, while new factories were set up in rural areas to ensure that production would continue even if urban factories were put out of action by enemy bombing. In this capacity, Banbury became intimately connected with aircraft production as a result of the presence of a Northern Aluminium Company factory. The latter facility had been opened in 1931 but it became particularly important during the war years.

As the war effort got into its full stride, some of the private sidings on the B&CDR line were pressed into use by the Ministry of Supply or other wartime organisations. The Duffield Iron Corporation Siding at Bloxham, for example, was requisitioned by the Ministry of Aircraft Production for use by the Northern Aluminium Company.

The presence of so many aerodromes on or near the route of the Banbury to Cheltenham line inevitably attracted the attention of enemy bombers. Chipping Norton airfield was bombed on several occasions, notably on the night of 29th October 1940, while RAF Barford St John was hit by ten high explosive bombs on the night of 24th August 1941. A few months earlier, on 11th December 1940, an overbridge near Cheltenham South & Leckhampton was destroyed during a raid on Cheltenham and the railway was closed for several days thereafter. Banbury was also a target and, on one occasion, an enemy bomb landed on the town's gas works and destroyed a gas holder with spectacular results.

It had been decided at the very start of the war that bombing decoys would be constructed near all major airfields and, following the attack on Coventry on 14th November 1940, similar decoys were constructed as a means of passive protection for many towns and industrial centres. One of these decoys was built at Tadmarton as a means of protection

After the war, the sidings alongside the Worcester main line to the north of Kingham station played host to long lines of stored ex-War Department locomotives awaiting disposal. The sidings themselves were provided for WD use in 1943, transferred to BR in 1962 and taken out of use in 1964.
Bob Brown collection

for the Northern Aluminium Company, the decoy in question taking the form of a dummy factory, complete with railway sidings, offices, a works canteen and a smoking chimney.

The Banbury to Cheltenham route carried large amounts of coal, ironstone and other forms of heavy freight traffic during the years of conflict, its value as a diversionary route being fully exploited. Wartime conditions resulted in a general reduction in engine weight restrictions and in this context, locomotives in the GWR 'Red' route category were allowed to work over the entire length of the B&CDR, which had hitherto been regarded as a 'Blue' route between King's Sutton and Kingham, and a 'Dotted Red' route between Kingham and Lansdown Junction.

The ironstone carried over the B&CDR during World War Two came from both the Hook Norton and Wroxham quarries – Hook Norton ore being transported to Brymbo Steelworks, while much of the Oxfordshire Ironstone Company's output was conveyed to South Wales via Banbury and the Banbury & Cheltenham Direct line.

Heavy ironstone trains were typically hauled by eight-coupled engines and in this context, the Banbury to Cheltenham route was worked by a number of different locomotive classes. The commonest heavy freight engines were still the hard-working '28XX' Class 2-8-0s, some random examples from the 1940s being Nos. 2805, 2817, 2818, 2833, 2852, 2869, 2871, 2878, 2882, 2883, 2885, 2897, 2895, 2898, 2898, 3802, 3825 and 3861, all of which were stationed at Banbury during the years of conflict. By 1944, no less than twenty five of these engines had been allocated to Banbury for heavy freight duties.

The eight-coupled '72XX' Class tank locomotives were originally built for work on South Wales coal trains but they were used on various long distance goods workings during the 1930s and 1940s, these duties bringing them onto the Banbury & Cheltenham line during World War Two. Banbury had an allocation of four '72XX' Class 2-8-2Ts in 1938, while other members of the class seen on the line were shedded in South Wales. The engines sometimes worked in conjunction with '28XX' Class 2-8-0s on double-headed workings over the B&CDR. In June 1945, for instance, '72XX' 2-8-2T No. 7246 was noted double-heading a heavy westbound freight with '28XX' 2-8-0 No. 2867.

It is a well-known fact that William Stanier was a former Great Western man, who took many GWR ideas with him when he accepted a new job with the London, Midland & Scottish Railway. His standard LMS 2-6-2T, 4-6-0 and 2-8-0 classes were, in effect, modified GWR designs, the Stanier '8F' Class 2-8-0s being based on the much older '28XX' Class 2-8-0s. Ironically, some Stanier '8F' Class locomotives were allocated to Banbury during the war years for heavy freight work and it is believed that these sometimes appeared on the Banbury & Cheltenham route.

Another 2-8-0 type seen on the B&CDR route during the war years were the 'WD' Class 2-8-0s and their American equivalents the 'USA' Transportation Corps 2-8-0s. At the start of the war, the Ministry of Supply had adopted the Stanier Class '8F' 2-8-0 design as a suitable type for wartime service but it was later decided that a simpler 'austerity' design was needed and in consequence, R.A. Riddles introduced the 'WD' Class 2-8-0s. No less than 932 of these engines were constructed by the North British Locomotive Company and the Vulcan Foundry, together with a further 103 2-10-0s of similar design.

Despite their wartime origins, the 'WD' Class 2-8-0s were visually-pleasing locomotives, with parallel boilers and massive, eight-wheeled tenders. In addition to the British 'WD' locomotives, 920 Class 'S160' 2-8-0s were imported from the United States in preparation for the D-Day invasion of Europe. Constructed by manufacturers such as Alco, Lima and Baldwins, the American 2-8-0s were superficially-similar to their British counterparts, although their high running plates and other external details were of classic American appearance.

Banbury had received an allocation of ten 'S160' 2-8-0s by June 1944, the engines in question being Nos. 1647, 1649, 1654, 1658, 2132, 2134, 2147, 2431, 2440 and 2441. The American engines were a powerful design but they were not particularly popular with British locomotive crews. There was a problem with their water gauges, which could show false readings if the steam valves were not fully open, and this led to an explosion at Honeybourne on 17th November 1943, when the firebox of a Banbury-based engine collapsed. The train involved in this incident was travelling from Banbury to Margam via Leamington and Stratford-upon-Avon, although other services were routed via the B&CDR line.

Photographic evidence shows that both American and British-built war locomotives appeared on the Banbury & Cheltenham Direct line during the 1940s, together with the indigenous Great Western '28XX' Class 2-8-0s. It is likely that Robinson 'O4' Class 2-8-0s were also employed on Banbury to South Wales ironstone workings over the B&CDR route, five of these locomotives having been transferred to Banbury shed in 1940, pending the arrival of additional '28XX' 2-8-0s for wartime duties.

An interesting working took place on the evening of Wednesday 22nd October 1941, when the Banbury & Cheltenham line was traversed by the LMS royal train *en route* from Monmouth Troy to Kingham. As usual on such occasions, the arrangements for working the royal special were shrouded in secrecy, although the elaborate preparations at Kingham and elsewhere served only to draw attention to the unusual proceedings at an otherwise quiet country junction. The formation of the royal train on this occasion comprised brake first No. 5155, royal saloon No. 800, dining saloon No. 76, saloon No. 907, sleeping saloon No. 477, saloon No. 806, dining saloon No. 77 and brake first No. 5154.

Leaving Monmouth Troy at 6.05 pm, the royal special travelled via Ross-on-Wye, Grange Court, Hatherley Junction, Gloucester Loop Junction, Notgrove and Bourton-on-the Water, the arrival time at Kingham being 9.38 pm. Motive power was provided by 'Hall' Class 4-6-0s Nos. 6917 *Oldlands Hall* and 6921 *Borwick Hall*, No. 6917 being the leading engine (neither of the engines had received their names). The train was limited to a speed of twenty miles per hour on the Banbury & Cheltenham Direct route and special arrangements were in force for the inspection of Sandywell Tunnel immediately prior to the passage of the royal working.

Chapter Five

THE ROUTE FROM CHELTENHAM TO KINGHAM

Cheltenham & District Light Railway tramcar No. 5 has just paused at the tram stop outside St James station around 1905. The wonderfully ornate cast-iron lamp post is worthy of note.
Mrs. Freda Gittos collection

Having described the history of the Banbury & Cheltenham Direct Line from its inception until the 1950s, it would now be appropriate to examine the physical appearance of the line in greater detail, with particular reference to the stations and other infrastructure. The following sections will therefore take readers on an imaginary guided tour along the line from Cheltenham St. James to Banbury. The topographical details that follow will be correct for the later Great Western and early British Railways period, and the datum point for the calculation of distances will be Cheltenham St. James.

CHELTENHAM SPA ST. JAMES

Cheltenham St. James station was well-sited near the centre of the town. The station was orientated from east to west, and its layout incorporated two double-sided terminal platforms providing two arrival and two departure platforms. The terminus was signalled in such a way that trains could arrive at the two arrival platforms on the north side and depart from any of the four platform faces. Two dead-end sidings, known as 'The Middle Lines', were sited between the platform roads, and there were further sidings to the north and south of the passenger platforms.

The three main platforms were around 450 feet in length but the outer face on the south (departure) side was somewhat shorter, with a length of around 375 feet; the latter platform was normally used by local trains to Kingham and Honeybourne. In British Railways days, the northern (arrival) platforms were extended by 150 feet, giving them a total length of 600 feet. All four platforms were covered, for much of their length, by typical Great Western canopies.

The station building was an extensive L-shaped structure, with one wing parallel to the 'departure' platforms and the other at right angles to the terminal buffer stops; the building sported an ornate *porte cochere* on its main street frontage. Internally, the station building contained a wide range of accommodation; entering the station from St. James Square, travellers found themselves in a booking hall, with

The road frontage as it appeared in the early 1950s. The station was very well positioned for the centre of this attractive Georgian spa town, being merely a couple of minutes walk from the famous Promenade. However, its role as a terminus, not directly accessible from the north, meant that it was eventually to lose out to the less well sited ex-Midland station at Lansdown. The distinctive design of the station building was similar to such stations as Ross-on-Wye and Ealing Broadway, and was the result of a major rebuilding carried out in 1894, when the original wooden terminus was demolished and the station resited slightly to the east. Until 1908, the station was called simply Cheltenham but, from 11th May that year, the name was changed to Cheltenham St. James. On 1st February 1925 it changed again, to Cheltenham Spa (St. James), although the BR nameboards on the valancing here do not seem to agree. *Bob Brown collection*

cloakrooms and a parcels office to the right, and the ticket office to the left. The projecting wing alongside the departure platform contained general waiting rooms, the station master's office, toilets and various other facilities.

The terminus was signalled from a standard GWR signal cabin on the north side of the arrival platforms. This brick and timber structure was a typical late Victorian box, with a gable roof and small-paned windows. Internally, it contained a 52-lever frame, with seven spare spaces.

The main goods yard, with room for no less than 494 short-wheelbase goods vehicles, was situated on the south side of the passenger station. There was a large goods shed, with a 200 foot internal loading platform and four fixed 1 ton 10 cwt hand cranes, together with an array of sidings for coal and other forms of 'mileage' traffic. A powerful 12 ton yard crane was available for use when timber, drain pipes or other large or bulky consignments were received or despatched by rail. An additional goods loading dock, with a length of around 200 feet, was situated between the goods shed and the departure platforms.

Further goods sidings, on the north side of the station, fanned out into a separate yard at the rear of the signal box, which was known as 'The New Street Coal Yard'. Nearby, a short spur served as a headshunt for the 'Cattle Dock Siding', while a Cheltenham Corporation depot to the south of the station was served by a private siding link. There was no engine shed, as such, at Cheltenham Spa St. James, although a long siding known as the 'Pilot Road' was

The frontal aspect to the station circa 1960, showing the fine *porte cochere*, which lent the station an air of importance, with its ornate columns facing onto St. James' Square. The station was built on the site of Jessop's Pleasure Gardens, which were the work of Mr Charles Hale Jessop, and included vast greenhouses, aviaries, oriental pagodas and even a small zoo. The Georgian building to the right in this view was Depository No. 1 for Barnby, Bendall & Co., the removers and storage concern whose poster appeared on the early view of Stow-on-the-Wold station, with the Burton Brewery Inn on the corner. Note that the nameboards now carry the station's correct full name. *The Lens of Sutton Collection*

In 1955 a new kiosk was provided on the station concourse, behind the buffer stops, for Wyman's Newsagents. This official view, taken on 3rd June that year, shows the newsagent's stand with adjoining storeroom on the right and ticket inspector's office just behind, plus a pair of telephone booths at the far end. The design was typical of the 1950s and rather at odds with the station around it. Note the board on the right containing timetables for passengers' use and the array of advertising placards high up on the wall for products such as 'Aspro', *Esquire,* and *The Listener*. The *Radio Times* was advertising a chart for election results; Anthony Eden was re-elected Prime Minister a couple of weeks later. *Neil Parkhouse collection*

available for locomotives in front of the signal box on the north side of the station. This, in turn, gave access to a short engine siding, with an ashpit and turntable.

Great Western working appendices reveal that the hand-worked points giving access to the New Street Yard sidings were normally secured by a padlock, the key to which was kept in the nearby signal box. The Corporation Sidings on the other side of the station were protected by a gate, which was also kept locked. The station was not equipped with many carriage storage facilities but a long siding, known as 'The Up Siding', was normally used for carriage stabling purposes. Photographic evidence also suggests that spare coaches were sometimes parked in the neighbouring goods yard if no room could be found elsewhere in the station.

St. James was served by main line services to and from Paddington, as well as local services to Honeybourne, Gloucester and Kingham. In later years it was also used by M&SWJ services to Southampton, which had been diverted from the Midland station at Cheltenham Lansdown. Other services ran between Cheltenham St. James and South Wales, while the extensive goods yard gave rise to a considerable amount of traffic, including the B&CDR branch freight services to Kingham, which started and finished their journeys at Cheltenham St. James goods yard.

On walking out onto Platform 3 from the concourse, this was the view which greeted the prospective traveller in the mid 1950s. Note the array of starting signals in the distance and also the auto coach standing on one of the centre roads. *Bob Brown collection*

An interesting photograph taken circa 1910 from platform 3 facing east towards the buffer stops, showing the spacious and well laid out nature of the station. A 'Cordon' gas tank wagon is parked against the buffer stops, these distinctive vehicles being utilised for replenishing the gas used in coach lighting. The two coaches on the left may be slip carriages, waiting to be returned to London. The tall spire of St. Gregory's Roman Catholic church can be seen to the left, while the much plainer spire of St. Matthew's Anglican church appears in the centre background. Both of these places of worship were of Victorian origin, St. Gregory's having been designed by Charles F. Hansom and built between 1854 and the 1870s, while St. Matthew's was designed by Ewan Christian and constructed in 1876–9. An adjacent property, No. 10 St. James Square, was the home of Alfred Tennyson, the Victorian poet, from 1845 until 1850, when he became Poet Laureate and moved to a new abode in Sussex.

Bob Brown collection

Above: A panoramic view westwards from Platforms 3 and 4 on 30th December 1965. On the right can be seen the turntable road, which was accessed from the engine release road alongside Platform 4. It was used chiefly by trains arriving from the M&SWJR route, the turntable being too small for anything larger than a 'Manor' Class 4-6-0. Larger types were turned on the triangular junction with the Banbury & Cheltenham Line. Immediately behind the turntable is St. Gregory's School. Note the hand-lettered travelling safe, in the left foreground, this particular example being labelled for use between St. James and Cardiff General. At the date of this photograph, the M&SWJR and Kingham line trains were just a memory. *Courtesy Stations UK*

Above: A rainy day in Cheltenham around 1960, with the generous platform canopies at St. James providing shelter whilst the station is quiet between trains. The obligatory 'Cordon' gas tank wagon rests against the buffers on one of the centre roads, with the tail end of a rake of Mk1 stock on the right.
The Lens of Sutton Collection

Left: On 1st October 1960, the Casserleys paid a visit to the station. The coaches for a Kingham service wait in Platform 4 on the left and the end of the turntable can just be seen behind them. Note that St. Matthew's Church had by this time lost its pyramidal spire.
H.C. Casserley, courtesy Richard Casserley

Two slightly different views of St. James station in GWR days, circa the 1930s. The top view is looking towards Platforms 3 and 4 from Platform 2. **Below**, an unidentified prairie tank waits to leave from Platform 2, probably with a Gloucester-bound local, whilst the coaches on the right wait alongside Platform 1. Note that the end of the nearest carriage is lettered 'CHELTENHAM AND KINGHAM BRANCH'. For some reason, far fewer photograhs seem to have been taken of Platforms 1/2 than of 3/4. The piece of equipment in front of the screen at the end of the canopy is thought to be an oil dispenser for filling the carriage lamp reservoirs. *Both The Lens of Sutton Collection*

Collett '51XX' Class large prairie No. 4101 of Gloucester (Horton Road) shed is seen running round its train after arrival from Kingham on 1st October 1960. Note the unusual position of the disc signal, attached high up on the building on the right, due to the cramped nature of the location and also the signal in the right background for engines coming off the turntable. *H.C. Casserley, courtesy Richard Casserley*

Right: The '45XX' Class 2-6-2Ts were synonymous with the Cheltenham to Kingham section of the line during the 1930s; No. 4573, seen here alongside Cheltenham Spa Station Signal Box was a regular visitor. However, this view was taken on 10th July 1959, by which time most duties on the B&CDR line were in the hands of '51XX' Class large prairies and it is likely that No. 4573 had worked in from Gloucester. The flat-topped tanks mark the engine out as one of the smaller water capacity examples. Of particular note in this view is New Street coal yard to the left of the locomotive, a location rarely photographed. *Courtesy Richard Casserley*

Left: Cheltenham Spa Station Signal Box seen shortly after the station had closed to passenger services. This 53-lever cabin dated from the remodelling of the station in 1894 and was a standard GWR design of the period, built largely of brick with wooden window frames and gable ends, and a slated gabled roof. It was well positioned with a view over the platform roads and the lines entering the station, as well as the whole of the goods yard. The last passenger service ran on New Years Day 1966 but goods services continued until 31st October that year. The 16-ton mineral wagons in this view are standing in part of New Street coal yard, the only trackage that ran behind the box. *Bob Brown collection*

The sweeping curves, on the final approach to St. James, made for a stylish entrance into the station. Photographed from St. George's Road bridge in 1932, the two main running lines, arrivals on the left and departures on the right, straddle the Malvern Road Junction Home signal in the foreground. Trains could leave from any of the four platforms but the signalling only permitted arrivals in Platforms 1 and 2. The siding on the left served the cattle dock, in the foreground, and Snowells Brewery beyond. However, the brewery had closed by the date of this photograph and it is not known who later occupied the premises or if they used the siding. To its right, the line on which the two siphons are standing in the centre background provided access to New Street coal yard. The empty coaching stock is parked on a dedicated 500 foot long siding, to the right of which was the goods yard, with the end of the goods shed just visible. The corrugated iron shed with a curved roof just in front of it was also used for goods traffic. The entrance line to the goods yard made a junction with the running lines just the other side of St. George's Road bridge. It also acted as a headshunt, for which purpose it extended some distance past the junction. The siding curving sharply round to the right past the permanent way hut gave access to several other sidings in the goods yard and also, via a gated entrance, to the Corporation Yard tucked alongside the southern boundary of the station.

Neil Parkhouse collection

This aerial view of Cheltenham, showing Christchurch Anglican church and St. James station, was taken circa 1930. On the left, the Honeybourne line can be seen curving away from Malvern Road Junction, whilst the rarely photographed New Street coal yard can be seen at the top of the picture. Three passenger trains can be seen waiting to depart from Platforms 2, 3 and 4; that at Platform 2 is most likely to be destined for the line to Kingham. The goods yard seems to be particularly crowded. It had a capacity of 494 wagons and must be well on the way to achieving that here. The sheds of the Corporation Yard, another rarely photographed part of the station, can just be seen between the trees above the last row of houses, along the northern edge of St. George's Road.

Neil Parkhouse collection

This is the view looking south-westwards from St Georges Road bridge towards Malvern Road station, showing Malvern Road Junction and Malvern Road East Signal Box on 21st August 1960. From the left, the lines are the St James goods yard headshunt and the two running lines into the station, with the twin tracks of the Honeybourne line diverging to the right. The ground on the right, as well as this first section of the Honeybourne trackbed, was the site of the original Cheltenham GWR locomotive shed. The light engine is probably reversing into the station to head a departing service, having come off Malvern Road shed. *Bob Brown collection*

CHELTENHAM MALVERN ROAD

Leaving Cheltenham St. James, Up trains ran westwards for a short distance to Malvern Road Junction, at which point the GWR main line from Honeybourne converged from the north-east. Malvern Road station was only a few chains further on. This station, which was opened on 3rd March 1908, was used by long distance through trains between the Midlands and West of England. The principal service was an early morning express from Wolverhampton Low Level to Penzance which, in British Railways days, was designated 'The Cornishman'. This prestigious service ran on weekdays as a through restaurant car express via Cheltenham, Gloucester and Bristol, the usual motive power being an immaculate 'Castle' Class 4-6-0.

The layout at Cheltenham Malvern Road consisted of one long island platform, with a short bay at the northern end

The GWR was obliged to widen the bridge carrying Malvern Road over the line when building the new station. The original arch was extended by means of two curved ferro-concrete beams, the first time the GWR had used this medium for bridge construction. The red brick parapet matched the one on the other side. The illustrations appeared in the *Great Western Railway Magazine* of August 1908. Although the line has closed, the bridge still survives in this condition today. *Neil Parkhouse collection*

An overall view of the north end of Malvern Road station, taken from Malvern Road Bridge on a warm, hazy day in 1932. The rather unusual layout (for a GWR station) is evident, with the southbound line passing through the station on the left and the northbound line to the right of the island platform. The booking office was above the line on the left, passengers reaching the platform via the footbridge. The three loop sidings were used for sorting wagons, while two further sidings for local coal traffic were situated on the other side of the locomotive shed. The *RCH Handbook* listed the station as handling general goods traffic, although there was never a goods shed here. The locomotive shed can be seen on the right, while the ramped coaling stage with water tower on top is visible in the centre of the view. It can be seen that the coaling stage has a lean-to covered roof over the ramp, in order that coal wagons could be unloaded under shelter; this was a later addition. The water column near the end of the platform was later replaced with a standard GWR conical tower. The bay platform was built for the Steam Rail Motor trains, which provided the local stopping service to Stratford when the line opened in 1908. These would start from St. James and work into the bay here at Malvern Road, before heading northwards to Honeybourne. *Neil Parkhouse collection*

Above: Whilst ostensibly it would appear that the Malvern Road station staff have come out to greet an arriving south-bound service, most of them seem more interested in the presence of the photographer in this circa 1910 view. The train is being hauled by what appears to be one of the numerous 4-4-0 types favoured by the GWR at the time. Also awaiting the arrival is a horse-drawn carriage and a couple of motor cars, which can be seen parked outside the station entrance. In the right foreground is the carriage loading dock, which saw much use until the motor car took over completely from horse-drawn carriages as a means of personal transport. In their description of the new station in the March 1908 issue of the *Great Western Railway Magazine*, the company commented on its unusual layout: '*This new station, which is rapidly nearing completion, is of rather special design. It comprises a slightly curved island platform 700 feet long, served by a footbridge from the booking office, which is situated on the opposite side of the line. The station buildings are located in the centre of the platform, and a verandah roof affords satisfactory covering on either side and at the ends of these buildings. ... the general design of the building, which has a red tile roof, was prepared with an eye to its suitability for the attractive surroundings. The work has been carried out, under control of the New Works Engineer, Mr. W. Armstrong, by Messrs. Scott & Middleton, of Westminster.*'
Michael Mitchell collection

Right: The station was not situated in an area prone to flooding, so this spectacular scene must have been the result of a sustained torrential downpour, with water gathering in the cutting beyond, as well as gushing down the entrance road and cascading over the carriage loading dock. The date on the back of the original photograph simply read May 19th but, at a guess, the year would be around 1912. The motor car visible in the background certainly appears to be a pre-First World War model. *Neil Parkhouse collection*

The station still looks quite new in this view, which was taken on a wet day around 1908. The unusual arrangement of the station buildings is well illustrated. Note the screen in front of the Gentlemen's toilets at the nearer end and the loading gauge sited over the carriage truck bay, to check that any carriages loaded onto wagons here remained within gauge. *Mrs Freda Gittos collection*

A view of the south-west end of the station, showing the handsome Malvern Road West Signal Box, probably taken around 1912. The photographer was standing on the footpath from Queens Road that ran along the top of the cutting. The long rake of wagons in the loop behind the box includes at least two belonging to the Pyx Granite Company of Malvern. Malvern Road shed can be discerned in the background, with the coaling stage in the centre seen prior to gaining its lean-to addition. *The Lens of Sutton Collection*

The Great Western's new line from Cheltenham to Stratford-on-Avon, or 'the Honeybourne line' as it is often called, was opened in stages. The Stratford to Honeybourne section had been built as long ago as 1859 but south from there a new line was constructed in the early years of the 20th century, opening progressively southwards between 1904 and 1906. The station at Malvern Road was not opened until 1908 but, in the meantime, new locomotive servicing facilities had to be built, as the old shed had been in the way of the new line. These official views of the new complex at Malvern Road were taken on 26th July 1907. The picture, **above**, shows the two-road, brick-built shed, with stores and offices alongside, over which the sloping roof extended. It was 180 feet long and 40 feet wide. The view, **left**, shows the interior of the new shed looking spick and span, prior to the arrival of its locomotive allocation.
Courtesy National Railway Museum

THE BANBURY & CHELTENHAM DIRECT RAILWAY

Another official view, taken on the same day as the previous two, showing the new coaling stage and water tower. The shed never had a turntable, although space was left for one. Tender locomotives were turned on the turntable at St. James, or sent down to the Gloucester Loop triangle for turning. For the first three decades of its existence, the shed was mainly home to the tank engines used on the B&CDR line and Cheltenham-Gloucester local trains. In 1936, the ex-M&SWJR shed at Cheltenham High Street was closed and its allocation transferred to Malvern Road, which brought an influx of small tender engine types. At around the same time, the shed lost its CHEL code, becoming a sub-shed to Gloucester (GLO). Incidentally, the use of inside keyed track, on the centre siding only, seems odd. *Courtesy National Railway Museum*

that had originally been used by railmotor services to and from Honeybourne. The main station buildings were situated at a higher level on the south side of the line, a footbridge being provided in order that passengers could reach the platform. A carriage dock, used for unloading horse boxes or similar forms of traffic, was situated a short distance to the west of the main station building and this was served by a siding that formed a trailing connection with the adjacent running line.

There were three goods marshalling loops on the north side of the platform, together with a further loop line that gave access to the adjacent Malvern Road engine shed. The station was signalled from two standard Great Western signal cabins, known as Malvern Road East and Malvern Road West boxes. These two cabins were of similar external appearance; they were of brick and timber construction, with hipped, slate-covered roofs and five-pane windows.

Malvern Road engine shed, a sub-shed of Gloucester, was built in 1907 as a two road shed with the usual coaling and watering facilities, although no turntable was ever installed. The shed building was enlarged in 1936, in order to provide sufficient covered accommodation for locomotives employed on the Midland & South Western Junction line that had hitherto used the former M&SWJR engine shed at Cheltenham High Street. In its extended form, the shed housed four roads, the original brick building being flanked by a typical 1930s-style prefabricated structure.

Malvern Road shed normally housed an assortment of local passenger and freight locomotives, many of which would have been used on the Banbury & Cheltenham route, together with visiting engines from other sheds. In 1921, the allocation included 'Metro' Class 2-4-0Ts Nos. 458, 464, 628, 1449, 1461 and 1497; '517' Class 0-4-2T No. 1160, and '3521' Class 4-4-0s Nos. 3539 and 3545.

In 1947, the shed had an allocation of seventeen engines, including 'Manor' Class 4-6-0 No. 7808 *Cookham Manor*; 'Bulldog' Class 4-4-0 No. 3449 *Nightingale*; '43XX' Class 2-6-0s Nos. 4320, 5345, 6326, 6341, 7303 and 7312; '41XX' Class 2-6-2T No. 4101; '45XX' Class 2-6-2Ts Nos. 4534, 4564, 4567, 4578, 5515, 5538 and 5574; Collett '14XX' Class 0-4-2T No. 1402; and Diesel Railcar No. 25. Improved facilities for diesel multiple units were added in 1958, when BR constructed new workshops, storage buildings, two 7,000 gallon fuel tanks and a 280 foot inspection pit.

LANSDOWN JUNCTION

Leaving Cheltenham Malvern Road, trains reached Lansdown Junction. Here, the Great Western line converged with the former Midland Railway Bristol to Birmingham route. The line between Lansdown Junction

Another early overall view of Malvern Road station, looking north-east and showing the rear of the West Box, again probably taken just before the First World War. A GWR 4-4-0 waits with an Up express which, as it has stopped here, has most likely come down the Honeybourne line. The goods loops are empty apart from the three open wagons, the nearest of which is a private owner vehicle belonging to Stevens of Oxford. The earth ramp up to the coaling stage is shown in its entirety, with a further handful of coal wagons nearby, whilst a small Permanent Way depot seems to have been established in the triangle between the lines in the centre. In the foreground, the line leading off to the two sidings that ran adjacent to the Old Gloucester Road can just be seen. The station nameboard can just be made out under magnification, reading 'MALVERN ROAD CHELTENHAM'; the Spa was not added until 1925. The sweep of the lines as they curve through the station lent it a definite dramatic air. *Neil Parkhouse collection*

Malvern Road shed in August 1953, showing the later asbestos clad addition on the left, which increased the width of the building to 66 feet. This was added around 1936, following the closure of High Street shed and the reallocation of its locomotives to Malvern Road. Several locomotives can be seen including, from left to right, an unidentified BR standard Class '4MT' 4-6-0, '51XX' Class 2-6-2T No. 4141, Hawksworth '94XX' Class 0-6-0PT No. 8488 and '51XX' Class 2-6-2T No. 4140. The two prairie tanks would certainly have worked over the Cheltenham to Kingham line, whereas the BR Standard 4-6-0 would probably have arrived via the M&SWJ route. *Bob Brown collection*

The two long sidings behind the locomotive shed were used by coal merchants Crook & Greenway as one of their main depots serving the town. This photograph appeared in the *Cheltenham Chronicle & Graphic* on 7th January 1922 with a note recording it as their 21st anniversary. However, the company were supplied wagons by the Gloucester Carriage & Wagon Co. and their records indicate build dates for Crook & Greenway from 1898 at least. This impressive line up of a number of their own railway wagons and horse-drawn delivery vehicles also features then proprietor Mr E.J.W. Greenway, standing behind the pile of coal in the centre. The company seem to have experimented with a number of different liveries over the years, including chocolate, blue and light grey. Those seen here were most likely to have been in chocolate with white lettering. The company was still in business in 1931 but had ceased trading by 1935. Their other main depot was at the Midland yard, alongside the Tewkesbury Road bridge. The houses in the background face onto Malvern Road, whilst part of the engine shed can be seen on the right. The later extension was built onto this side of it. *Ian Pope collection*

These two views along Platform 1 both date from the mid 1950s. The view, **above**, looking towards St. James, shows a pre-fabricated structure on the platform, which was probably a wartime addition. It seems to have gone by the late 1950s. The picture, **below**, gives a good view of the rear of the booking office. Note the loudspeaker for train announcements suspended beneath the footbridge, which is also likely to have been a wartime addition. The station was generally kept in a tidy condition, with neat, stone-bordered flower beds along the platform.

Both The Lens of Sutton Collection

Above: Another of Gloucester (Horton Road) shed's '51XX' Class 2-6-2Ts, No. 5182, is seen departing from Malvern Road on the last leg of a service from Kingham on 26th August 1961. On shed in the background can just be seen a '94XX' Class pannier tank and another '51XX' Class prairie. *W. Potter*

Left: On 25th September 1962, '51XX' Class 2-6-2T No. 4163 pauses at Malvern Road en route to Kingham. Note the well-tended garden and the poster with that well-remembered 1960s slogan 'Drinka pinta milka day'. *R.K. Blencowe*

Right: One of the '45Xx' Class small prairies of the later '4575' series, No. 5514, stands at Malvern Road with a service from Kingham on 6th November 1958. These versatile engines were the mainstay of many branch line and cross-country routes throughout the former GWR system. The short footbridge was the only means of access for the public to the island platform. This view also demonstrates that the southbound platform was signalled for what is today referred to as 'bi-directional working'. *Courtesy Roger Carpenter*

A poor quality but unusual view of Malvern Road showing the approach to the station from the south-west, probably taken circa 1930. The photographer was standing on the bridge carrying Queens Road over the line and up to the right can be seen the rear of the houses in Eldorado Road. The yard headshunt is in the left foreground. The bracket signal on the right is unusual and presumably positioned where it is for sighting purposes. From right to left, the arms were for Platform 2, the goods loops and the locomotive shed. Lower down the post there is a distant arm, which was the advanced warning for St. James Junction.
Courtesy
Historical Model Railway Society

and Gloucester Engine Shed Junction was quadrupled in World War Two and this resulted in a particularly complex junction layout, with several route permutations. The junction arrangements incorporated a simple double track connection for GWR trains proceeding from Cheltenham Malvern Road towards Kingham but through workings from the LMS line had to leave their own line by means of a double track junction, cross the Up and Down Great Western lines on the level, and then converge with the Kingham route.

Over the years, Lansdown Junction was controlled from as diverse a selection of signal boxes as it would have been possible to find. The Gloucester Railway Carriage & Wagon Company provided the first box, for the opening of the Kingham line in 1881. It was sited immediately adjacent to and just to the north side of Lansdown Road bridge, and was of exceptional height to allow the signalmen to see over the bridge. Apart from its height, it was a typical GRC&W all timber construction, with a slated roof and originally two staircases, one leading from track level all the way up to the lever floor and the other for the locking room below. This arrangement had changed by the time the box closed in May 1914, with the opening of a new GWR standard design brick-built cabin, with hipped slated roof, situated about 50 yards further north east towards Malvern Road.

This poor quality but rare photograph was recently discovered, showing the original Lansdown Junction box in its final form and dating from circa 1905. Note some of the embankment has been dug away to allow for a new set of steps to be provided, running straight up to the operating floor. The lower set of panes in the cabin windows have been blanked off and the box has also acquired a new paint scheme and a new cast iron nameboard – Lansdown Junction Signal Box. A Midland 2-4-0 is passing, having just left Lansdown station, bound for Gloucester and Bristol.
Courtesy Cheltenham Museum

THE BANBURY & CHELTENHAM DIRECT RAILWAY

Lansdown Junction in 1932, looking towards Malvern Road. Much has changed since the late 19th century view on page 48. The tall GRC&W Co. box has gone, replaced by a standard GWR brick-built cabin opened in May 1914. The bracket signal controlling entry to the junction from the east has also been moved from the top of the cutting and positioned alongside the track. On the left is the former MR Birmingham to Bristol main line with Lansdown station just out of view around the curve. What can be seen is the bay used by M&SWJ line trains, which continued to run into Lansdown even after the closure of High Street shed. It was only in the final years of the M&SWJ route that they were diverted into St. James station. Note the single slip point in centre of the junction. *Bob Brown collection*

This box had a life of less than thirty years, being swept away when Lansdown Junction was extensively remodelled during the Second World War, with the junction being moved about a quarter of a mile south west, nearer Gloucester. A new brick signal cabin was sited in the 'V' where the Kingham route diverged. The box was a typical Great Western wartime structure, with a flat, reinforced concrete roof and a fully enclosed locking room. Although such buildings would not have survived a direct hit by a high explosive bomb, they were intended to give at least some protection from blast and shrapnel damage, for which reason they were generally known as 'ARP' (or Air Raid

During the Second World War, the line between Cheltenham and Gloucester was quadrupled and at Lansdown the site of the junction changed dramatically. The signal box was swept away to make room for the realignment of the GWR line and a crossover was put in to allow M&SWJ line trains to run into the bay at Lansdown station. This view of '45XX' Class 2-6-2T No. 5514 with a train for Kingham was taken in early 1959, the crossover to Lansdown having been removed in late 1958. Evidence of this extensive PW work is clear, the signals controlling the exit from Lansdown station to the Kingham line also having been removed. They were positioned on the gantry, immediately to the right of the two posts on the left. *Bob Brown collection*

The corresponding view to the top picture on the previous page is this photograph also taken in 1932 from Lansdown Road bridge, looking south-west towards Gloucester. The Kingham line swings off to the left, with the jointly owned GWR/L&MSR line between Cheltenham and Gloucester on the right. The signals are all of Great Western design; the bracket on the right signalled trains into Lansdown station, via the right hand post, or through Malvern Road as indicated by the lowered arm here. The arrangement for the Kingham line was a little more unusual, with trains being able to approach the junction on either of the running lines, which explains the presence of the single slip shown on page 132 and also of the runaway siding seen here on the Up line.
Bob Brown collection

Above: The remodelled junction on 10th April 1964. The whole layout has changed extensively from the previous picture and the junction between the Birmingham and Honeybourne lines had been moved some distance further east, with the new Lansdown Junction Signal Box right. Here, ex-GWR '43XX' Class mogul No 7319 is coming off the Kingham line with lifted rails from Notgrove. In the 1950s, especially on Saturdays, there would be up to 50 or 60 trainspotters sitting on the path leading to the signal box – officialdom was more flexible in those days! *D.R. Lewis*

Right: The driver of ex-WD 'Austerity' 2-8-0 No. 90471 has paused behind Lansdown Junction Signal Box on 21st May 1964 to allow the guard to inspect the load of rails recovered from the Kingham branch. The box was commissioned in July 1942 as part of the Cheltenham to Gloucester widening scheme and was built to the standard GWR 'air-raid precaution' design capable of withstanding a bomb blast – although not a direct hit. It still stands disused today. *D.R. Lewis*

Right: Taken a few moments after the lower picture on the previous page, with the guard having completed his inspection, the 'Austerity' 2-8-0 moves off towards Malvern Road with its load of rails. The train is about to pass under Lansdown Road bridge; the original arch is on the right, the left-hand one being built as part of the war-time widening. *D.R. Lewis*

Above: The view of Lansdown Junction from the Kingham line. 'Manor' Class 4-6-0 No. 7808 *Cookham Manor* has just been given the road to proceed onto the Honeybourne Line with a brake van, after delivering more empty wagons for track recovery at Andoversford on New Years Day 1965. Behind the trees on the right are some of the buildings of the renowned Dean Close School. *D.R. Lewis*

Left: '45XX' Class small prairie No. 4573 of Gloucester (Horton Road) shed gets well into its stride accelerating away from Lansdown Junction with the 9.50 am train to Kingham on Whit Sunday 1960. The locomotive has just crossed the bridge over Hatherley Road. No trace remains today at this point to suggest that a railway ever existed here. *D.R. Lewis*

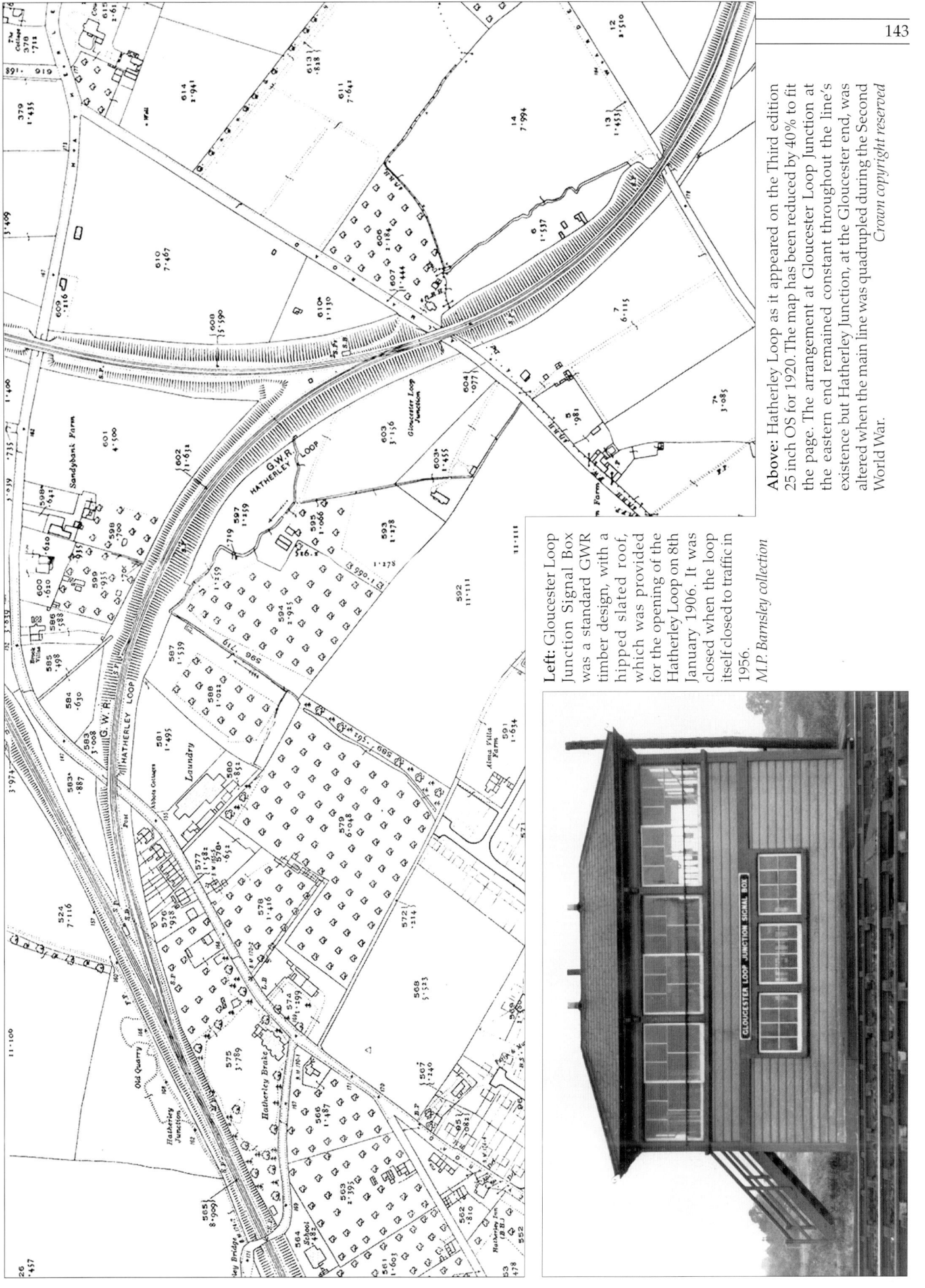

Above: Hatherley Loop as it appeared on the Third edition 25 inch OS for 1920. The map has been reduced by 40% to fit the page. The arrangement at Gloucester Loop Junction at the eastern end remained constant throughout the line's existence but Hatherley Junction, at the Gloucester end, was altered when the main line was quadrupled during the Second World War.
Crown copyright reserved

Left: Gloucester Loop Junction Signal Box was a standard GWR timber design, with a hipped slated roof, which was provided for the opening of the Hatherley Loop on 8th January 1906. It was closed when the loop itself closed to traffic in 1956.
M.P. Barnsley collection

A circa 1950 view of Gloucester Loop Junction and signal box, looking towards Cheltenham with the spire of St. Marks Church in the right background. Most unusually, the points are set for a Gloucester-bound train. *M.P. Barnsley collection*

Precaution) boxes. A similar cabin was also built further west at Hatherley Junction, where the Hatherley Loop joined the main line, as a replacement for a standard GWR timber box, but this saw very little use after the war as the traffic using the loop either ceased or was diverted away.

Kingham trains diverged south-westwards onto their own route and negotiated a ninety degree curve as they followed the double track line onto an easterly alignment. At Gloucester Loop Junction (1 mile 37 chains), the double track Hatherley Curve converged from the west; this east-to-west loop formed the south side of a triangle that was sometimes used for turning engines, although its main purpose was to permit through running between Banbury, Kingham and the Gloucester line. A signal cabin was provided on the up (eastbound) side of the line at Gloucester Loop Junction; the box, of standard Great Western design, was of all-timber construction, with a hipped, slate-covered roof.

In practice, the Hatherley Loop saw little regular use although, prior to World War Two, it carried the 'Ports-to-Ports Express' (one a day in each direction) on its way between Newcastle and Swansea. This 39 chain east-to-west connection was also used by the heavy ironstone workings *en route* from Oxfordshire to South Wales. It came into its own during the war years, when the Banbury & Cheltenham Direct and Midland & South Western Junction lines were both pressed into use as important diversionary routes for heavy freight traffic. The curve saw little use after World War Two and in British Railways days it was abandoned as a running connection, the junctions at each end being reduced to simple, trailing connections.

Gloucester Loop Junction and box looking towards Kingham, taken on the same occasion as the previous view. Interestingly, although named Gloucester Loop Junction, the Gloucester-bound curve was officially called Hatherley Loop but to have named this box Hatherley Loop Junction would have created confusion with Hatherley Junction Box, where the curve joined the main line. *M.P. Barnsley collection*

Above: Express services leaving Cheltenham St. James were often hauled as far as Gloucester by a tank engine, which made for a rather incongruous sight. However, with no large passenger classes allocated to Malvern Road shed, it saved sending a light engine from Gloucester, the train engine instead being coupled to the coaches there. Here a Cheltenham to Paddington express heads for Gloucester with a prairie tank performing the 'drag', circa 1950. To the right of the engine, the Hatherley Loop comes in to join the main line at Hatherley Junction. This was the 'direct line' used by the 'Ports-to-Ports express' and ironstone trains heading for South Wales but, after the Second World War, with the former routed away from the B&CDR line and the ironstone quarries ceasing operations, it saw even less use. Hatherley Junction Signal Box was another 'ARP' design, which was a replacement in 1942 for a timber cabin of the same pattern as Gloucester Loop Junction Box. This was dismantled for re-use at Exeter Riverside, where it was still standing in the early 1990s. Heron Close is now built on this part of the Loop. *M.P. Barnsley collection*

Above: The daily pick-up freight from Cheltenham to Kingham left St. James' yard at 8.10 am. This train was usually well loaded and the engine crew would charge the 1 in 60 gradient up from Lansdown Junction, making a fine spectacle as it crossed Hatherley Road. This June 1960 view shows a typical formation headed by '57XX' Class pannier No. 8717, seen approaching the site of Gloucester Loop Junction Signal Box. *D.R. Lewis*

Right: Collett '57XX' Class 0-6-0 pannier tank No. 8743 of Gloucester shed heads towards Cheltenham with a short pick-up goods working from the Kingham branch in 1960. The train consists of a United Dairies milk tank, a 16 ton mineral wagon and a Toad brake van. It has just passed beneath Bourneside Farm bridge, which was reputedly used a year or so after this by the late Brian Jones (a local lad), for some early publicity shots for The Rolling Stones. *D.R. Lewis*

Two more of William Nash's photographs, showing trains bound for the ex-M&SWJR line approaching Leckhampton. GWR 0-6-0 No. 1004, **above**, is passing Bournside and approaching the bridge seen in the background of the lower photograph (from which Nash also took the view, looking east, which appears on page 73). Gloucester Loop Junction is just out of sight round the corner in the distance. No. 1004 was part of a class of ten goods locomotives built by Beyer Peacock for the M&SWJR, their No. 20. It was heavily rebuilt by the GWR in December 1925, this photograph dating from 1926. **Below**, GWR 4-4-0 No. 1123 shows a turn of speed with a Cheltenham to Southampton train as it leans into the curve taking the line under Shurdington Road bridge. Originally M&SWJR No. 5, the engine shows little sign of being 'Swindonised' in this 1925 photograph, not being rebuilt until 1929. The train comprises four smart looking GWR clerestory carriages.

Both William Nash collection, courtesy Kate Robinson

An obviously posed view of the station, showing the extensive saw mills at Maida Vale behind. The photograph, the earliest so far discovered of Leckhampton station, appeared in the *Cheltenham Chronicle & Graphic* of 8th July 1905 and was almost certainly taken especially for publication. The saw mills seem to have been closed and the site cleared a year or so later. The station gardens are worthy of note, complete with greenhouse behind the Up platform and the archway leading onto it.   *Courtesy Gloucester Local Studies Library*

CHELTENHAM SOUTH & LECKHAMPTON

Running more or less due east, the double track branch skirted the southern edges of Cheltenham as it neared the first intermediate stopping place at Cheltenham South & Leckhampton. The station was preceded by five overline bridges in close succession, one of which carried the busy A46 road across the railway. Two slightly curved platforms were provided here, the station being situated in a cutting some 2 miles 69 chains from Cheltenham St. James. The B4070 Leckhampton Road crossed the line on a single-span, brick-arched bridge immediately to the west of the platforms and an occupation bridge crossed the railway at the east end of the station.

The main station building was sited on the Up or east-bound platform and there was a small waiting room on the westbound platform. Both of these buildings were single-storey brick structures, the main block having a low-pitched gable roof, with raised copings at each end. The main building, which contained the usual booking office, waiting room and public toilet facilities, dated from the opening of the line in 1881, and it featured three tall chimney stacks and a projecting platform canopy. The front of the building was slightly recessed to form a sort of loggia beneath the generously-proportioned platform canopy. The booking office was to the left, when viewed from the platform.

On the Down side, a standard Great Western hip-roofed building was provided. It was of brick construction, with a slated roof and a full length platform canopy. Internally, this subsidiary structure contained additional waiting room and toilet facilities for passengers waiting on the westbound platform. The double track through Cheltenham South was brought into use in September 1902, and it is reasonable to assume that the Down platform and its standard GWR building were constructed in that same year.

The track layout at Cheltenham South was unusual. The goods yard, on the Up side, contained four sidings; there were two west-facing sidings entered by means of a trailing connection from the Up main line, whilst a similar trailing connection left the Down main line and, crossing the Up line, split into two east-facing sidings. These two sets of sidings were linked by a double-slip, which enabled wagons to be shunted from one end of the yard to the other without fouling the main running lines. The yard contained coal wharves, cattle pens, an end-loading dock, a weigh-house and a 5-ton yard crane.

There was a standard Great Western gable-roofed signal box at the east end of the Up platform. The cabin was a typical late Victorian structure, provided in 1902 when the line was doubled, with small-paned windows and a 23-lever frame (including five spaces). At night, the platforms were originally gas-lit by traditional tapered glass lanterns but these were later replaced by hemispherical lamps with circular metal shields. Passengers were able to cross between the Up and Down sides by means of a wooden barrow

Proof that the sun did not always shine back then! Cheltenham South & Leckhampton station on a wet day around 1910. Although the change of name from plain Leckhampton occurred prior to the commencement of the 'Ports-to-Ports express' service, it proved useful for the GWR who were able to thereby claim a Cheltenham stop for the train. It otherwise bypassed the town, by heading south at Gloucester Loop Junction. The name was changed yet again in 1952 to Cheltenham Leckhampton. The diminutive goods shed can also be seen just behind the Up platform. It faced onto a siding running directly behind the platform. In the background, all trace of the saw mills has gone and the stationmaster's garden adornments also appear to have been done away with. *Neil Parkhouse collection*

A view of the eastern end of the station looking towards Charlton Kings in 1932. Both the Up and Down signals are in the off position, probably due to the box being switched out and therefore lengthening the section. The double slip that permitted shunting of the yard without using the running lines is visible just beyond the signal box and the 5-ton yard crane can just be made out behind the lead wagon. The gas lamps on the platform are also worthy of note, the lanterns being quite large and ornate. The bridge in the distance carried a track over the line. It exists to this day but sadly all trace of the station itself has been swept aside to make way for the inevitable cluster of industrial units.
The Lens of Sutton Collection

Cheltenham South & Leckhampton station looking east towards Banbury on 9th April 1932. On this bright spring day, the station looks very neat with its well-tended gardens and in its still essentially rural loocation. In the days when every household relied on coal for heating and hot water, even small stations such as this boasted several coal merchants plying their trade. On the left, behind the telegraph pole, can be seen the offices of three coal merchants – B. Beaumont, W.D. Farrar and Henry Jordan. Beaumont traded as Leckhampton Coal Depot and appears in *Kelly's Directories* throughout the 1930s. William Farrar had several depots in Cheltenham and seems to have begun trading around 1906, with listings still appearing in 1939. Henry Jordan had started his business by 1879 at least and again had depots all over the town. His company also appears in the 1939 edition of *Kelly's Directory*. The signal box dated from the doubling of the line in 1902.

Bob Brown collection

crossing at the east end of the platforms, or via the road bridge at the opposite end of the station.

In pre-Grouping days, Cheltenham South & Leckhampton was served by Midland & South Western Junction trains between Cheltenham Lansdown and Andover, as well as GWR branch services to Kingham. In addition, local travellers were able to make use of the celebrated 'Ports-to-Ports Express', which did not call at any of the other Cheltenham stations. In view of this, it is perhaps surprising that Cheltenham South did not generate much passenger traffic. On the other hand, many local residents preferred to use the competing electric tramway, which passed through the area, and offered a cheap and frequent service to and from Cheltenham town centre.

In its first years of operation the station was officially known as 'Leckhampton' but GWR timetables reveal that 'Cheltenham South & Leckhampton' was in widespread use by the 1890s. This name was displayed in full on the station nameboards until World War Two, when they were taken down as an anti-invasion measure. In 1952, the station was renamed 'Cheltenham Leckhampton', this slightly abbreviated appellation being displayed in timetables and on a new set of station nameboards.

The goods yard handled modest amounts of coal and general merchandise traffic. Domestic coal was distributed by several local merchants. A free cartage service provided collection and delivery facilities for traders and residents in Leckhampton and the surrounding district. In the 1930s, the station typically handled around 7,000 tons of freight per annum, including about 4,750 tons of coal.

Passenger traffic decreased steadily from around 10,500 bookings a year during the pre-Grouping period, to around 5,000 per annum during the mid-1930s and just 3,366 bookings in 1938. The overall pattern of decline is underlined by the following traffic statistics:

TRAFFIC DEALT WITH AT CHELTENHAM SOUTH & LECKHAMPTON

YEAR	STAFF	RECEIPTS (£)	TICKETS	PARCELS	GOODS (TONS)
1903	5	2,282	10,434	4,668	7,359
1913	4	2,324	9,484	4,802	3,971
1923	4	10,216	11,037	3,213	17,548
1933	3	3,479	5,651	1,342	6,566
1938	3	3,495	3,366	5,150	7,080

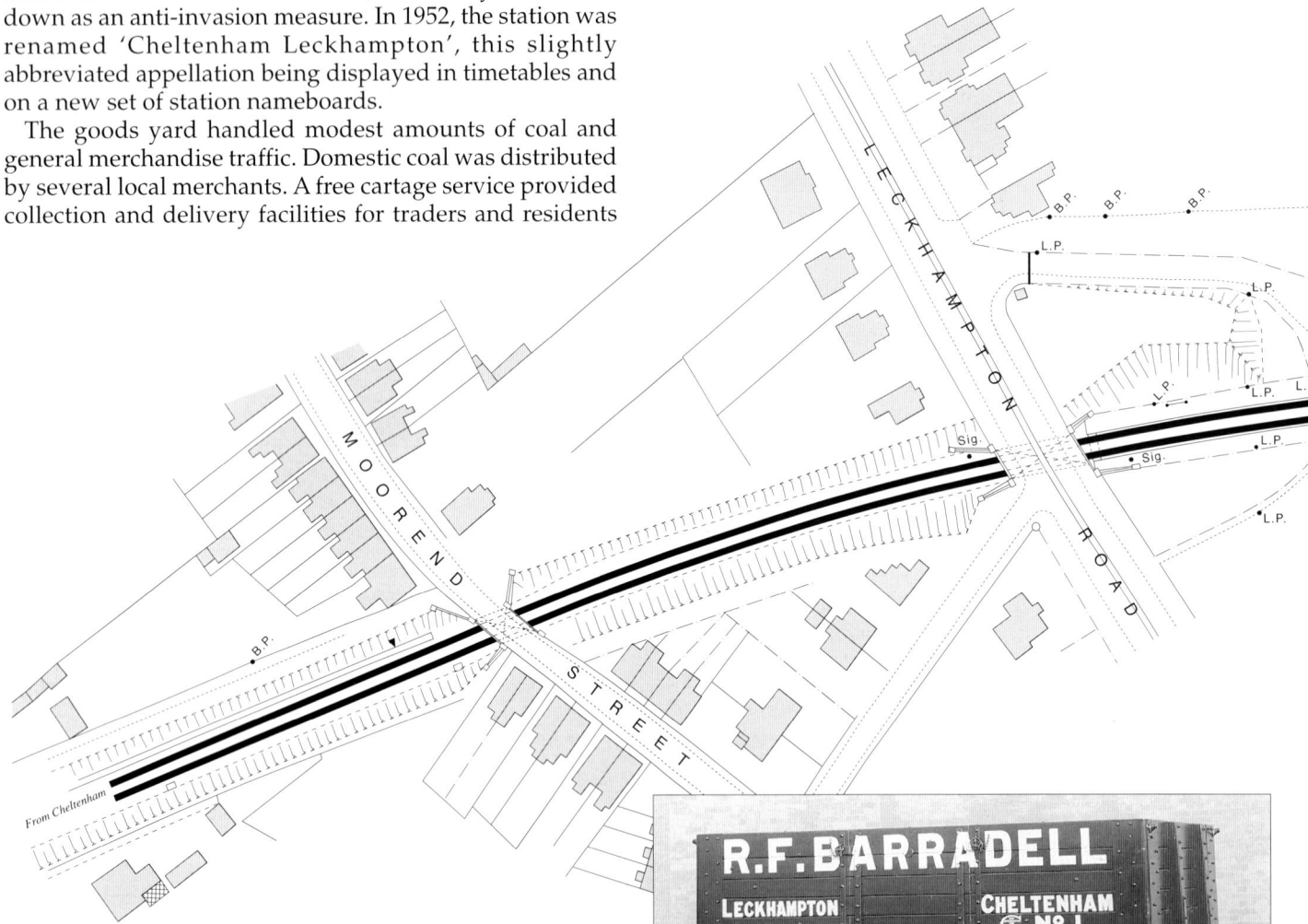

Nothing is known of R.F. Barradell, who ordered this wagon, painted black with white lettering, from the Gloucester RC&W Co. in 1902. It is thought that he may have been in the timber business and possibly owned the Maida Vale saw mills for a short time but his name does not appear in any of the trade directories.

Courtesy Gloucestershire Record Office

Left: Grimy looking '45XX' Class small prairie No. 4573 arrives at Leckhampton station on a sunny 5th March 1960 with the 10.50 am Up service to Kingham. The plans seem to indicate that the bridge carrying Leckhampton Road over the line, in the background, was built to double track width from the outset. *D.R. Lewis*

Below: This 1885 advertisement for Smith Brothers, timber and general builders merchants of Cheltenham, indicates they also had a base at Leckhampton station. They are known to have purchased one 8-ton wagon secondhand wagon from the GRC&WCo. as well as having at least two others.
Neil Parkhouse collection

SMITH BROTHERS,
Albion Street, & Leckhampton Station,
CHELTENHAM.
English and Foreign Timber Merchants,
BRICK & DRAIN PIPE MAKERS,
SLATE, BROSELEY TILE, & CEMENT MERCHANTS,
Dealers in all kinds of Building Materials.
DRY CONVERTED TIMBER OF ALL KINDS IN STOCK.
Gates, Fencing, & Rustic Summer Houses made to order & fixed on the shortest notice.
CASH BUYERS OF ANY DESCRIPTION OF ENGLISH TIMBER.

LECKHAMPTON STATION
Above: After doubling. Redrawn from the 2 chain survey, 1914.

Below: Before doubling. Redrawn from the Board of Trade survey circa 1902.

A '51XX' Class 2-6-2T nears Leckhampton with the 5.15 pm Kingham to Cheltenham service on 20th August 1962. The train has just passed beneath a small iron aqueduct. In the background is Pilley Bridge, which was a replacement structure for one destroyed by a direct hit from a German bomb on December 11th 1940. Astonishingly, the bridge was not replaced until 1955, a temporary footbridge spanning the line until then. This section of track is now a nature walk offering an opportunity for a peaceful stroll as far as the bridge, which survives intact despite being on a tight bend between two road junctions. *W. Potter*

CHARLTON KINGS

Turning onto a south-easterly heading, trains ran through further cuttings as they left Cheltenham and entered the outlying suburb of Charlton Kings; Charlton Park, once the seat of Sir William Russell, who had played such a pivotal role in the East Gloucestershire Railway saga, was situated about half a mile to the north of the line. Climbing into the Cotswold Hills, the double track railway passed beneath five more overbridges, before a gentle, eastwards curve brought Up trains into the platforms at Charlton Kings station (4 miles 1 chain).

This small stopping place was sited in a tree-lined cutting, with its main station building on the Down side. The A435 road crossed the line on a single-span brick and girder bridge at the east end of the platforms. The single-storey station building was a diminutive, timber framed structure, clad in horizontal weather boarding. Its low-pitched gable roof was extended forward over the platform frontage for a

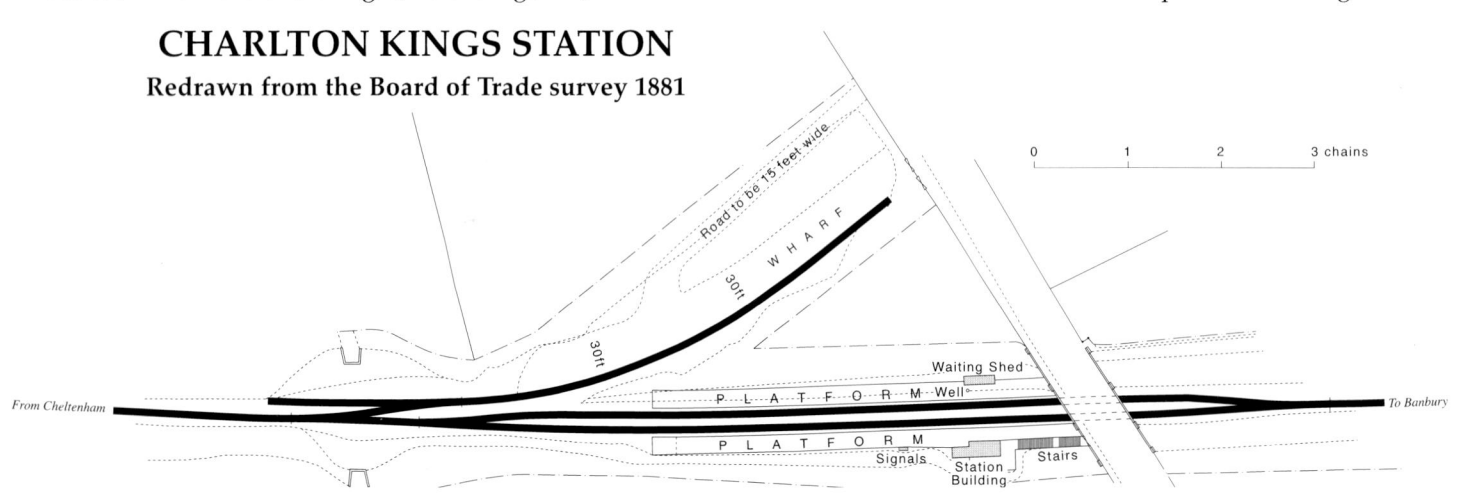

CHARLTON KINGS STATION
Redrawn from the Board of Trade survey 1881

The earliest known view of Charlton Kings station, looking east towards Banbury and probably taken around 1905. The signal box, which shows little sign of age, was provided in 1902 when the line was doubled, replacing the original GRC&W cabin which was sited on the Down platform. The brick-built goods lock-up on the left was similar to that at Leckhampton station. The yard consisted of two sidings, the longer one being used for coal whilst the shorter served a loading dock. A yard crane was never provided here and there were no cattle pens although the station was listed as being available for livestock traffic. One of Cheltenham's grander hotels, the Lilleybrook, lay behind the trees on the right and it must have provided at least some custom for the station, particularly in the years prior to the First World War. Only two station nameboards are in evidence, one on the Up platform by the goods shed and one on the Down platform just the other side of the wooden station building. The bridge carrying the Cirencester Road over the line in the background – brick abutments and wing walls, with brick parapets carried on wrought iron girders – is the only surviving piece of railway infrastructure here today.

Mrs Freda Gittos collection

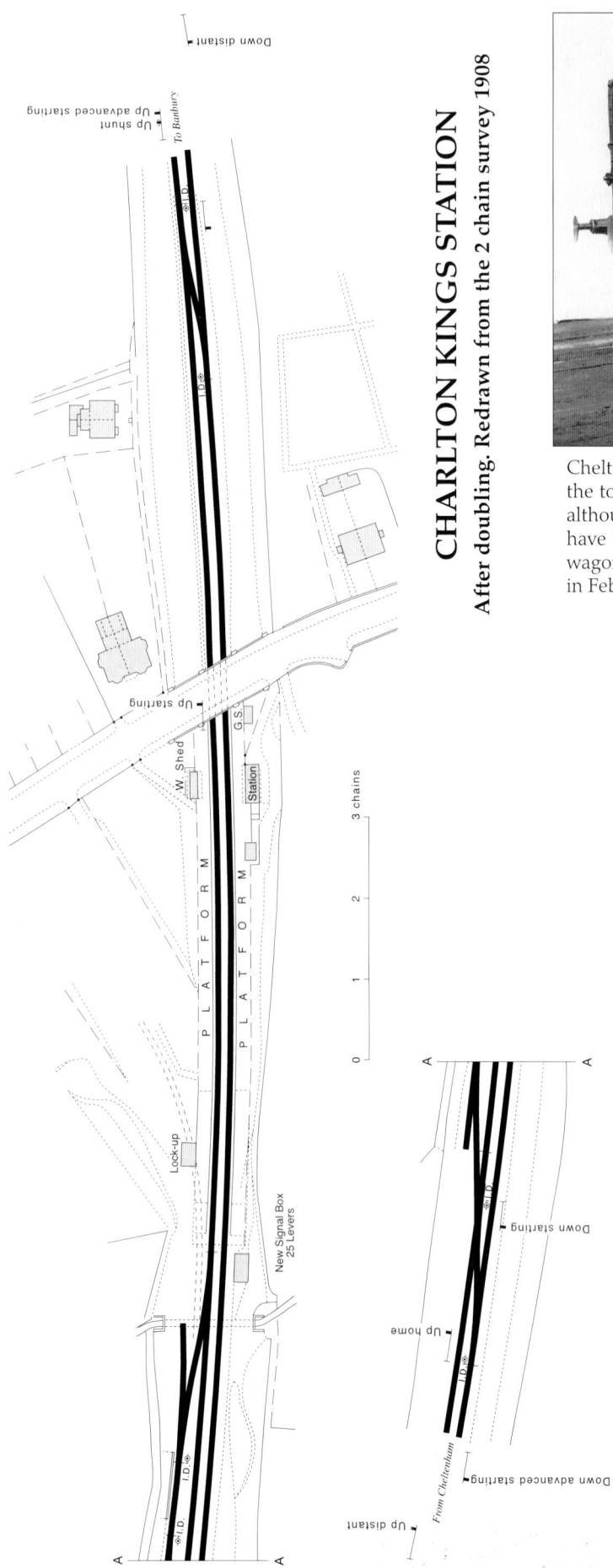

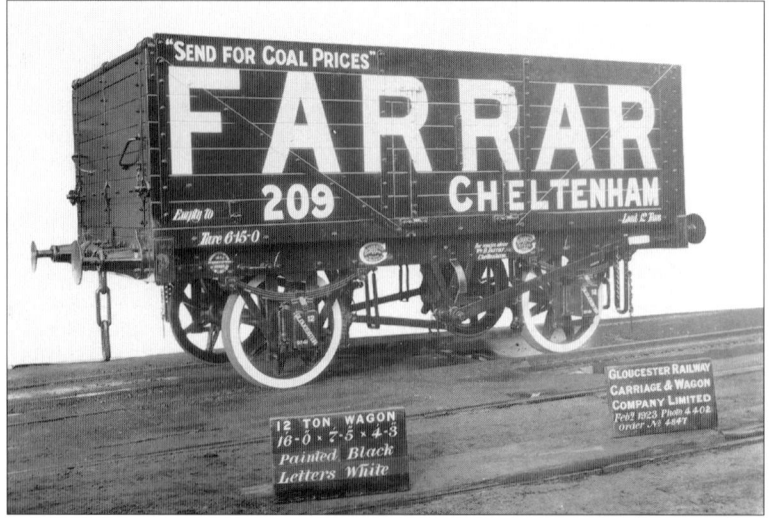

CHARLTON KINGS STATION
After doubling. Redrawn from the 2 chain survey 1908

Cheltenham coal merchant W.D. Farrar traded from a number of bases in the town. He was in business by 1897 and continued until at least 1927, although his offices at Charlton Kings and Leckhampton only seem to have been in operation for a short period around 1905-7. This 12-ton wagon, painted black with white lettering, was delivered from Gloucester in February 1923. *Courtesy Gloucestershire Record Office*

distance of about three feet to form a vestigial platform canopy, while a brick chimney stack was asymmetrically positioned at the front of the building.

The Up side station building was also of timber-framed construction. It was little more than a large shed, with a single-pitch roof that formed a full-length canopy. The Up and Down platforms were linked by a barrow crossing at the west end of the station, although passengers could also cross the line via the road overbridge at the Banbury end. Until World War Two, the platforms were fenced with tubular metal railings, while at night the station was lit by gas. A good deal of the platform railings had disappeared by the British Railways era – presumably as a result of the wartime requirement for scrap metal.

The goods yard, with provision for coal, horse boxes and general merchandise traffic, was on the Up side of the running lines. It had just one siding, which was originally linked to the single running line by means of a connection that was facing to Up trains. At that time, the layout at Charlton Kings consisted of this one siding and a crossing loop but modifications were required in connection with the doubling of the line in 1902 and, as a result, the siding was extended westwards and linked to the Up and Down running lines by means of trailing connections.

Dead-end spurs extended from each end of the main goods siding, the western spur being no more that a very short headshunt, whereas the eastern-facing spur was much longer. The goods shed was merely a brick store at the west end of the Up platform, while the signal box, dating from 1902, was sited on the Down side of the running lines at the west end of the platforms. This standard Great Western structure replaced an earlier box, which had been sited beside the station building on the Down platform. The site of the old signal box was later occupied by a single-storey shed, which may have incorporated timber components from the redundant cabin.

Charlton Kings station on 20th August 1952, in happier times before being reduced to an unstaffed halt. The gardens are still tended and the station appears well kept, although the buildings look in need of a lick of paint, no doubt a result of war-time restrictions. The white platform edges are also a left-over from the war, being painted on as a visual aid during the blackout. *John Alsop collection*

By the mid 1950s, the station buildings had been repainted, as had the various signs and the station nameboards. The bridge carrying the main A435 Cirencester Road across the line at the east end of the station also served as the footbridge. The steps ascending from the Down platform can be seen, along with one of the large cast iron signs that warned passengers not to cross the line. *L.B. Lapper*

The main station building viewed from the other direction, from a passing Kingham-bound train on 1st May 1956. The store beyond the station building marks the site of the original signal box which was closed in 1902. It can be seen that the replacement box, at the far end of the platform, had also been quickly removed following its closure on 30th January 1955. The station had been reduced to the status of an unstaffed halt a month before this picture was taken.

H.C. Casserley, courtesy Richard Casserley

Right: An unidentified '51XX' Class 2-6-2T arrives at Charlton Kings with a Kingham to Cheltenham train towards the end of the line's life. Latterly, the Gentlemen's lavatory on the Down platform was boarded-up, whilst one of the warning notices lies cast aside on the Up platform. *Bob Brown collection*

Above: This circa 1960 view through the station shows the line curving away towards Dowdeswell and beneath the overbridge in the middle distance that carried Little Herberts Lane (later Road) over the railway. Note that the left-hand abutment of this bridge bears a square of white paint. There had been a signal on the Up line at this point and it was common practice to paint the brickwork behind the signal white in order to aid sighting by footplate crews. For many years, a trailing crossover was in place between the two bridges but it had been removed by the 1950s. This was originally a temporary connection provided during the doubling of the line between here and Andoversford. The fir trees lining the station were a standard feature throughout the former GWR system and, together with the sunlight on the Up platform waiting shelter, make this a particularly pleasant scene. The site today houses some light industrial units but the 'Great Western' pines are still a feature. *Bob Brown collection*

Left: Collett '51XX' Class prairie tank No. 5154 accelerates away from Charlton Kings bound for Cheltenham with the 5.15 pm service from Kingham. The overgrown area to the right of the train was the site of the exchange sidings for the Leckhampton Quarries line. *W. Potter*

For a short period during the 1920s, a pair of private quarry sidings existed on the Down side of the line and there was also a connection directly to the private gated branch serving the quarry. This facility was linked to the Up running line via a trailing connection and to the Down line by means of a complex arrangement involving the sidings and a single slip. The history of the Leckhampton Quarries Company is detailed in the following section but the sidings had fallen into disuse by the late 1920s.

In 1903, Charlton Kings issued 8,910 tickets but this fairly respectable figure had dropped to just 1,803 tickets by 1930. Thereafter, there were around 1,800 passenger bookings per annum throughout the early and middle 1930s, while season ticket sales amounted to around four a year. By 1938, sales of ordinary tickets had dropped to 1,368, although the number of season tickets sold had increased to eight. In practice, the apparent decline in the number of passengers can probably be attributed to the increased use of season tickets by a handful of regular travellers – one three month season being the equivalent of 60 return journeys, while a six month season equated to 120 daily journeys.

The amount of goods traffic handled at Charlton Kings fluctuated between 4,100 and 6,100 tons during the 1930s. In 1936, a typical year, the station dealt with 4,889 tons of freight, 3,423 tons being in the form of coal traffic. In an attempt to reduce operating costs, the staffing establishment at this small station was cut from five in 1903, to four by the early 1930s and just two by 1938. Despite these economies, the staff paybill expenses in that year totalled £335, whereas total receipts were only £1,064.

Left: Two more late views of the station, both taken circa 1960 and looking west towards Cheltenham. Here, the A435 road bridge frames a rather unkempt looking station, with nature beginning to encroach on the platforms and buildings. The signal box has gone and so have the staff.
Bob Brown collection

Right: With the line curving away towards Cheltenham, this view shows the station waiting out its final days. All the original wooden station buildings, including the delightful waiting shelter on the Up platform, survived until the end. In the distance, there is another glimpse of the brick-built goods shed, whilst the wooden shed just visible beyond seems to have been a late addition to the station site, which does not appear in any of the other photographs and the purpose of which is not known.
Bob Brown collection

THE LECKHAMPTON QUARRIES BRANCH

The history of stone quarrying on Leckhampton Hill can be traced back to the early 1800s at least and was largely responsible for the building of one of the country's earliest tramroads. The Gloucester & Cheltenham Tramroad opened in 1811 and a branch joined with already existing tramroads bringing stone down from Leckhampton Quarries. It is not proposed to delve into the history of these operations here, not least because they have been well documented elsewhere by the industrial archeaologist David Bick. In any case, in1881, when the Banbury & Cheltenham Direct Railway was opened between Bourton-on-the-Water and Cheltenham, the quarries and the new line had no connection with each other whatsoever.

However, in the early 1920s, after some 120 years of quarrying the hillside high above southern Cheltenham for fine quality building stone, a new operation was set up to crush and burn limestone here, to produce lime. Henry Dale, who had owned the quarries since 1894, established this new concern, following a reorganisation of his Dale's Leckhampton Quarries Company after the First World War. He also took advantage of the ready availability of Government loans put in place to help alleviate the chronic unemployment problems that were then prevalent.

It was anticipated that vast tonnages of lime would be produced, which would need to be quickly despatched to eager customers; indeed, the prospectus promised that this would be the case. Acordingly, Dale decided that the antiquated system of tramroads and inclines, which were in use bringing building stone down the hill, needed

Above: A close-up of Manning Wardle 0-6-0ST *Fashoda*, built in 1899 (Works No. 1432). It was delivered new to the contractors Walter Scott & Co. and used on the contract to build the GCR branch from Woodford to Banbury (see Chapter Three). The locomotive remained with Scott until 1917 and is then believed to have been in Government use for some years, until purchased by Caffins circa 1922. After finishing work at Leckhampton, *Fashoda* left for a contract in Newport.
The late Humphrey Household

Above: On 15th January 1923, *Fashoda* shunts contractors wagons into position for filling with spoil by the Ruston steam navvy excavating the route of the quarry line near Sandy Lane.

Right: On the flatter middle section, narrow gauge tracks were laid and a petrol locomotive, named *Caffin & Co.*, was used to haul the side tipping wagons carrying the spoil. The track looks extremely rudimentary but was quite typical of contractor's lines.
Both the late Humphrey Household

replacing. Instead, he intended to build a standard gauge railway on a completely new alignment, dropping down from the proposed calcining kilns up on the hillside by means of an electrically powered incline of nearly two thirds of a mile in length, to run across the fields to the south-east of Leckhampton for about half a mile and connect with the B&CDR line at Charlton Kings.

With the plans accepted and money having been raised from Government loans and by private subscription, construction of the whole enterprise commenced in 1922. Fortunately, having been fascinated by the quarries and their tramroads from a very young age, Humphrey Household, when still only a teenager, took a long series of photographs of the new line under construction. These now mostly reside in the National Railway Museum at York, although they by no means have a full set – it is thought the photographer lent some of them out in later years. He also left a detailed record of his observations of the work, which formed a chapter in his 1984 book *Gloucestershire Railways in the Twenties* (Alan Sutton).

The contractors for the line were Caffin & Co. of London. Work commenced in late 1922 and they made use of a Ruston steam navvy and a Manning Wardle 0-6-0ST *Fashoda* during the construction. *Fashoda* was delivered by rail to Leckhampton station, placed on a wooden trolley and then hauled by a traction engine to the work site. The construction work was not without its difficulties, involving the building of a new incline, a substantial embankment and a cutting near Sandy

Top: Opening up the cutting to connect with the B&CDR line, 14th June 1923. The Ruston steam navvy appears to be under the operation of a crew of 3 (hopefully it was not one of those wonderful Roland Emmett types which could do the work of 3 men!) and is standing on its own short length of track.

Centre: The Ruston steam navvy at work alongside the B&CDR line at Charlton Kings on 20th June 1923, loading spoil into wooden bodied, side-tipping contractors wagons.

Left: Removing the bank alongside the main line on 4th July 1923. The steam navvy is loading spoil into a rake of contractor's wagons hauled by *Fashoda*. Although just a glimpse, this is the only known view showing the extent of the goods yard at Charlton Kings, in the background.
All Humphrey Household collection, courtesy National Railway Museum

Left: The track being laid in the cutting leading to the B&CDR line in early August 1923. Work is also proceeding on strengthening and grading the cutting sides.

Below: Looking in the opposite direction, this bridge was built to carry a footpath over the line. Work has just begun on the nearer abutment and it can be seen that the bridge was on a sharp skew.
Both Humphrey Household collection, courtesy NRM

Lane. The underlying clay and the inclement weather – excavations at the Charlton Kings end commenced in January 1923 – led to flooding and temporary abandonment of the works until the flood water could be cleared. It was also labour intensive, although this was partly due to the requirements of the Government loan, which was specifically to create jobs. Nevertheless, the initial £50,000 loan soon disappeared and much more was to follow, mostly from the Treasury but some also from private investors.

By August of 1923, a GWR permanent way gang was laying in the new junction at Charlton Kings. Two sidings

A GWR permanent way gang at work laying in the new junction and sidings on 10th August 1923. According to Household's own notes, the goods train had been *'shunted 'Wrong Line' to allow a passenger train to overtake'*, which seems an unusual manoeuvre to undertake at a work location such as this but possibly some wagons had to be dropped off or picked up from Charlton Kings yard.
Humphrey Household collection, courtesy National Railway Museum

The bridge carrying Daisy Bank Road over the incline under construction on 6th July 1923. The stone abutments were solidly built, with the road being carried on steel girders. The bottom section of the incline was steeper than the middle section and can be seen dropping away in the distance. Daisy Bank Road was diverted around the site whilst the bridge was being built, with the narrow gauge contractors line running underneath it in a short tunnel, which the men in the foreground are digging away.

were laid in running almost up to Charlton Kings Signal Box and other work on the line included a footbridge over a path close to the junction, a level crossing complete with gates over Sandy Lane and a substantial bridge carrying Daisy Bank Road over the incline about midway up. The electrical equipment installed for operation of the incline gives an indication of the money lavished on the new line. Four new calcining kilns, supplied by Priest Furnaces, were erected on a specially built stone platform at the head of the incline. Dale purchased a Peckett 0-4-0ST *Lightmoor* from Lightmoor Colliery in the Forest of Dean, for use on the new line, plus a couple of second-hand wagons, including one from the Great North of Scotland Railway which retained its lettering. With everything completed, the new operation had begun production by late September 1924. The total cost of the construction and new plant was estimated to be £270,000.

By October 1925, the company was facing bankruptcy. Neither output nor profit had matched the lavish expectations of the

Taken a couple of weeks earlier, the earth bank carrying Daisy Bank Road can be seen through the arch, whilst only one of the steel side girders is in place. The quarry faces can be seen in the background. This was only about the mid-point of the incline, which gives some idea of how high above the town the quarries were situated. *Both Humphrey Household collection, courtesy NRM*

Right: The incline in operation on 10th September 1924, with two wagons about to begin the ascent. Common practice with inclines was to utilise three rails, with the centre rail being common to ascending and descending wagons and a passing loop at mid point, and that was the system adopted here. However, the self-acting principle could not be employed (loaded wagons going down pulling empty wagons back up) because loaded wagons were also coming up, with coal for the calcining kilns. Consequently, the incline was electrically powered, using an 80 hp motor to drive the winding drum at the head of the incline. There was a small yard off to the right of this view, at Southfields Farm, with a locomotive shed and workshops, and the generating plant for operating the incline was also situated here.

Left: The same two wagons are seen nearing the top of the incline, with the main steel haulage cable connected to the chain link coupling and the tension cable passing beneath the wagons. The photographer recalled seeing the ex-Great North of Scotland Railway 3-plank open No. 2185 on numerous occasions, it having been bought by the quarry company as an internal user wagon. Its main use is likely to have been as a barrier wagon on the incline. Coupled behind is a GW 3-plank wagon, with tarpaulin bar and sheet, which is likely to have been loaded with stores for the quarry.

Below: This spectacular view from above the quarry, looking down on the calcining kilns and the whole of the incline, was taken on 19th September 1924. The passing loop was on the shallower section just below Daisy Bank Road bridge. The winding drum at the top of the incline was disused at this date. It had been used during the building of the incline, lowering contractors wagons for tipping. Just to the left of it is the shed housing the winding gear for the Middle Incline of the old tramroad. *All the late Humphrey Household*

company's prospectus, whilst local opposition to the noise and smoke created up on the picturesque hillside by the continual blasting and calcining operations was not helping either. The company staggered on for another year but, in November 1926, work finally ceased. The concern was put up for sale but no interest was shown and an auction of the plant and effects in late 1927 realised a meagre £8,000. The local council bought the Leckhampton Estate, including the hillside and quarry sites, very cheaply and, with the quarry plant, rails and other reminders of the operation removed, the whole area was turned into a public amenity. It was essentially what the local people had been campaigning for and met with great favour.

Today, little remains to be found of this financially disastrous enterprise, apart from the embankment built to lift the line towards the hillside, the course of the incline running down from the quarry and under Daisy Bank Road, and the quarry faces themselves.

As for the GWR, they had probably seen very little extra traffic from the enterprise and the Private Siding Agreement, which had been signed on 27th November 1922, was noted as being '*regarded as terminated*' on 23rd September 1929.

Right: Peckett 0-4-0ST *Lightmoor*, built in 1902 (Works No. 906) for Henry Crawshay's Lightmoor Colliery, near Cinderford, in the Forest of Dean. It seems to have been displaced from its original home by the arrival of a new Peckett 0-4-0ST in 1922 named *Crawshay*, being sold to Leckhampton Quarries shortly afterwards, in January 1923. After the failure of the quarry enterprise, *Lightmoor* was purchased at auction in late 1927 by the contractors Henry Boot & Sons (London) Ltd, of Foxton, Cambridgeshire. They used it on the contract to build the light railway serving Eastwood Cement Ltd's Barrington Cement Works. The engine seems to have then been sold to Eastwood's, because it remained there to work the new line.
Humphrey Household collection, courtesy NRM

Left: *Lightmoor* rattles over the level crossing at Sandy Lane on 2nd September 1924 bound for the exchange sidings at Charlton Kings. Once again, it is obvious from the substantial nature of the crossing gates that no expense was spared in building the line. After just a few years at Eastwood's Barrington Cement Works, around 1930 *Lightmoor* was sold or transferred to Kempston Hardwick Brickworks in Bedfordshire, which was owned by Eastwood Flettons Ltd, a related company, where it survived in use until scrapped in 1944.
The late Humphrey Household

The new track layout at the west end of Charlton Kings station, soon after completion in September 1923, showing the junction for the quarry branch and the exchange sidings. The branch, being privately owned and operated, was gated, with the quarry locomotive's crew needing permission from the Charlton Kings signalman to work into the sidings. The connection with the B&CDR was removed by the end of 1929, with the two exchange sidings lasting a little longer, being taken out by the end of 1932.
M.P. Barnsley collection

DOWDESWELL VIADUCT

From Charlton Kings, the double track route ran through cuttings and on embankments, as it climbed the scarp slope of the Cotswolds on a rising gradient of 1 in 70 that extended for almost four miles. As the line at last left the environs of Cheltenham, it passed to the south of and above Dowdeswell Reservoir. Built in 1886 at the instigation of Cheltenham Corporation, the reservoir has a capacity of 100,000,000 gallons and was provided to keep the town supplied with water. It was formed by the construction of an earth embankment dam across the end of the valley and its building obliterated the original route of the Cheltenham to London coach road. Although still in use today, its role now is as an overflow reservoir and reserve supply only, and at the time of writing it is destined to become the centrepiece of a new country park.

Passing over the twelve brick arches of Dowdeswell Viaduct, the line curved first left and then rightwards, and with the A40 running parallel on the north side, trains plunged into the 384 yard long Sandywell Tunnel. The viaduct was known locally as 'Woodbank Viaduct', while the tunnel was also known as Andoversford Tunnel. Emerging from the eastern portal, the line continued towards Andoversford, the next stopping place.

Above: '51XX' Class prairie No. 4101 passes Dowdeswell Reservoir on its way to Kingham on Saturday 6th October 1962. The view from the train was particularly beautiful at this point, looking down the Chelt Valley with the glistening expanse of Dowdeswell Reservoir below, and today would have made a fine cycle path if only the viaduct had not been needlessly demolished in 1967. *W. Potter*

Right: A view along the track at the same point, with classmate 2-6-2T No. 4161 having just cleared Dowdeswell Viaduct with the 10.50 am Up working to Kingham on 13th October 1962. This was the last day of service and a third carriage was added to cope with the expected extra passengers wanting a final ride on the line. *D.R. Lewis*

DOWDESWELL RESERVOIR & VIADUCT.   JCW 13-39.

The railway in the landscape. The timeless beauty of the Chelt Valley, with a pick-up goods heading for Kingham labouring eastwards up the hill and about to cross Dowdeswell Viaduct, some time in the 1930s. Part of Dowdeswell Reservoir can be seen to the right.
Mrs Freda Gittos collection

Contrasting views in the life of the viaduct. **Above**, the Cotswold Hounds are seen getting ready to set off on a hunt round the Dowdeswell area around 1910. The view is looking up the lane leading to Dowdeswell village. Note the group of lads up on the viaduct watching proceedings. The view, **below**, shows the structure's working life about to end. The last day of services was Saturday 13th October 1962, with the official closure date being the following Monday. '51XX' Class prairie tank No. 4109 is seen crossing with a Kingham-bound service, which has additional coaches attached to cater for the enthusiasts making a final pilgrimage to the line.

Top: Michael Mitchell collection
Bottom: W. Potter, courtesy Kidderminster Railway Museum

The western portal of Sandywell Park Tunnel on 12th August 1914, being guarded against the possibility of sabotage by boy scouts! Whilst such a scene today would surely send both the Scouting movement and the Health & Safety Executive into apoplexy, it may well be that the boys are involved in some sort of officially sanctioned military exercise, with war having broken out in Europe. The fact the photograph carries a date caption obviously had some significance to the scene depicted but of what exactly we cannot now be sure. The tunnel was built in preference to a cutting to retain the view from the adjacent Sandywell Park House. Built for double track from the outset, it included recesses for p-way men at intervals of 105 feet on alternate sides.
Neil Parkhouse collection

On occasions, the relentless rising gradients between Charlton Kings and Andoversford caused problems for eastbound freight workings, and if necessary Up trains would be divided. The front portion would be hauled into Andoversford station and left in the Up sidings, while the engine returned westwards under a 'wrong line' order. Having retrieved the rearmost wagons, the locomotive would then reassemble the two halves of its train at Andoversford before resuming its journey.

ANDOVERSFORD

In operational terms, Andoversford (7 miles 60 chains) was important in that it was the junction for M&SWJR services to Southampton, which diverged southwards onto their own line at the eastern end of the station. No Midland & South Western Junction trains called at Andoversford Great Western station until 1904 – the M&SWJR company having a separate station known as Andoversford & Dowdeswell, which remained in use until 1927. Thereafter, all trains used the GWR station and the M&SWJR station was closed. The latter station was situated on the M&SWJR route, about half a mile beyond the junction. Incidentally, although often referred to as Andoversford Junction, the station itself was always named simply Andoversford.

The station incorporated Up and Down platforms, with the main buildings on the Down (westbound) side and a small waiting shelter on the Up platform. The goods yard was situated on the Down side to the east of the passenger station and there was an Up running loop on the opposite side of the line. The station building was very similar to its counterpart at Cheltenham South, being a gable-roofed structure with a recessed front and a projecting canopy. The Up side building, in contrast, was a simple wooden waiting shelter with a projecting, single-pitch roof.

Internally, the main station building contained the usual range of accommodation for staff and travellers. When viewed from the platform, the booking office was located at the left hand end of the building, while the waiting room was situated more or less in the centre, public access being by means of a doorway within the recessed loggia or waiting area. There was a ladies' waiting room immediately to the right of the general waiting room and the gentlemen's toilets were on the extreme right. A small room at the rear of the building served as additional staff accommodation.

The most prominent feature in Andoversford village is the Andoversford Hotel, seen here on a postcard of circa 1905. Regular livestock markets were held in the hotel's yard, with many of the animals bought and sold, as well as the market clientele, arriving and departing by train.
Neil Parkhouse collection

This early 1930s view of Andoversford Junction station, looking westwards towards Cheltenham, shows it looking distinctly careworn. The fittings, paintwork and ballast all look tired, no doubt a sign of the privations which pervaded the country as a whole at this period. There is still, however, an impressive display of enamel advertising signs to be seen. At the far end of the Up platform, the pre-1935 Andoversford Station Signal Box can be seen. Its replacement was sited a few feet away off the end of the platform and slightly closer to the track. The photograph was taken by C.L. Mowat and appeared in the Locomotive & General Railway Photographs series. *John Alsop collection*

Water columns were available at the east end of the Up platform and the west end of the Down, and there was a standard GWR-type raised water tank at the east end of the Up platform. The goods shed was a simple lock-up beside the station building on the Down platform, while the goods yard contained a full range of facilities for coal, livestock and general merchandise traffic; the yard crane had a capacity of 1 ton 10 cwt.

Other features of interest at Andoversford Junction included a standard Great Western signal cabin at the west end of the Up platform ramp, and an assortment of huts and stores alongside the weigh-house at the rear of the goods yard. The signal cabin was known as Andoversford Station Signal Box to distinguish it from the nearby Junction Box and was of all-timber construction, with a gabled slated roof. Despite its traditional appearance, Andoversford Station Box was of comparatively recent construction, having been erected in 1935 to replace an earlier cabin positioned on a contiguous site.

Andoversford Junction Signal Box was situated just 15 chains along the line, near the point of bifurcation between the Banbury and M&SWJR routes. The box had been opened in conjunction with the Midland & South Western Junction line in 1891, and it was a wooden structure with a gable roof and nine-pane window frames. Internally, the Junction Box contained a 35-lever frame with 34 working levers and one white-painted 'spare'.

Andoversford was one of the stations selected by the Great Western for development as a Country Lorry Centre and, as such, it served a small but distinct hinterland. In the late 1930s, collections and deliveries were made within a radius of about four miles around the station. The GWR lorries ran northwards to Charlton Abbots, via Syreford, Sevenhampton and Brockhampton, while on the south side of the railway, the country lorries served places such as Shipton Solers, Shipton Oliffe, Compton Abdale and Hazleton. The 1938 GWR publication *Towns, Villages & Outlying Works Etc* reveals that Andoversford residents did not enjoy a free cartage service but local collections and deliveries could be made by railway porter.

In later years, these arrangements were modified following the introduction of 'zonal' collection and delivery services. Under this system, British Railways road vehicles were based in a limited number of 'railheads' and 'sub-railheads', and small consignments were then collected and delivered by road. Full load traffic was, however, still handled at Andoversford and most of the other local stations, albeit with amended cartage boundaries. In practice, this new system meant that parcels and 'smalls' traffic was collected and delivered by railway motor vehicles from Cheltenham or Bourton-on-the-Water, while large consignments continued to be carted from Andoversford, Notgrove and Stow-on-the-Wold.

In the early 1900s, Andoversford had a staff of eight, and it issued around 9,000 tickets. This figure had declined to about 6,000 bookings per annum by the early 1930s, falling to about 2,000 tickets each year at the end of the decade. In 1938, for instance, 2,172 ordinary tickets were sold, together with just two seasons. Goods traffic declined from 11,054 tons in 1913, to an average of around 6,000 tons per year during the later 1930s. Traffic from the former M&SWJR station at Andoversford & Dowdeswell was included with that from the GWR station after 1926 but this revised arrangement could not hide the steady loss of traffic during the 1920s and 1930s.

As mentioned in Chapter Two, the section of line between Cheltenham and Andoversford had a curious history, having been authorised in the 1860s as part of the East Gloucestershire Railway. East Gloucestershire documents reveal that 'considerable progress' had been made at Andoversford by the end of 1865, although it remains unclear how advanced the EGR earthworks were at the time of their abandonment. On balance, it seems likely that the formation had been substantially completed between the eastern end of Sandywell Tunnel and the site of Andoversford station, and most of the earlier cuttings and embankments were probably utilised by the Banbury & Cheltenham company.

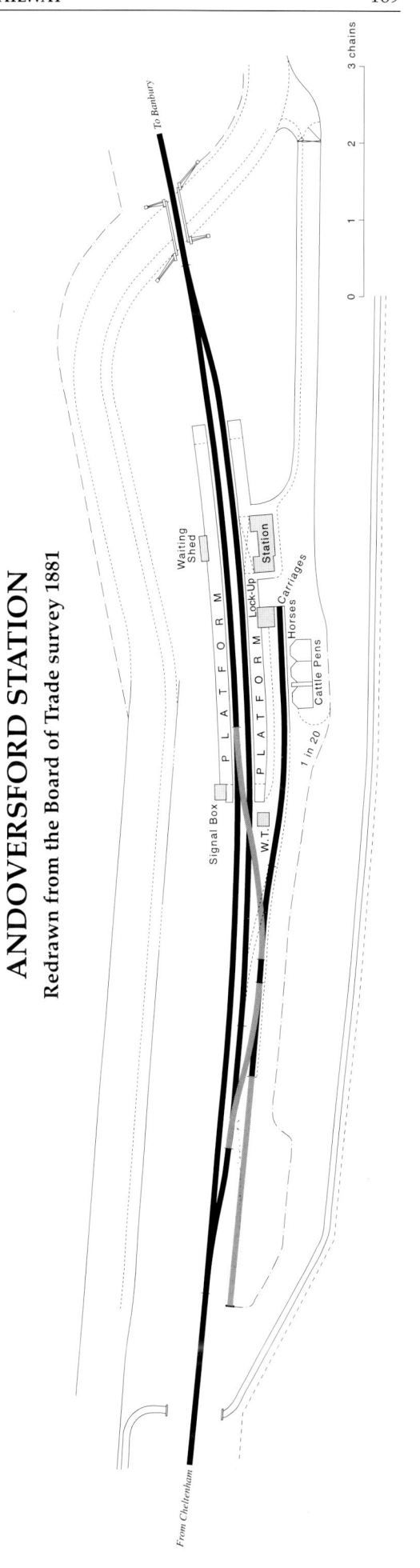

ANDOVERSFORD STATION
Redrawn from the Board of Trade survey 1881

Top and left: Two examples of Finch family private owner wagons. H. Finch & Son No. 14 was supplied by the Glos RC&W Co. in April 1898, whilst William J. Finch No. 1 dates from October 1906, suggesting the 'Son' had taken over the business in the interim. Both vehicles were painted red, with white lettering shaded black. This was a fairly long lived concern; H. Finch was in business by 1894 and William was still trading in 1939.

Courtesy Gloucestershire Record Office

This view looking east towards Andoversford Junction was taken on 11th September 1935, showing the B&CDR line bearing off to the left and the ex-M&SWJR line to the right. The Junction Home bracket signal stands just in front of the bridge carrying the line over the main A40 road. Andoversford Junction Signal Box can be seen in the distance. *John Alsop collection*

ANDOVERSFORD STATION

Andoversford station and junction falls across the corners of four sheets of the 25 inch OS. Having joined them all back together, this is how it appeared on the Third edition OS of 1921.

Neil Parkhouse collection, Crown copyright reserved

Above: Andoversford Station Signal Box and the western approaches to the station in 1962. Beyond the Outer Home signal, the line drops away towards Sandywell Park Tunnel and Charlton Kings. The signal box appears to be switched out as all the signals are 'off', whilst a solitary steel mineral wagon inhabits the yard. *Joe Moss collection, courtesy Roger Carpenter*

Left: A close-up of the Up Inner Home signal, seen centre right in the previous view. It also carried a fixed distant arm for the signals controlling the junction of the Kingham and M&SWJR lines. *Bob Brown collection*

Right: Looking east along the platforms towards the junction in the mid 1950s, with the waiting shelter now devoid of its stove-pipe; presumably heating was no longer supplied for waiting passengers in the winter months. On the right is the brick-built goods shed which was sited at the end of the cattle dock siding. *Bob Brown collection*

The main station building, seen here in 1962, was unusual in that its brickwork was cement rendered, giving it a rather dull look. Note the 25 mph speed restriction sign in the 4 foot. *Joe Moss collection, courtesy Roger Carpenter*

A '43XX' Class mogul shunts the yard at Andoversford, in this circa 1960 view looking west towards Cheltenham. *The Lens of Sutton Collection*

Left: A frontal view of Andoversford Station Signal Box, a GWR standard wooden cabin which was a replacement structure dating from November 1935. Behind it is the water tank which supplied the columns on both Up and Down platforms. *Bob Brown collection*

Right: A northwards facing view of the box, showing the steps and the entrance porch. In later years it was painted all over Western Region cream. *The Lens of Sutton Collection*

'51XX' Class prairie tank No. 4101 pulls into Andoversford with a Cheltenham to Kingham service in 1962. *R.K. Blencowe*

Left: Ex-GWR '45XX' Class small prairie No. 5514 arrives at Andoversford from Charlton Kings with a train for Kingham in the late 1950s. The porter waits with a single small parcel to hand to the guard.
David Lawrence, courtesy Hugh Davies

Right: A close-up view of the standard GWR water column which stood at the end of the Down platform. In the left background are the cattle pens which would once have been busy with livestock traffic to and from the cattle markets held in the village at the Andoversford Hotel. *Bob Brown ollection*

Left: An unidentified Collett '51XX' Class 2-6-2 prairie tank stands in the station with a Cheltenham-bound train in June 1960, hauling the usual two coaches which sufficed for the passenger service by this date.
R.K. Blencowe

Right: The junction end of the station in 1962. By this date, the M&SWJR line to the right had closed completely to through traffic, although the small goods yard at Andoversford & Dowdeswell station, about half a mile on from here alongside the A40 road, remained open until October 1962.
Joe Moss collection, courtesy Roger Carpenter

Left: The signalman stands ready to exchange the token with the crew of a train taking the M&SWJR route. Andoversford Junction Signal Box was provided in 1891, at the expense of the M&SWJR, in order to control the converging traffic between the two lines. The relationship at the outset was certainly not a happy one, with the GWR refusing to allow the M&SWJR use of its stations from here to Lansdown Junction. It was not until October 1904 that the GWR allowed use of its station and subsequently, following the 1923 Grouping, the M&SWJR station at Andoversford & Dowdeswell was closed to passengers on 1st April 1927. *R.K. Blencowe*

Right: The fireman of a Cheltenham-bound train leans out to exchange the token with the Andoversford Junction signalman. Unusually, the Down Inner Home and Distant signal was sited on the inside of the curve approaching the junction. This was probably due to the limited spacing between the Down running line and adjacent sidings at this point, which prevented it being placed on the outside of the curve.
R.K. Blencowe

THE BANBURY & CHELTENHAM DIRECT RAILWAY

The Banbury & Cheltenham route diverged eastwards at the Banbury end of the station, and this left a large section of East Gloucestershire embankment in the middle of a field to the south-east of the station, which was in the wrong position *vis-á-vis* the B&CDR. The isolated earthwork was therefore left *in situ* and it has remained to this day as a memorial to the abortive East Gloucestershire scheme. Other relics of the East Gloucestershire works included a row of unfinished shafts to the north of Sandywell Tunnel – the route chosen for the original EGR bore being on a slightly diverging alignment in relation to the Banbury & Cheltenham Direct line.

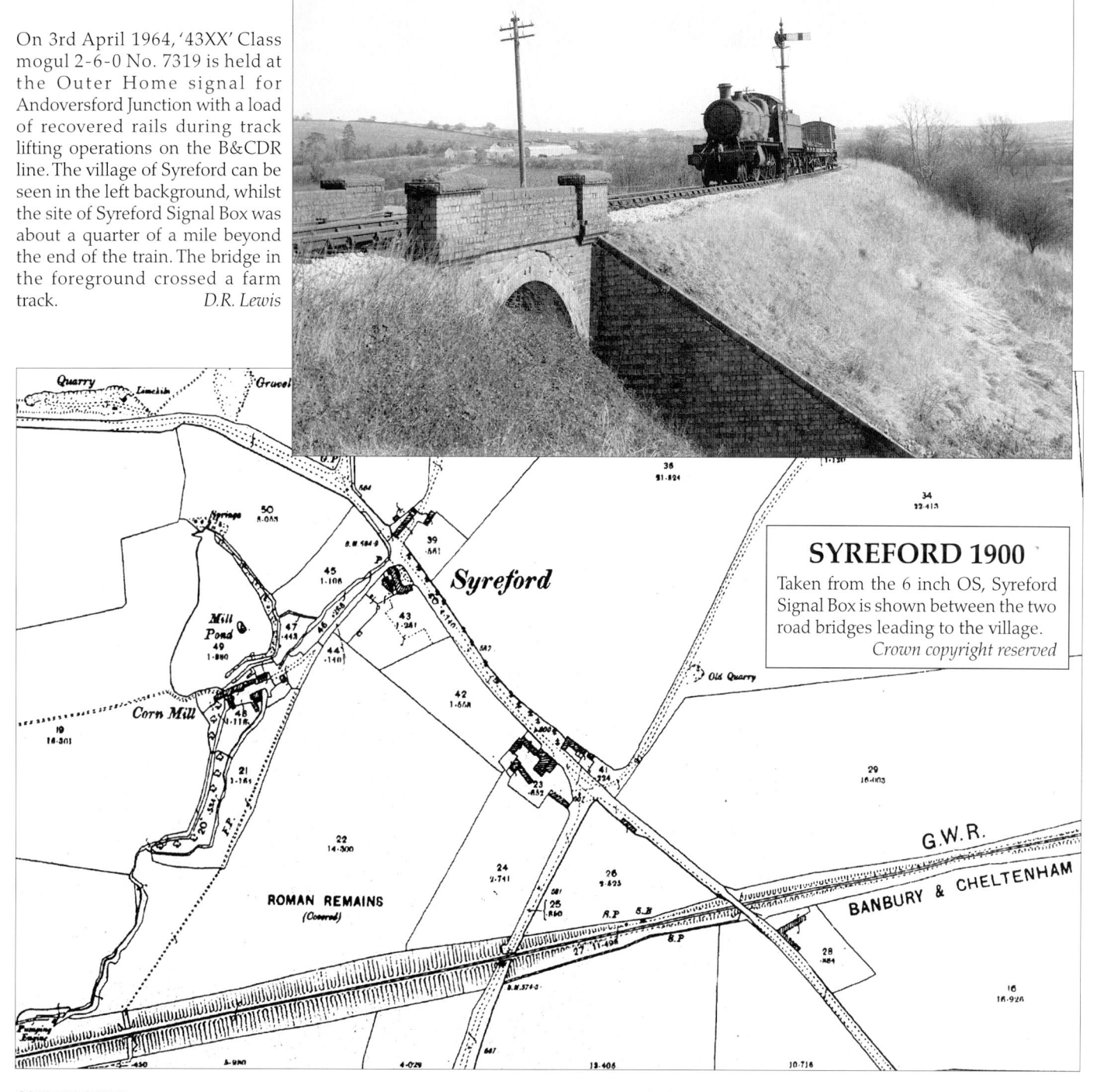

On 3rd April 1964, '43XX' Class mogul 2-6-0 No. 7319 is held at the Outer Home signal for Andoversford Junction with a load of recovered rails during track lifting operations on the B&CDR line. The village of Syreford can be seen in the left background, whilst the site of Syreford Signal Box was about a quarter of a mile beyond the end of the train. The bridge in the foreground crossed a farm track. *D.R. Lewis*

SYREFORD 1900
Taken from the 6 inch OS, Syreford Signal Box is shown between the two road bridges leading to the village. *Crown copyright reserved*

SYREFORD

On leaving Andoversford, Up trains crossed the busy A40 road on a girder bridge with a span of 35 feet, beyond which the M&SWJR line diverged south-eastwards from the Banbury 'main line'. The route became single track a little way beyond the junction and, having crossed the River Colne, trains set off along a length of embankment as they continued their ascent towards the Cotswold uplands on a 1 in 60 rising gradient. On 17th October 1899, a signal box was opened at Syreford (also possibly spelt 'Sierford' in some records), which was only three quarters of a mile from Andoversford. Little is known of it and this relatively short-lived cabin was closed on 29th April 1924, after a life of barely twenty-five years.

It is not entirely clear why a signal box should have been considered necessary at Syreford, the likeliest explanation being that it provided an additional element of safety when loose-coupled iron ore trains were descending the 1 in 60 towards Andoversford Junction. Perhaps significantly, the box was closed during a period of severe depression in the iron and steel industry. Thereafter, the eastern approaches to Andoversford were protected by an outer home signal, sited 664 yards from Andoversford Junction Signal Box, and a fixed distant near the site of the abandoned Syreford Box.

A deserted Notgrove station around 1930, looking west towards Andoversford and Cheltenham. This view graphically demonstrates the remoteness of the location, Notgrove village itself being a mile and a quarter away. Note the milk churns on the Down platform and the Cotswold stone walls in place of the usual platform fencing. *Neil Parkhouse collection*

NOTGROVE

The area traversed by the railway was unusually rich in antiquities, the surrounding hills being littered with long barrows, tumuli and other monuments, while the valleys and other more sheltered spots were invariably associated with Roman remains. A small villa was sited on the north side of the railway near Andoversford station, while a further Roman site was discovered west of Syreford.

Cuttings alternated with embankments as the route climbed steadily towards its summit – the 700 foot contour being passed as the line crossed the A436 road on a single span bridge. Beyond, the railway climbed still higher onto the Cotswolds; passing beneath two minor road bridges in succession, the line reached its 784 foot summit near Salperton, after which the route continued eastwards on a further series of cuttings and embankments.

Salperton, a tiny village, could be glimpsed to the right of the line as trains commenced their descent. It consisted of little more than a cluster of cottages, the church of All Saints and a Jacobean mansion in a park of 83 acres. The church and mansion were said to be haunted by several ghosts, including the spectral figure of a young woman with long dark hair, who could sometimes be seen wandering in the church yard before disappearing into a convenient grave. In similar vein, the church contained a mysterious immovable stain, which was said to have been the blood of an unfortunate murder victim!

Running through surprisingly remote upland, with an

Opposite page: Looking west from the B4068 road bridge at the east end of Notgrove station just after closure in 1962. Notgrove was not quite the highest point on the line, the summit being situated in a deep cutting near Salperton, about one and a half miles to the west of the station. If one stands on this spot today (the bridge has been replaced by a road embankment, although supposedly the bridge still exists beneath the soil), it is easy to appreciate just how remote and windswept the station must have seemed to the traveller. The layout here was extensively remodelled in 1906; the works included the lengthening of the passing loop at both ends, amending the siding connections and the complete re-signalling of the station. In his letter to the GWR dated 6th June that year, Colonel Yorke of the Board of Trade sanctioned the use of the new works subject to the condition that no mineral train should be brought to a stand at the Down Home signal (on a 1 in 60 inclination) without a locomotive attached at the rear. In other words, no mineral train was allowed to leave Bourton unassisted without the road being clear into the loop at Notgrove. *Joe Moss collection, courtesy Roger Carpenter*

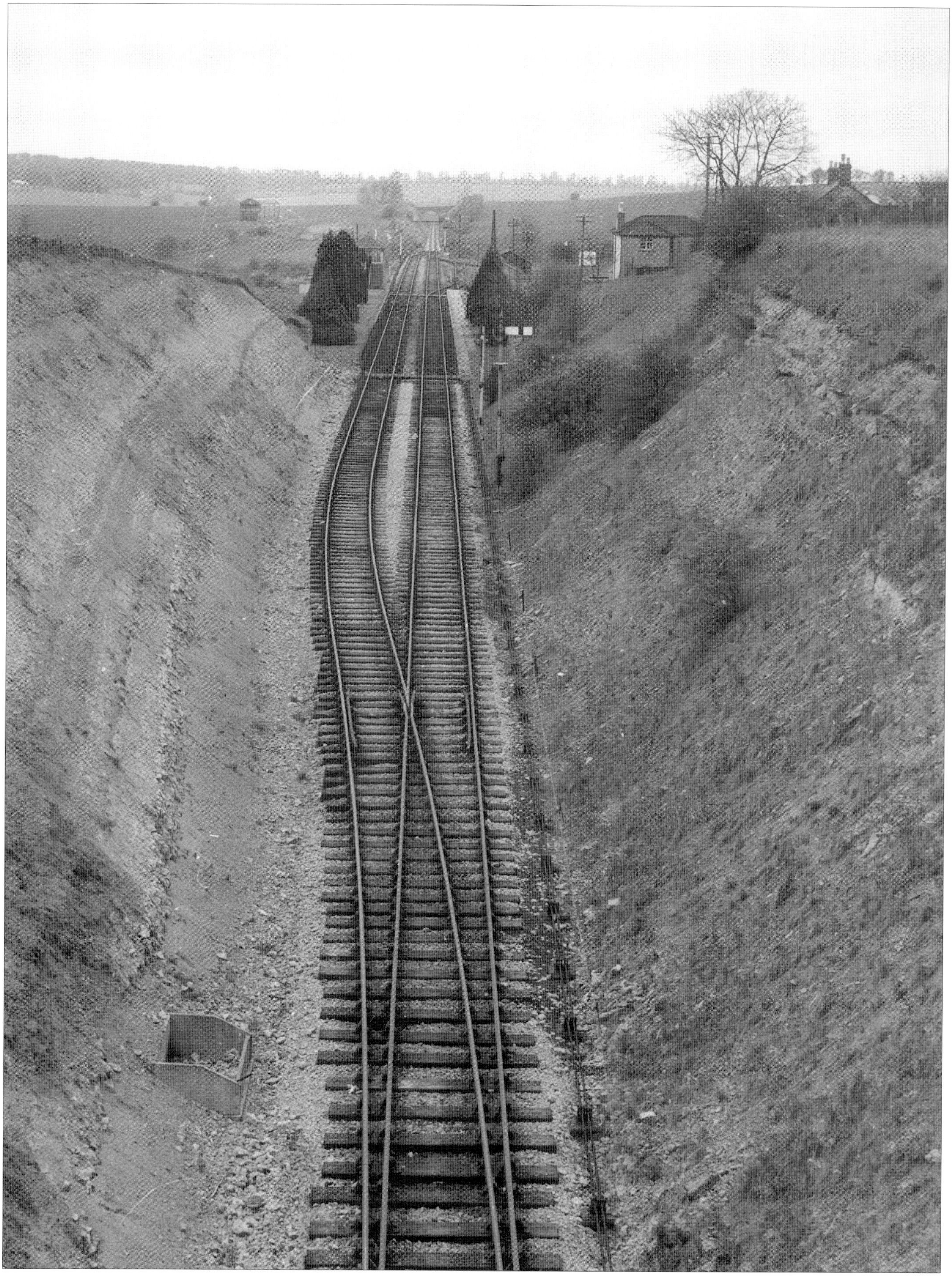

BR Mk. 1 coaching stock was often seen on the line from around 1959. The Kingham to Cheltenham service seen here calling at Notgrove late one summer afternoon in 1962 is composed of two Mk. 1 coaches, in the charge of an unidentified '51XX' Class 2-6-2T. *R.K. Blencowe*

The view from the signal box steps on 3rd March 1962 (compare with the picture on page 70), with both platforms still well maintained. In the distance, the standard tubular post Up Starting signal was a 1952 replacement for the old lattice post one. *E. Wilmshurst*

average elevation of 750-800 feet above mean sea level, Up trains passed beneath a tall brick overbridge before coming to rest in the isolated station at Notgrove (12 miles 38 chains from Cheltenham St. James).

The facilities provided here consisted of a lengthy crossing loop, with a two-siding goods yard on the Up side. There was an underline bridge with a single span of 8 feet at the west end of the station, while the B4068 road was carried across the line on a lofty triple arched brick bridge beyond the east end of the platforms. The main station building was sited on the Up platform and there was a small waiting shelter on the Down, or westbound platform. Pedestrian access between the Up and Down sides of the station was by means of barrow crossings at each end of the platforms.

Notgrove was provided with a simple wooden station building which was, in most respects, similar to the building at Charlton Kings. This single-storey, timber framed structure was clad in horizontal weather boarding; it had a slated, gable roof and its overall dimensions at ground level were approximately 30 feet by 10 feet wide. The gentlemen's toilets were accommodated in a small projecting wing at the west end. The internal layout of the station building was entirely conventional, in that a central waiting room was flanked on one side by the ticket office and on the other by the ladies' toilets.

The Down side building was a simple wooden shelter, with a single-pitched roof that was carried forward to form a modest platform canopy. The platform frontage was filled by a glass and timber screen, presumably intended to shield waiting travellers from the harsh Cotswold winters. A two-storey, hip-roofed house in the station approach provided domestic accommodation for the station master and his family. The platforms were backed, for most of their length, by Cotswold stone walls rather than wooden fencing – a most unusual feature in England, although such walls were relatively common on many of the Irish railways.

A close up of Notgrove Down Home signal and the road bridge spanning the cutting taken in May 1952. The view is looking west.
J.F. Russell-Smith, courtesy National Railway Museum

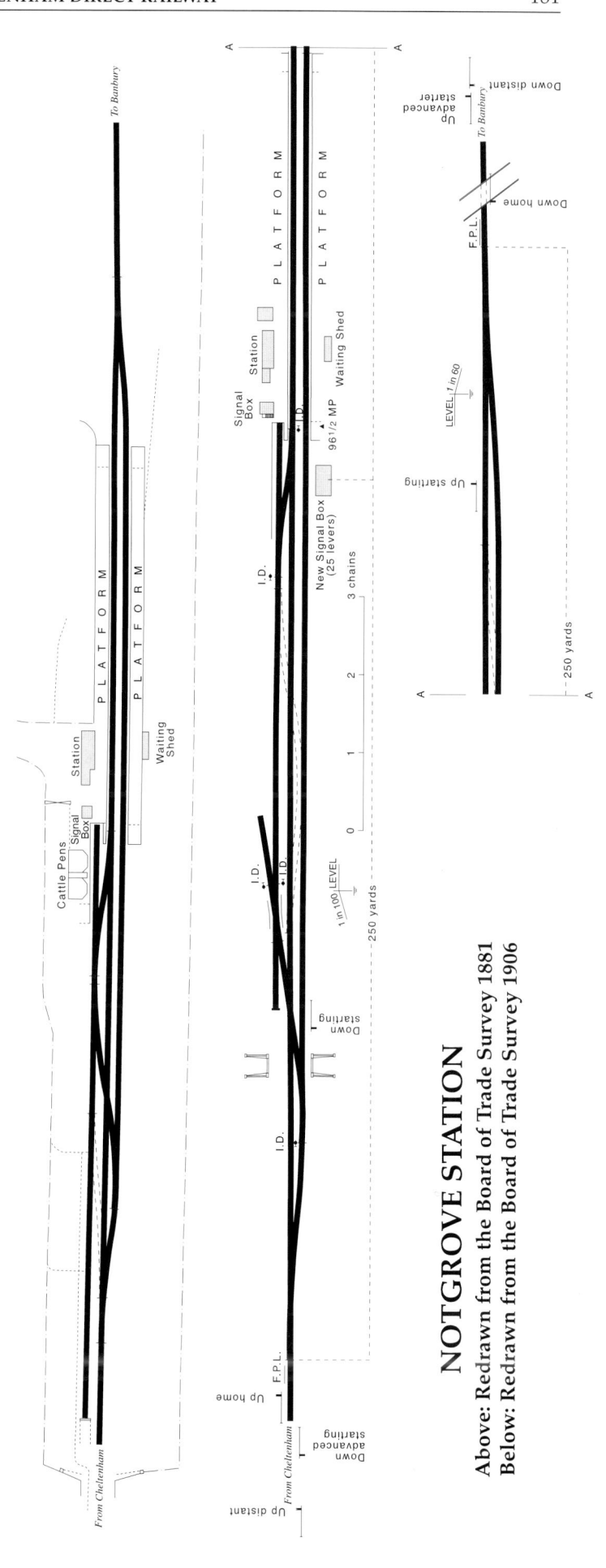

NOTGROVE STATION

Above: Redrawn from the Board of Trade Survey 1881
Below: Redrawn from the Board of Trade Survey 1906

Above: A 1962 study of the western end of the station. There was a sharp dip of 1 in 60 away from the platforms in this direction, just past the Down Starting signal. The standard GWR brick-built signal box was a 1906 replacement for the original cabin, which had been sited about where the photographer was standing. On the right are the end loading dock, cattle pens and corrugated iron goods shed. *Joe Moss, courtesy Roger Carpenter*

Above: At least four coal merchants are known to have operated from Notgrove at various times but it is not known if any of them had the station name painted on their wagons. H. Burlingham & Co. of Evesham was one of them and they also had an office at Bourton-on-the-Water, so the 1896-built 4-plank wagon seen here may well have appeared on the line at some stage. Burlingham & Co. are known to have been in operation for the two decades leading up to the First World War.

Above & right: Similarly, the South Wales & Cannock Chase Coal & Coke Co. Ltd of Worcester had offices at Notgrove, Andoversford and Bourton. The 1892 wagon is unusual in being in plain varnished wood, with black lettering shaded red. By the time that wagon No. 353 was built five months later, the livery was noted as red, with white lettering shaded black. The company seem to have ceased serving these stations around 1910, although they remained in business for many more years.
All Glos RC&W Co. collection, courtesy Gloucestershire Record Office

The track layout at Notgrove incorporated a loop siding, which was linked to the Up and Down running lines by trailing connections at each end, together with a dead end siding for coal and other forms of mileage traffic. A short spur extended eastwards from the east end of the main loop siding and this terminated in a loading dock at the end of the Up platform. The loading bank was equipped with cattle pens and a gable-roofed store that functioned as a goods shed. There was, in addition, a small weigh house and an 8-ton yard crane.

The crossing loop, originally around 16 chains in length, was extended to 23 chains in April 1906, in connection with the programme of improvements carried out on the Banbury & Cheltenham Direct line at that time. The extended loop had a length of approximately 1,350 feet, this being sufficient to cross two sixty-wagon freight trains, together with their engines and brake vans.

The station was a block post and crossing place on the single line, the loop being fully signalled with the usual Up and Down home and starting signals. There were, in addition, Up and Down advanced starting signals, together with fixed distant signals in each direction. The Up home signal was a bracketed assembly carrying an additional siding arm, while the Up starting signal was, for many years, a rare example of a Great Western lattice post signal.

The signal box, a standard Great Western hip-roofed structure, dating from April 1906, was situated to the west of the Down platform on the south side of the line. It was a brick and timber structure, with characteristic five-paned windows and a low-pitched, slated roof. Internally, Notgrove Signal Box was equipped with a 25-lever frame containing 16 working levers and nine spaces. Prior to 1906, the station had been signalled from a gabled cabin on the Up platform.

Like many other country stations, Notgrove was designed as a convenient railhead for a group of villages and hamlets, including Salperton (2 miles to the west), Westfield (half a mile to the north) and Notgrove itself (2 miles to the southeast). The station was originally called 'Notgrove & Westfield' and, indeed, the station building was sited on the Westfield side of the line, in which position it was less convenient for the inhabitants of Notgrove. The name was officially shortened to 'Notgrove' on 24th June 1896.

As Notgrove boasted a relatively powerful 8-ton yard crane, the station was sometimes called upon to deal with furniture containers, timber, drain pipes, or other large and bulky consignments that could not easily be handled at neighbouring Bourton-on-the-Water. In the late 1930s, parcels and 'smalls' traffic for Notgrove, and the surrounding area, was collected and delivered by railway lorries based at Bourton-on-the-Water, although smaller items could also be collected or delivered within a radius

'51XX' Class prairie tank No. 5182 leaves Notgrove *en route* for Kingham with the 10.50am Up service from Cheltenham on 7th February 1962. Note how the maturing conifers have softened the station's appearance from its earlier years. *Ben Ashworth*

A detailed view of the wooden station building, which dated from the opening of the line in 1881, taken just after closure in 1962. Although not definitely confirmed, it may well have been a Gloucester RC&W Co. product. It is still adorned with a variety of posters, amongst which are examples advertising camping coaches, cheap day return tickets and the 'Condor' overnight freight service between London and Glasgow. Quite how effective the latter was to the line's users we shall never know!   *Joe Moss, courtesy Roger Carpenter*

of half a mile of the station by railway porter, no charge being levied for this service. In British Railways days, collections and deliveries were carried out by 'zonal' lorries from Cheltenham.

On a minor point of interest, it has sometimes been stated that Notgrove was 'the highest through station on the Great Western system'. In reality, several stations on the Welsh lines absorbed at the Grouping had very much higher elevations; one thinks, for example, of places such as Torpantau on the Brecon & Merthyr section. Notgrove was sited at an elevation of approximately 750 feet above mean sea level, which was considerably lower than Dolygaer, Torpantau, Craigynos, Pantydwr, Arenig and other stations in Wales, though by English standards, it must be admitted that this Gloucestershire station was a surprisingly bleak and windswept place.

Traffic levels here were modest in the extreme, around 6,000 tickets a year being issued during the Edwardian period, falling to only 2,282 bookings in 1929 and 1,412 in the following year. The loss of passenger traffic continued during the 1930s and, in 1938, Notgrove sold just 770 tickets; there were no season ticket holders at any time during the 1930s. The amount of goods traffic handled in 1929 was 4,542 tons, though in the following year the total rose to 6,233 tons; in 1938, the annual total was 2,748 tons. Coal traffic was fairly constant, at about 1,300 tons per annum, while livestock traffic typically consisted of about 160 wagon loads a year during the 1930s.

| TRAFFIC DEALT WITH AT NOTGROVE ||||||
YEAR	STAFF	RECEIPTS (£)	TICKETS	PARCELS	GOODS (TONS)
1913	4	2,667	6,229	4,342	6,840
1923	4	4,031	5,216	5,522	6,962
1930	4	4,416	1,412	17,182	6,223
1937	4	2,045	709	2,188	3,467
1938	4	1,625	770	2,071	2,748

The figure for parcels despatched in 1930 merits some comment, being three times the total for 1923 and measured against a general drop off in trade shown in all the other totals. The massive increase is seen through 1929-31, the most likely explanation being agricultural goods. The GWR classified small animals such as lambs and chickens in consignments of less than 2 cwt as parcels, and it may well be the establishment of a chicken farm in the area at this period resulted in the despatch of large quantities of eggs or boxes of chicks. As the figures show, by 1937 sleepy normality had returned and whatever activity had been responsible for the sudden upturn in parcels traffic had either failed or moved away.

A regular performer on the line in the late 1950s and early 1960s was '45XX' Class small prairie No. 4573, seen here at Notgrove circa 1960 with a Kingham-bound train. The station master has come out to greet its arrival, whilst the signalman ambles along the platform with the Notgrove to Bourton-on-the-Water token in his hand. Note he is not even looking at the train but heading to the point where he expects the driver to halt the locomotive, where the token exchange will then take place. Having collected the Andoversford to Notgrove token in return, he will then return to the box and insert it into the electric token apparatus to clear the section, before pulling off the Down Starter allowing No. 4573 to proceed on its way to Bourton-on-the-Water. Note the Cotswold stone walling behind the platforms.

R.K. Blencowe

Right: Notgrove Signal Box viewed from a train pulling in to the station on 22nd September 1962. Note the line already beginning to dip down the slope towards Bourton-on-the-Water under the road bridge in the extreme left distance.

Below centre: Collett '51XX' Class prairie tank No. 4109 arrives with the 1.15 pm ex-Kingham service, bound for Cheltenham St. James, on 10th October 1962.

Bottom left: A few minutes later, having exchanged tokens, No. 4109 departs on its way under the watchful eye of the Notgrove signalman. Note the locomotive is in fully lined BR green passenger livery.
All Paul Strong

Above: This view from one of the rear windows of a locomotive approaching Notgrove with a train from Bourton gives a clear indication of the steep climb and the height of the road bridge. The tubular posted Down Home signal is on the left of this view, taken on 22nd September 1962. *Paul Strong*

A 'Metro' tank, with a Down train consisting of five 6-wheeled carriages, leaves Bourton-on-the-Water for Cheltenham sometime during the first decade of the 20th century. A long straight section of embankment lifted the line out of the village, past the houses forming the area known as Lansdown and across the Fosse Way, the bridge parapets being just discernible in the left distance. This fascinating view, taken from the tower of the 18th century parish church of St. Lawrence, also shows The Mousetrap Inn immediately below the centre of the train. This popular hostelry, originally called The Lansdown Inn, was reputedly renamed as railway gangers would have extended lunch breaks and risked being caught, as there was only one door in and one out! *Bob Brown collection*

BOURTON-ON-THE-WATER

From Notgrove, the railway continued its descent through a tract of typical Cotswold countryside. In the summer months, these Gloucestershire uplands were an idyllic place for walking or riding but in the depths of winter the landscape became cold and sombre, with a pervading feeling of isolation. Reaching the Windrush Valley, the line entered a more intimate landscape, the river itself being only a short distance away on the north side of the line. On a footnote, the name 'Windrush' is thought to have been derived from *Gwen-risc* – a Celtic river name meaning the white stream or morass – a reference, perhaps, to abundant white flowers which may once have bloomed along the course of the river.

Nearing Bourton-on-the-Water, the railway crossed from the south side of the Windrush to the north bank, and having passed a Roman site and crossed the A429 road on a girder bridge, the route curved north-eastwards into Bourton-on-the-Water station (17 miles 44 chains). This was another crossing station, with Up and Down platforms, and a single-storey station building on the Down side. A minor road crossed the line on a single-span, brick arch bridge at the west end of the station, and there was a three-siding goods yard on the Down side of the running lines.

When first opened by the West Midland Railway in 1862, Bourton-on-the-Water had boasted an ornate 'Tudor' style station building with decorative timber framing but photographs suggest that this distinctive structure had become somewhat decrepit by the 1930s and, perhaps for this reason, the Great Western erected an entirely new Cotswold stone station building in 1938. Although the replacement building was of modern construction, it was solidly built in traditional materials, in the familiar Cotswold architectural style. There was a projecting canopy on the platform side of the building and three squat chimney stacks protruded through the stone-slated roof.

Internally, the new station building incorporated the usual booking office and waiting room facilities, together with toilets and a parcels room. The parcels office was at the left hand end of the building (when viewed from the platform), while the general waiting room was sited towards the centre of the main block. The gentlemen's toilets and ladies' waiting room occupied the area between the parcels office and waiting room, and the ticket office was situated towards the right hand end of the building. An adjoining room to the right of the ticket office functioned as a goods office.

The Up side building was a modest, timber-framed structure, with a single-pitch roof that sloped towards the rear wall an at angle of approximately 20 degrees. This small but attractive waiting room featured a fully-glazed frontage and it was entered by means of a single door at the west end. The building measured approximately 25 feet by 7 feet

The approach to Bourton-on-the-Water station, looking westwards from Station Road Bridge past the Up Inner Home signal towards Notgrove, on a lazy summer's day in the mid 1950s. The long sweeping curve by Lansdown actually took the line away from the village, which lay off to the left. Note the vegetable patch on the right, the work of one of the station staff no doubt. *Joe Moss, courtesy Roger Carpenter*

6 inches at ground level; there was a brick chimney stack at the east end and the doorway was graced by a miniature platform canopy.

The layout at Bourton-on-the-Water was relatively simple. There was a lengthy crossing loop, which was extended from 16 chains to 22 chains in the early 1900s. There was, at one time, a connection between the Up loop line and the goods yard but this facility was removed around 1932, when the Great Western modified the pointwork at each end of the crossing loop.

The goods shed siding was arranged as a loop, with access from the running lines at each end, while the two mileage sidings for coal and other wagon load traffic were dead end roads. The goods shed siding was extended at each end, a short headshunt being provided at the east end, whereas a much longer extension at the west end served cattle pens and an end loading dock at the rear of the Down platform.

In the late 1930s, the eastern end of the headshunt formed a convenient place to stable Bourton's popular camping coach. This vehicle could be hired throughout the summer from April to October by holidaymakers who purchased ordinary return tickets in advance of their stay and it could be booked for periods of one or two weeks. Towels, bed linen, cutlery and other essentials were provided by the railway company but people staying in the coach had to use the nearby station building for their ablution facilities.

A view of Station Road bridge around 1960, with '51XX' Class 2-6-2T No. 4109 running into the Up loop on a service from Cheltenham. *A.W.V. Mace collection, courtesy Milepost*

The original station building is seen towards the end of its life in this circa 1930 view, **above**, looking east from Station Road Bridge. Note the Down Starting signal with its lattice post which, along with other similar examples on the B&CDR route, had been replaced by the early 1950s by a standard tubular post example. The seemingly unnecessary 'kink' in the running lines was probably a legacy of the station's original role as a terminus, a slight realignment being required when extending beyond the station's bounds on to Cheltenham. **Below**, a turn of the century study of the original Bourton-on-the-Water Railway station building. This distinctive style of timber-framed architecture was adopted as a standard design by the West Midland Railway in the 1860s (Kidderminster was a notable example), which may well have influenced the buildings seen here and at Stow-on-the-Wold. Note the cattle wagons in the yard.
Top: The Lens of Sutton Collection; Bottom: Neil Parkhouse collection

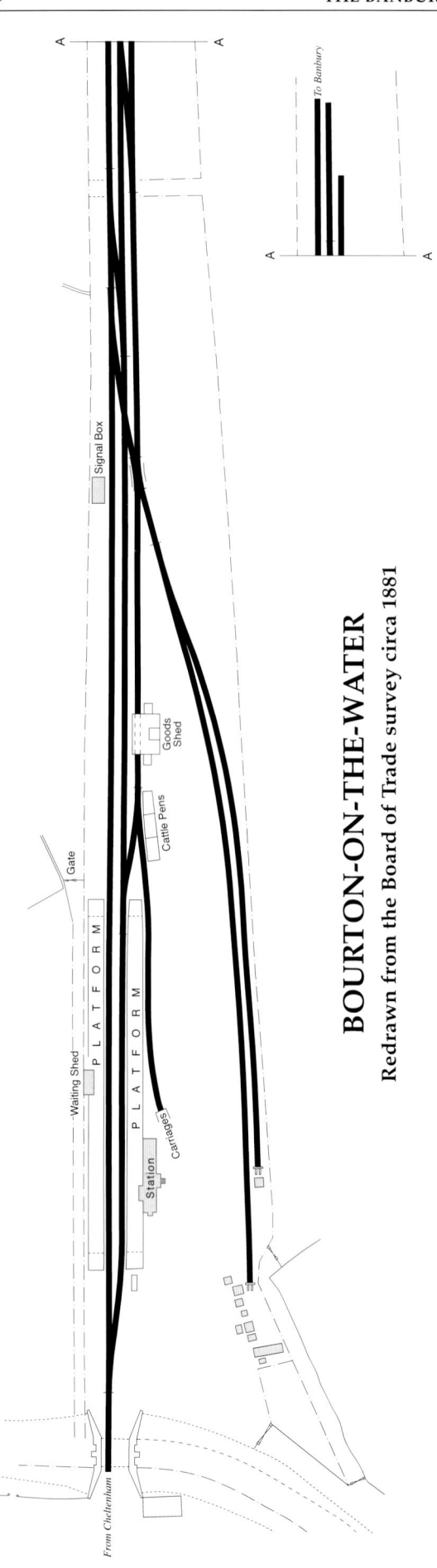

Three examples of privately owned coal wagons belonging to merchants based at Bourton-on-the-Water station. George Clifford, **top**, also had offices at Shipton-under-Wychwood. Wagon No. 31, supplied in September 1902, was painted red with white letters shaded black. Chas. Collett & Sons (later Ltd), **centre and bottom**, were in business from the early 1900s at least and the company was still trading in 1939. They were a small concern, trading solely from the yard at Bourton and there was a nine year gap between the construction of wagons Nos. 5 and 6. The wagons were in an attractive chocolate brown livery, with white letters shaded black. The strapping was also picked out in black.

All courtesy Gloucestershire Record Office

BOURTON-ON-THE-WATER
Redrawn from the Board of Trade survey circa 1881

Two GWR official views at Bourton-on-the-Water showing the platform and forecourt elevations of the new replacement station building, taken on 7th September 1938. It was positively austere compared to its predecessor, whilst even the canopy was basic by GWR standards. It did, however, blend with the local architecture, even down to the stone slates on the roof. *Both Bob Brown collection*

Looking eastwards from the embankment carrying Station Road up to the bridge at the approach to the forecourt in 1946, prior to the construction of the extension to the eastern end of the station building in 1947. The weighbridge is on the right and this view makes an interesting comparison with that on page 89. To the right of the end loading dock is one of the grounded coach bodies used for storage of animal feeds, which were replaced by a concrete provender store. The wartime buildings on the right were used for the manufacture of bomb crates. Coal and agricultural products are still the main commodities handled. *Joe Moss, courtesy Roger Carpenter*

Looking eastwards through the station in the direction of Banbury on 30th May 1958. *R.M. Casserley*

Bourton-on-the-Water Signal Box was a standard Great Western brick and timber design, with a hipped roof and characteristic five-pane 'high visibility' windows, which were supposed to give signalmen an unimpeded view. The signal box was built in 1912 in place of an earlier structure, which had been sited in roughly the same position. Internally, the new box contained a 26-lever frame. As mentioned above, the single line section between Notgrove and Bourton-on-the-Water was worked by electric train staff, and this mode of operation was also in force between Bourton-on-the-Water and Stow-on-the-Wold.

The goods shed, to the east of the station building on the Down side, was a small, timber structure with an internal loading platform and a projecting checker's office at its west end; the loading platform was equipped with a 1 ton 10 cwt fixed hand crane. The building sported a low-pitched, gable roof, that was swept down on its south side to form a protective canopy over the cart entrance, while the walls were clad in vertical matchboarding, the joins between each narrow plank being covered by thin laths or 'cover strips'.

Other buildings in the goods yard included some ramshackle wooden huts used by the local coal merchants and a distinctive brick weigh house with a pyramidal roof. The weigh house was similar to those found along the Oxford, Worcester & Wolverhampton main line and it is therefore reasonable to assume that it was an original West Midland Railway structure, dating back to the opening of the Bourton-on-the-Water branch in 1862. The weighing equipment, on the other hand, was definitely not original, a new 20-ton weighbridge having been installed by the GWR in connection with the introduction of motor vehicles.

In World War Two, a field immediately to the south of the goods yard became the site of a makeshift collection of Nissen huts and other temporary buildings. These were used as workshops for the manufacture of bomb crates, while after the war the site was taken over by a firm known as 'Sona', which made kitchenware.

In later years, a traders' store was erected in the goods yard for the benefit of farmers and agricultural traders, who were able to rent warehouse space for the storage of cattle feed, fertilizers and other commodities. In this context, it should be remembered that Bourton-on-the-Water was a GWR Country Lorry Centre, with railway-owned road vehicles being used for the collection and delivery of goods and parcels within a wide rural hinterland. Towns and villages served by Bourton-based lorries included Naunton (4 miles), Upper Slaughter (2 miles), Guiting Power (5 miles) and Temple Guiting ($5^1/_2$ miles from the station).

In general terms, the area covered by the Bourton country lorries during the 1930s corresponded with the upper Windrush valley, all of the above-mentioned villages being situated within a mile or so of the river on the north side of the station. To the south of the railway, Bourton's hinterland followed the Windrush valley via Little Rissington, Clapton, Great Barrington and Windrush, while collections and deliveries were also carried out in an area extending south-westwards as far as Northleach, Farmington and Hampnett. All of these villages and hamlets were situated within a

Left: A detailed view of the Up platform in the mid 1930s, prior to the station building being rebuilt. Note the unusual design of the wooden waiting shelter, with its tiny canopy that extended over the entrance door only – although the decorative valancing was carried round the whole of the building. Note also the standard GWR nameboard, with cast iron letters. The enamel sign advertises Palethorpe's sausages.
The Lens of Sutton Collection

Left: The Down platform looking westwards towards Cheltenham on 30th May 1958. This end of the waiting shelter was partly constructed of brick to accommodate the fireplace and chimney. *R.M. Casserley*

Below: Another view of the road side of the replacement station building in 1958, with a couple of period motor cars also to be seen. Note how the colour of the stonework has 'aged' in the twenty years since the station had been built and also the new stonework of an extension to the eastern end of the building. Added in the 1950s, it housed a new parcels office. On the right is the pre-fabricated concrete provender store, which replaced the grounded coach body seen in the earlier view.
H.C. Casserley

THE BANBURY & CHELTENHAM DIRECT RAILWAY 195

Right: A very similar view to that on page 189 but taken on a warm day in the late 1940s and showing the replacement station building. Otherwise, little has changed, including the Down Starter signal which still has its lattice post.
Joe Moss, courtesy Roger Carpenter

Right: An Up train for Kingham can just be seen heading into the distance in this circa 1960 view, as the porter deals with the parcels from a Down train, on the right. Note the replacement BR enamel nameboard, the length of which required two intermediate posts. The wooden pale-and-space fencing to the rear of the platform has also been replaced with post and wire. *Bob Brown collection*

Below: Another circa 1960 study of the station, with the line to Cheltenham curving away to the right beyond Station Road bridge. *Bob Brown collection*

Busy platforms at Bourton-on-the-Water in this June 1960 view, **above**. Passengers on the Up platform, on the left, await their afternoon train from Cheltenham as '45XX' Class small prairie No. 4573 coasts into the opposite platform with a service from Kingham. **Below**, hauled by '51XX' Class large prairie No. 6137, the Kingham-bound train draws to a stop a couple of minutes later, as signalman Denis Coles stands ready with the single line token recently deposited on the catching apparatus by the fireman of No. 4573. As both trains departed, peace would descend upon the station for another couple of hours. The single daily each way pick-up freights had already been and gone. *Both E.T. Gill*

The fireman of '51XX' Class 2-6-2T No. 4142 leans well out of his cab to leave the Kingham to Bourton-on-the-Water token on the catching arm as the train prepares to stop at Bourton on 26th August 1961. Swift reflexes would then require him to pick up the token for the next section to Notgrove from its stand just in front of the goods shed. The signalman watches the operation taking place. He may be waiting to quickly pick up the token for an east-bound train due in on the Up platform. *M.P. Barnsley collection*

radius of about seven miles from the station.

In 1903, Bourton-on-the-Water issued 18,538 tickets, while in 1913 and 1923 the corresponding figures were 19,658 and 16,780 respectively. The amount of goods traffic handled over that same period rose from 13,791 tons in 1903 to 15,397 tons by 1923. Parcels traffic was relatively healthy, around 30,000 small parcels and packages being dealt with each year during the period under review, while staff numbers rose from six in 1903 to eight by 1913.

This Cotswold station typically issued around 8,000 tickets per annum during the mid to late 1930s, while goods traffic amounted to approximately 13,000 tons each year, most of this being in the form of incoming coal. There were also about 200 wagon loads of livestock per annum during the early 1930s. Domestic coal was distributed by at least two local firms which, in GWR days, operated their own small fleets of privately-owned wagons.

George Clifford, who also traded from Shipton-under-Wychwood station on the OW&WR main line, owned at least half a dozen 6- or 7-plank open wagons. Clifford's wagons were painted in an attractive red livery, with white lettering shaded in black; some of these vehicles were allocated to Bourton-on-the-Water, while others worked from Shipton-under-Wychwood, the appropriate station names being applied in full along the wagon sides. The other Bourton-based coal merchants were Messrs C. Collett &

Sons and they owned at least two wagons. Colletts' livery was chocolate brown, with white lettering shaded in black.

The introduction of the post-war 'zonal' scheme meant that sundries traffic for Bourton-on-the-Water and Stow-on-the-Wold was dealt with at Chipping Norton, which became the 'sub-railhead' for local smalls traffic. Full load cartage work continued to be handled at Bourton-on-the-Water, a Thornycroft 'half-tilt' lorry and other road vehicles being retained for that purpose.

Bourton-on-the-Water station was a relatively important employment centre in a predominantly agricultural area, its status being considerably enhanced by the introduction of country lorry services. The 1881 census reveals the names of several GWR employees, including station master George Pope, clerk George Amey, and porters Edward Burden, Henry Porfteeor, Frederick Hamm, and brothers Henry and Edwin Fifield. There was also an engine driver by the name of Thomas Vaughan, who lived in 'Railway Cottages' and was presumably based at Bourton whilst the station was still a terminus, in order that he could drive the first up and last down daily workings.

The apparent absence of any signalmen in 1881 may be a reflection of the primitive signalling arrangements that had pertained on the Bourton-on-the-Water Railway during its earlier years of operation. Alternatively, some or all of the employees described as 'porters' by the census enumerators may in fact have acted as 'porter-signalmen' in the days when the station was the terminus of a short and simple branch from Chipping Norton Junction.

In later years, around 1939, the staffing establishment normally comprised two clerks, two signalmen, three porters, one checker, and two motor drivers. This labour force of around eleven people was supervised by a 'class three' station master – the usual grade for a Great Western country station. There was, in addition, a locally-based permanent way gang consisting of one ganger, one sub-ganger and three or four lengthmen. The station master, in 1939, was Mr Spencer, while station masters in charge of Bourton-on-the-Water during the British Railways period included F.A.J. Poole and Mr A. Harris.

People arriving at Bourton-on-the-Water by train were faced with a short walk into the town, although the station was relatively well sited in relation to the urban area. Bourton had a population of about 2,000 at the end of World War Two, though in summer time the town was often thronged with tourists who came to admire this famous Cotswold beauty spot. Unusually, the River Windrush actually flows through the main street, the Cotswold stone houses and cottages being set back behind lawns and flower beds on either side of the sparkling stream. Bourton's many attractions include a model of the village in the garden of the 'Old New Inn'.

A Collett '45XX' Class small prairie hurries in to Stow-on-the-Wold station with a Kingham-bound Up working in July 1956. The goods yard here consisted simply of two loops, the outer one on the extreme right, known as 'No. 2 Siding', having a kick back spur that ended in the loading dock seen in the bottom right hand corner of the picture.
Gregory collection

STOW-ON-THE-WOLD

Resuming their journey, Up trains ran north-eastwards for about two miles, the River Dikler being crossed on a small bridge roughly mid-way between Bourton-on-the-Water and the next station at Stow-on-the-Wold. After crossing this small tributary of the Windrush, the railway passed beneath a road overbridge that carried the minor road from Lower Slaughter to Wick Rissington. Both of these places were typical Cotswold villages, Lower Slaughter, barely half a mile to the north of the railway, being attractively situated on the banks of the River Eye – a small stream which flows into the River Dikler.

Wick Rissington, a mile to the south-east, was associated with the Cheltenham composer Gustav Holst (1874-1934) who, in 1892, began his professional career as the organist and choirmaster at the Church of St. Laurence at a salary of £4 per annum.

With the Fosse Way running parallel away to the left, the route began to climb once more as it approached Stow-on-the-Wold, the station (19 miles 53 chains), being situated approximately 500 feet above mean sea level.

Stow-on-the-Wold station was similar to Bourton-on-the-Water, although there was just one platform on the Up side of the running line. The goods yard, which was also on the Up side, had two loop sidings, one of these being extended at its east end to terminate alongside cattle loading pens and a carriage dock. The sidings were known as 'No. 1' and 'No. 2', No. 1 Siding being long enough to hold thirty short-wheelbase goods wagons, while the slightly shorter No. 2 Siding could hold twenty-three vehicles. The loading dock, which formed an eastwards continuation of No. 2 Siding, could hold a further four short-wheelbase wagons.

The goods yard was laid out in such a way that No. 1 Siding could not easily be used for loading or unloading purposes, as it had no road access. In practice, goods traffic was dealt with in No. 2 Siding or the loading dock. The yard contained a 30 cwt hand crane, together with a small brick weigh-house with a pyramidal roof that appeared to

Looking east along the goods loading dock, **below**, with the station in the background. Stow was a far more modest affair than Bourton, as this view shows. When first opened, facilities were even more basic, with the goods lock-up on the platform, signal box, loading dock and crane all being later GWR additions. RCH Handbooks for the early 20th century give the capacity of the crane provided as being 4 tons; the plate on the side of this crane, **right**, reads 'Load Not To Exceed 5 Tons', so it may have been a later replacement. It would appear there was the occasional load of agricultural scrap metal from here.
Right: Joe Moss, courtesy Roger Carpenter
Below: Bob Brown collection

be of West Midland origin. A large, arc-roofed corrugated iron lock-up served as a goods shed, the latter structure being sited on the platform beside the station building.

The substantial station building was another Cotswold stone GWR design that had been erected in the 1930s to replace the original timber-framed West Midland building. The walls were formed of regular courses and the gable roof was covered in traditional Cotswold stone slates. The rear facade sported an asymmetrically-placed gable, while a projecting canopy was provided on the platform frontage. A further length of canopy was attached to the adjacent corrugated iron goods shed and this formed a convenient parking area for platform trolleys or other equipment.

Stow-on-the-Wold was not a crossing station but it had a small signal box to release the siding points, and work home and starting signals in each direction (the distants being fixed). The signal box was a typical Great Western branch line-style cabin, with a gable roof and small-paned windows; it was sited on the platform and was of just one storey. Such boxes were built towards the end of the Victorian period between 1890 and 1900, after which they were superseded by the GWR hip-roofed signal box design. The small box at Stow-on-the-Wold was opened in 1893 and ceased to be used as a signal cabin in 1948.

The connections to Nos.1 and 2 sidings were worked from ground frames following the closure of the signal cabin, the

200 THE BANBURY & CHELTENHAM DIRECT RAILWAY

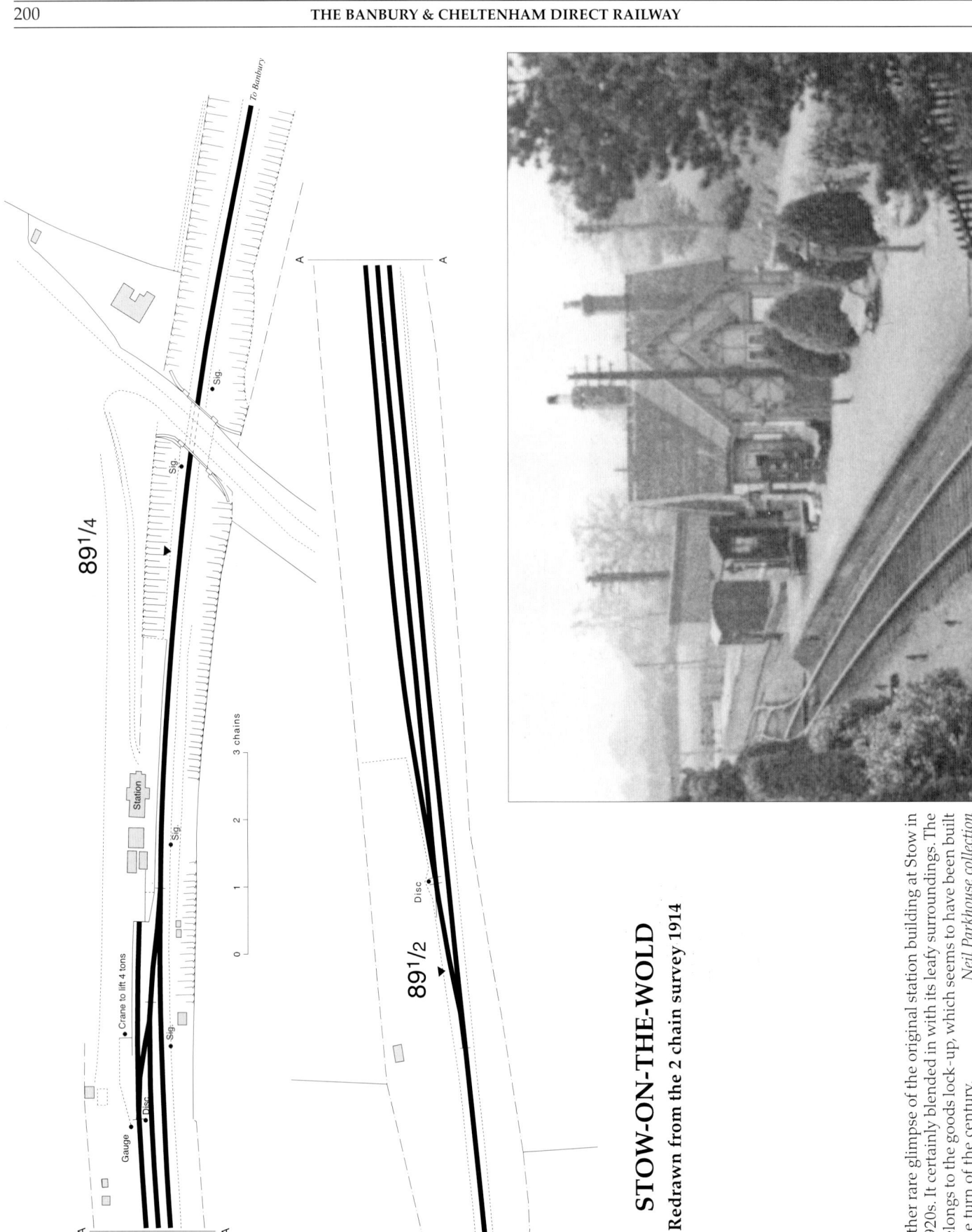

STOW-ON-THE-WOLD
Redrawn from the 2 chain survey 1914

Left: Another rare glimpse of the original station building at Stow in the late 1920s. It certainly blended in with its leafy surroundings. The canopy belongs to the goods lock-up, which seems to have been built around the turn of the century. *Neil Parkhouse collection*

The 1938 replacement station building was constructed of dressed Cotswold stone blocks with a simple undecorated canopy, in a style identical to that built at Bourton. Rather austere by Great Western standards, it served its purpose well in being simple yet functional. Note that the corrugated iron goods lock-up remained, whilst the Edwardian vending machine, dispensing cigarettes, matches and sweets, a wonderful example of its type, also survived in place. *Bob Brown collection*

The forecourt side presented a quite unrailway-like aspect. Suitably extended, the building survives today as a private residence. *Bob Brown collection*

Two photographs of Stow-on-the-Wold in early British Railways days, both taken on 22nd August 1948. In the first view, **left**, the line curves away south-westerly towards Bourton-on-the-Water, past the Down Starter and Up Home signals, and the tablet exchange apparatus in between. The gangers hut for this section of the line is set back behind this lineside equipment. The only known private owner wagon user based here was the Stow Coal Co., which appears to have ceased trading in the early 1920s. They are known to have been in business by 1869, when they ordered a single wagon from the Birmingham Wagon Co. No other wagon orders have been traced. From around 1897 to when they finished, the manager was listed as one Jabez Roff.

The photograph, **below**, was taken from the Up Home signal, again looking at the tablet exchange apparatus with the station beyond. Following closure of Stow-on-the-Wold Signal Box in 1948 (authorised the previous year on 18th July), the tablet apparatus and the signals were all removed.

Both courtesy Kidderminster Railway Museum

frames in question being designated 'Stow-on-the-Wold East Ground Frame' and 'Stow-on-the-Wold West Ground Frame'. A degree of sophistication was introduced, insofar as Intermediate Token Instruments were provided at each ground frame. In general, the siding points were released by the Electric Train Token for the Bourton-on-the-Water to Kingham West Junction single line section but the provision of the Intermediate Token Instruments meant that, if necessary, a train could be locked into the sidings to allow another working to run through the station in either direction.

When a goods train was required to call at Stow-on-the-Wold for traffic purposes, the porter on duty would telephone the Bourton-on-the-Water signalmen to ascertain if the train would need to be shunted clear of the main line. He would then meet the train and work the ground frames. After any necessary shunting had been carried out, the porter would again telephone Bourton-on-the-Water to inform the signalman, who then forwarded a special (3-3-3) bell signal to his counterpart in Kingham West Box. On receiving the acknowledgment, both signalmen pressed the plungers of their respective Train Token Instruments in order that the Token could be withdrawn from the Intermediate Instrument.

This wayside station was, for many years, regarded as important enough to justify the employment of a station master but, in the 1960s, it was placed under the control of Mr A. Harris, the Bourton-on-the-Water station master. In earlier years, around 1880, the local station master had been George Tibbs, while clerical duties were undertaken by his son William Tibbs. The staffing establishment comprised just three men during the late 19th and early 20th centuries, rising to four by the 1930s and five in 1938.

One of the last station masters at Stow was John Perry, who worked at the station in the 1950s. In its final years, the station was staffed by leading porters Bill Close and John Wilsdon – Mr Close being a former signalman who had worked at Stow-on-the-Wold since 1920; in 1948 he had become a leading porter so that he could remain at Stow after the closure of his signal box.

Stow-on-the-Wold station was poorly-sited in relation to

Above: The station was sheltered by a belt of high trees facing the single platform, as can clearly be seen in this view, looking east towards the A424 road bridge. Upon alighting here, the traveller was faced with a mile long journey up the steep Stow Hill to reach the town itself, which did not help with passenger receipts, particularly in later years. In this late 1950s view, the Stow porter readies some parcels for collection by the next train.

Right: '45XX' Class small prairie No. 4573 from Gloucester shed runs into the station with a Kingham-bound train in 1960. Note that the GWR nameboard was still in place. Stow never received new BR enamel signs as had Bourton.
Both Bob Brown collection

the community that it purported to serve, not only in terms of the one mile distance between the town and the railway but also because the intervening distance was steeply uphill for most of the way. Travellers arriving at the station were inevitably faced with a long and wearisome trek before they could even catch a glimpse of the town and, for this reason, many local people preferred to catch their trains at nearby stations on the OW&WR main line, such as Kingham or Moreton-in-Marsh.

As one might expect, the amount of traffic handled here was relatively modest. In 1903, the station issued 14,136 tickets, falling to 5,568 in 1930 and 4,615 by 1938. There were, on the other hand, ten season ticket holders in the early 1930s, suggesting that the small number of regular passengers may have preferred to pay their travelling expenses in this convenient way. As Great Western season tickets were normally available for periods of one, two, three, six or twelve months, it follows that ten season ticket sales could easily have been the equivalent of 2,500 ordinary returns (assuming ten annual season ticket holders travelling on a daily basis).

In terms of freight traffic, Stow handled around 9,500 tons of freight per annum, this figure being fairly constant for many years. In 1903, for example, the station dealt with 10,196 tons of freight while, in 1938, 12,591 tons were handled. There was also a considerable amount of livestock traffic, an average of 200 wagon loads being received or despatched each year during the first three decades of the 20th century. In 1933, livestock traffic amounted to only 57 wagon loads but this meagre total had increased to 95 in

Stow-on-the-Wold station, in all its sylvan glory, basking in hot sunshine in the late Spring of 1958. The goods shed, of corrugated iron construction, was unusually situated on the station platform and had a canopy, complete with valancing, extending from it. Places where goods traffic was dealt with on the main running line were rare but this was obviously one, although presumably the amount of goods handled here was small enough for it not to cause a problem. It most probably amounted mainly to small parcels, any vans requiring unloading of perishable goods for storage in the shed no doubt being dealt with from the short bay platform. The small 17 lever signal box dated from 1892 and replaced two ground frames which had controlled the ends of the goods yard loops. Although the box was shut in 1948, the building survived until the line's final closure in 1964. The corrugated iron structure behind the signal box was used as a lamp hut.

H.C. Casserley

Two later views of the road frontage of the replacement station building. The photograph, **above**, taken on 30th May 1958, is looking eastwards up the station approach road. The station was quite well hidden from the Stow to Burford road even then; today it is all to easy to drive by the site without even noticing. The rising road necessitated the steps from the forecourt leading down to platform level, whilst the Ladies' and Gents' conveniences were sited at the nearer end. The 1956 view, **below**, is looking in the opposite direction and also shows the rear of the goods lock-up with its large sliding door. *Top: R.M. Casserley; bottom: Bob Brown collection*

1933, and as many as 229 by 1936.

TRAFFIC DEALT WITH AT STOW-ON-THE-WOLD					
YEAR	STAFF	RECEIPTS (£)	TICKETS	PARCELS	GOODS (TONS)
1913	3	5,113	12,580	13,526	9,150
1923	4	7,548	11,733	12,538	9,085
1929	4	6,899	7,334	12,688	8,436
1937	4	14,840	4,271	9,588	16,181
1938	5	12,945	4,615	11,314	12,591

Stow-on-the-Wold is one of the most attractive small towns in the Cotswolds. It is situated in an exposed position, about 800 ft above mean sea level, at the intersection of the Fosse Way and several minor roads. This hill-top location gave rise to the local rhyme '*Stow-on-the-Wold, where the wind blows cold*' and in the depths of winter this saying has more than a grain of truth. (An alternative version referred to '*Stow-on-the-Wold, where the Devil caught cold*').

The town was originally called St. Edward's Stow after Edward the Martyr, the 10th century boy king of Wessex who was murdered at Corfe in 978, allegedly at the behest of his own brother. There are many interesting old buildings, representing all periods from the 16th to the 19th centuries, most of these being constructed in the familiar Cotswold stone style. The parish church of St. Edward reflects all periods of ecclesiastical architecture from the Norman period onwards, while the large market place recalls the days when this fine old town was a venue for Cotswold sheep fairs and wool markets.

In recent years, Stow's annual fairs, held on 12th May and 24th October, have become associated with horse sales – as many as three hundred animals being sold at a single auction to dealers from all over the British Isles.

Film enthusiasts will perhaps be aware of a World War Two British film entitled *The Tawny Pipit*, which was one of the most effective propaganda films made during the 1939-45 war. This simple, semi-documentary was filmed in and around Stow, with at least one good shot of the branch train entering Stow-on-the-Wold station.

Left: A general view of Stow-on-the-Wold station, looking westwards along the single platform towards Cheltenham in the late 1950s. The small goods yard looks quite busy, with several wagons in the sidings and a rigid wheelbase lorry backed up for loading from one of the vans.
Bob Brown collection

Right: On 7th September 1954, '45XX' Class 2-6-2T No. 5530 ambles away from Stow with the 10.30 am ex-Cheltenham service for Kingham. The train consists of a two coach 'B Set' and the view also provides good detail of the A424 road bridge. The abutments and wing walls were built of local stone, with the road supported on cast iron girders and the parapet made up of timber with a cast iron framework. It no longer exists, the cutting having been filled in and the road widened at this point.
Bob Brown collection

Chapter Six

KINGHAM AND THE CHIPPING NORTON BRANCH

A postcard study of Kingham village centre by Frank Packer. The Royal Mail van is making a delivery to Eaton's general stores early one sunny morning, circa 1930.
Neil Parkhouse collection

Departing from Stow-on-the-Wold, eastbound trains entered a deep cutting which, towards its western end, was crossed by a single-span girder bridge carrying the A424 road over the line. Emerging from the cutting, the route curved towards the east as it descended into the Evenlode Valley. The cutting was followed by a length of embankment, which was pierced part way along by an underline occupation bridge. To the right, travellers were rewarded with a good view of the wooded slopes of Maugersbury Hill, with the 799 foot summit of Icomb Hill discernible in the distance. To the left, the ground rose in similar fashion towards the hill-top town of Stow.

With Ash Farm visible to the south of the railway, trains passed beneath the B4450 road bridge, beyond which the route turned south-eastwards for the approach to Kingham. There were two gated level crossings on this section of the line, both of these being regarded merely as occupation crossings, although they carried unclassified roads leading from Bledington to Oddington across the railway.

KINGHAM

After about two miles, the route turned eastwards and, as it neared the River Evenlode, the railway bifurcated at Kingham West Junction (23 miles 48 chains); to the left, the double track Kingham Avoiding Line continued due east towards Chipping Norton, while to the right a double track curve turned through eighty degrees in order that branch trains could reach Kingham station. The Avoiding Line, which had been built in 1906, was used only by through freight workings and the 'Ports-to-Ports Express' – the latter service being the only passenger train that did not call at Kingham station during the normal course of operations.

The two double track routes continued more or less due eastwards for a distance of about a quarter of a mile, the Kingham West Curve being a low level line, whereas the Avoiding Line climbed onto a raised embankment in order that it could be carried across the OW&WR main line on a girder bridge with brick abutments and a single clear span of 76 feet. Diverging at an angle of about five degrees, the two routes were carried across the River Evenlode on separate bridges, after which the West Curve crossed a tributary stream. This smaller stream delineated the county boundary between Gloucestershire and Oxfordshire for a short distance on the south side of the railway.

The 1906 cut-off formed the north side of a triangle, with double track curves on each side. This triangle was controlled from three signal boxes, Kingham West and Kingham East boxes being sited at each end of the direct line, while the southern end of the triangle was controlled from Kingham Station Signal Box. Trains from Cheltenham took the right hand fork at Kingham West Junction and, having crossed the Up and Down main lines, they finally came to rest in the branch platforms on the east side of this surprisingly complex rural junction station. The distance from Cheltenham St. James was 24 miles 17 chains.

Above: Kingham West Junction and tablet exchange apparatus in the early 1950s, looking west towards Stow. The photograph was taken from the steps of Kingham West Signal Box. The line further divided into two double tracks a little way beyond the box, one pair crossing the bridge, while the other curved round to Kingham station. The box was closed in September 1953 and the direct junction then taken out.
Joe Moss, courtesy Roger Carpenter

Right: Looking from a train entering Kingham station from the west, on 22nd September 1962, with Kingham Station Signal Box (originally Kingham North) on the left. The sidings visible on the right formed part of Kingham goods yard and were also used for marshalling wagons to and from the Cheltenham line. *Paul Strong*

Kingham station (Chipping Norton Junction until 1909) was dominated by its impressive footbridge, which spanned four platforms and four running lines, as this circa 1910 view looking northwards clearly shows. B&CDR trains ran into Platform 3, on the right, leaving the main OW&WR line clear. The direct line bridge can be seen in the left distance. *Barry Davis collection*

Kingham was not an original OW&WR station, having opened in connection with the Chipping Norton branch in 1855. Seven years later, the opening of the Bourton-on-the-Water branch led to a further increase of facilities, though the station buildings appear to have been relatively simple structures. The station originally had just two platforms for main line traffic, which were later designated Platforms One and Two. Platform Three, the Chipping Norton branch platform, was subsequently added behind the main Up platform, which became an island with two faces.

An important stage in the development of the station came in the 1880s, when the Great Western carried out a comprehensive rebuilding scheme which resulted in the provision of extensive new station buildings on both platforms. These new structures were single-storey, hipped roof buildings, with tall chimneys and projecting platform canopies; the main building was completed in 1883. At about the same time, Platform Four was constructed on the east side of the station, which thereby became a quadruple-platform junction station, with two platforms on the west side for main line traffic, and two additional platforms for Cheltenham and Banbury branch line services to the east.

The railway facilities at Kingham were further increased in the early 1900s, when the East and West branch line curves were doubled, and the Kingham Avoiding Line was built to allow through workings to run directly between Banbury and Cheltenham without having to reverse in the station. The station's signalling was up-graded in connection with these new works, and various new loops and sidings were installed. The improvement scheme included the provision of a new engine shed, in place of an earlier structure that had been opened in 1881. The final phase of development here took place during World War Two, with the addition of seven new sidings for wartime goods traffic.

Kingham's main goods handling facilities were situated on the Down side, where three dead-end sidings were available for a range of traffic including coal, livestock and general merchandise. The yard area featured a raised surface, which greatly facilitated the loading and unloading of livestock. Buildings in the yard included a standard GWR weigh-house, and the usual collection of huts and sheds, some of which were used by the local coal merchants. A further goods siding was provided to the south of the road bridge, serving a horse loading dock on the Up side.

The War Department sidings were situated to the north of the station, on the Up side, and entered by means of a northwards extension from an existing loop near the engine shed sidings. Opened in 1943, the sidings were used for a variety of traffic, including supplies and equipment for nearby aerodromes such as RAF Little Rissington, as well as for a huge range of material needed by the army in connection with the D-Day invasion of Europe. Mr M.C. Jenkins, of the Royal Army Ordnance Corps, particularly remembered *'wagon loads of camouflage netting'*, which were unloaded at Kingham and taken by military vehicles to an anonymous-looking store behind one of the houses in the village.

The range of accommodation provided within the hipped-roof building on the Down side originally comprised (from left to right when viewed from the platform): a ticket office, a general waiting room, the ladies waiting room and toilets, further office accommodation, and the gentlemen's toilets. The office next to the gentlemen's ablutions was equipped with a 6 foot wide doorway and double doors, suggesting that it was intended to be used as a parcels office and cloakroom.

THE BANBURY & CHELTENHAM DIRECT RAILWAY

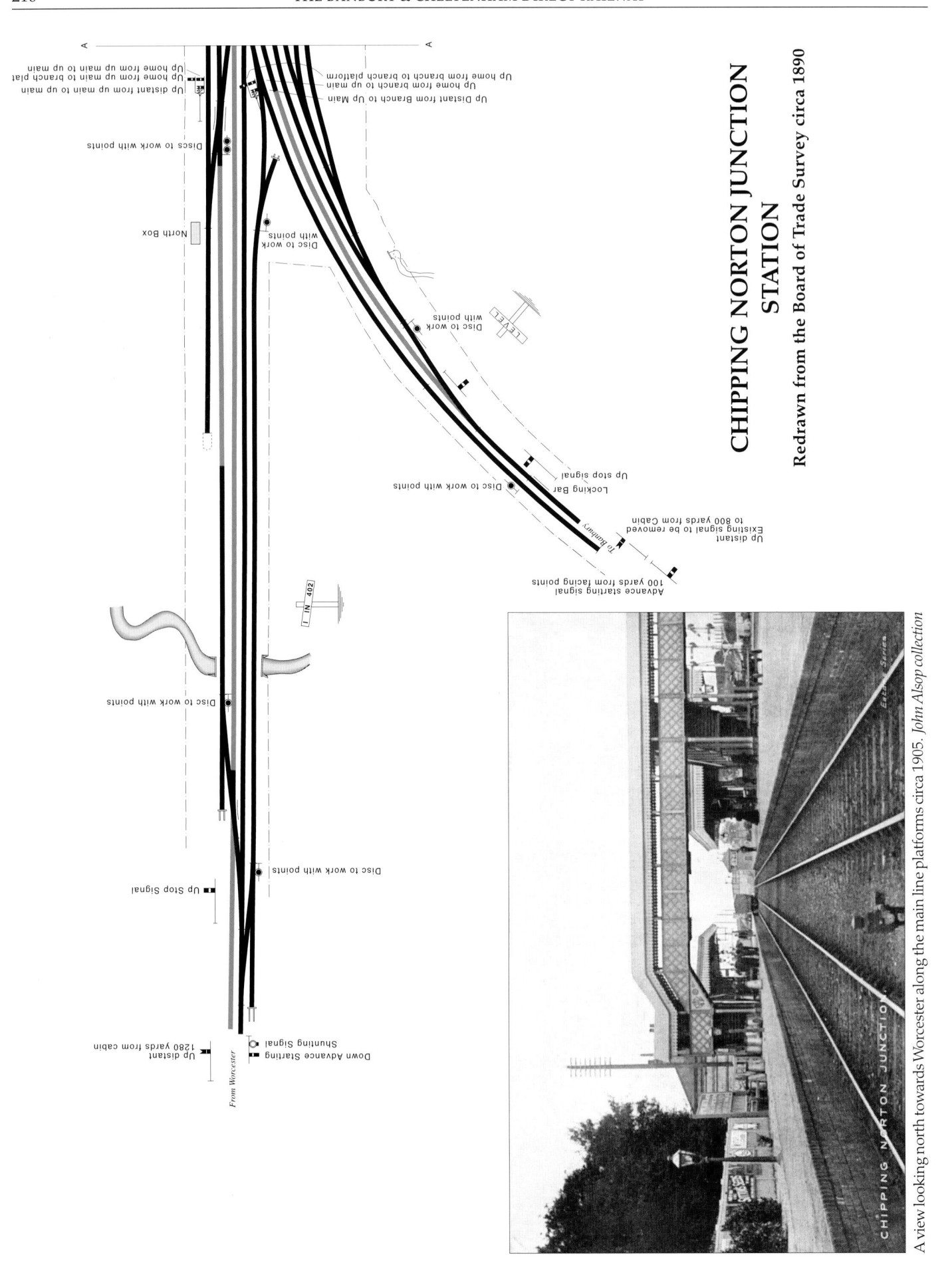

CHIPPING NORTON JUNCTION STATION
Redrawn from the Board of Trade Survey circa 1890

A view looking north towards Worcester along the main line platforms circa 1905. *John Alsop collection*

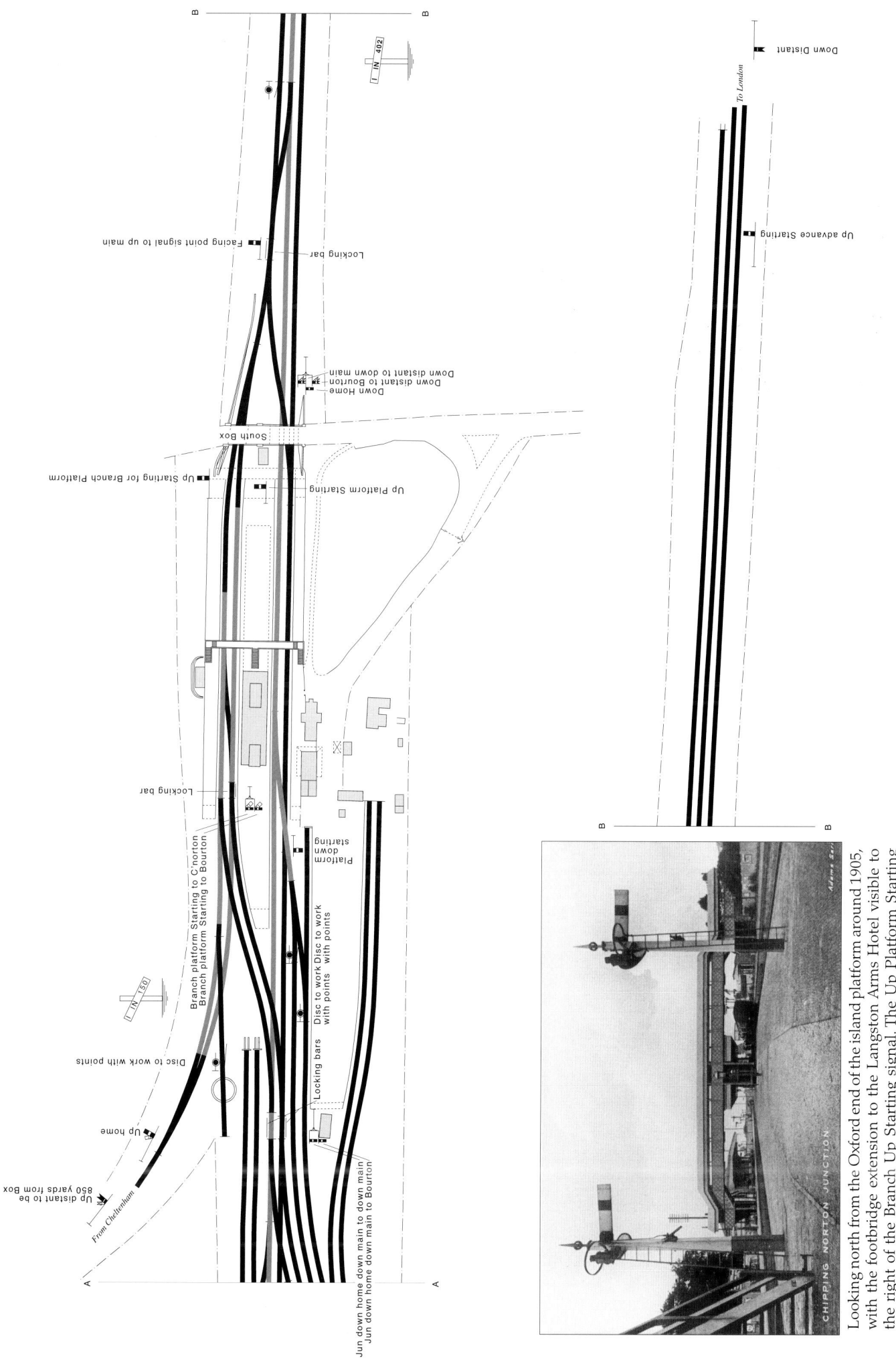

Looking north from the Oxford end of the island platform around 1905, with the footbridge extension to the Langston Arms Hotel visible to the right of the Branch Up Starting signal. The Up Platform Starting signal and part of the South box steps are on the left. *John Alsop collection*

This busy Edwardian scene, circa 1910, was taken from the steps up to Kingham South Signal Box and shows a rake of 4- and 6-wheel passenger stock waiting to depart for Cheltenham from Platform Three. The southbound main line train in Platform Two consists of a mixture of bogie clerestory carriages and 6-wheel stock, whilst a northbound service occupies Platform One on the far left. Above the footbridge, a long section of the avoiding line is in view. *Courtesy Kidderminster Railway Museum*

However, in 1946 it was agreed that a new parcels office would be added at the Paddington end of the buildings and, when this addition was finally completed around 1951, the old parcels room became the station master's office.

Externally, this stylish structure was a standard Great Western building, its architectural details being very similar to those found at Cheltenham Malvern Road and on the down side at Cheltenham South & Leckhampton. It was of yellow brick construction with contrasting red brick string courses and a hipped, slated roof. The building was sub-divided into ten bays, eight of these having a width of 10 feet, whereas the two end bays were both 14 feet in length. Most of the window and door apertures were grouped in pairs beneath a single curved-topped lintel, fenestration of this kind being typical of GWR architectural practice during the 1880s and 1890s.

Although the new parcels office at the south end of the main block had not been completed until the British Railways period, it was built of the same materials as the older part of the structure and uninitiated travellers would have assumed that it was part of the original Victorian fabric. The general waiting room could be entered through 3 foot wide doorways at the front and rear, whereas the new parcels room, office, ladies' room and station master's office had no means of access from the station approach. The gentlemen's urinals were entered via a door in the north wall, beside which a second door gave access to a small porters' mess room at the north-west corner of the building.

The main block was approximately 88 feet long and its platform facade was covered for most of its length by a projecting canopy. A similar, slightly shorter canopy extended from the rear wall of the building and both were adorned with wooden 'tongue-and-groove' valancing.

The standard hipped roof building on the Up side contained further accommodation for waiting passengers, including another general waiting room, a ladies' waiting room and toilets for both sexes. The main brick buildings were separated by a 120 foot long open waiting area, which was covered by a continuous roof with generously-proportioned canopies on both sides. The easternmost platform, in contrast, was equipped only with a simple waiting shelter. All of these 1880s buildings were constructed of yellow brickwork with contrasting orange and black string courses.

The four platforms were linked by a standard GWR lattice girder footbridge, which continued eastwards into the reception area of the adjacent Langston Arms Hotel. The footbridge was fully roofed, and in the 1920s and 1930s a small, privately-run refreshment kiosk was provided in the restricted space beneath the steps on the island platform. The station was originally lit by oil lamps but gas lighting had appeared by the early 20th century. Electric lighting had been introduced by the British Railways era, some of the platform lamps being of the 'swan-necked' type, while others were mounted on concrete standards.

The lines in and around Kingham station were at one time controlled from four signal cabins. In addition to the East and West junction boxes and the main station box, there had also been a signal box at the south end of the island platform. The last mentioned cabin, known as Kingham South Box, was opened in 1884 and abolished in 1922. Photographs show it to have been an unusually tall three-storey structure, which allowed signalmen an unimpeded view over the adjacent road overbridge. The South Box had been of brick and timber construction, with a gable roof and small-paned windows.

Following the demise of Kingham South Box, the former North Box was renamed 'Kingham Station Box'. The latter was sited immediately to the north of the platforms, on the Up side of the running lines. Like its counterparts at Kingham East and Kingham West junctions, the Station Box was a standard Great Western hip-roofed cabin dating from 1906. It was an entirely typical design, of red brick construction with a grey slate roof, its window frames being of the usual 'five-pane' type. As it was situated in the 'V' of the diverging Worcester and Chipping Norton lines, this box featured windows on all four sides, to ensure signalmen were able to obtain a clear view of the surrounding tracks.

The station was signalled in such a way that Cheltenham branch workings normally arrived in Platform Three, while Banbury trains arrived in the adjacent Platform Four. Platform Three was the usual departure platform for both Cheltenham and Banbury services, although Cheltenham trains could also use the Down main line platform, which had a direct connection to the Down Cheltenham line. As mentioned earlier, Chipping Norton and Banbury branch services were typically worked by auto-trains, whereas Cheltenham trains had to run-round in the platforms at Kingham.

Kingham engine shed was a small single-road structure, situated on the Up side of the main line; it was of brick construction and measured approximately 75 feet by 20 feet at ground level. A lean-to office and mess room adjoined the main building on its west side. Although the shed was a sub-shed of Worcester, the resident locomotives were supplied by Gloucester. The shed normally housed a 'Dean Goods' Class 0-6-0 for local goods work, although in the late 1940s there were two resident locomotives, one of which worked the Chipping Norton route while the other was used on the Shipston-on-Stour branch. These locomotives could be turned on a 45 foot diameter turntable positioned in front of the shed building.

Water columns were strategically sited at the north end of Platform One and the south end of Platform Four. There was no provision for watering on the centre island platform, although an additional column was available near the engine shed. Water was supplied from a stilted metal tank supported on six tubular metal columns, this structure being sited between the engine shed and Kingham East Curve.

In May 1926, the Kingham station master was one of the very few Great Western station masters to support the General Strike. Unfortunately, a GWR director turned up at the station at the beginning of the strike and asked to speak to the station master; when told he was not at work, he declared that the man should be sacked. In the event the station master was down-graded to the status of a Class Five clerk at Pershore but in due course he was reinstated as a Class Two station master at Droitwich Spa – allegedly as the result of a personal intervention by Felix Pole, the GWR General Manager, who did not believe that individual employees should be punished for their political beliefs.

In the 1930s, Kingham gave employment to over 30 people including two clerks, two foremen, two ticket collectors, four porters, seven signalmen, two relief signalmen, one lampman and two shunters. There were also two locally-based train crews, together with several permanent way men. In late Victorian days, the station master had been John G. Brecknell, while in the 1930s the station was supervised by Mr Curnock. A later station master, from 1949 until 1966, was Mr T.W.H. Lane, who had worked at Kingham in 1926 as a junior clerk.

The station fulfilled an important role as an interchange point between the Cheltenham and Kingham, Banbury and Kingham, and Oxford, Worcester & Wolverhampton routes. In 1903, the station issued 21,925 tickets, falling to 12,396 by 1930 and just 9,572 by 1939. On the other hand, there were by that time around forty season ticket holders who travelled regularly to Oxford or London. As GWR season tickets were issued for periods of one, two, three, six or even twelve months, season ticket sales may have amounted to around 2,400 journeys per annum (assuming that most customers had purchased three month tickets).

Kingham handled around 6,000 tons of freight during the early 1900s but this very modest figure had declined to 4,817 tons per annum by 1930 and barely 3,000 tons a year during the later 1930s. The main sources of traffic were coal and general merchandise inwards, and sugar beet outwards, together with fairly regular consignments of agricultural equipment made by Lainchbury & Sons of Kingham, a local engineering firm. There were, in addition, around 300 wagons loads of cattle each year during the period under review, while in 1930, Kingham dealt with over 18,000 parcels and small consignments.

The station was located in a rural setting amid verdant agricultural land, its only significant neighbour being a large Victorian hotel called The Langston Arms. The hotel, sited immediately to the east of the station and connected to it by an extension of the lattice footbridge, had been erected in the 1870s at the expense of the third Earl of Ducie. It was an elaborate Tudor-style structure, with prominent gables and a profusion of towering chimney stacks. A small cattle market was established to the east of the hotel and this brought extra traffic to the railway in the form of livestock consignments, as well as additional passenger traffic.

Cattle markets were held at the Langston Arms on a monthly basis, normally on the third Monday. These tended to be small-scale, localised affairs but the hotel was also the venue for bi-annual cattle sales, which attracted farmers and

A rare view of the lofty Chipping Norton Junction South Signal Box circa 1905, its position adjoining the road bridge necessitating an extra storey in order for the signalmen to obtain a good view of the station's southern approaches. The box was opened in 1884, being provided as part of the revision and extension of the station layout carried out in that year. It was at this time that the fourth platform was added and the lines running into Platforms Three and Four brought through the station to connect with the main line to the south of the station, as can be seen in the right background. The connections and crossovers to the Cheltenham line were remodelled at the same time and these were controlled from a second new box, known as Chipping Norton Junction North. The latter had closed by 1906 but the South box seen here remained in use until October 1922. A horse dock was also provided just to the south of the bridge on the eastern side of the line in 1903 (it is obscured from view here), for the benefit of members of the Heythrop Hunt. It is likely that the station's full complement of staff are on view here, a rare quiet moment between trains at this busy junction. *John Alsop collection*

Two wonderful views of the station master and his pet pig, which incidentally provide some good detail of the infrastructure here. It was not unusual for staff at country stations to keep animals but the tame pig seen here was a novelty and a portion of this first photograph appeared in the *Great Western Railway Magazine* edition for October 1907. Chipping Norton Junction North Signal Box was opened on 8th January 1906, replacing the 1884 North box situated a little further north, which was closed because it was in the way of the new direct line. In 1908, when the station name changed, this box was renamed Kingham North and then in 1922, on closure of the South box, it became Kingham Station Signal Box. *John Alsop collection*

Taken on the same day, the station master and his porcine companion are seen here at the back of the goods yard. The *Great Western Railway Magazine* remarked 'We trust such affection will be rewarded by deferring the butcher's visit as long as possible.' No goods shed was ever provided here, the large loading bay sufficing for the commodities generally handled, mainly coal and agricultural produce. There were also livestock pens, visible in the background. A crane of 10 tons capacity was originally installed, which had been replaced by a 5-ton one by 1904 and removed altogether by 1912. In the background, behind the signal box, the new engine shed has yet to be built, that provided in 1881 on the same site having been dismantled in 1905-6. It was of mainly timber construction with a water tank above. The signal box closed in 1966, with the final removal of the last remaining sidings in the old branch platforms. *John Alsop collection*

Prior to the 1st May 1909, the station was called Chipping Norton Junction but the GWR took the decision to rename it apparently to avoid confusion with Chipping Norton station, on the Banbury & Cheltenham line. In this rather damp scene taken circa 1906 facing Oxford, the large nameboard announcing all the destinations which could be reached from here can be seen. Note the 'Junction' of the title is in smaller lettering than the rest of the station name. In the left background is the rather stately Langston Arms Hotel. As much of its clientele was quite grand and brought a good deal of useful business to the station, the Great Western extended the footbridge across to it. As well as allowing easy access from the station for the baggage, servants etc. that the well-off Edwardian tourist travelled with, gentlemen and ladies could get to within feet of the hotel entrance entirely under cover. In the right background, the horse dock can just be glimpsed through the bridge arch, whilst a Banbury line train headed by one of the ubiquitous 'Metro' tanks waits to leave from Platform Three.

Bob Brown collection

Right: The entire Chipping Norton Junction staff assembled for a group photograph in April 1906, on the occasion of the retirement of station master J.G. Brecknell, 5th from left in the front row. He was presented with the handsome marble clock, visible above his head, and other mementoes, in recognition of his service, having been station master here since July 1879. Mr Brecknell had dealings with many members of the landed gentry who regularly used the station, his courteous manner being recognised by the testimonial address he received, which was organised and presented by Lord Moreton.
Barry Davis collection

Left: The platform staff assembled for another group portrait circa 1906. The occasion, if any, is not known but it may have been to record the arrival of the new station master. Both photographs were taken by Frank Packer. *Barry Davis collection*

Below: This delightful wintry scene, looking towards Oxford from the Station Signal Box, was taken on March 7th 1937. It shows the earlier Down bracket signal on the right hand platform. This was later replaced by the famous under-slung example aiding sighting under the platform canopy for fast Down trains. Note, no trains have yet disturbed the snow. *Bob Brown collection*

The new brick-built locomotive shed at Kingham, **above**, just prior to opening in June 1913. The turntable remained from the 1881-built shed, which had closed in 1905 and was dismantled the following year, probably because it was considered too small and something of a fire hazard, being built of timber. The turntable saw little use and was removed in the mid 1940s. The direct line can be seen in the background. **Below**, the new shed again from the front, with the attendant water crane on the right. In the immediate foreground is the ash pit, looking beautifully clean with the shed still waiting for its first locomotives. *Courtesy National Railway Museum*

Left: The inside of the shed looking far too clean, although within a week of housing locomotives it undoubtedly had quickly changed. It provides a nice clear view of the area around the roof before being blackened by smoke and soot. The smoke trough, with its stay rods from the side walls, shows up particularly clearly. The main shed building measured 75 feet in length by 20 feet wide, whilst the offices on the front western side were 20 feet long by 15 feet wide. Although provided for engines working to both Cheltenham and Banbury, changes in traffic working meant that, particularly in its latter years, it was used primarily by locomotives from the Chipping Norton branch. The shed closed at the same time as passenger services over the Chipping Norton line, in December 1962.
Courtesy National Railway Museum

Right: A side view of the shed, looking east, in later years. On 30th May 1958, BR standard Class '2MT' mogul No. 78009 is seen alongside the coaling stage, which was a later addition following removal of the turntable. *R.M. Casserley*

Below: A circa 1960 view of the shed, with another Class '2MT' 2-6-0 at rest alongside the coaling stage. The line to Cheltenham can just be seen curving off behind the signal, left.
Courtesy Kidderminster Railway Museum

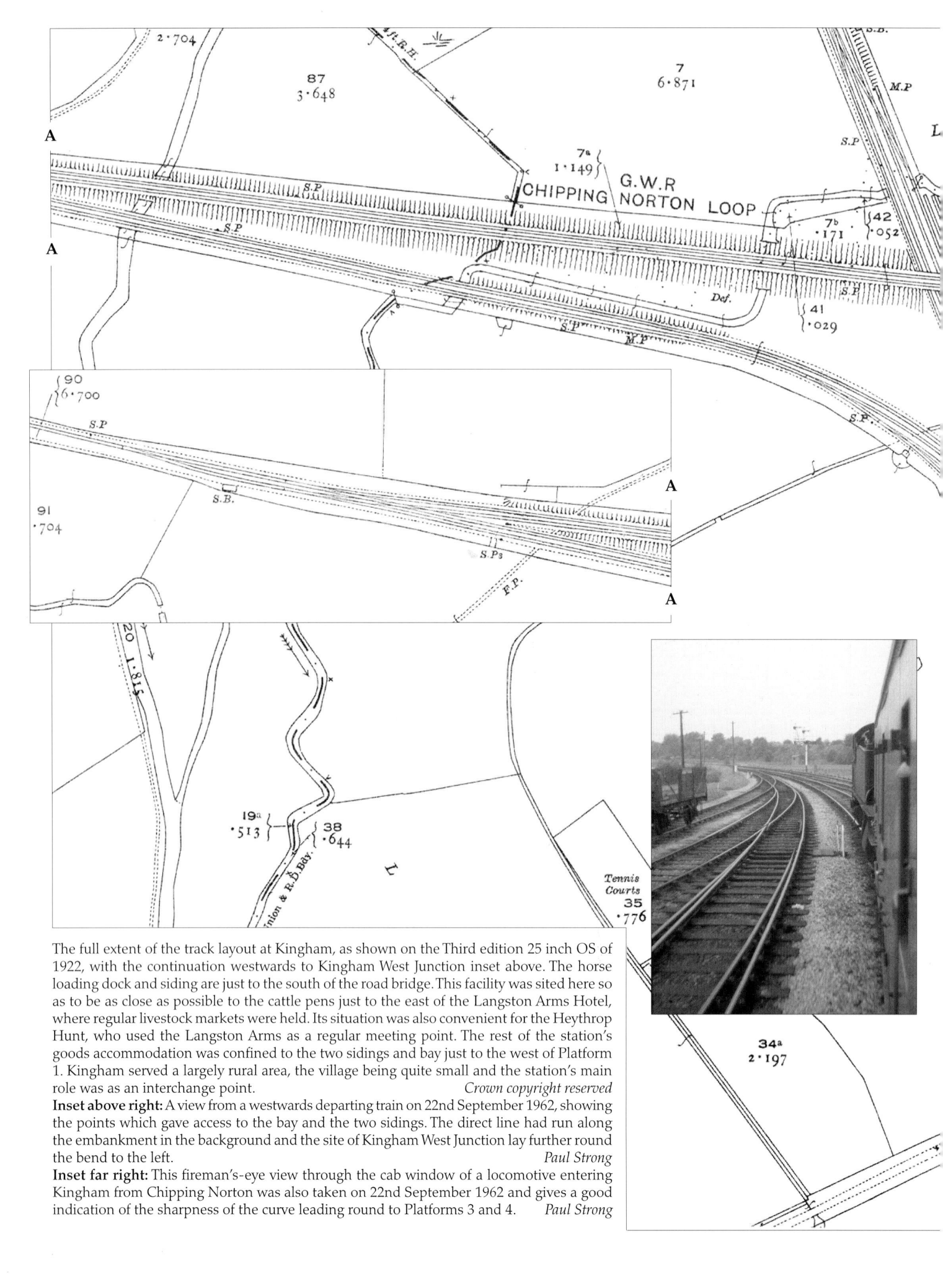

The full extent of the track layout at Kingham, as shown on the Third edition 25 inch OS of 1922, with the continuation westwards to Kingham West Junction inset above. The horse loading dock and siding are just to the south of the road bridge. This facility was sited here so as to be as close as possible to the cattle pens just to the east of the Langston Arms Hotel, where regular livestock markets were held. Its situation was also convenient for the Heythrop Hunt, who used the Langston Arms as a regular meeting point. The rest of the station's goods accommodation was confined to the two sidings and bay just to the west of Platform 1. Kingham served a largely rural area, the village being quite small and the station's main role was as an interchange point. *Crown copyright reserved*

Inset above right: A view from a westwards departing train on 22nd September 1962, showing the points which gave access to the bay and the two sidings. The direct line had run along the embankment in the background and the site of Kingham West Junction lay further round the bend to the left. *Paul Strong*

Inset far right: This fireman's-eye view through the cab window of a locomotive entering Kingham from Chipping Norton was also taken on 22nd September 1962 and gives a good indication of the sharpness of the curve leading round to Platforms 3 and 4. *Paul Strong*

10·322

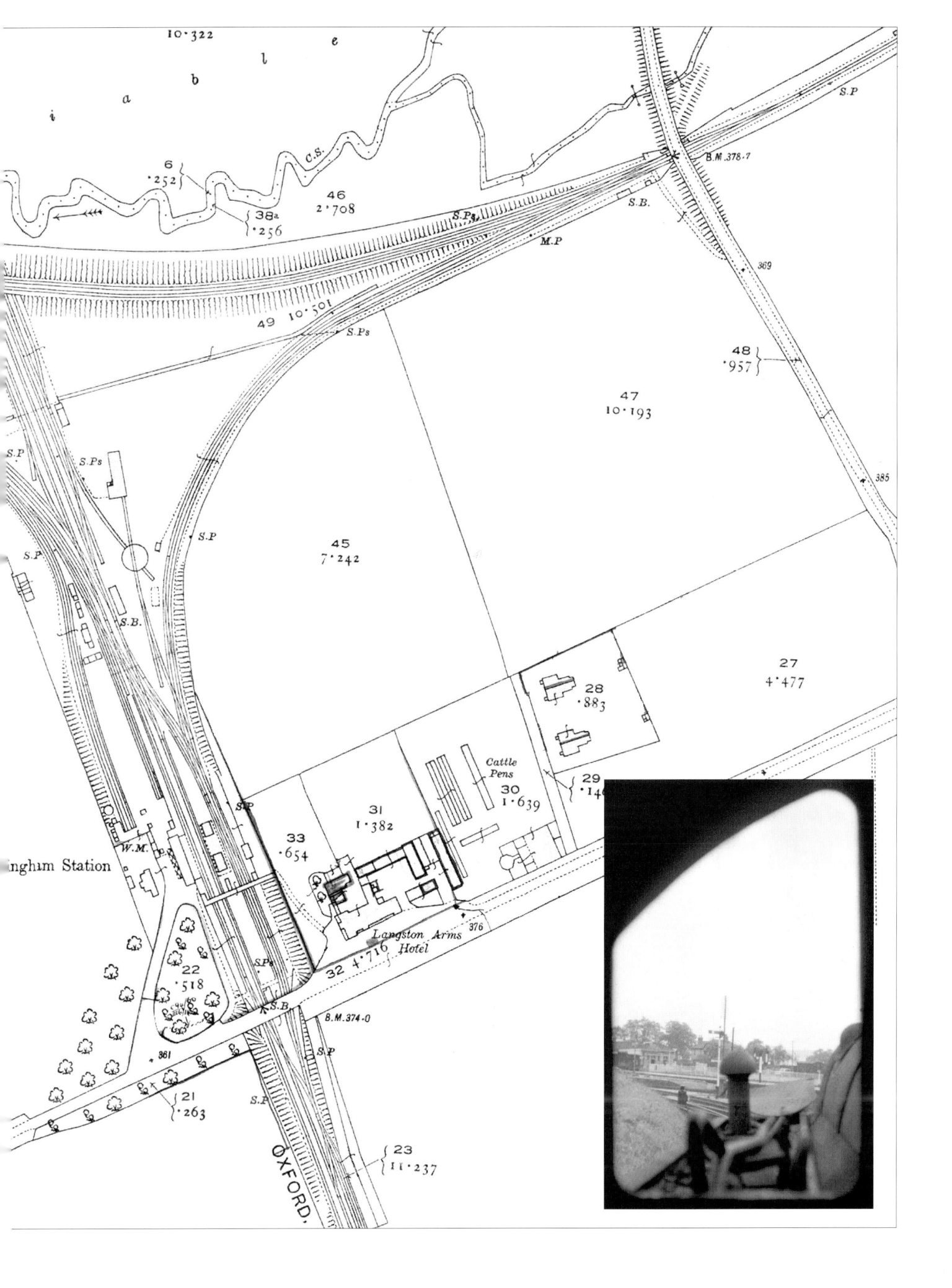

6
·252
38a
·256

46
2·708

49 10·501

48
·957

47
10·193

45
7·242

27
4·477

28
·883

Cattle Pens
30
1·639

29
·146

31
1·382

33
·654

22
·518

Langston Arms Hotel
32 4·716

...ingham Station

21
·263

23
11·237

OXFORD

B.M. 378·7

369

385

376

B.M. 374·0

361

S.P S.B. M.P W.M.

Kingham East Signal Box in the early 1950s, with the Chipping Norton branch curving round towards the station on the left and the direct line heading west towards Cheltenham on the right. No photograph has been found of Kingham West Signal Box but it is presumed to have been identical to Kingham East, as it was provided at the same time. They also both closed on the same day, 23rd September 1953.

Joe Moss, courtesy Roger Carpenter

THE BANBURY & CHELTENHAM DIRECT RAILWAY

Above: A view of the simplified junction on 9th July 1960, with all trace of the signal box having gone. By this date, the direct line was only being used for turning engines, such as the standard class 2-6-0s and Collett '2251' Class 0-6-0s which appeared on Chipping Norton goods trains. This line terminated at buffer stops just behind the photographer. West Junction was similarly remodelled, so that engines rejoined the running line via a trailing connection. *Michael Hale*

Left: Another fireman's-eye view from the cab of '51XX' Class large prairie No. 4142 on 22nd September 1962. The train is approaching the road bridge from which the views of Kingham East Junction were taken. The engine turning triangle and the junctions were finally removed in November 1961. *Paul Strong*

traders from a much wider area. On these occasions, Kingham's extensive cattle loading facilities could often be filled to capacity with standard Great Western 'Mex' cattle wagons, together with the company's less-familiar 'Beetle' prize cattle vans. The latter vehicles resembled horse boxes, in that they sported passenger brown livery and contained a small passenger compartment for the convenience of stockmen who accompanied the animals.

Another form of traffic generated by The Langston Arms arose, albeit indirectly, from the activities of the Heythrop Hunt. The Heythrop had started in 1835, as an offshoot of the Badminton Hunt which had once met regularly in north Oxfordshire. In those days, the Duke of Beaufort had hunted regularly in the north of the county, moving his dogs, horses and servants between Heythrop Park and Badminton. When this practice was abandoned by the 6th Duke, Lord Redesdale and other hunting enthusiasts formed the Heythrop Hunt to cover the country north of the Oxford to

Cheltenham road. The huntsmen and whippers-in nevertheless continued to wear Badminton-style green coats, in recognition of their origins.

The Heythrop kennels were subsequently moved from Heythrop Park to Chipping Norton and, perhaps for this reason, the hunt began to meet regularly at the Langston Arms. In this context, the availability of a rail link was clearly of great importance and many hunt members would travel to and from Kingham by train, their horses being unloaded from 'Paco' horse boxes in the Horse Dock on the Up side of the line.

The Great Western Railway was always regarded as an aristocratic company, its directors being drawn largely from the ranks of the landowning classes. Many of these individuals were enthusiastic horsemen and hunt meetings in GWR territory would invariably attract at least some of the company's own directors, or members of their families. One such director was Michael Mason of Eynsham Hall, who rode with the Heythrop and would habitually send his horse by train over the short distance between Handborough and Kingham stations – presumably making full use of his director's travel concessions!

Kingham's secluded location, and its extensive system of loops and sidings, made it an ideal overnight stopping place for the royal train and, in this context, the station was visited by royal specials on several occasions. On Tuesday January 16th 1940, for instance, King George VI made a wartime morale-boosting visit to factories and military installations in the Oxfordshire area. It was decided that the royal party would travel by train from Paddington to Kingham on the night of 16th January, arriving at Kingham at 1.10 am on the morning of the following day. The royal special was then stabled in the Down Cheltenham branch loop, where the King and his party were able to spend the night.

On the following morning, the 6.32 am branch train from

Above: A view of the main line and platforms 1 and 2, looking north from the footbridge probably in the late 1930s. A clerestory carriage can be seen in the bay on the left and the Down Starter bracket signal has yet to be replaced. *The Lens of Sutton Collection*
Top: The rear of the station building from the station approach road circa 1970. The yellow brickwork used in its construction is particularly evident in this view. The parcels office at the extreme right hand end of the building was added after World War Two, the extension being authorised in 1946 and completed in 1951. The doorway visible beneath the canopy gave access to the waiting room, the ticket window being on the right as one entered the room. *Stanley C. Jenkins*

Cheltenham to Kingham and the 8.36 am return working to Cheltenham were routed via Kingham East Junction and the Avoiding Loop, while the royal train remained safely berthed on the West Loop. At 9.15 am, the royal train was drawn into Kingham Down platform and the royal party alighted prior to travelling to Witney by road transport. The royal train then ran empty from Kingham to Witney, where the King rejoined the train for his return journey to London.

As usual, the royal special was composed of a mixture of special saloons, sleeping cars and brake firsts. The formation on arrival at Kingham consisted of brake composite No. 7061, sleeping composite No. 9090, brake saloon No. 9004, the royal saloon, brake saloon No. 9005, sleeping composite No. 9091, and brake first No. 8020. The two brake saloons were interesting, self-contained vehicles, boasting kitchen and pantry facilities suitable for VIPs, while the locomotive was 'Castle' Class 4-6-0 No. 5045 *The Earl of Dudley*.

The arrangements for stabling the royal special that ran over the western section of the B&CDR line on 22nd October 1941 (see previous chapter), were similar to those that had pertained on 16th January 1940, the West Loop again being used as the designated overnight stabling point. The special instructions issued in connection with the October 1941 visit stipulated that 'Hall' Class 4-6-0 No. 6917 would attach a battery van to the rear of the LMS royal train, '*the engine remaining on the train throughout the night for steam-heating purposes*', while second engine No. 6921 was '*released and sent to Kingham station*', where it was '*employed throughout the night*'.

Curiously, the copious set of special working instructions issued in January 1940 made no mention of a battery van – possibly because the electrical systems on the LMS royal train differed from those on the GWR train (alternatively, the battery van may have been needed in connection with some form of wireless telegraphy apparatus, whereby the King was able to maintain contact with his ministers).

The use of Kingham as a stabling point for the royal train continued after the war and former station master T.W. Lane recalled that '*in 1950, the royal train with the King and Queen arrived late one evening, and they spent the night on the train, which was parked on the curve to Cheltenham. I had to remain on duty all night with many others and saw them safely away next morning on their way to Stratford-upon-Avon*'.

The picturesque village of Kingham was about a mile to the north-east of the station. It consisted chiefly of one long, main street, a large village green and a heavily-restored 15th century parish church. The limestone cottages were similar to their counterparts in the Gloucestershire Cotswolds, although many of them had thatched roofs instead of the limestone slates seen further west. The village's population during the mid 20th century was barely 500, although this meagre figure does not seem to have detracted from Kingham's importance as a passenger station.

The station also served the hamlet of Foscot, about half a mile to the south-west, and the village of Bledington, a mile

This close-up of one of the station nameboards was taken on 2nd June 1951, the final day of passenger services beyond Chipping Norton and thus the letters spelling out 'Banbury' were about to be removed. The auto-coach used was adorned with union flags and a wreath to commemorate the last day.

Bob Brown collection

Above: The later underslung Down Starter bracket signal, photographed on 29th May 1964 from an Oxford-bound train. This unusual design allowed drivers of fast Down trains to sight the signals under the station's canopies much more easily. Also by this date, the branch to Cheltenham going off to the left was now freight only and in use only as far as Bourton-on-the-Water, whilst the avoiding line bridge has been dismantled. *A.A. Vickers*

Above right: The Up Starting signal on Platform Four, photographed on 6th October 1951. The shunting arm controlled entry to the Up siding and horse dock. *P. J. Garland, courtesy Roger Carpenter*

Below: This 1920s view from the eastern end of the footbridge clearly shows the sinuous path taken by trains from Cheltenham to reach Platform Three. Coming down the West curve (by the van parked outside the goods yard), they ran briefly onto the main line before swinging off onto the double crossover, which was used to gain access to the platform. The small brick building on Platform 4 (right) comprised a public waiting area and a gentlemen's urinal. The triple-arm Starting signal at the end of Platform 4 actually applied to Platform 3. *Roger Carpenter collection*

The 4.50 pm service to Chipping Norton about to leave Kingham on 9th July 1960, with '45XX' Class 2-6-2T No. 4573 in charge. Note the nameboard is now missing its 'Banbury' destination. *Michael Hale*

Left: The Down Starting signal on the north end of Platform 3, complete with its theatre type route indicator. This single-armed signal, and the double bracket signal on the extreme right, replaced the 3-armed bracket signal seen previously at the end of Platform 4. *Bob Brown collection*

Below: A '51XX' Class prairie with a service from Cheltenham winds its way across the main line to enter the branch platform in 1962. Another 2-6-2T sits in the locomotive shed in the background, waiting for its next turn of duty, probably to Chipping Norton, the branch to which can be seen curving away on the right. The huge water tower supplied four water columns on the platforms, as well as one outside the shed and latterly was painted the yellowy cream beloved by BR (Western Region), with the base of the columns in chocolate. In earlier years it would have been in GWR light and dark stone. Note the platform flower beds are in full bloom, a feature of so many stations in the days when the staff took pride in their surroundings and had the time to look after them. Note also the slight drop in height on this end of the Up platform. *Bob Brown collection*

Left: Collett '54XX' Class 0-6-0 pannier tank No. 5404 waits in Platform Three with the 12.35 pm auto train to Banbury on 30th May 1951. The auto train service was affectionately known as the 'Chippy Dick' by staff and passengers alike. With the demise of the Banbury trains, prairie tanks took over most of the passenger duties on the remaining services to Chipping Norton.

T.J. Edgington, courtesy Roger Carpenter

Right: Having just brought in a service from Cheltenham, '51XX' Class 2-6-2T No. 4142 is seen in the process of running round its train on 22nd September 1962. With closure of both branches to passenger services imminent, No. 4142's train was an enthusiasts' special and, instead of heading straight back to Cheltenham, it was due to carry on to Chipping Norton.

Paul Strong

Left: A pick-up goods service from the Chipping Norton branch waits alongside Platform Four in 1954. Bound for the yards at Oxford, the crew of '2251' Class 0-6-0 No. 2202 have paused to wait for the road, which, as can be seen from the Up Branch Platform Starter on the right, has just been given. It will be noted that No. 2202 is in clean external condition. These attractively proportioned engines were regularly used on goods services along the line, having taken over from the 'Dean Goods' 0-6-0s.

Adrian Vaughan collection

By the late 1950s, the footbridge roof had become life expired and was removed. Although less spectacular in appearance as a result, the bridge certainly fitted in to the overall scene more easily in its reduced state. Following final closure of the Cheltenham and Chipping Norton lines, the original station buildings were demolished in 1975, to be replaced by a rather bland single storey ticket office. The footbridge survives, although it now only spans the main line platforms. Altogether, as with many medium sized main line stations fallen on reduced circumstances, Kingham now presents a rather depressing scene, although it is well-served by trains between Worcester and Oxford. Indeed, it is lucky to survive, as complete closure of the route was mooted in the 1960s. However, thanks in no small part to the efforts of the Cotswold Line Promotion Group, the line still provides a useful service. In this circa 1960 general view of the station from the road bridge, a Cheltenham train can be seen waiting in Platform Three. *Bob Brown collection*

to the west. Curiously, the 1938 GWR publication *Towns, Villages, Outlying Works Etc* reveals there were at that time no formal collection or delivery arrangements for either Kingham or Foscot, though Bledington was served by Great Western country lorries from Bourton-on-the-Water. Perhaps for this reason, private taxi operators became well-established in the vicinity, one such operator being based in a small garage in the station approach.

City of Oxford Motor Services buses also called at the station on a regular basis, Kingham being on several City of Oxford routes, including those from Chipping Norton to Stow-on-the-Wold (Route 45), Chipping Norton to Little Rissington (Route 50) and Chipping Norton to Witney (Route 55). The buses normally pulled up in front of the Down side station building, affording travellers a convenient interchange facility.

On a minor point of interest, it may be remarked that City of Oxford vehicles sported a most attractive livery, incorporating maroon bodywork and purple-brown roofs, these two main colours being relieved by horizontal bands of contrasting apple green. The bus company was part-owned by the Great Western Railway, which had purchased 49 per cent of its shares in 1930 but, despite this close association, there was little attempt to co-ordinate rail and bus services in this part of Oxfordshire.

In practice, the station functioned as a railhead for people living in a wide rural area, this process being encouraged by the fact that Kingham enjoyed a main line service to Paddington. For this reason, it attracted passengers from towns and villages such as Chipping Norton and Bourton-on-the-Water, many of whom used road transport to and from Kingham in preference to the Banbury & Cheltenham branch services. In the longer term, Kingham was destined to survive as a main line station and, in this context, it has remained an important part of the local railway infrastructure.

A final view looking north towards Worcester, on 9th July 1960 with, from left to right, the line to Cheltenham curving away to the west, the main line going straight on under the direct line bridge, Kingham Station Signal Box, the engine shed and water tower, and the Chipping Norton branch curving away to the north-east. Note that, by this date, the track leading from Platform 3 had been changed to a single line splitting into two for the junction with the main line. Note also the check rails on the sharply curving Chipping Norton line. *Bob Brown collection*

Kingham was, for many years, the home of William Warde Fowler, the author of *A Year with the Birds* (1885). This famous book, which did much to popularise ornithology, described the bird life of two districts, one of these being Oxford (where the author taught classics), while the other was Kingham and its surroundings. Fowler had lived in Kingham since the 1870s and, as a frequent traveller to and from Oxford, his observations contain various references to the local railways. He had obviously watched the Banbury & Cheltenham Direct line being built, and he noted that '*both cuttings and embankments*', as soon as they were '*well overgrown with grass*', afforded '*secure and sunny nesting places to a number of birds which build their nests on the ground*'.

He added that nests found in and around the station and goods yard were '*carefully protected by the employees of the company*', while at one time the wagtails used to build their nests in the crevices of the sacks of coal. On one occasion, there was a nest in the buffer stops near the signal cabin – or as Warde Fowler quaintly put it, '*just beneath the massive wooden posts fixed at the end of a siding to resist the force of shunted trucks*'. Warde Fowler's other noted work was *Kingham Old & New* (1921), which also contains several contemporary references to the local railway system, including an account of an epic, six hour journey between Oxford and Chipping Norton Junction during the great snow storm of 18th January 1881.

Before leaving Kingham, it may be worth mentioning that the station was the setting for a spectacular incident on Friday 15th July 1966, when the rear coach of the 12.30 pm express from Hereford to Paddington was derailed by defective trackwork. The vehicle came off the rails as the train was passing the signal box, finally coming to rest against the Down platform. The remaining part of the train continued to London after a 45 minute delay but both lines were blocked for a further 24 hours. Several passengers were taken to Chipping Norton hospital but there were no serious injuries. The accident was caused by the negligence of permanent way men, who were removing redundant pointwork at the time.

On departure from Kingham, Banbury trains immediately swung north-eastwards through a full ninety degree turn as they left the OW&WR main line. Following the route of the original Chipping Norton Railway, eastbound workings soon reached Kingham East Junction (24 miles 46 chains), where the east-to-west Avoiding Line converged from the left. The junction was controlled from a standard GWR hipped-roof signal cabin known as Kingham East Junction Box, which was sited on the Down side of the line near the actual point of convergence.

The East Curve and the east-to-west Avoiding Line were both double track but the line became single immediately beyond Kingham East Junction. Kingham East and Kingham West Junction boxes were abolished in September 1953 and the East Curve was then reduced to two single tracks. The Down Avoiding Line was lifted but the former Up line was left *in situ* to form an engine turning line, in conjunction with the East Curve and one of the single lines on the neighbouring West Curve.

CHURCHILL CROSSING

Passing a minor road bridge, eastbound (or Up) services set off across open countryside, with the village of Kingham visible across fields to the left. After about a mile, the single line crossed Churchill Lane by means of a gated level crossing (25 miles 57 chains), the crossing gates being controlled by a resident gatekeeper who lived in a single-storey cottage on the Up side of the line. As usual in such cases, the gate-keeper was warned of approaching trains by means of an indicator and repeater bell. The gate-keeper's cottage was of red brick construction, with a gabled, slated roof.

The 1881 census reveals that the crossing keeper at that time was William Dickens, aged 67, who lived in the gate lodge with his wife Ann, aged 63, and unmarried daughter Frances, aged 25. William Dickens had been born in the nearby parish of Bledington and his occupation was given as *'railway policeman'* – an archaic term denoting a railway signalman. Frances Dickens was described as a *'dressmaker'*. The gate-keeper at the time of closure in 1964 was William Cook, who had lived and worked at Churchill Crossing since the Great Western period.

Top right: Churchill Crossing circa 1900, with the crossing keeper, his wife and baby posed for the photographer in front of their cottage. Note the 'S' and 'T' plates on the wall behind the baby's head.
Courtesy Kidderminster Railway Museum
Right: Churchill Crossing ground frame, not long before closure but looking newly painted, on 13th May 1962.
P.J. Garland, courtesy Roger Carpenter

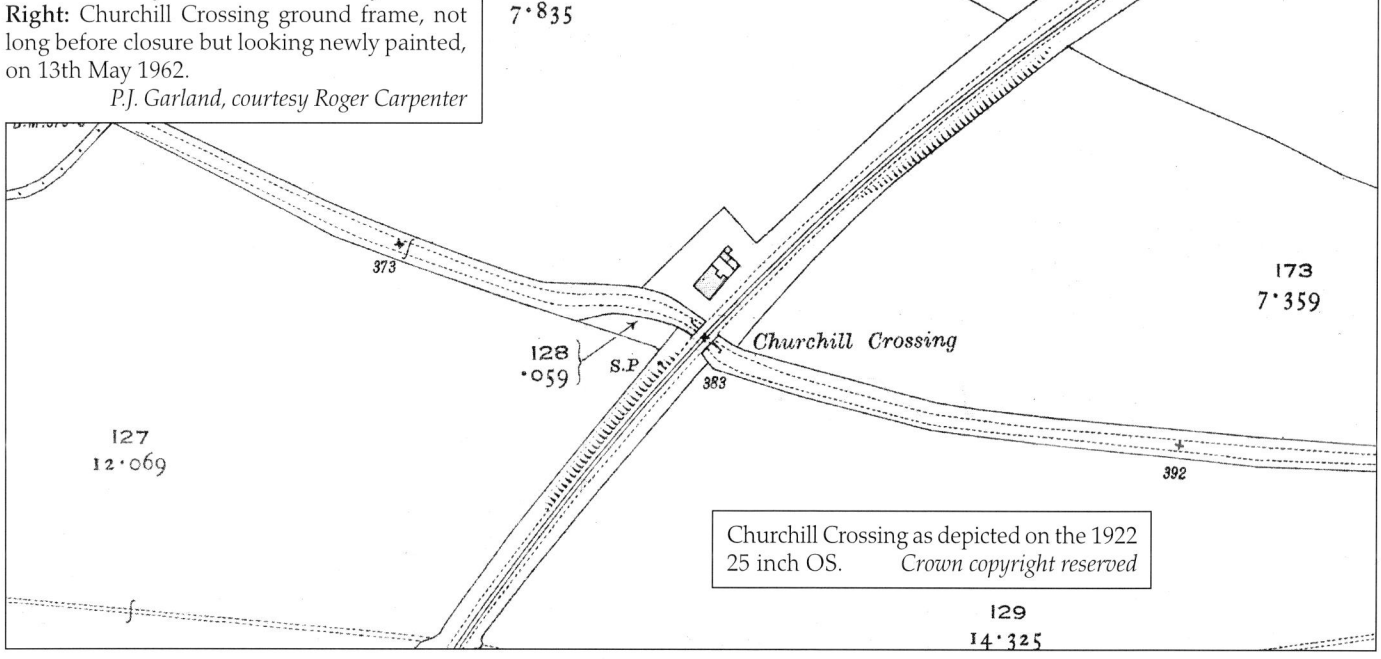

Churchill Crossing as depicted on the 1922 25 inch OS. *Crown copyright reserved*

Sarsden Halt actually served the small village of Churchill but was so named because the local landowner, Earl Ducie, who lived at nearby Sarsden House, requested it carry that name. It was originally the site of a short platform for goods traffic, which was replaced by the timber passenger platform seen here in 1906. A '517' Class 0-4-2T waits obligingly at the halt with the 3.15pm from Chipping Norton Junction around 1908. Note the grubby Toomer, R. & Co. wagon on the right: they were coal merchants based in the Reading area but with depots and agents from London to the Forest of Dean. *John Alsop collection*

SARSDEN HALT

Beyond, the route continued north-eastwards to Sarsden Halt, some 26 miles 5 chains from Cheltenham. The halt had been opened on 2nd July 1906, and its modest facilities consisted of a single platform for passengers and a loop siding for goods traffic. The platform, of sleeper construction, was 150 feet in length and situated on the Up side, while the goods siding was sited on the opposite side of the running line. The siding had a length of about 480 feet.

The halt was equipped with a typical Great Western corrugated iron 'pagoda' shed for the convenience of waiting passengers, while at night the wooden platform was illuminated by simple oil lamps, resting in four glass lanterns supported on wooden uprights. For operational purposes, Sarsden was under the supervision of the station master at Chipping Norton.

A minor road crossed the line on the level at the west end of the platform and there was a small signal box on the Up side. The box, which pre-dated the halt by several years, was a GWR brick and timber design, with a gable roof and small-

The timetable board for the Rail Motor Cars (generally today referred to as auto trains). In later years certainly, it was placed on the old goods office, situated on the Up side of the railway by the road entrance to the station. The board is today a remarkable survivor from this tiny halt and can be found in the collection at the Winchcombe Railway Museum.

Phil Coutanche

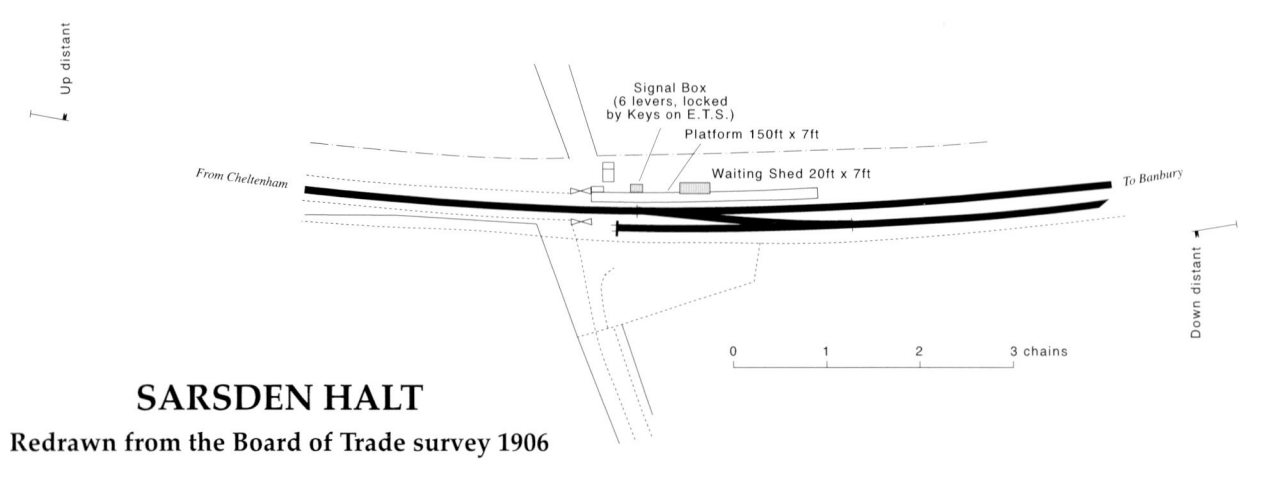

SARSDEN HALT
Redrawn from the Board of Trade survey 1906

A charming scene from around 1908, portraying a relaxed way of life that has sadly gone forever. The signal box pre-dated the passenger halt, having been opened in 1893. It was reduced to the status of a crossing ground frame in March 1899. The metal plates located either side of the nameplate indicate the state of the signalling and telegraph equipment in the box. If all was well, the plates would show an 'S' or 'T' in white on a black background; if there was a fault they would be reversed to show red letters on a white background, the idea being that passing inspectors or linesmen would see there was a fault and so report it. It would thus appear that there was a problem with the telegraph equipment when this picture was taken. Is the lad bringing the newspaper for his dad to read? *John Alsop collection*

paned windows. It was very similar to the signal cabin at Stow-on-the-Wold, both boxes having been constructed during the 1890s as part of a programme of improvements carried out at that time. Sarsden Crossing Box was opened in 1893 and reduced to 'ground frame' status in March 1899. A crossing keeper's house was authorised on 31st October 1929 and completed in the following year at a cost of £480. It was sited on the Down side of the line.

The loop siding was linked to the running line by connections at each end, the siding points being locked from a frame in the signal cabin and released by a key on the single line staff. The signal box also controlled working Up and Down distant signals, which protected Churchill level crossing and were interlocked with the crossing gates. A 15 ton cart weighbridge was authorised at Sarsden in 1913 at a cost of £152, and this facility was conveniently sited beside the goods siding; there was no weigh-house as such, the wooden hut provided being barely large enough to cover the weighing machine.

Sarsden Siding was used for occasional consignments of coal, sugar beet or other full wagon load traffic that was loaded or unloaded by individual farmers or traders. The siding appears never to have been listed in the *Railway Clearing House Handbook of Stations* as being available for

Close inspection of this photograph suggests that it depicts the same gentleman as in the picture above but a little older and greyer. If so, the picture would date from circa 1920. With the box having by now been reduced to crossing ground frame status, he was presumably acting as signalman, crossing keeper and porter at the halt, and may have also taken on the goods office duties by this date as well.

John Alsop collection

234 THE BANBURY & CHELTENHAM DIRECT RAILWAY

A young porter poses with his pet cat on the steps of the signal box, in this view showing almost the full extent of the layout at Sarsden, circa 1908. It is likely that his duties included the running of the tiny goods office here. A rake of open wagons can just be seen on the right in the process of being unloaded. Coal inwards and agricultural produce outwards would have been the main forms of traffic. Worthy of note are the oil lamps complete with the halt's name on the glass, quite extravagant for such a small stopping place as this, and also the inside-chaired track. The wagon tarpaulin seen slung over the platform railing in the view on the previous page is here in use protecting some small boxes on the platform, whilst the 'T' plate is still showing red on white. The young lady on the platform, in typical Edwardian costume of hat and dress, is unusually oblivious to the photographer; it was still a novelty to have one's picture taken at this date.

John Alsop collection

Above: The GWR finally provided a crossing keeper's cottage in 1930 following the acquisition of more land. The cottage was to a standard design, being brick built (with cement rendering) and having a half-hipped roof. On the extreme right is the mill and just beyond the crossing is the Distant signal for Churchill crossing, just over half a mile away.

Right: A well known view of the halt looking towards the crossing, taken soon after opening in 1906. The two men with shovels are probably local coal merchants or agricultural workers, unloading a wagon in the siding and taking the opportunity to have their picture taken.
Both Bob Brown collection

public goods traffic. In general, goods and parcels were collected and delivered in the Churchill and Sarsden areas by Great Western county lorries from Bourton-on-the-Water or Shipton (for Burford) stations.

In earlier years, Sarsden had dealt with a considerable amount of milk traffic, milk churns being brought to the halt twice a day in two-wheeled farmers' carts. This traffic declined after World War One, in part because of the effects of road transport but also because of the introduction of glass-lined milk tank wagons and the development of centralised dairies at nearby stations such as Moreton-in-the-Marsh.

Sarsden served the nearby village of Churchill, although its name was apparently derived from nearby Sarsden House, a 17th century mansion which was extensively remodelled during the 1820s at the behest of James Langston, the then owner. Neighbouring Churchill was the birthplace of Warren Hastings (1732-1818), the first Governor-General of India, who upheld the prestige of the British Empire at the time of the disastrous American War.

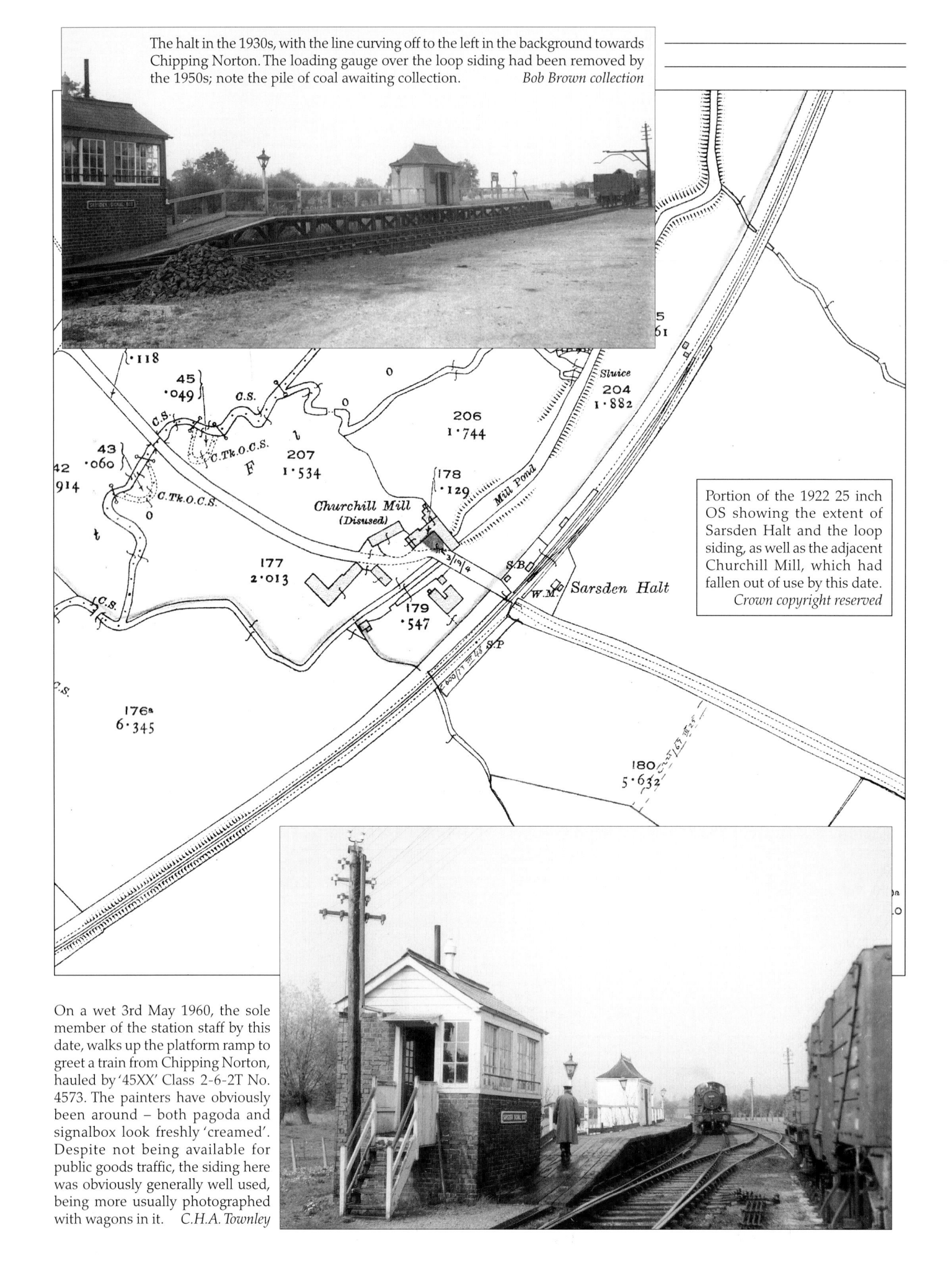

The halt in the 1930s, with the line curving off to the left in the background towards Chipping Norton. The loading gauge over the loop siding had been removed by the 1950s; note the pile of coal awaiting collection. *Bob Brown collection*

Portion of the 1922 25 inch OS showing the extent of Sarsden Halt and the loop siding, as well as the adjacent Churchill Mill, which had fallen out of use by this date. *Crown copyright reserved*

On a wet 3rd May 1960, the sole member of the station staff by this date, walks up the platform ramp to greet a train from Chipping Norton, hauled by '45XX' Class 2-6-2T No. 4573. The painters have obviously been around – both pagoda and signalbox look freshly 'creamed'. Despite not being available for public goods traffic, the siding here was obviously generally well used, being more usually photographed with wagons in it. *C.H.A. Townley*

Above: Coal traffic is evident in this circa 1960 view of the halt, with a lone 16-ton mineral wagon fulfilling the day's needs. The local coal merchant is unloading it by hand directly into his Morris pick-up truck. Note that the siding in the foreground is laid with concrete pots and tie bars rather than conventional sleepers, following relaying in the early 1940s. The pollarded willow trees seen behind the platform mark the course of the mill stream. *Bob Brown collection*

Right: On another dismal day, 27th March 1960, '45XX' Class 2-6-2T No. 4573 is again the branch engine, arriving at Sarsden Halt with the 4.53 pm from Chipping Norton to Cheltenham. *D.R. Lewis*

This tiny Cotswold village was also the birthplace of William Smith (1769-1839), the 'Father of British Geology', who made the first geological maps and introduced many of the names by which we know the various rock strata.

Sarsden Halt was also conveniently sited in relation to Kingham Hill School, a little over one mile to the north of the railway. Kingham Hill was originally founded as a charitable school for orphans and slum children. The founder, the wealthy Victorian philanthropist Charles Baring-Young (who sought no personal credit for his work) hoped that 'The Kingham Homes' would enable deprived boys to learn profitable trades in healthy rural surroundings and, in 1886, the architect W. Howard Seth Smith was commissioned to design the necessary boarding houses, school rooms and workshops in a traditional Cotswold style.

The school was richly-endowed and in the fullness of time it came to be regarded as a conventional boy's boarding school, although its charitable origins were never entirely forgotten. Like most boarding schools, it generated a certain amount of traffic for the railway, particularly at the beginning and end of term when the scholars and their trunks arrived or departed by train. In practice, the main line station at Kingham probably handled most of this traffic, though the 1938 *Book of Towns, Villages & Outlying Works* lists Chipping Norton or Sarsden Siding as the normal railheads for Kingham Hill.

On Sunday April 24th 1955, the Railway Enthusiasts Club ran the 'South Midlander', a railtour starting from Oxford which travelled over the Kingham to Kings Sutton line. It provided a rare chance to travel over the section east from Chipping Norton, which had been closed to passengers three years previously. For added interest, hauling the train was 'Dukedog' 4-4-0 No. 9015, a type which had probably not appeared on the line since the heyday of the 'Ports-to-Ports express'. From King's Sutton, the tour then ran onto the old Stratford & Midland Junction line at Fenny Compton, taking the avoiding curve at Broom to reach Evesham (Midland) station. A reversal onto the ex-GWR Worcester to Oxford line followed, with the train then heading to Moreton-in-Marsh. Here, a journey was taken along the Shipston-on-Stour branch, for which the motive power was 'Dean Goods' 0-6-0 No. 2474 making its last ever trip. The 'Dukedogs' were actually a hybrid, being rebuilds using 'Bulldog' frames and 'Duke' boilers, hence the nickname. Built between 1936-9, the GWR classed them as 'Earls', allocating them Earl names. No. 9015, built in 1937 and originally numbered 3215, was allocated the name *Earl of Clancarty* but, in common with several others of the class, never carried its plates. Here, the train is seen approaching Chipping Norton amidst some classic English countryside. *J.F. Russell Smith, courtesy NRM*

CHIPPING NORTON

Leaving Sarsden Halt in a north-easterly direction, trains continued their ascent towards Chipping Norton which, with an elevation of around 600 feet above mean sea level, is Oxfordshire's highest town. Crossing the 400 foot contour, the railway passed beneath another minor road bridge, beyond which the single line curved rightwards onto an easterly heading. A little over one mile further on, the route turned northwards through a full ninety degrees and, having passed William Bliss's striking Italianate mill on the left hand side of the line, trains came to rest in the curved platforms at Chipping Norton station (28 miles 59 chains).

The layout here was dictated by geography and by the historical development of railways in the Chipping Norton area. As previously mentioned, Chipping Norton was the terminus of the line from 1855 until 1887, when the original Chipping Norton Railway was extended to King's Sutton by the Banbury & Cheltenham Direct Railway. The 1855 terminus then became part of an enlarged goods yard, which diverged north-eastwards from the B&CDR route on a tangential alignment.

On a footnote, it may be remarked that virtually none of the earlier infrastructure was retained when the former terminus was adapted for its new role. The platform, station building, train shed and goods shed were removed in their entirety, though the engine shed appears to have been retained, in modified form, for several years. This drastic reconstruction was presumably considered necessary because the authorised Banbury & Cheltenham route cut through the original goods yard. Moreover, the redundant terminal buildings could not be adapted for loading or unloading coal or other types of goods traffic and they were therefore demolished.

The resited passenger station incorporated a long crossing loop, with Up and Down platforms on each side. The main station building was sited on the Down platform and the Up and Down platforms were linked by an elegant, lattice girder footbridge. At the north end of the platforms, the line entered a deep cutting, which was crossed by a brick overbridge with a single arched span of 25 feet. A 20 mph speed restriction applied to trains running through the passenger station, which was sited on a sharp curve.

This poorly printed circa 1905 postcard view is included simply because it is unusual. It is the only picture we have seen from this particular viewpoint and shows the reverse of Bliss Mill, with a portion of the gas works on the left and the railway approach to Chipping Norton running across the centre of the view. The housing was for mill workers. *Neil Parkhouse collection*

In architectural terms, Chipping Norton station building could be described as an enlarged version of the Banbury & Cheltenham Direct Railway buildings at Leckhampton and Andoversford. It was of brick construction, with a gable roof and a recessed loggia in the platform frontage. The booking hall and general waiting room were situated in the central part of the building, while the ticket office was situated to the right of the booking hall (when viewed from the platform). The ladies' room was to the left of the general waiting room, and the gentlemen's urinals were sited at the very end of the building.

The platform frontage was covered by a full length canopy and, as usual on Victorian railway buildings, this featured wooden valancing with fretwork decoration. The only accommodation for waiting travellers on the Up side comprised a small brick waiting room with a single pitch roof. The roof was carried forward over the platform to form a small canopy and this was edged with ovular fretwork that matched that on the main station building.

At night, the platforms were lit by gas lamps fitted with traditional, tapered glass lanterns, while circular 'mushroom' style water tanks were sited at the north end of the Up platform and the south end of the Down. Both of these water tanks were fitted with rotating booms and flexible hoses, by means of which locomotives were able to replenish their tanks.

Chipping Norton was at one time signalled from two signal boxes, known as Chipping Norton West Box and Chipping Norton East Box. The East Box was sited on the Down platform next to the station building, whereas the West Box was situated at the west end of the crossing loop, near the goods yard throat. These arrangements were modified in August 1929 when the West Box was abolished and the station was then signalled from the former East Box, which was renamed Chipping Norton Signal Box.

The surviving signal box was a diminutive, one-and-

Looking along New Street from the town centre, with the Baptist chapel visible above the trees on the right, circa 1910. The station entrance was on the left around the bend in the distance. In the foreground, one of the local coal merchants is making a delivery, whilst the other carts and wagons visible are most probably either heading to or from the station, some with passengers and others bound for the goods yard.
Oxfordshire County Council Photographic Archive

A view of the station from the road circa 1910, with the lane leading to Bliss Mill dropping down on the right and running behind the Up platform. A '517' Class 0-4-2T is just pulling into the platform with a Kingham-bound train. Note the traction engine in steam in the goods yard in the centre background. *John Alsop collection*

The original 1855 terminus at Chipping Norton was replaced by this station in 1887, when the line opened through to King's Sutton. This postcard view dates from circa 1905 and shows the Down platform with quite a crowd of passengers in typical Edwardian dress, waiting for the arrival of the next service from Banbury to the junction. The ornate non-standard (in GWR terms) footbridge may well have been an 'off the shelf' purchase from one of the companies specialising in the manufacture of such hardware. *John Alsop collection*

THE BANBURY & CHELTENHAM DIRECT RAILWAY

Photographed on a hot summer's day, sometime between the wars – the station is seen nearing the end of its prime. Regular train services were running over the whole of the route, as well as the Up and Down 'Ports-to-Ports' expresses' passing through on a daily basis, and GWR country bus services were feeding passengers into the station from outlying villages. The goods shed, in the centre background, had connections to the running lines from both directions. However, this eastern end was only connected directly to the Up line, with a single slip on the Down line to allow it also to be used as a crossover between the two lines. The eastern end of this loop was removed on 30th September 1956 and for the last few years of the yard's life it was shunted from the western end only. For many years, a short stub siding had existed, running from the loop to near the end of the Down platform but this had been removed by 1923 and there is no sign of it in this view. Note also that the Distant signal at the end of the Down platform is painted in the earlier style with a white 'V' on a red background. This practice ceased in favour of yellow arms with a black 'V' from 1927 onwards in the provinces, thus dating this photograph to circa 1930. *Neil Parkhouse collection*

Some of the employees of the Chipping Norton Gas & Coke Company Ltd pose in front of the works around 1905. The retort house and chimney can be seen on the right and there were two gas holders beyond, with a third seen here on the left. The private siding was authorised on 1st November 1871, with the agreement for its use being signed on 22nd May 1872. It was in use by 4th September that year but the company seemingly got into difficulties a few years later and the PSA was terminated on 12th September 1879. A new agreement was signed with a company of the same name on 26th April 1883, which was renewed four years later. Further renewal on 3rd February 1892 also included authorisation for the extension of the siding by 40 feet. It was renewed again in 1902 and then on 8th May 1907, a new agreement was signed with the Mid Oxfordshire Gas, Light & Coke Company Ltd. The siding was worked by its own ground frame, situated on the Down side of the line – to the right in this view. The three nearer wagons all belong to the Wynnstay Colliery Co. This colliery was situated close by Ruabon station, in Denbighshire, and near also to Wynnstay House, the seat of GWR director Sir Watkin Williams-Wynn (1820–85), after whom it took its name. The colliery supplied gas coal to a number of gas works in the Oxfordshire and Berkshire area. *Bob Brown collection*

Left: A closer view of the gas works and siding, taken on the same day as the previous picture. Bliss Mill dominates the valley at this point and is seen in the right background, whilst the house visible to the right of the wagon was the residence of the Works Manager. One of the by-products of coal gas production was coke and a small works such as this seems to have found a market for what it was producing. The weighing scales positioned on the wooden platform would indicate that coke was being bagged and sent out from here, which is presumably what the GW 4-plank open will be used for. Coal deliveries were probably shovelled onto a stockpile near the end of the siding and then barrowed into the retort house for use. By 1924, the private siding agreement was with the Chipping Norton Gas Company, which concern ran the works until just after the Second World War. It is not thought any of the companies that had operated the works ever actually owned any wagons. However, there is a record of the Chipping Norton Gas Co. hiring two wagons from the Gloucester RC&W Co. in 1891 for a period of eight months. This may have been a trial to see if it was worth purchasing wagons of their own or because of a short term problem with their gas coal supply. On nationalisation of the gas producing industry in 1947, many small works were quickly closed down and the Chipping Norton Gas Company seems to have suffered the same fate. The PSA was terminated on 13th June 1952 and the removal of the siding was proposed just three months later. It had gone by the following year.

Bob Brown collection

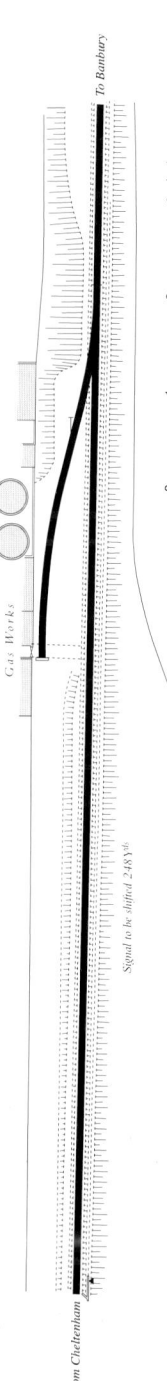

Right: Plan of the gas works siding circa 1885. A later version, showing the extended siding, appears on the OS map reproduced on pages 250-1.

Bliss's new Lower Mill opened on 7th February 1873, replacing the previous building which had been destroyed by fire. The fine Italianate structure is seen here around 1905, in view from across the railway and with a spot of permanent way maintenance underway on the left. The gated entrance to the mill private siding is on the right. The agreement for the siding was first signed with Bliss & Sons on 12th November 1884 and a further agreement was signed on 18th June 1889, which included authorisation to extend the siding. It is believed this refers to the siding on which the wagons can just be seen standing in the extreme left background, which was in any case an extension of the goods run round loop of the original terminus. By 1946, the PSA was with William Bliss & Son Ltd and it was terminated in 1964, when the rest of the branch was finally closed completely. *Barry Davies collection*

a-half storey structure with a brick base and a timber-framed upper storey. It had a gabled, slated roof and four-pane window frames, together with spike finials, and elaborate pierced and scalloped barge boards. The building was of non-Great Western origin, having clearly been supplied by a specialist signalling contractor such as the Railway Signalling Company. The abandoned West Box was, similarly, a contractor's cabin which had probably been supplied by the Gloucester Wagon Company. Photographic evidence reveals it to have been a typical gable-roofed, all-timber cabin with four-pane windows and ornate barge boards.

The goods yard, to the south of the platforms on the Down side, contained six long sidings and a short spur. One of these was a long reception siding while another served as the Goods Shed Road, both of these sidings being arranged as loops with connections at each end. A spur at the Banbury end of the reception loop continued northwards for a short distance, terminating in an end-loading dock near the end of the Down platform. Two more sidings, both dead end roads, fanned out behind the goods shed; one of these terminated alongside the cattle loading dock, whilst the other was used for various forms of wagon load traffic.

Two further sidings were available at the rear of the yard. One of these was used primarily for coal and mineral traffic, the other being the former engine shed road; these two sidings converged at their north end to form a loop. Finally, there was a short spur to the south-east of the old shed road. This had presumably functioned as a coaling road in the days when locomotives were sub-shedded at Chipping

The station staff's pride and joy. The attractive rock garden behind the Up platform circa 1912. *Neil Parkhouse collection*

Norton, although it served no real purpose after the closure of the engine shed. Indeed, the shed siding could not be used for loading or unloading purposes, as it had no road access and for this reason it served as a spare road on which wagons could be parked during shunting operations.

Chipping Norton goods shed was a large and impressive structure, with a spacious loading platform. It was of standard GWR brick construction and measured around 121 feet overall. The internal loading platform was equipped with two fixed hand cranes and, as originally constructed, it incorporated two cart docks for road vehicles, these being entered through large doorways in the east wall. In British Railways days, further apertures were cut through the east-facing wall, five of the original windows being filled in to facilitate this modification.

A two-storey office wing adjoined the north gable of the

Above: A view from the roof of the mill, looking across to the goods yard, with Bliss's private siding in the right foreground and the station just coming in to view on the far left. Note the chimney of Bliss's Upper Mill amongst the trees just right of centre. *John Alsop collection*

Right: Although only a minor incident in railway terms, the accident of 23rd May 1907 alongside Chipping Norton West Box was recorded on a number of different postcard views by Frank Packer. This one is looking in the opposite direction to that on page 93 and shows the box in particular in more detail. *Nigel Oram collection*

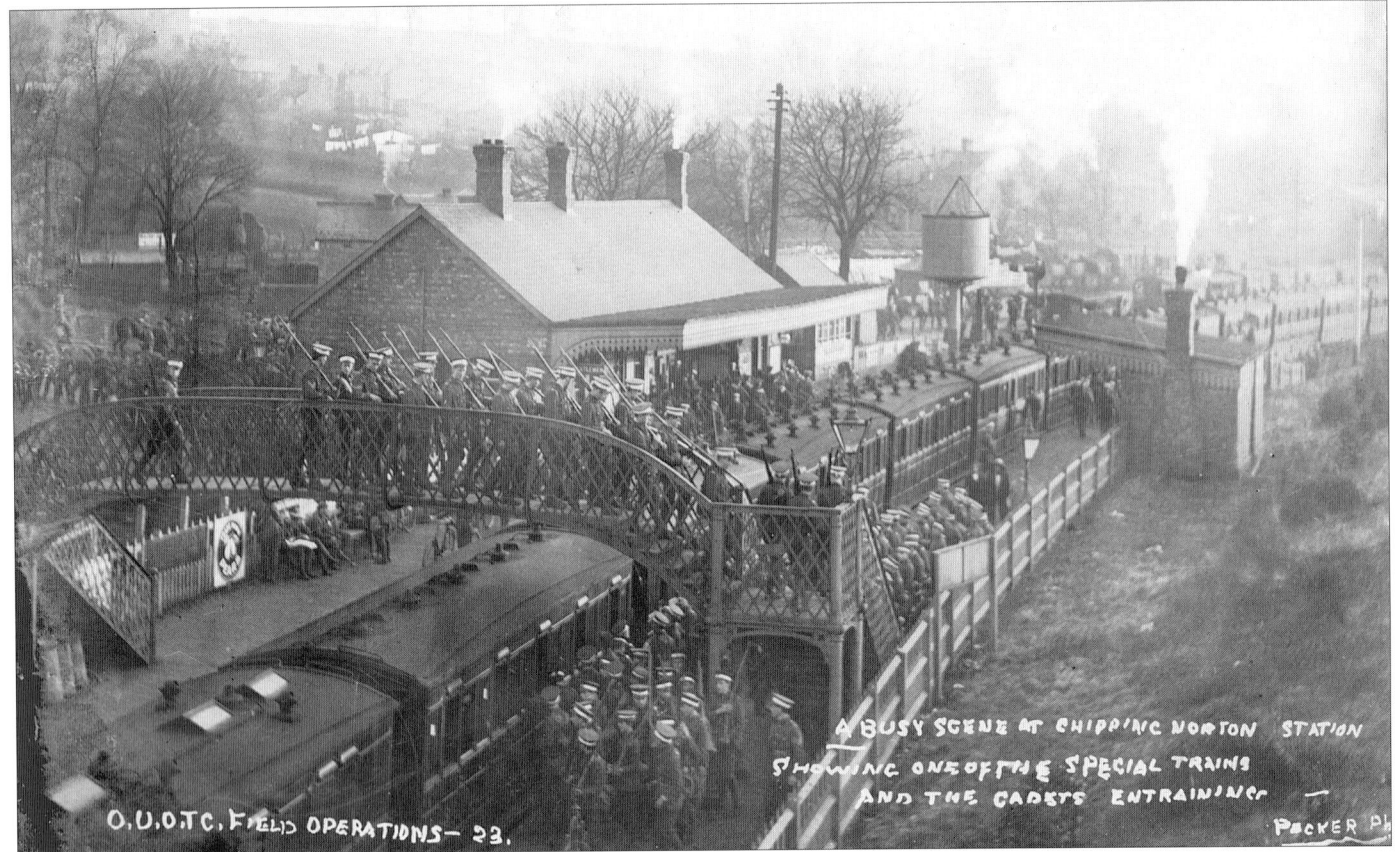

Above: Chipping Norton station's heyday was in the two decades covering the period from 1900 to just after the First World War. The selection of photographs on these two pages illustrate a few aspects of the station's life during that time. This *'busy scene at Chipping Norton station'* shows cadets of the Oxford University Officers' Training Corps boarding one of the trains carrying them back from camp, around 1910. Presumably the train of 4-wheel stock is destined for Oxford via Kingham, so is in the 'wrong' platform. Horses and equipment are being prepared for loading in the background, quite probably aboard the wagons seen on the Down line. These were jolly scenes compared to those a few years later when men started to catch trains taking them away to fight in some foreign field – some never to return. *Bob Brown collection*

Above: Volunteers waiting on the Up platform to be taken off to war. The number of men (and boys) in civilian dress suggests this may be a Territorial battalion, with probably a 3-4 month sojourn in training camp before being sent to France. *Paul Laming collection*

Right: Whilst on a recruiting drive for volunteers during World War One, a Sergeant Baker posed with various members of staff and others at Chipping Norton station. Baker was a decorated war hero, having won the Victoria Cross, probably in the Boer War campaigns in South Africa. Such 'old soldiers' were routinely used by the army to persuade young men to sign up to fight. He is said to have recruited three volunteers during his visit to Chipping Norton, quite possibly the three standing to the right of him (his left) in this view. Did they make it back from the killing fields of France?
Oxfordshire County Council Photographic Archive

Right: As a company, the GWR took their responsibilities towards passengers and staff seriously and the welfare of both was paramount. In an age long before ambulances and paramedics, station staff were expected to have a good working knowledge of first aid and most stations of any size on the system had an Ambulance Class, with staff being encouraged to join. Competitions were held between the stations in an area to foster the interest and for those keen on climbing the promotional ladder it was a must to join the group. For others, it was simply a useful social activity when radio was in its infancy and televisions did not exist. Here, Chipping Norton's Ambulance Class of 1921 pose for Frank Packer, along with the station cat!
Oxfordshire County Council Photographic Archive

Left: This fine body of men is the Chipping Norton St. John's Ambulance brigade, who were photographed circa 1911 as they were about to depart for Windsor to take part in a Royal Review. Spit, polish and belt whitener much in evidence and you would not get away with standing on the track like this today!
Paul Laming collection

Below: As the German army rampaged through Belgium in 1914, many of the civilian population became refugees and some, mostly women and children, left their country to seek safe haven. The Chipping Norton area seems to have played host to a sizeable group for a number of years and this is just one of another long series of Packer postcards showing refugees arriving at the station. *Neil Parkhouse collection*

The station from the road bridge around 1930, with a Banbury to Kingham auto service making a smokey departure. As well as the road approach to the station, there were also two pedestrian entrances from the main road, that to the Down platform leading in from the left, whilst the one to the Up platform dropped steeply down behind the footbridge. *Neil Parkhouse collection*

main shed building. The lower floor was used as the goods office, whereas the floor above was intended for use as a 'book loft'. By analogy with other large GWR goods sheds (such as Redruth Drump Lane), the loft area would originally have been entered by means of an angled wooden stairway from the loading platform. In later years, the stairway was apparently removed and access to the book loft was then made with the aid of a portable ladder.

Other features of interest in the goods yard included a standard GWR stable block, with a gable roof and the usual accommodation for shunting and dray horses; the slated roof was surmounted by two small square ventilators. Nearby, the rectangular brick weigh-house was very similar to the one at Bourton-on-the-Water, being an OW&WR style structure with a pyramidal, slated roof. The weighbridge itself measured roughly 18 feet by 8 feet. Early prints suggest that this humble brick hut was the only one of the original Chipping Norton Railway buildings to survive into the British Railways era.

The 1938 *Railway Clearing House Handbook of Stations* suggests that Chipping Norton did not have a large yard crane at that time and no such cranes are shown on contemporary Ordnance Survey maps. There were, on the other hand, the two 1 ton 10 cwt hand cranes within the goods shed and these would clearly have been sufficient for all but the largest or bulkiest consignments. It was later decided that a 6 ton yard crane, that had hitherto been sited at Shipton, would be moved to Chipping Norton. The crane in question was installed in Chipping Norton goods yard by 1950, the altered crane power being duly recorded in a list of amendments to the *RCH Handbook of Stations* issued in January 1951.

Photographic evidence indicates that the long-demolished engine shed had been of stone construction, with a gable roof. The single-road shed was long enough to accommodate two tank locomotives, or one tank engine and an 0-6-0 tender locomotive. A 'stilted' water tank, similar to that at Kingham, was situated to the west of the shed. This typical Great Western style structure was a relatively late addition to the station's infrastructure, the original OW&WR 'tank house' having been on a different site, to the north of the shed building.

The types of freight traffic dealt with at Chipping Norton included coal, iron castings from a local iron foundry, textile fabrics from Bliss's Mill, livestock and general merchandise. There were also regular deliveries of wagonloads of coal to Chipping Norton Gas Works, which had its own private siding off the main running line just to the west of Bliss Mill. Certainly in earlier years, much of this arrived direct from the pithead in wagons privately owned by the colliery making the delivery. Domestic coal was distributed by a number of firms, including the Chipping Norton Co-operative Society and Bernard T. Frost. The Co-op owned several coal wagons, their livery being black bodywork with white lettering; the words 'CHIPPING NORTON CO-OPERATIVE SOCIETY LIMITED' were displayed on the second and fourth planks.

The Frost coal firm was owned by Bernard Tree Frost, a businessman who traded from offices in a former coaching inn at 27 Market Square, Witney. On a footnote, it may be

Right: A view of the pointwork forming the west entry to the goods yard, photographed from the Up Home signal in the late 1940s. The headshunt on the right was the one on which the accident occurred in 1907 but the West box had closed on 13th August 1929 and been removed by the date of this view. The long headshunt on the left originally ran from the crossover at the west end of the platforms, with only Bliss Mill siding running off it. In 1929, at the same date the West box was closed, the crossover seen here in the left middle distance was installed, shortening this siding by over half its length. A couple of wagons can be seen at the far end of it in the view on page 244 but in later years it was little used. *Bob Brown collection*

Below: A view of the yard in the early 1950s, surprisingly bereft of wagons. The goods shed was a sizeable and imposing standard GWR brick-built structure, containing two cranes in addition to the one shown here in the yard, which was of 6 ton capacity and had only recently been installed. *Oxfordshire County Council Photographic Archive*

remarked that Mr Frost rarely used his unusual middle name! The firm owned a large number of coal wagons, ordering two dozen in 1924 alone from the Gloucester RC&W Co. They bore the name 'FROST' in large unshaded white letters on a black background. The legend 'Bernard T' appeared on the top planks, whilst wagon numbers and other details were displayed on the bottom planks.

Frosts, who were probably at their peak during the 1930s, rented coal wharves at a number of local stations, including Witney, Banbury, Chipping Norton and Charlbury. They also owned a fleet of road delivery vehicles which, in later years at least, were painted in a bright red livery that remained surprisingly unsullied by the effects of coal dust.

The authorised staff establishment at Chipping Norton during the 1920s generally comprised one station master, one senior clerk, three clerks, three porters and one checker. There were, in addition, two signalmen, five permanent way men and several road motor

Chipping Norton Co-operative Society had their own wagons by 1891 at least, in which year they signed a repair contract with Gloucester RC&W Co. for the maintenance of two 6 ton and two 8 ton wagons. The builder of these wagons is not known. In 1898, they renewed the repair contract and then in 1902 they hired two 8 ton wagons from Gloucester, seemingly to replace their earlier small fleet. In February 1909, they made their first purchase from Gloucester, wagon No. 9 seen above. This would suggest that they may have bought or hired two further wagons in the interim, which would have been from another wagon builder as there is nothing in the Gloucester records. In February 1914, they bought three further wagons from Gloucester, one of which was No. 1 illustrated below. These may have been as replacements for their original four wagons, two of which had been of 6 ton capacity as already noted. The Co-operative paid cash for all their wagons, as CWS's tended to do, rather than having them on deferred purchase. Wagon No. 9 returned to Gloucester for repair in 1916, whilst wagon No. 1 also appears in the lower illustration on page 253, taken circa 1930, by which time it had been repainted in a different livery. In *Private Owner Wagons Vol. Four* (1987), Bill Hudson suggests the livery may have been red, whilst the lettering was still white but with a shading, probably in black.

Courtesy Gloucestershire Record Office

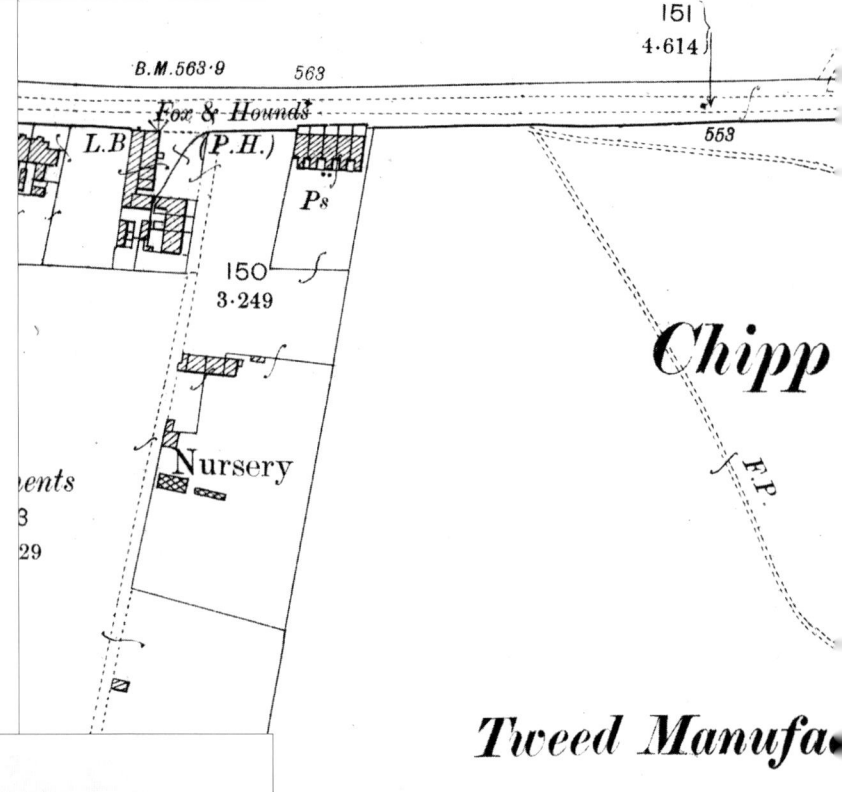

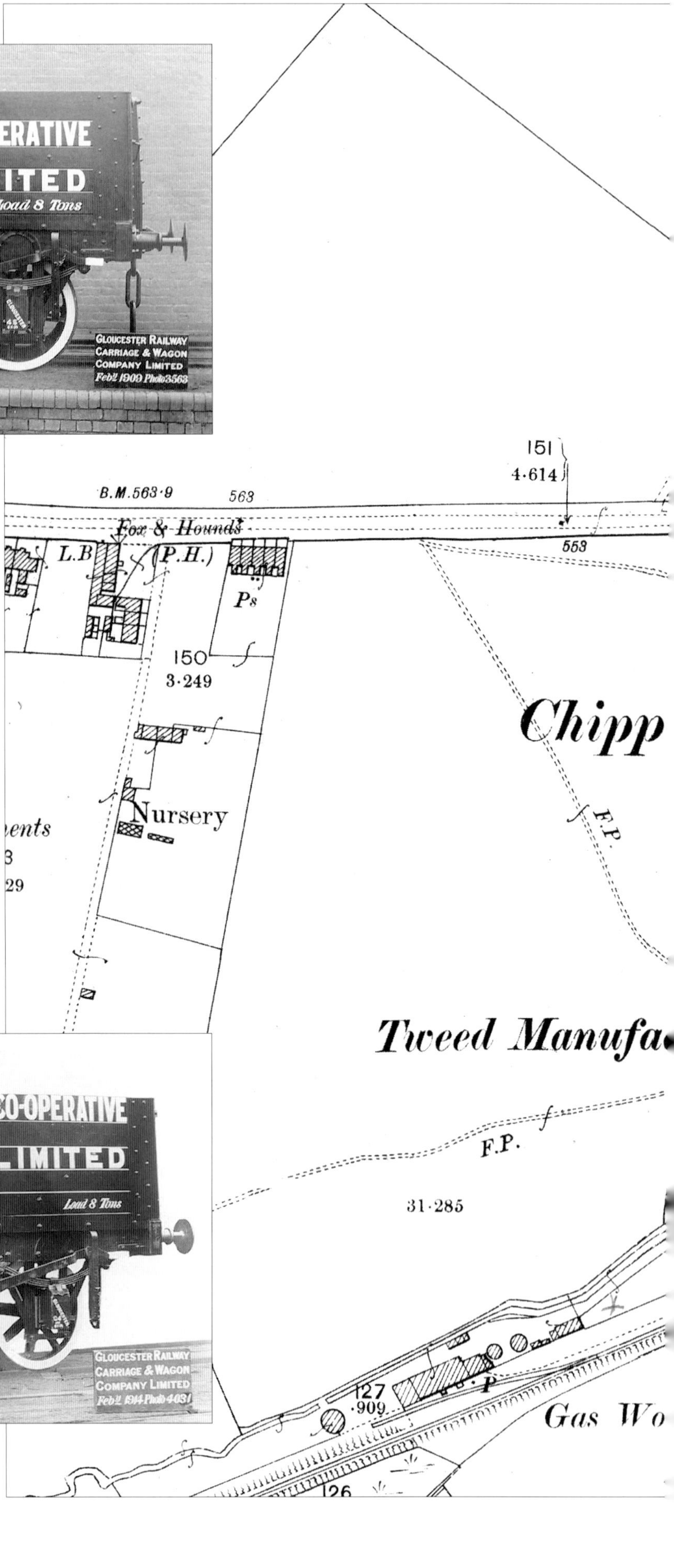

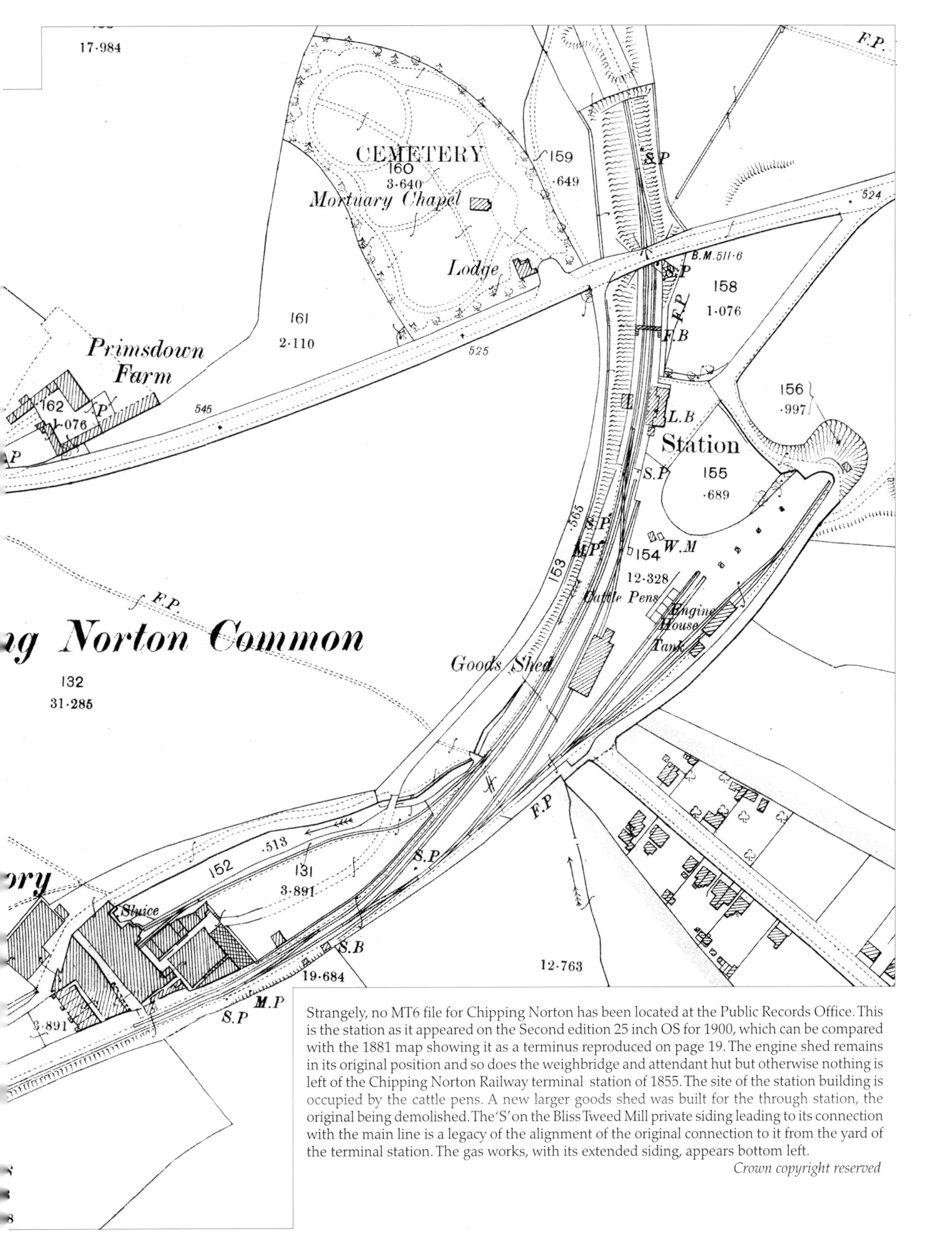

Strangely, no MT6 file for Chipping Norton has been located at the Public Records Office. This is the station as it appeared on the Second edition 25 inch OS for 1900, which can be compared with the 1881 map showing it as a terminus reproduced on page 19. The engine shed remains in its original position and so does the weighbridge and attendant hut but otherwise nothing is left of the Chipping Norton Railway terminal station of 1855. The site of the station building is occupied by the cattle pens. A new larger goods shed was built for the through station, the original being demolished. The 'S' on the Bliss Tweed Mill private siding leading to its connection with the main line is a legacy of the alignment of the original connection to it from the yard of the terminal station. The gas works, with its extended siding, appears bottom left.

Crown copyright reserved

The Leys, a steep residential street running down from Churchill Road to the station area, was the subject of many postcard views which, fortunately for railway historians, included part of the goods yard in the foreground. A record of some of the wagons visiting the yard can be built up from their incidental inclusion in these pictures and a selection is presented here. In the first view, **above**, dating from circa 1908, two Bliss Tweed Mills wagons can be seen on the right, Nos. 5 and 2 respectively. They were painted lead grey, with white lettering shaded black and black strapping. Also, just behind the two 'Iron Minks' can be seen a George Clifford of Bourton-on-the-Water wagon, No. 29. The second view, **below**, dates from around 1912 and it can be seen that a new terrace of houses has sprung up midway up on the left side of the road. In the yard, there is a 'Mink' on the far left lettered 'something C$^{\circ}$', possibly a cement company wagon and a Great Central 3-plank open on the right. The Eveson Ltd, Birmingham, wagon No. 3041 next to it is interesting, being still dumb buffered. An RCH edict requiring final removal of these from the network was issued in 1913. The lettering on the top plank reads 'WRITE FOR PRICE'. To its right is the end of a GWR 6-wheel 'Toad' brake van.

Both Bob Brown collection

THE BANBURY & CHELTENHAM DIRECT RAILWAY

These two views are both post-Grouping, probably circa 1930. **Above**, amongst the selection of 'big four' wagons is a Warwickshire Coal Co. Ltd Coventry Collieries wagon, No. 563, which was black with white lettering, with one belonging to the Dean Forest Coal Co., Lydney, behind. It is thought this may be in a red livery, with white lettering shaded black, introduced by the company from 1927 onwards. In the second view, **below**, there is a comparison in cattle wagon styles with, ironically, only a GWR example missing. The private owners again provide a colourful contrast, with a CWS Ltd, London, wagon No. 708, supplementing the local Chipping Norton Cooperative Society Limited wagon, the repainted No. 1. There is another from Coventry Collieries, No. 334, and one belonging to Griff of Nuneaton, No. 1908, painted black with white lettering. *Top: Bob Brown collection; bottom: Neil Parkhouse collection*

A final view of The Leys from the Packer archive, taken circa 1952 and therefore from the early British Railways period. The 1930s Crafts Corn Mill stands out to the left of this view but the locomotive shed which stood in front of it has been demolished. Note the two cars parked in The Leys; today both sides of the road are one continuous line of vehicles. *Oxfordshire County Council Photographic Archive*

The water tower and locomotive shed were the only substantial survivors from the original terminal station and are seen here on 27th August 1936. The shed opened in August 1855 and was built substantially of stone, with brick lined arches and quoins, and a slated roof. It was 68½ feet in length. The water tower, supported on cast iron columns, was a later addition, the original tank built by the Chipping Norton Railway being situated just to the left of and behind the shed in this view. There was a wooden coaling platform built into the base of the columns, onto which coal had first to be shovelled from a wagon before locomotive bunkers could be replenished. The shed was normally home to one of the 'Metro' tanks or other small tank engines which featured on the branch from the 1890s. It was closed in July 1922 and was reportedly intended to be converted into a house but was instead used as a garage for a time. The building had been demolished by 1947. In the coal yard in the left background can just be seen Bernard T. Frost's office. *W.A. Camwell*

staff – although the latter men were subsequently transferred to the City of Oxford Motor Services. Collection and delivery services in and around Chipping Norton were carried out under contract by private cartage agents and, perhaps for this reason, the station was not developed as a country lorry centre during the 1930s. Conversely, after World War Two, the station became a sub railhead under the 'zonal' scheme.

Chipping Norton's first station master was the unfortunate Mr Wheeler, who had very nearly lost his life in the 1855 buffer stop collision. In 1887, the station master was Thomas Henry Hunt and he remained in charge for several years thereafter. Later, around 1930, the station was supervised by David D. Davis, while in the 1960s the local station master was Mr W.T. Chamberlain.

In general, Chipping Norton handled around 27,000 tons of freight per annum during the first three decades of the 20th century, much of this traffic being in the form of coal. In 1932, for instance, 26,171 tons of freight were handled, including 14,132 tons of coal. There was a surprisingly large amount of parcels traffic, around 25,000 small parcels and packages being dealt with in an average year. It is assumed that many of these consignments were sent by Bliss Tweed Mill, clothing products being lightweight items that could easily be sent to customers in individual parcels.

In 1903, Chipping Norton issued 31,433 tickets, this figure being fairly typical during the early years of the 20th century. Passenger bookings fell from about 30,000 tickets per year during the early 1920s, to just 9,951 bookings in 1929. Most of this decline can be attributed to the loss of the station's road transport services, though at the same time it is perhaps unreasonable to expect Chipping Norton – a small town with just 3,489 inhabitants at the time of the 1931 census – to have contributed much passenger traffic during a period of economic depression.

The table below underlines the sudden loss of passenger traffic from Chipping Norton after the transfer of the GWR road transport services to the local bus company:

TRAFFIC DEALT WITH AT CHIPPING NORTON						
YEAR	STAFF	RECEIPTS (£)	TICKETS	PARCELS	GOODS (TONS)
1903	15	13,899	31,443	27,589	27,308
1913	23	15,722	35,596	30,449	32,081
1923	17	22,517	30,455	26,957	28,325
1929	15	20,099	9,951	29,167	32,243
1937	12	12,372	6,807	25,498	27,550
1938	13	10,822	6,176	25,741	23,810

Chipping Norton is situated in an elevated position, about 650 feet above sea level; in winter it can be a surprisingly bleak place. The word 'Chipping' is old English for a market, the name of the town meaning 'The North Market'. The Church of St. Mary is one of the finest Perpendicular

Looking west towards Cheltenham from the footbridge in the late 1940s, showing the trailing connection to the goods yard and the accompanying single slip over the Down line. There was a similar arrangement in the yard, allowing access to the two loops inside and alongside the goods shed, with the outside loop continuing eastwards to a set of buffer stops just beyond the end of the Down platform. *Bob Brown collection*

Looking through the station towards Banbury in the early 1950s, around the time of the cessation of the passenger service eastwards from Chipping Norton. The station appears to be in rather grubby GWR colours but note that some improvement is underway, as the footbridge is blocked off out of use whilst a number of the steps are being renewed. This is probably following the wartime maintenance hiatus, which saw only essential work carried out. The station structures had certainly been repainted by the mid 1950s, as other photographs show. Passengers would have crossed the line by means of the barrow crossing at the Kingham end of the platforms while the footbridge was closed. Chipping Norton Signal Box, on the right, was originally named Chipping Norton East Box but this was changed when the West box closed in 1929.

Joe Moss, Courtesy Roger Carpenter

A Collett '57XX' Class 0-6-0 pannier tank arriving from Banbury with an auto-trailer in tow, probably in 1951. The Up Starting signal on the right, situated 'wrong side' because of the water tower, carried a shunt arm lower down the post, which until 1950 at least, had been of the GWR pattern with large 'S' attached to it. The rest of the signal, however, appears to have remained unchanged. The '57XX' Class locomotives were not auto-fitted and so the engine would have to run-round its one coach train at Kingham in order to make the return trip.

Adrian Vaughan collection

Right: The forecourt aspect of the main station building circa 1950. Just peeping into view on the left is a corner of the small 'Nissen' hut used as a military post in World War Two. The station was built mainly of red brick but with blue engineering bricks used for the base. The roof was of slate and there was a small canopy with decorative valancing over the main entrance door. Note how the centre section of the building was inset slightly from the two outer sections, this applied on the platform side as well.
The Lens of Sutton Collection

Left: Looking west through the platforms towards Kingham and Cheltenham from track level on 1st November 1956.
R.M. Casserley

Right: Taken on the same day as the previous picture, this is the corresponding view in the opposite direction. It can be seen that the station woodwork, signal box, lamp posts and fencing had been painted in British Railways cream at some stage, probably a year or so prior to these photographs being taken. Surprisingly, there were no water columns at the stations east of here, so the water tower must have provided a welcome sight for the crews of westbound trains, as it would have been the first one encountered since leaving Banbury.
R.M. Casserley

churches in Oxfordshire, while other notable buildings in and around the town include the early Victorian Town Hall and the spectacular Bliss Tweed Mill. The town's population remained static at around 3,500-3,700 for several years.

Like most other English country towns, Chipping Norton once boasted a grammar school, in which promising children could be groomed for university entrance and careers in the learned professions. Sadly, this establishment was virtually moribund by the late 1850s, although it is interesting to note that its *alumni* from that period included Charles Stewart Parnell (1846-1891), the patrician Irishman who, despite his Protestant background, became leader of the Parliamentary Irish Party. For twenty years, Parnell dominated the House of Commons, becoming one of the most famous figures in Victorian politics, until his career was destroyed in 1890, when it was finally revealed that he was an adulterer.

In 1891, the fallen leader caught a chill and died at Brighton; if his vision of Irish Home Rule had been realised during the late Victorian era, a hundred years of conflict might well have been averted. On a footnote of history, it may also be added that, although Parnell was a cold and reserved figure who often seemed to despise the vulgar masses, the great politician was also a notorious womaniser – one of his very first romantic conquests being a Chipping Norton girl. Parnell's descendants are said to be living in and around Chipping Norton to this very day.

Top: Collett '45XX' Class 2-6-2T No. 4573 pulls into the Down platform with the 4.35 pm to Kingham on 18th July 1959. The line beyond here had closed to passengers in June 1951 and, whilst the train appears to have worked in from beyond the tunnel, it was normal practice for trains from Kingham to arrive in the Up platform, run round and then propel the stock into the tunnel before drawing forward as here into the 'correct' platform.
H.C. Casserley

Middle: Henry Casserley is seen standing on the footbridge in the process of taking the previous shot, in this photograph taken by his son Richard on 18th July 1959. *R.M. Casserley*

Bottom: '41XX' Class 2-6-2T No. 4106 is seen pulling into the Down platform with a Kingham service in 1962, completing the run round manoeuvre shown in the previous pictures. Note that the paraphernalia of the Victorian railway survived to the very end – gas lamps, footbridge, stone setts, etc. being much in evidence.
Joe Moss, courtesy Roger Carpenter

THE BANBURY & CHELTENHAM DIRECT RAILWAY

Right and below: The station building and the Up platform shelter were crudely shorn of their canopies in the latter half of the 1950s, which certainly spoilt their appearance. They were probably deemed life expired although painted only a few years previously. These two views show the main station building and signal box circa 1960. In the lower view, just to the right of the signal box, can be seen the corrugated iron lamp room, whilst to the right of that the weighbridge office, dating from 1926, can be glimpsed behind the water tower.
Both The Lens of Sutton Collection

Below: This view through the station on 18th July 1956 shows how the removal of the canopies spoilt its appearance, although the growth of the evergreens and other trees surrounding the station in its valley setting went some way towards off-setting this. '45XX' Class small prairie No. 4573 is waiting with the 4.25 pm to Kingham. *H.C. Casserley*

Left: A view of the rather forlorn looking waiting shelter on the Up platform, shorn of the overhang to its canopy, around 1960.
The Lens of Sutton Collection

Right: The main station building viewed from the forecourt in 1962. The small canopy over the entrance door was removed at the same time as the one over the platform. Clearly it was done without too much thought as to how the finished job would look, the damage being only too evident.

Below: '51XX' Class prairie tank No. 4106 waiting to leave for Kingham in 1962. Note that the connection to the goods shed from this end has gone, having been taken out in 1956.
Both Joe Moss, courtesy Roger Carpenter

THE BLISS MILLS

In addition to its public goods facilities, the station had two private sidings, the most important of which served Bliss's Lower Mills on the south-west side of the station. Chipping Norton can be seen as a detached outpost of the West of England textile industry and, in this context, it is significant that William Bliss (senior) owned two mills in the town by 1810. The Upper Mill was powered by a 'horse engine' but the somewhat smaller Lower Mill, on the site of a much older corn mill, was water-powered.

Unfortunately, the tiny stream which flows through Chipping Norton, known locally as 'The Common Brook', was a feeble source of power and, for this reason, a small steam engine had been installed at the Upper Mill by the 1830s. The Lower Mill continued in operation as a water-powered fulling mill, albeit with frequent stoppages due to an insufficient flow of water.

As recounted in Chapter One, William Bliss's son, also called William, was acutely aware of the need for a rail link for his thriving textile mills and he became a major supporter of the Chipping Norton Railway. When opened in 1855, the new line terminated roughly midway between the Upper and Lower mills, and the opportunity was taken to rebuild the Lower Mill as a steam powered mill, with a direct siding connection from the station. In this way, coal could be delivered to the doors of the boiler room. The mill building was already a towering five-storey edifice but in the next few years the structure was doubled in size.

Disaster struck on 7th February 1872, when the huge Lower Mill caught fire. Mill boilers were often installed in detached engine houses for safety reasons but this was apparently not the case at Chipping Norton, where the engine room was integral with the main structure. The fire is said to have been started by a boiler explosion and, in view of the layout at the old mill, the conflagration rapidly spread to the main parts of the building. The primitive fire-fighting equipment available at the time was virtually useless and nothing could be done to prevent the ensuing destruction. Three men were killed in the disaster and the Lower Mill was gutted within a matter of hours.

Undeterred by this catastrophe, William Bliss immediately applied to the Factory Commissioners for permission to work his remaining mill on a two-shift system and for the next few months, the Upper Mill worked day-and-night. Just twelve months later, on 7th February 1873, the new Bliss Mill was ceremonially opened, over 900 people being invited to an event that recalled the triumphant opening of the Chipping Norton Railway, some eighteen years before.

The new Lower Mill was a massive, five-storey structure incorporating an ornate, circular chimney stack, rising from an engaged semi-circular tower. The transition from tower to chimney was effected by means of a distinctive ribbed dome, while the 165 foot high chimney was designed in the form of a Tuscan column. Rectangular towers, positioned at each end of the main facade, were adorned with balustraded parapets with ornate urn finials, the resulting effect being reminiscent of an Italianate palace.

The main block measured approximately 189 feet by 68 feet at ground level, the building being formed of seventeen bays, each with an external width of around 11 feet. The individual bays were filled by generously-proportioned windows – those on the uppermost floor being two-light windows with arched, Italianate heads. The boldly-projecting chimney tower was asymmetrically-placed towards the right of the main facade, perhaps because the rebuilt mill incorporated substantial fragments of its ill-fated predecessor. Moreover, the position of the chimney and associated boiler house had an obvious relationship to the railway siding, which was laid on a narrow strip of land between the headrace and the mill yard.

This architecturally accomplished and technically advanced building contained 'fireproof' floors supported by rows of cast iron columns, each floor being formed of transverse cast iron beams which, in turn, provided support

The mill as viewed from the common, on a picture postcard from around 1905. It still stands today but no longer serves as a working mill and was converted to luxury flats in the 1980s. In the valley, to the left, can just be seen the Chipping Norton Up Home signal. *Bob Brown collection*

This 1920s view of the mill offers a closer look at its fine architectural features, which happily have largely been retained in the redeveloped structure which survives today, although the anciliary buildings have been demolished. The Up Home signal is visible again on the left; the lower arm was the Up Distant for Chipping Norton Tunnel. *Bob Brown collection*

for a system of longitudinal rolled iron beams. The spaces between the rolled iron beams were filled with shallow brick vaulting, while the external walls were built of brick, faced with Cotswold stone. The new mill was built by Messrs Davies & Sons of Banbury, to a design by the northern architect George Woodhouse (1829-83), who had carried out many similar commissions in Lancashire.

The rebuilt Lower Mill was just one part of a larger industrial complex that included a large weaving shed, a wool store, offices, a boiler house and a willey house. The main block was aligned more or less at right angles to the railway line, with its main facade orientated towards the north-east. Chipping Norton Gas Works was sited a short distance to the west of the Lower Mill, on land owned by the Bliss family.

Further development took place at Bliss's Mill throughout the years, notably around 1910, when a large new weaving shed was built to the north-east of the original weaving shed. The latter building, dating from 1865, was then adapted for use as a warping shed. The mill was run by a limited company following the death of William Bliss, whilst the Bliss family eventually decided to emigrate to Canada. However, Bliss Tweed Mill remained in production for many more years, the principal products being tweeds and other forms of cloth.

The private siding connection to the Bliss Tweed Mill diverged westwards from the Up loop line, while a further mill siding extended for a short distance from the west end of the crossing loop. Chipping Norton Gas Works was also served by a direct rail connection that diverged from the running line at a point some 31 chains to the west of the passenger station.

Wagon supplied to Bliss' Tweed Mills in 1897, with the company trade mark included in the design. The livery was green with white lettering shaded tan. The strapping is painted a darker colour, possibly tan, as well. The logo painted on the wagon was also used on their earlier batch of wagons, supplied by the Midland C&W Co. The pentangle device is used in masonic circles and it is thought that William Bliss may have been advertising his masonic connections by its use on the wagons. *Courtesy Gloucestershire Record Office*

Bliss Tweed Mill was well covered photographically but seldom so artistically as here. The private siding to the mill followed the left hand bank of the mill race and the rails can just be seen in the grass, with the end of a wagon visible between the house in the centre and the base of the mill chimney.
Oxfordshire County Council Photographic Archive

All three sidings were facing to the direction of Down trains proceeding towards Kingham. The main mill siding passed through a gate and then ran alongside the headrace for a short distance, before terminating near the base of the chimney tower. The main traffic was coal, which was unloaded into bunkers at the end of the line. The private sidings were shunted by the branch freight engine, which propelled loaded wagons inwards, or drew empty vehicles outwards, during the course of its normal shunting operations.

The mill owned a number of wooden bodied private owner wagons. They placed their first order in May 1871, for a dozen wagons from the Midland Carriage & Wagon Company. In 1897, a dozen 12 ton wagons were ordered from the Gloucester RC&W Co., which appear to have been numbered 1 to 12. They may not have been straight replacements however, rather the older wagons may have been re-numbered 13 to 24. Some of the Bliss wagons were painted black with 'BLISS TWEED MILL' written in large white letters; wagon numbers etc, and the words 'CHIPPING NORTON' were displayed in smaller white lettering. One of the photographs included in this section shows that, by about 1908, some of the Bliss wagons were painted in a lighter colour, possibly a lead grey livery with white lettering shaded black. These much simpler design were a complete change from the livery shown on the Gloucester wagon on the previous page and did not include the pentangle logo with its possible masonic connection.

WILLIAM BLISS & HIS FAMILY

The Bliss family originated in the Stroudwater area of Gloucestershire, where they had enjoyed a long association with the West of England textile trade. The first member of the family to have been associated with Chipping Norton was Thomas Bliss, who, around 1750, was sent to Oxfordshire in connection with his father's business. While staying in Chipping Norton he met and subsequently married Ann Insell, an inn keeper's daughter, and the couple embarked on a business career as inn keepers and textile traders. In the latter capacity, Thomas Bliss eventually took over an existing business and, by the end of the 18th century, he was manufacturing cloth on a domestic basis.

The business was further developed by William Bliss (1764-1825), Thomas's fourth son, who started the process of industrialisation by introducing a horse gin. The firm was, by this time, engaged in the production of a range of products, including rugs, mops, wagon tilts and 'kerseys' – a type of coarse heavy cloth, woven from long-staple wool. William's particular innovation concerned the introduction of 'kersey checks', a multi-coloured textile product that made a pleasant change from the plain red, brown, green or white cloth that had hitherto predominated. Chipping Norton kerseys became extremely popular as horse clothing and the Bliss business went from strength to strength.

At the beginning of the 19th century, Chipping Norton cloth was taken to a mill at Swinbrook, near Witney, for the finishing process known as 'tucking' or 'fulling'. Swinbrook, about eleven miles to the south, was situated on the fast-flowing River Windrush, which was ideal for driving water mills, whereas the Common Brook at Chipping Norton was hardly suited for that purpose. Nevertheless, William Bliss decided to purchase a corn mill at Chipping Norton to obviate the tiresome journeys to and from Swinbrook; the old mill was adapted for use as a water-powered textile mill and as such, it became the direct ancestor of the Bliss Lower Mill.

William Bliss (senior) had nine children and, on his premature retirement as a result of ill health, the firm was taken over by his son Robert Bliss. Unfortunately, Robert does not seem to have been particularly interested in the textile industry and, after an extended stay in the United States, he decided to emigrate permanently. The family business was therefore taken over in 1839 by William Bliss (1810-83), old William's eighth son, who was destined to become Chipping Norton's most famous benefactor. As we have seen, William Bliss (junior) was instrumental in bringing the railway to Chipping Norton and turning the family firm into a major industrial concern.

It is said that when he took over in 1839 the firm employed only eleven people but when he died in 1883 there were over seven hundred employees working in the two Bliss mills. Furthermore, William Bliss was, by any standards, a model employer who refused to employ children younger than thirteen, and introduced a range of sickness and pension schemes for his workers. He also built model dwellings for Bliss employees, and provided night schools, libraries, institutes, a reading room, and a Baptist chapel.

His work was formally recognised in 1851, when he was awarded two medals at the Great Exhibition, and again in 1867, when he won the Emperor Napoleon's prize at the Amsterdam Exhibition of Domestic Economy. The latter award was made in recognition of his outstanding role as an employer, the following tribute being paid in a report of the exhibition:

> To their honour, then, let it again be recorded that the firm of Messrs Bliss & Son was founded in 1757, and that in 1867 it could be proved that during the 110 years that it had flourished, no dispute had ever occurred between the masters and the 500 hands they had employed; that during that time none of the workmen had joined Trades Unions, nor had unions had any effect on their wages.
>
> There had been no combination; no hands had been allowed to go to the workhouse – families had worked for three generations – duration of life had been above average; workmen had saved money and bought life insurances; children had never been employed under thirteen years of age, and women employed had not been required to work before breakfast in the winter. Schools, reading-rooms, lectures, concerts, cricket, football, had been liberally promoted.
>
> That a gold medal should fall to such a firm, and that their tweeds and cloths should be both cheap and excellent, and not suffer in repute from Continental products cannot excite surprise; but the fact is none the less a source of international gratification, conducive, let us hope, to the promotion, the continuance, and the adoption by others of the most remunerative and the only Christian treatment of their workpeople by their employers.

Sadly, Britain and France were in the middle of a major diplomatic row in 1867, the international situation being so strained that William was not allowed to receive the prestigious award directly from the hands of the Emperor Napoleon III.

Like many other Victorian industrialists, the Bliss family were religious Nonconformists and this factor undoubtedly influenced every aspect of their activities. They were 'outsiders' in terms of Victorian society and yet, as a Baptist, William Bliss would have had much in common with Sir S. Morton Peto. Viewed in this light, the apparent ease with which the Chipping Norton Railway was brought into existence as an appendage of the Oxford, Worcester & Wolverhampton Railway can be readily understood.

The Bliss business empire was at its very peak around 1872, when the rebuilt Lower Mill was brought into operation. Sadly, the cost of rebuilding came at a time in which Britain's industries were faced with competition from rapidly industrialising nations such as Germany and the United States and, in retrospect, the Bliss firm never fully recovered. William's son was unable to continue in business without taking partners and turning the firm into a limited company. Control eventually passed out of the family's hands and, although the 'Bliss' name was retained, the new style of management resulted in poor industrial relations and a bitter eight month strike in 1913-14.

At length, the Bliss Mill passed into the hands of Fox Brothers of Wellington in Somerset, who retained the historic name 'William Bliss & Son Ltd'. In the 1970s, the Lower Mill was still producing traditional tweed products, as well as lighter weight, modern fabrics. Sadly, the mill was closed in 1980 as part of a 'restructuring' scheme which transferred all business to the parent company in Somerset. The fact that the mill's order books were full at the time of its demise left a legacy of bitterness that has never dissipated.

The mill was stripped of machinery and fittings, and left as an empty shell, though as a Grade II listed building it could not be demolished. In 1989, approval was granted for a conversion scheme whereby the main building would be adapted for use as 35 luxury residential apartments. Although some ancillary buildings were to be demolished, a further eight dwellings would be created out of the former warping house, while the wool house would be turned into a swimming pool and leisure complex. The conversion was duly carried out and the historic Bliss Tweed Mill thereby became a residential building.

The Upper Mill, which was sited about three quarters of a mile to the north-east of the Lower Mill, has disappeared in its entirety. The Bliss family formerly resided in an Italianate house near the Upper Mill but this too has been demolished, leaving a pair of stone gate posts to mark its site. William Bliss himself is buried behind the Baptist Chapel in which he had once worshipped.

Having arrived at Chipping Norton Up platform bunker first, '45XX' Class small prairie No. 5538, a resident of Gloucester (Horton Road) shed, has run round its two-coach 'B-set' in the station, before propelling it backwards into the tunnel, clear of the point at the east end of the loop. The 2-6-2T is then seen as it draws forward into the Down platform, prior to returning to Kingham sometime in July 1954. Note the fireman leaning right out of the cab, probably acknowledging the signalman.

C.H.A. Townley

The west portal of the 685-yard long Chipping Norton Tunnel framed by the blue-brick bridge carrying the Worcester Road over the line. The water tower here was well used by eastbound crews in the days when trains ran through to Banbury, as it was their last chance to fill up before the long run through Hook Norton, Bloxham and Adderbury, to the main line at King's Sutton.

Courtesy Historical Model Railway Society

'Dukedog' 4-4-0 No. 9015 about to plunge into Chipping Norton Tunnel shortly after leaving the station with the 'South Midlander' railtour on 24th April 1955. This was one of the last passenger trains to travel through the tunnel, although pick-up goods trains serving Rollright Siding continued to use it until November 1962.
J.F. Russell Smith, courtesy NRM

Above: A rare shot of the north end of the 685-yard Chipping Norton Tunnel, on 18th July 1959, which is also shown on the 1900 25 inch OS, **right**, which has been reduced by 40% to fit the page). It was nowhere near as accessible as the station end and consequently was only photographed by the occasional intrepid enthusiast. There was a rising gradient through the tunnel in the King's Sutton direction of 1 in 80. The tunnel survives today and is now a bat sanctuary, a use to which quite a number of old railway tunnels have been adapted. The downside from the railway enthusiast's point of view is that bats are a protected species and thus any chance of opening up these old tunnels – not necessarily for rail use – is therefore precluded. *R.M. Casserley*

Chapter Seven

THE ROUTE FROM CHIPPING NORTON TO BANBURY

This 1920s multiview picture postcard of Great Rollright village by Percy Simms also included a view of the halt. *Neil Parkhouse collection*

On leaving Chipping Norton, Up workings rumbled beneath the A44 road overbridge and into a cutting, at the end of which the single line entered the 685-yard Chipping Norton Tunnel. The line was, at this point, on a 1 in 80 rising gradient, which sometimes caused difficulties for heavily-laden eastbound freight trains. Emerging into daylight at the other end of the tunnel, up trains initially headed in a north-westerly direction but, after passing through a short cutting that was spanned, at its approximate mid-point, by an accommodation bridge, the railway curved rightwards onto a north-easterly alignment.

ROLLRIGHT HALT

Running along a length of embankment that was pierced by two underline bridges or cattle creeps, the line passed beneath a minor road bridge and, still climbing, trains laboured towards their next stopping place at Rollright Halt. The famous stone circle known as 'The Rollright Stones' lay about one mile to the north of the railway, on the summit of a hill above Great Rollright village. As mysterious as the monuments at Stonehenge and Avebury, the Rollright Stones consist of two circles, one about 100 feet in diameter, while the other encloses an area about six feet across; these are known as 'The King's Men' and 'The Whispering Knights' respectively.

Nearby, a gaunt monolith, standing about 8 feet high, inevitably became known as 'The King Stone'. The stones were said to have been the remains of a king and his army, who were turned to stone by a witch known as Old Mother Shipton. Many of these legends were collected by the archaeologist Sir Arthur Evans, who published them in *Folklore* in March 1895. In reality, the stone circle is thought to date from about the 3rd century BC, while the Whispering Knights are the remnants of a burial mound; the King Stone may be the sole survivor of a ceremonial avenue that once led to the main stone circle.

This panoramic view of Rollright Halt was taken in wintertime, the trees looking naked without their summer foliage. Note the heaps in the field beyond, these are possibly limestone and manure being left over the winter prior to spreading in the spring. The full length of the platform as built is apparent in this view, being capable of taking an engine and two bogie coaches. Amongst the handful of waiting passengers, two painters in white overalls can be seen with a step ladder, part way through the task of applying a coat of Great Western light stone to the pagoda waiting shelter. This may indicate that the halt was just being completed following its opening in December 1906, suggesting perhaps an early 1907 date for the photograph. The view is looking north; Rollright Siding was situated 200 yards to the right or east of here. Also shown is the underline bridge over the lane leading to Great Rollright. The abutments and wing walls were of brick, with two cast iron girders forming the span. *Barry Davies collection*

The Rollright Stones comprise three main constituent monuments – the Whispering Knights, which consist of five upright stones, the King Stone, which is actually situated across the modern county boundary in Warwickshire, and the King's Men, a late Neolithic ceremonial stone circle which is seen here on this 1920s postcard view by Percy Simms of Chipping Norton. This perfect circle of 104 feet in diameter consists of 77 pieces of limestone. *Neil Parkhouse collection*

Passing beneath the A34 Oxford to Stratford-upon-Avon road, trains soon reached Rollright Halt (31 miles 52 chains). Rollright had been opened on 12th December 1906 and its facilities were very similar to those at nearby Sarsden Halt. There was a single platform for passenger traffic, 192 feet in length, on the Up side of the line, together with a loop siding for coal and other forms of wagon load traffic. The platform was of sleeper construction and it was sited in an elevated position on the side of a tall embankment. The platform, originally a full length structure, was later reduced in length at its west end, modifications of this kind being fairly common in the case of sleeper-built halts.

The lane to Great Rollright village passed beneath the line by means of an underline bridge on the west side of the halt. The passenger platform boasted another Great Western 'pagoda' shelter, measuring approximately 20 feet by 8 feet at ground level. At night, the lonely platform was illuminated by oil lamps, which were lit and trimmed by

Although this postcard view is labelled Great Rollright, the halt was always known simply as Rollright Halt. It was a classic GWR halt, with a corrugated iron 'pagoda' style waiting shelter resting on a sleeper-built platform. This view is circa 1930, by which time it will be noted that the platform had been shortened at its west end. *Oxfordshire County Council Photographic Archive*

Right: A view of the platform and pagoda shelter from a passing train, probably in the late 1940s.
Bob Brown collection

Below: A final glimpse of the halt, looking down the hill in a circa 1930 Frank Packer postcard view. Southwards, the lane – now the B4026 – led ultimately back to Chipping Norton, taking a somewhat more direct route than the railway whose way was more dictated by the local topography. *Bob Brown collection*

the guards of passing trains. For administrative purposes, Rollright Halt was under the control of the station master at nearby Chipping Norton.

Rollright Siding was on the Up side of the running line, about 12 chains to the east of the platform. The siding post-dated the halt by three years, having been opened on 1st January 1909. It was worked from two ground frames, known as Rollright East and Rollright West frames. When goods trains called at the siding, the points were released by a key on the single line staff for the Hook Norton to Chipping Norton section.

A short loading bank was available for use when sugar beet or other agricultural traffic was loaded and there was a small goods lock-up. The latter structure was an arc-roofed corrugated iron shed, of standard corrugated iron design, with sliding doors at front and rear. Other accommodation for freight traffic included a brick-built weigh-house and coal wharves for the local coal merchants. A sleeper-built platelayers' hut was sited opposite the goods siding, on the Down side of the line.

BANBURY & CHELTENHAM DIRECT RAILWAY

Below: Rollright Siding was slightly divorced from the halt, partly because the latter, which had opened three years earlier, was sited on an embankment. It was actually listed in the *RCH Handbook* as Great Rollright Siding and was noted simply as being a goods station. This view is looking east towards King's Sutton in about 1950, with the West Ground Frame in the foreground. A key on the end of the single line train staff, which had to be inserted into a keyway in the frame, released the point levers allowing access to the single loop. Also to be seen in this view is the loading gauge and weighbridge hut, with a stack of coal in the yard beyond. *J.H. Russell, courtesy Roger Carpenter*

Right: Rollright Halt and Great Rollright Siding as shown on the Third edition 25 inch OS of 1922 (reduced by 40% to fit the page). Note the lane providing road access to the siding. *Crown copyright reserved*

Right and below: Front and rear views of the tiny corrugated iron goods shed which was provided here, atop a small loading dock. This had brick walls with the edges formed by old sleepers and a gravel infill. Note that there was also a second loading gauge in the background which, unlike the other one appears to be metal posted. The regular traffic was coal coming in but no doubt there were also deliveries of fertiliser from time to time and agricultural machinery. In season, agricultural produce such as sugar beet was loaded here, for onward transport to the sugar beet processing factory on the Severn Valley line at Kidderminster.

Both J.H. Russell, courtesy Roger Carpenter

Below: After the passenger service along this section ceased in 1951, Rollright Siding was still served by the pick-up goods trains from Banbury to Kingham. These ceased in August 1958 when the line was blocked by a landslide between Rollright and Hook Norton and thereafter, the siding was served from Kingham only. By the early 1960s, the regular goods service was not booked to travel here and it would appear the siding was served on an 'as required' basis. That it still generated traffic is apparent in this view of the siding taken on 10th July 1960, with two steel mineral wagons and a wooden coal wagon sandwiching a box van. Coal deliveries kept the tiny yard open, whilst the box van may have brought in a load of bagged fertiliser. Note that the goods shed had by now gone and just the weighbridge hut remained.

Michael Hale

THE BANBURY & CHELTENHAM DIRECT RAILWAY

HOOK NORTON TUNNEL

From Rollright Halt, the railway maintained an east-north-easterly heading for a distance of about two miles. With the tiny River Swere flowing alongside on the right hand side, the route crossed the 600 foot contour as it swung towards the north. As trains left the Swere valley, travellers may have glimpsed the picturesque Cotswold village of Swerford, with the elegant 18th century Swerford House standing in parkland between the village and the railway line. Entering a cutting, the railway then curved leftwards as it entered the 418 yard Hook Norton Tunnel. The cutting was wide and relatively shallow-sided but nevertheless susceptible to landslips and, in an attempt to reduce this problem, its sides were revetted with rough stonework.

Above: Ex-Great Western '43XX' Class 2-6-0 No. 5391 leaves the south portal of Hook Norton Tunnel and heads towards Chipping Norton with a Banbury to Kingham pick-up goods working in the early 1950s. *Bob Brown collection*

Left: Looking back at the overline bridge from which the previous view was taken, with '54XX' Class 0-6-0PT No. 5404 propelling its auto train down the slight bank towards Rollright Halt. The stone revetments built to try and hold the cutting back can be clearly seen in both these views. Although shallow sided and covered in grass and bushes which should have aided binding of the top layer, the shale stone through which the cutting was dug had a tendency to slip, with the line being closed on several occasions between 1890 and 1906. *Neil Parkhouse collection*

Left: This is almost certainly the same auto train seen in the previous view but photographed a few moments earlier, with the '54XX' class pannier tank propelling its coach away from the tunnel. The date is circa 1950 and the photographer was standing on top of one of the stone revetments. It was on this section that the landslide occurred in 1958 which was to ultimately close the line as a through route. *Bob Brown collection*

Below: The northern portal of Hook Norton Tunnel was about half a mile to the left. This general view of Hook Norton village circa 1910, also shows the Earl of Dudley's private siding in the foreground, with loaded coal wagons waiting to be emptied. There was a continuous rope haulage system serving the kiln on the valley floor, with coal going down and calcined ore coming up.

Mrs Freda Gittos collection

THE EARL OF DUDLEY'S SIDING

Emerging from Hook Norton Tunnel, the single line ran through a section of cutting, which was quickly followed by a lofty embankment. As they approached the two towering Hook Norton viaducts, trains passed the site of an abandoned private siding on the Down side. This was the former South Hill Ironstone Siding, which had been installed in 1900 in connection with the Earl of Dudley's nearby ironstone workings. The siding was entered by means of a single line connection that was facing to Down trains, the connection being released from a ground frame on the Up side of the running line. This facility was used from 1901 until the closure of the quarries in 1916.

The Earl of Dudley's Quarries were named after the Second Earl of Dudley (1867-1932), the son of William Humble Ward, the first Earl of Dudley, and the owner of

THE BANBURY & CHELTENHAM DIRECT RAILWAY

This panoramic circa 1920 view shows the gated entrance to the siding, with Hook Norton No. 2 Viaduct in the background. The siding opened on 17th July 1900 and was officially known as South Hill Siding, access to it being controlled from South Hill Siding Ground Frame – the hut visible in the centre distance. The incline down to the Earl of Dudley's kiln is out of sight on the right. The siding went out of use when the works closed in 1916 but was not removed until 1926. *Oxfordshire County Council Photographic Archive*

extensive industrial interests in the West Midlands. Lord Dudley's father had, at one time, been chairman of the Oxford, Worcester & Wolverhampton Railway. The Dudleys, who resided at Witley Court, near Worcester, also owned Round Oak Steelworks near Stourbridge. Like other large steelworks, Round Oak received its ore from a variety of sources but, for a short time at least, most of its calcined ore came from the Dudley Quarries at Hook Norton.

It should be explained that 'calcination' is the process whereby water and other volatile constituents are expelled from ironstone, this essential purification process being achieved by roasting in kilns. Calcination was not normally carried out in iron quarries but when ore was transported over relatively long distances, it made sense for this initial process to take place before carriage, as calcined ore weighed less than raw ironstone. For this reason, ore was calcined on site at many of the Oxfordshire ironstone quarries, the Earl of Dudley's Quarry being equipped with a single, coal-fired calcining kiln.

Although the Earl of Dudley's quarry workings were in operation for only fifteen years, they were of considerable interest from an industrial archaeological point of view. The site extended east and west of the Banbury & Cheltenham line, a double track, cable-worked narrow gauge tramway being laid beneath the No. 2 Viaduct. The tramway was linked to the calcining kiln by an inclined ramp, while two similar ramps, one of which was gravity-operated, linked the quarry tramway to the standard gauge siding. Steam power was employed to work the cable system, coal for use in the engine house and in the kiln being delivered regularly by the GWR.

A rare view on the valley floor at this point, with No. 2 Viaduct in the background and the Earl of Dudley's kiln on the left. Leading up to it is the charging ramp, up which narrow gauge tubs carried successive loads of ore and coal, which were then tipped in the top until the kiln was full and allowed to roast over a period of several days. Unlike larger kilns, this one was operated on the batch process; when the roast was completed it was emptied from the base and then refilled again. Part of the route of the narrow gauge tramway can just be made out on the right, marked by the curving hedge and with wooden buffer stops visible in the centre. *Barry Davies collection*

A postcard showing part of No. 2 Viaduct looking south-west, with the kiln visible again through the piers. It is obviously still in operation, which would put the date of the postcard as circa 1912. The incline is out of sight in the right background. A fuller account of this and all the other ironstone operations which connected with the B&CDR can be found in Tonks Part II (see bibliography). The slender nature of the viaduct girders is very apparent in this view. Only the piers remain today. *Barry Davies collection*

THE HOOK NORTON VIADUCTS

Still heading more or less due north, trains then crossed the impressive Hook Norton No. 2 Viaduct, which carried the line over the valley of a small stream. The viaduct consisted of eight lattice girder spans, the horizontal girders being supported on seven gently-tapering stone columns; No. 2 Viaduct was 296 yards long and it carried the railway about 90 feet above ground level. In the heyday of the local ironstone industry, the valley below the two Hook Norton viaducts was traversed by a network of narrow gauge tramways, serving the Earl of Dudley, Hook Norton and Brymbo quarry systems.

The No. 2 Viaduct was followed by a length of embankment, beyond which trains crossed Hook Norton No. 1 Viaduct. This was slightly shorter than its neighbour, the five lattice spans, which rested on four stone piers, totalling 188 yards in length. The track across both viaducts was formed of conventional chaired rails, bolted to longitudinal timber sleepers and ballasted in the usual way; spacers were employed at intervals to maintain the gauge. The Hook Norton Up Home signal was sited just a few feet beyond the northern abutment of the No. 1 Viaduct.

No. 2 Viaduct from the south-west, with Hook Norton village and parish church in the background. The kiln appears to be out of use, suggesting a date of circa 1920. Part of the incline to the siding can just be seen on the extreme left. *Oxfordshire County Council Photographic Archive*

Right and below: These two postcards of No. 2 Viaduct are from similar viewpoints, on the south side of Hook Norton village. Along with the ironstone quarries, they were notable local landmarks and both were thus well photographed for posterity.
Right: Bob Brown collection
Below: Barry Davies collection

Below: The classic view of No. 2 Viaduct, showing its full 296-yard length, with all eight spans and seven stone-built piers. The photograph was taken by Frank Packer around 1910 and is looking east towards Hook Norton station.
Bob Brown collection

This superb panoramic view of the centre of Hook Norton village and No. 2 Viaduct was taken from the church tower, looking south west around 1920. The Earl of Dudley's works can just be seen through the centre spans. The somewhat flimsy appearance of both viaducts, with their narrow stone piers and spidery ironwork, belied their strength to a certain extent, although crossing them was something of an experience, particularly in later years as they advanced in age and especially for locomotive crews. Trains passing over, as well as being restricted to 20 mph maximum, were also expected to stop before proceeding onto the girder spans, so as not to have to undertake any unneccesary braking whilst on the bridges. In an attempt perhaps to dispel some of these fears, load deflection tests were carried out by running four '28XX' Class 2-8-0s over the viaducts at speed. It is recorded that neither the onlookers nor the enginemen were ever to forget the event. The village roofs are a mixture of Cotswold stone tiles and thatch, Welsh slate then being an expensive commodity which had to be brought in. Today, the manufacture of stone tiles and thatching are both local crafts which have all but died out, as a consequence of which slate is now the cheaper option and reconstituted slate cheaper still.

Oxfordshire County Council Photographic Archive

A better idea of the scale of the viaducts is given in this view, with a Banbury to Kingham auto-train about to rumble onto No. 2 Viaduct. The '517' Class 0-4-2T and auto trailer have already crossed the No. 1 Viaduct, visible in the right background. Being less spectacular, with only five spans although otherwise visually similar, No. 1 seems to have been far less photographed. *Barry Davies collection*

Another breathtaking study from the Packer archive, confirming what a magnificent legacy he has left for future generations. This is the view across No. 1 Viaduct circa 1910, with the line curving gently to the right at the far end, past the Hook Norton Up Home signal and into the station. In the right foreground is the Down Home signal for No. 2 Viaduct. *Oxfordshire County Council Photographic Archive*

Looking westwards from the station towards No. 1 Viaduct, just prior to the end of passenger services in 1951. In the distance, '54XX' Class 0-6-0PT No. 5404 can be seen between the two viaducts, approaching with a Banbury-bound auto service. The large hut in the foreground housed a gangers' trolley. In the bottom of the valley to the left can be seen the track bed of the old standard gauge line belonging to the long defunct Hook Norton Ironstone Partnership Ltd, which was wound up in 1903. The appearance of rails is probably an illusion, however, as they were reportedly taken up around 1903; it is more likely that what can be seen is a farm track. *W.A. Camwell*

HOOK NORTON

Having safely negotiated both bridges, Up trains entered Hook Norton station (35 miles 17 chains). The layout provided here consisted of a long crossing loop, with Up and Down platforms on either side. The goods yard, with two sidings, was situated to the west of the platforms on the Up side, while further sidings were available for ironstone traffic on the Down side of the line. The main station building was on the Up side and the minor road from Hook Norton to Milcombe passed beneath the Up and Down loop lines, on a skewed alignment, by means of an underline bridge at the Banbury end of the station. The bridge was formed of transverse girders resting on brick abutments.

Observant travellers could tell that they had left the former Oxford, Worcester & Wolverhampton system simply by looking at the station building, which was a single-storey, brick structure reflecting Banbury & Cheltenham architectural practice. There was, in fact, a marked similarity to Andoversford and Cheltenham South stations – which had also been constructed by the B&CDR – although the stations east of Kingham were of somewhat plainer external appearance.

As we have seen, the Banbury & Cheltenham Direct Railway had been opened to traffic as a close ally of the GWR and it is, perhaps, hardly surprising that the stations built under B&CDR auspices should have reflected Great Western traditions. These modest structures were in effect a simplified version of a design that had earlier been employed in the West Country on lines such as the Cornwall Railway. In essence, the Banbury & Cheltenham station buildings were rectangular brick structures, with projecting canopies and low-pitched, slated roofs. However, the basic design also featured a recessed loggia, which formed a waiting area for passengers and added an element of visual interest to these small structures.

Internally, the buildings contained the usual range of accommodation found at Victorian railway stations, including a booking office, general and ladies' waiting rooms and toilets for both sexes. The booking office was at the right hand end of the building (when viewed from the platform), with the waiting room to the left. The gentlemen's toilets were on the extreme left, then the ladies' room and next the waiting room. Access to the waiting room was obtained via doorways in the front and rear of the building, separate entrances being provided in the left hand gable in connection with the urinals and an adjacent store room.

The window and door apertures featured slightly-arched heads, the windows themselves having large-paned sliding sash frames. The office was heated by a fireplace in the east gable, while similar fireplaces were provided in the waiting room and the ladies' room. In the case of Hook Norton, the station was situated on an artificial embankment and perhaps for this reason, part of the void beneath the station building was adapted for use as a 20 foot deep cellar.

The Down platform was equipped with a waiting shelter,

THE BANBURY & CHELTENHAM DIRECT RAILWAY

The goods yard and station at Hook Norton, as seen from the end of No. 1 Viaduct around 1925, showing the sidings originally installed for the Hook Norton Ironstone Partnership running behind the Down platform to the right. The Partnership's standard gauge locomotive, an 0-6-0ST appropriately named *Hook Norton*, could only bring loaded wagons up to the sidings two or three at a time, so steep was the incline. Following closure of this operation and removal of the rails in the valley, the sidings were left in place. The rather awkward looking pointwork in the foreground, leading to the goods shed, was arranged like this so as to avoid another facing point on the running line. The foreshortening effect of this viewpoint also emphasises the 'S' bend that the railway made as it negotiated its way through the station. *John Alsop collection*

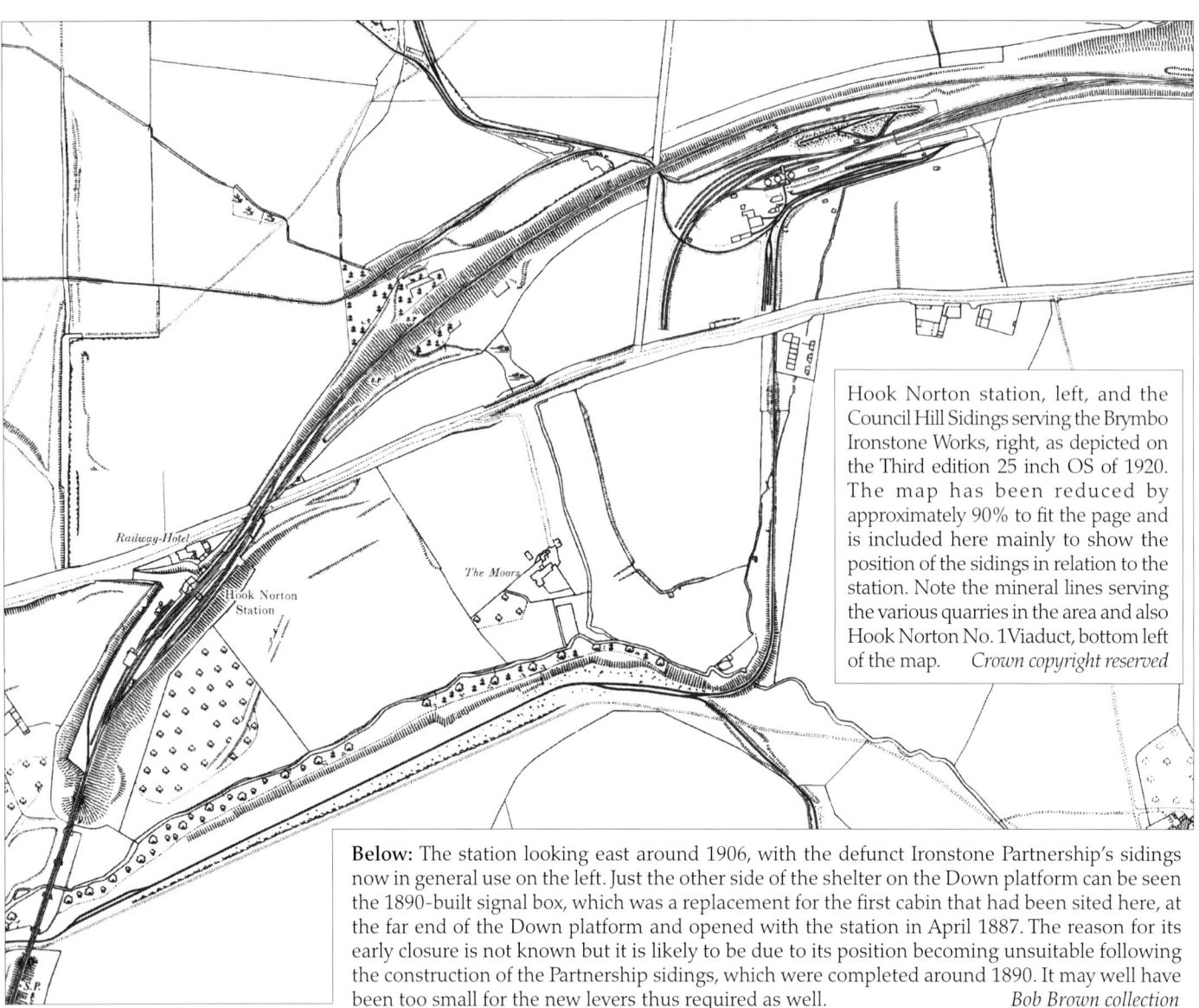

Hook Norton station, left, and the Council Hill Sidings serving the Brymbo Ironstone Works, right, as depicted on the Third edition 25 inch OS of 1920. The map has been reduced by approximately 90% to fit the page and is included here mainly to show the position of the sidings in relation to the station. Note the mineral lines serving the various quarries in the area and also Hook Norton No. 1 Viaduct, bottom left of the map. *Crown copyright reserved*

Below: The station looking east around 1906, with the defunct Ironstone Partnership's sidings now in general use on the left. Just the other side of the shelter on the Down platform can be seen the 1890-built signal box, which was a replacement for the first cabin that had been sited here, at the far end of the Down platform and opened with the station in April 1887. The reason for its early closure is not known but it is likely to be due to its position becoming unsuitable following the construction of the Partnership sidings, which were completed around 1890. It may well have been too small for the new levers thus required as well. *Bob Brown collection*

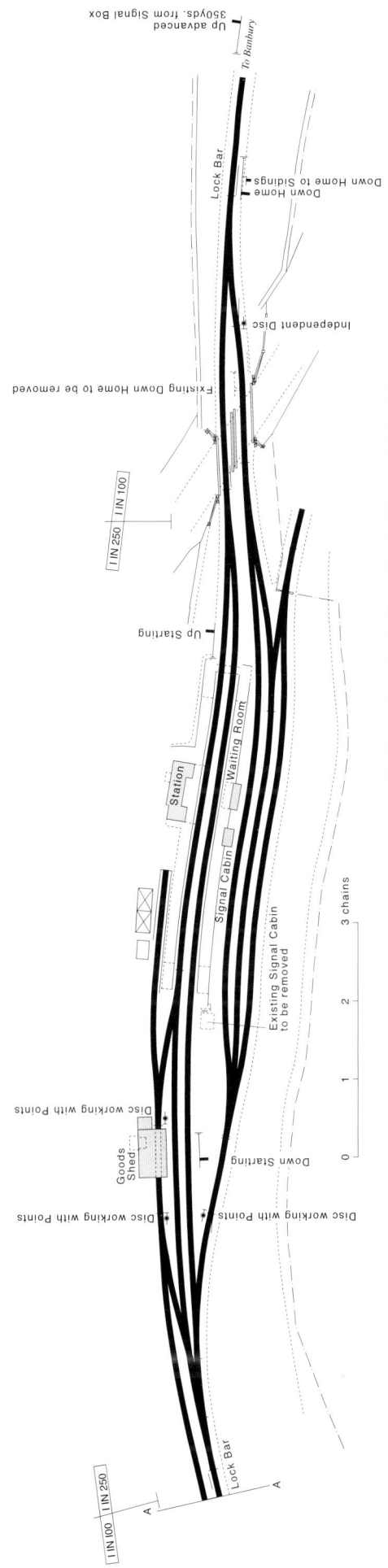

HOOK NORTON STATION

Redrawn from the Board of Trade survey 1907

A number of improvements were put in hand on the eastern section of the Banbury & Cheltenham route in the period 1906-7, largely to accommodate the expected extra traffic from the development of the ironstone fields. At Hook Norton, the crossing loop was almost doubled in order to hold a 60-wagon plus train and a new signal box, the third in less than two decades, was built. It is just visible here, at the end of the Up platform, behind the station building, whilst the lengthened loop passed over the road bridge in the background.

John Alsop collection

Below: A delightful early study of the road entrance to Hook Norton station dating from around 1906 and providing another tantalising glimpse of the 1890 signal box on the Down platform. Note the tiny canopy over the front entrance, very similar to that at Chipping Norton. The Railway Hotel, the only other building in the vicinity of the station, is on the left. The gates protecting the station entrance are also worthy of note, being of a decidedly non-standard design. The doorway at the rear of the building gave access to the waiting room; the ticket office was to the left and the ladies waiting room to the right, while the extension at the right hand end of the building contained a store and the gentlemen's urinal.

Right: This view dates from circa 1930 and shows how the foliage matured around the entrance, largely obscuring the view of the station. However, the rear of the 1907-built Hook Norton Signal Box can be seen, along with the bridge carrying the line over the road to Milcombe. There also appears to be litter on the verge, at least forty years before there should be!

Both Barry Davies collection

The Up platform and main station building looking east, sometime prior to the First World War. Behind the platform is the Railway Hotel, almost certainly built at the same time as, or shortly after, the railway itself. Note the decorative fish scale pattern of the red clay tiles which covered the upper storey. It would appear that some work is about to take place on the station building, although quite what the single piece of wooden scaffolding is for is anyone's guess! Note how well tended the platform flower borders are in all these early views of the station and also the mix of fencing styles along the back of the platform. *Paul Laming collection*

with a single-pitched roof that was continued forward over the platform to create a small platform canopy. The Up and Down sides were linked by a barrow crossing at the east end of the platforms. An array of three parallel sidings at the rear of the Down platform were installed around 1890, to serve the newly-created Hook Norton Ironstone Partnership Ltd. The ironstone sidings were initially entered via a connection at the east end of the station but a further connection was subsequently brought into use at the west of the Down platform and the three sidings were thereby turned into loops, with connections at each end.

Hook Norton Signal Box was situated beside the station building on the Up platform. It was again of standard Great Western design, though of all-wood construction, instead of the more usual brick-and-timber. It featured a hipped, slated roof, together with the usual five-pane high visibility windows. When first opened in 1887, the station had been equipped with a gable-roofed Gloucester Wagon Company-type signal cabin to the west of the station on the Down side but this was replaced in 1890 when a new box was opened sited on the Down platform. This was itself replaced on 8th February 1907, on which date the third and last signal box was brought into use, positioned at the eastern end of the Up platform.

The goods shed was distinctive in appearance and, like the station building, reflected B&CDR architectural practice. It was a small brick structure, with a low-pitched gable roof and an internal loading platform. Unusually, for such a small shed, the goods office was accommodated within a projecting two-storey extension at the east end, the size of the office being out of proportion in relation to the rest of the building. Other features of interest in the goods yard included a weigh-house and a cattle loading dock, the last-mentioned facility being situated beside a loading dock at the rear of the Up platform.

The track layout at Hook Norton was modified in a number of ways in the years preceding World War One, the principal alterations being the addition of the Ironstone Partnership exchange sidings around 1890, the construction of a second goods siding for mileage traffic in 1901 and an extension of the crossing loop in 1907. As a result of the last-mentioned work, the loop was lengthened from 13 chains to 23 chains, the resulting length of around 1,500 feet being sufficient to hold a train of over sixty mineral wagons, together with the engine and brake van.

The goods shed siding was originally linked to the Up and Down running lines by trailing connections, while the mileage or 'back' siding that ran along the northern edge of the goods yard was entered via a connection from the single line. Two short spurs extended eastwards and westwards from the Goods Shed Road, that at the west end being a sort of headshunt, while the other terminated in the aforementioned end-loading dock. In later years, these arrangements were simplified, the eastern spur being extended to form a connection with the Back Road, the advantage of this modified layout being that it produced a

This view of the station looking west towards Cheltenham is contemporaneous with the photograph of Chipping Norton on page 248. There is little sign of activity, on the station or in the sidings, and it all looks a bit shabby compared with the pre-1914 views. *Neil Parkhouse collection*

Right: Following on from the view on page 280, Collett '54XX' Class 0-6-0PT No. 5404 and auto-trailer pause at Hook Norton whilst *en route* for Banbury in 1951. *W.A. Camwell*

lengthened Goods Shed Road.

The types of freight traffic dealt with at Hook Norton included coal inwards and agricultural products outwards. The now-famous Hook Norton Brewery, founded by John Harris in 1849, contributed a certain amount of traffic, although much of the brewery's output was delivered locally by horse-drawn vehicles. In 1918, the brewery was granted a licence to supply beer to Coventry clubs and rail transport was used for this traffic until 1924, when a motor lorry was hired for the regular Coventry deliveries. Otherwise, the principal source of freight traffic at this Oxfordshire station was ironstone from the Hook Norton Ironstone Partnership and other rail-connected ironstone firms in the vicinity.

The amount of freight traffic dealt with at Hook Norton varied from year to year, according to the amount of ironstone being excavated. Thus, in 1903, 87,844 tons of freight were handled, while in 1923 this figure had increased to 154,820 tons. There was, thereafter, a perceptible decline, although as a general rule Hook Norton dealt with around 50,000 tons of freight per annum throughout the 1930s. Passenger bookings averaged about 8,000 – 9,500 per annum during the early 1900s, falling to about 2,800 a year by the 1930s – although with season ticket sales reaching 124 by 1937, the station remained relatively busy.

\multicolumn{6}{c}{TRAFFIC DEALT WITH AT HOOK NORTON}
YEAR	STAFF	RECEIPTS (£)	TICKETS	PARCELS	GOODS (TONS)
1913	7	19,217	9,646	5,160	105,943
1929	5	18,196	4,233	6,662	65,784
1936	4	8,944	2,096	3,432	32,601
1937	4	23,192	3,199	3,490	86,282
1938	4	7,638	2,944	3,232	25,864

The station was situated in a rural area to the east of the village, its only neighbour being the 'Railway Hotel', a

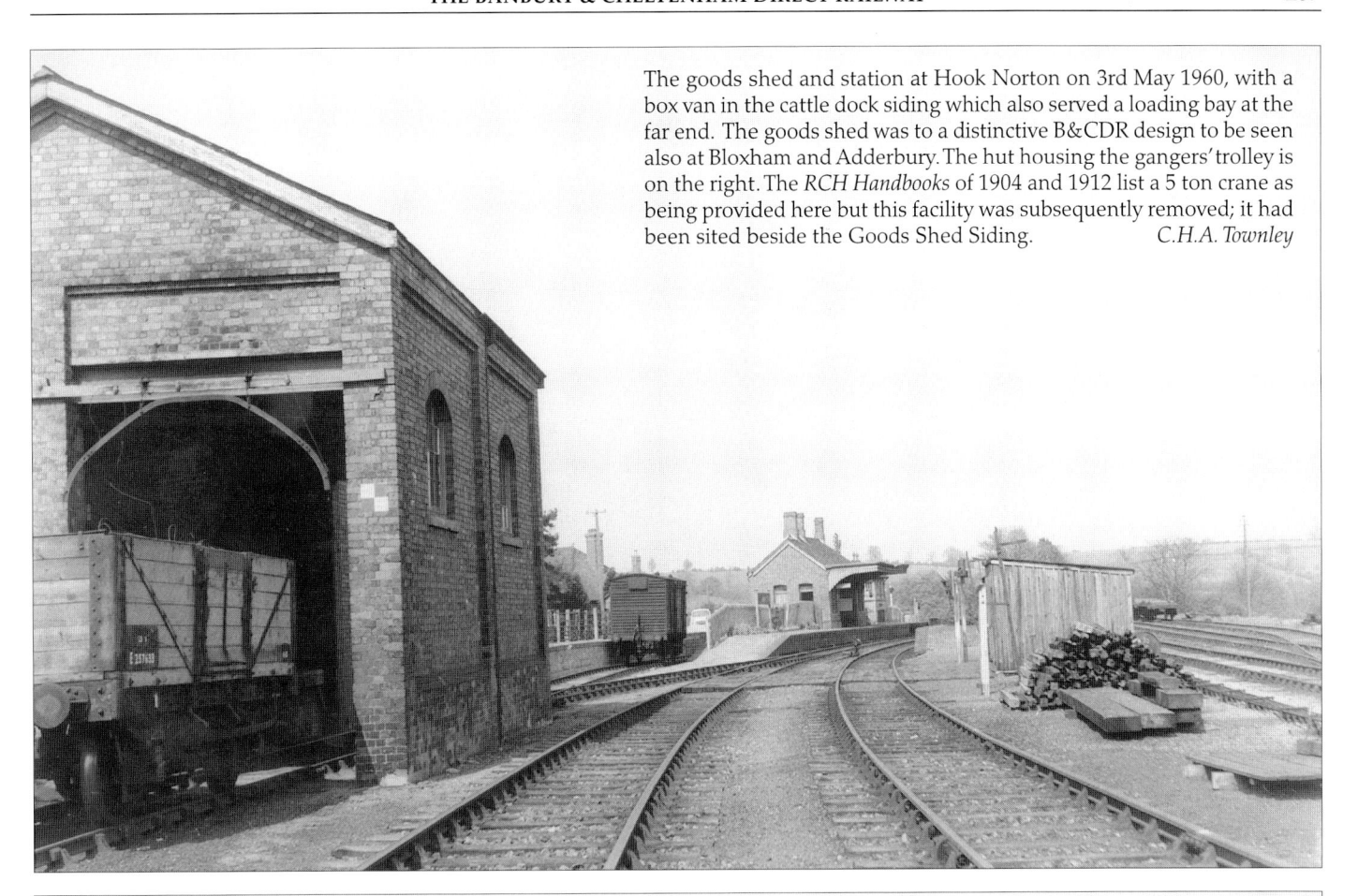

The goods shed and station at Hook Norton on 3rd May 1960, with a box van in the cattle dock siding which also served a loading bay at the far end. The goods shed was to a distinctive B&CDR design to be seen also at Bloxham and Adderbury. The hut housing the gangers' trolley is on the right. The *RCH Handbooks* of 1904 and 1912 list a 5 ton crane as being provided here but this facility was subsequently removed; it had been sited beside the Goods Shed Siding. *C.H.A. Townley*

Facing east towards Bloxham in 1962, the station looks in tidy condition considering passenger services had ceased eleven years earlier. The cattle dock is on the left, whilst the sleepered area in the foreground was to facilitate manhandling of the gangers' inspection trolley from the hut just out of view to the right. *Joe Moss, courtesy Roger Carpenter*

Above: This westward facing view from 1962 shows the 1907-built signal box in good detail. *Joe Moss, courtesy Roger Carpenter*
Below: Despite closure of the passenger service on 2nd June 1951, the stations between Chipping Norton and King's Sutton remained remarkably intact until the line closed completely. This is the Down platform and shelter in the late 1950s. *The Lens of Sutton Collection*

relatively large, hipped roof structure which occupied a roughly triangular plot of land on the Up side of the line, between the railway and the Hook Norton to Milcombe road. The building was of brick construction, with a tile-hung upper storey and generously-proportioned windows. Its late-Victorian, 'vernacular revival' features suggested that the hotel was contemporaneous with the railway.

Hook Norton itself was situated on the west side of the railway. A decayed town, rather than a purely agricultural village, Hook Norton was supposed to have been the scene of a massacre of the Danes during the Viking Wars. Later, in more peaceful times, the village was rebuilt in the characteristic honey-brown marlstone of the Oxfordshire ironstone district. The use of this material resulted in the appearance of typical 'Cotswold' style houses and cottages, albeit mostly with steeply-pitched thatched roofs in place of the stone-tiled roofs found elsewhere in Gloucestershire and west Oxfordshire. However, the photograph on page 278 shows that, by the Edwardian period, many of the houses had been given stone tiled roofs instead.

The church of St. Peter occupies a prominent site near the centre of the village, while Hook Norton manor house was situated a quarter of a mile to the south-west of the station. Although the name Hook Norton Manor would clearly have been familiar to locomotive enthusiasts, the building itself was not without interest, being a large, two-and-a-half storey, 'L'-shaped structure, with a triple-gabled frontage. A bay window at one end displayed the date '1656', suggesting that this was the year of construction.

The steps end of Hook Norton Signal Box, again in 1962, with the line snaking eastwards over Station Road towards Banbury. Note how the access to the south side sidings from the Up line – avoiding the need for a facing connection on the Down line (this was part of the 1907 improvements) – straddled the girders of the road bridge. The signal box appears to have had a recent coat of paint – a sure sign that final closure was imminent! *Joe Moss, courtesy Roger Carpenter*

THE HOOK NORTON IRONSTONE PARTNERSHIP

As recounted in Chapter Three, the Ironstone Partnership was formed by Richard Looker and other entrepreneurs with links to the Banbury & Cheltenham Direct Railway. Ironstone extraction was under way by 1889, a Manning Wardle 0-6-0ST named *Hook Norton* (Works No. 1127) having been obtained in that year to work the quarry system. As operations progressed, the workings extended to areas on the west side of the Banbury & Cheltenham line, and these were linked to the ironstone sidings via a single track branch that curved south-eastwards from the main line and passed beneath Hook Norton No. 1 Viaduct.

The workings on the west side of Hook Norton station were served by a 1 foot 8 inch gauge quarry system, incorporating a cable-worked incline and a short tunnel beneath the Hook Norton to Banbury road. Ironstone was transported along the tramway in narrow gauge wagons and tipped into standard gauge vehicles at a transshipment point near the viaduct. The loaded wagons were taken along the ironstone branch to the station, *Hook Norton* being used for that purpose. The physical connection between the quarry branch and the GWR was arranged via a long headshunt which extended north-eastwards from the exchange sidings.

In addition to *Hook Norton*, the Ironstone Partnership employed a narrow gauge Manning Wardle 0-4-0ST named *Florence* (Works No. 579) for work in the quarries at the north

Following liquidation of the Ironstone Partnership, their locomotive, *Hook Norton*, was taken into GWR ownership. Allocated the number 1337, it spent the rest of its days at Weymouth, where it was photographed in 1925. *Neil Parkhouse collection*

end of the narrow gauge tramway. This locomotive had been built in 1875 and its name recalled previous service with the Florence Coal & Iron Company of Trentham, Staffordshire. It was used for a short time in the Hook Norton Ironstone Partership's other quarries at Adderbury, after which the engine was transferred to Hook Norton.

When not at work, the two Ironstone Partnership engines were housed in single track locomotive sheds, the narrow gauge shed being sited at the upper part of the tramway, in a quarry known as Hiatt's Pit. This small structure is clearly depicted on the 1898 Ordnance Survey map, which reveals that the infrastructure at the northern end of the quarry tramway included a run-round loop, a headshunt at the end of the line and a curved siding into the quarry; the engine shed was sited at the end of a short spur, near the end of the siding. The standard gauge 0-6-0ST was housed in a corrugated iron shed beside the headshunt connection to the exchange sidings.

The Ironstone Partnership worked successfully for several years but, in 1903, it was wound up and placed in liquidation. As principal creditor, the GWR acquired the 0-6-0ST *Hook Norton*, which was numbered 1337 and sent to Weymouth, where it worked for many years on the quayside tramway. A large area of land to the north and west of the Banbury & Cheltenham line that had been owned by the Ironstone Partnership was sold by the liquidators. In 1909, this same land, known as Redlands, was purchased by the Brymbo Steel Company, which resumed mineral extraction around the former Hook Norton Ironstone Partnership workings at Hiatt's Pit.

The Brymbo Ironstone Works at Hook Norton around 1906, with the first two kilns in operation. They were of the gas-fired Davis Colby type and were mounted atop substantial stone bases, which were further strengthened with iron banding to prevent them spreading under the weight of a fully charged kiln. They were emptied via chutes around the base of the kiln, discharging directly into standard gauge wagons for onward transport to North Wales. Two sidings straddled the kilns – their level is most clearly seen to the left of the left hand water tank – and production of calcined ore began in December 1899. The B&CDR line passes by on the embankment in the background. To the right of the water tank, was the water softening plant on its square brick base and the gas producing plant can be seen just to the right of and behind that. *Barry Davies collection*

THE BRYMBO IRONSTONE WORKS

Resuming their journeys, eastbound trains left Hook Norton station in a northerly direction but, having traversed an eighty degree curve, they soon resumed an easterly heading. Council Hill Sidings, serving the Brymbo Steel Company's extensive ironstone workings, were about half a mile beyond Hook Norton station, at 35 miles 75 chains. Shortly before the sidings, trains passed over a girder bridge known as the 'Black Bridge'. This originally carried the railway across a minor road, although following the acquisition of Redlands, the Brymbo Company also laid a narrow gauge quarry tramway beneath its single girder span.

The Brymbo Ironworks near Wrexham, in North Wales, had been founded in the 1790s by John 'Iron Mad' Wilkinson (1728-1808), one of the leading figures in the Industrial Revolution. In 1841, the Brymbo Works and estate were purchased by Robert Roy (1795-1873), who reorganised the site and formed the Brymbo Mineral & Railway Company, in conjunction with Henry Robertson (1816-1888) and other entrepreneurs. Robertson was a business associate and close friend of Benjamin Piercy, who had been involved with some of the earlier surveys for lines between Cheltenham and Banbury, and it is conceivable that Piercy had informed Robertson and his colleagues of the presence of iron ore in and around Hook Norton.

An extensive narrow gauge system was laid down to carry the ore from the quarries to the kilns and a train of laden wagons can be seen in this circa 1908 photograph. The wagons were lifted to the top of the kilns for tipping by means of the wagon hoist, on the right, with short lengths of narrow gauge rail also being in place on the charging platform at the top. It would appear that only the left hand kiln is in operation in this view. In 1908, 70,000 tons of ore were mined from the Park Farm site. A detailed history of the Brymbo company's operations at Hook Norton can be found in the book by Paul Ingham (see bibliography).
Neil Parkhouse collection

In the event, it was not until their own local supplies of ironstone started to become exhausted that the Brymbo Company started operations in the Hook Norton area, beginning with the purchase of the 152-acre Park Farm, in 1898, an estate which it was calculated would yield just in excess of 1 million tons of iron ore and take some thirteen and a half years to extract. The company quickly commenced mining on the estate, to the east of the Hook Norton viaducts, whilst the Redlands quarries, to the west of the Great Western line, were in full production by 1917. The company also acquired land at Manor Farm, to the east of the Park Farm site.

The quarries were served by a narrow gauge railway system, as well as a system of standard gauge sidings that ran directly into the works. Access to the private quarry system was by means of a connection on the Down side of the Banbury & Cheltenham route, the sidings being worked from a ground frame that was locked and unlocked by a key on the electric train staff for the single line section.

In addition to the widely-dispersed ironstone quarries, the Brymbo Ironstone Works contained, by the 1920s, four large, gas-fired calcining kilns that seemed somewhat out of place in the bucolic Oxfordshire landscape. When the works first began production, there were only two kilns, increased later to three and eventually to four. The cylindrical metal kilns were slightly tapered and they stood on stone

Another view of the works prior to the installation of a third kiln, taken circa 1910 and showing the wagon hoist in good detail. The brick buildings with curved roofs on the left were the engine shed and workshops for the narrow gauge railway. They were extended and a further engine shed added in later years, with the acquisition of extra locomotives. Note the shed on top of the charging platform, for the benefit of the kiln loaders in inclement weather. The dumb-buffered private owner wagon with rounded ends, on the right, belongs to Joseph H. Pearson, Netherton Collieries, Dudley.
Barry Davies collection

Above: The exact date the third kiln was built has never been established but it is generally accepted to have been during the First World War, most probably in 1916-7. There was a significant jump in production in 1918, by 15,000 tons to 60,000 in total. It was added to the left, in this view, of the existing kilns, with the charging platform and gas pipes being extended across. This view dates from around 1920 and shows all three kilns in operation. On the left can just be seen the new locomotive shed, built circa 1915 for the arrival of *Joan*. *Neil Parkhouse collection*

Left: The acquisition of a second Hudswell Clarke 0-4-2T in 1915, to supplement the existing engine, *Gwen*, also indicates the increase in production in wartime. *Joan* was delivered by rail to the Ironstone sidings in late October of that year. This 1920s view is at Park Farm Quarry. *Oxfordshire County Council Photographic Archive*

bases between two standard gauge sidings. A wagon lift carried narrow gauge quarry wagons to the top of the kilns. A high level line was provided at the top, so that ore could be tipped into the kilns from the loaded wagons. Chutes at the bottom of the kilns enabled calcined ore to be discharged into standard gauge wagons, for onwards transport to the Brymbo Steel Works or other destinations.

Changing economic circumstances after World War One led to a reduction in the quantities of iron ore sent to Wrexham from Hook Norton and it was therefore decided that the Oxfordshire operation would be scaled down. The Great Depression dealt a major blow to the Brymbo Steel Company and the once-busy works at Brymbo were, in consequence, shut down from 1931 until 1934. The quarries were, however, able to supply reduced quantities of ironstone to other customers in the Midlands and South Wales, and in this way the Hook Norton site remained in use until World War Two, when a major revival took place.

The calcining kilns were shut down during the 1926 General Strike and never used again for full calcination. There were attempts to utilise one of the kilns for drying ore but most of the ironstone obtained from Hook Norton during the 1930s was transported in its raw state to the Midlands or South Wales. When full production resumed

Another 1920s view of *Joan*, collecting a train of laden tubs from the quarry face. The temporary nature of the track is evident; it was moved and extended as neccesary, in conjunction with the working faces of the quarries. *Joan*, along with the rest of the plant then on site – three other locomotives, the track, ore wagons and the kilns – was disposed of to scrap merchant G. Cohen & Sons Ltd in 1948. Apart from the wagons, which were sold abroad, everything else was dismantled and cut up on site in 1949. *Neil Parkhouse collection*

during World War Two, the Hook Norton quarries sent uncalcined ore to Brymbo.

The 2 foot gauge quarry system was worked by a variety of narrow gauge engines, including the former Welsh Highland Railway 2-6-2T *Russell*, which was sold to the Brymbo Company in 1942 and transferred to Oxfordshire in the following year. This Hunslet Engine Company locomotive (Works No. 901) was used as an 0-6-2T on the sharply-curved quarry network. Other engines used on the Brymbo quarry system were 0-4-2STs or 4-6-0Ts, the first to arrive, in August 1899, being a Hudswell Clarke 0-4-2ST known as *Gwen* (Works No. 523). This engine had 8 inch by 12 inch outside cylinders and 2 foot driving wheels; it was named *Gwen* after Mrs Gwen Littlebody, the quarry manager's wife.

A similar 0-4-2ST was ordered from Hudswell Clarke in 1915 and this second engine (Works No. 1173) was delivered to Hook Norton in October of that same year. Its leading dimensions were identical to those of *Gwen* and it was named *Joan*, after one of the quarry manager's daughters. A further engine was obtained from the Ministry of Munitions in 1919, the locomotive in question being standard Hunslet War Department 4-6-0T No. 352 (Works No. 1264). Locomotives of this type had been produced in large numbers for service on the Western

The Ruston 20 ton steam navvy and its attendant mobile rotary screen, circa 1920. It arrived at Hook Norton in the summer of 1915. *Barry Davies collection*

Front, the 4-6-0 configuration being ideal for use on the army's wartime ammunition-carrying lines.

The new locomotive was dubbed 'Black Bess', presumably because of its sombre livery, although this appellation remained entirely unofficial. The engine was altered slightly from 60 centimetre to 2 foot gauge, and reduced in height to allow it to pass beneath the tunnel near Brymbo Cottages. Otherwise, 'Black Bess' was a standard WD 4-6-0T, with $9^1/_2$ inch by 12 inch outside cylinders, 2 foot coupled wheels and a total weight of 14 tons 1 cwt.

Reverting briefly to the 2-6-2T *Russell*, it may be worth adding that this famous engine had initially been built for service on the abortive Portmadoc, Beddgelert & South Snowdon Railway. As this line was never constructed, the engine was put to work on the associated North Wales Narrow Gauge Railway. When the latter route became part of the Welsh Highland Railway, *Russell* was modified to allow through running onto the Festiniog Railway through Moelwyn Tunnel, its cab and boiler fittings being reduced in height. Following the closure of the Welsh Highland Railway in 1937, *Russell* was left in Dinas engine shed until 1941, when it was requisitioned by the Ministry of Supply. *Russell* is back on the new WHR today, the only engine that worked at Hook Norton to survive.

Left and below: A group of quarrymen standing in front of the rotary screen which was coupled to the steam navvy and able to move slowly along with it. It separated the ore stone from the dust and soil, which was then carried away on a conveyor belt and deposited to one side of the workings. It was a marvellous piece of machinery, bought at a time when production was being stepped up to meet wartime demand and which threatened to put many of the workforce out of a job, until it was discovered it did not function in damp conditions because the holes in the drum became blocked. Nevertheless, it was in operation with the steam navvy, which dug out the ore before emptying its bucket into the top of the drum, well into the 1920s. It was electrically powered and also lit up at night by a string of bulbs.

Left: Barry Davies collection
Below: Oxfordshire County Council Photographic Archive

Two final views of the Brymbo Ironstone Works, showing it at its fullest extent with four kilns in operation. The fourth kiln was working by the summer of 1922 and was built to the right of the original two. The view, **above**, is looking up the steep incline that loaded narrow gauge trains had to negotiate to reach the works from Park Farm Quarry. One of the Hunslets, either *Joan* or *Gwen* can be seen in the centre distance. The picture, **below**, probably dating from circa 1930, is looking from the other side of the kilns, with the B&CDR line behind the photographer. A selection of private owner wagons is on view, mostly taking calcined ore to the Shelton Steelworks at Stoke-on-Trent but at least one – seen in the process of being loaded from the chutes at the base of one of the kilns – is destined for the Margam Steelworks at Port Talbot. *Above: Oxfordshire County Council Photographic Archive; below: Barry Davies collection*

A westbound pick-up goods train is held in the loop whilst a '43XX' Class mogul runs through with the 7:40 am Swansea to Newcastle 'Ports-to-Ports Express' sometime in the 1920s. The occasion seems to have created some local interest, judging by the small group of station staff, wives, children and one or two others on the platform, whilst the express appears to be moving quite slowly – perhaps the crew had advance warning that their passage through Bloxham on this particular day was going to be recorded for posterity. Note the board advertising Palmerson's coal depot in the right background. *Barry Davies collection*

BLOXHAM

From Council Hill Sidings, the route ran due eastwards, with the minor road from Hook Norton to Milcombe running parallel across intervening fields on the right hand side of the line. Through travellers from Cheltenham might have noticed that subtle changes were now taking place in the scenery that could be viewed on either side of the line. Although the surrounding farms and villages were still noticeably 'Cotswold' in appearance, the West Country atmosphere was now less pronounced. The railway had not yet left the West of England, although one sensed that the Midlands were not far off.

Still heading eastwards, the route dropped towards Bloxham on a 1 in 100 descending gradient. The railway passed within half a mile of the village of Wigginton, which was situated to the right of the line in the Swere Valley. No stopping place was ever provided here although, in the 1930s, goods and parcels were collected or delivered by private carrier from Hook Norton, or by GWR country lorry service from Banbury, some six miles to the north-east. In the early 19th century, a Roman villa was discovered near the parish church of St. Giles; modern excavations have suggested that it was a large house with over fifteen rooms, dating from the middle of the 3rd century AD.

A stop board near Wigginton told the drivers of up freight trains to halt, so the guard could pin down an appropriate number of wagon brakes before the descent into Bloxham station. Beyond, the line passed through a cutting as it

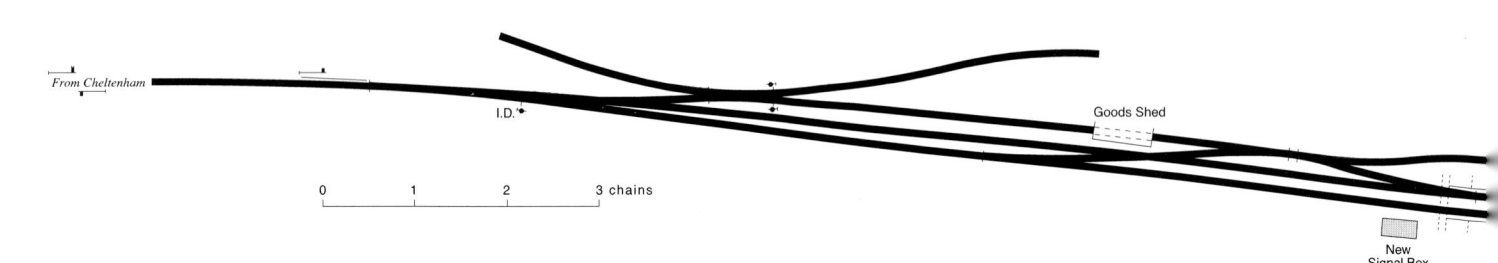

Looking east towards King's Sutton circa 1925, with several young children posing on the Up platform whilst a member of the station staff attends to a trolley laden with milk churns. The sighting of the Up Starting signal was greatly aided by the brickwork of the left hand abutment of the road bridge being painted white. The station building and Down platform shelter were identical to those at Hook Norton and, once again, well tended station gardens are much in evidence. *Mrs Freda Gittos collection*

skirted the village of Milcombe. Like Wigginton, Milcombe was served by Great Western country lorries from Banbury, or by private carriers.

Tadmarton Heath, about one mile to the north of Milcombe, was the site of the wartime bombing decoy mentioned in Chapter Four. Night decoys, known as 'QF' sites, were designed to lure enemy aircraft away from real targets such as airfields, factories and marshalling yards. In the event of an air attack, pyrotechnic effects were used to simulate fires and explosions, the idea being that the Germans would think that they had found their intended target – in this case Banbury. The Q-site was controlled from an underground bunker, and it was activated at least once during the conflict.

Bloxham, the next stop (39 miles 40 chains), was very similar to neighbouring Hook Norton. The layout incorporated Up and Down platforms on either side of a crossing loop, with a two-siding goods yard to the west of the Up platform. The station building, of identical appearance to its counterpart at Hook Norton, was on the Up platform, and there was a B&CDR-type waiting shelter on the Down side. The slightly curved Up and Down platforms were linked by barrow crossings and fenced with traditional pale-and-space fencing. At night, the platforms were lit by simple oil lamps.

The A361 road was carried across the line on a skew girder bridge at the east end of the station; this structure had brick abutments and a single span of 25 feet. Another overbridge, of brick arch construction, was sited only a short distance beyond, while a lattice girder footbridge spanned the line roughly midway between these two public road overbridges.

The goods yard contained the usual range of facilities for coal, livestock, vehicles, furniture and general merchandise

BLOXHAM STATION
Redrawn from the Board of Trade survey 1907

The station in its beautifully rural setting, looking west towards Cheltenham from the A361 Chipping Norton to Banbury road bridge on 3rd May 1960. Again, it is difficult to believe from this view that passenger services had finished nine years previously; the station looks neat and tidy with gardens and vegetation all well maintained. Note that the gas lamps are still in place too. Around the end of the First World War, a private standard gauge tramway serving the Bloxham Ironstone Quarries was laid, running from the outer siding in the yard (on which the wagons are standing) and running across the field on the right. No photographs have been found to illustrate it but, despite various ups and downs, the tramway continued in use until 1954. *C.H.A. Townley*

These two views of Bloxham, facing east, **above**, and west, **page right**, were both taken on 16th June 1956. The white paint behind the Up Starter has faded from the bridge abutment and the posters have gone but otherwise little seems to have changed over the three decades since the view on page 297. Although the line was now freight only, the signal box here still had to be manned for a full shift during the daytime. The daily 10.10 am ex-Banbury pick-up goods arrived at Bloxham at 11.20, pausing for 14 minutes to shunt the sidings before departing on its way west. It was due at Kingham at 1.43 pm. The return left Kingham eastwards at 2.30, stopping again at Bloxham at 3.54 but this time just for 10 minutes, before arriving back at Banbury at 4.53. Note the Wickham inspection trolley parked opposite the signal box in the view on the right. *Both R.M. Casserley*

traffic. There was a characteristic B&CDR-type brick goods shed, with a projecting two-storey office, the shed road being arranged as a loop with connections to the Up and Down loop lines; a dead end spur at the east end of the shed road served an end-loading dock and the station's cattle loading pens. A dead end siding at the back of the yard was used for coal and other forms of mileage traffic, while a connection at the west end of the coal siding gave access to another private ironstone siding, used by the Clay Cross Company. There was also a 5-ton crane provided at the western end of the yard, which seems to have been there for most of the station's working life.

The station was signalled from a gable roofed brick-and-timber cabin, sited just west of the platforms on the Down side. Dating from circa 1890-5, the box was a typical late Victorian GWR structure, with small paned windows. In 1907, the crossing loop was lengthened from 18 to 23 chains, entailing several changes in the signalling arrangements. The frame and interlocking equipment would clearly have been renewed but it seems likely the exterior shell of the signal box was retained, its architectural features being of unmistakable pre-1900 appearance.

In its pre-Grouping heyday, Bloxham station had functioned as a railhead for a group of villages and hamlets, including Tadmarton and Lower Tadmarton on the north side of the railway, and Barford St. John and Barford St. Michael to the south. In later years, however, the Great Western served these dispersed villages by country lorry service from Banbury. Although local collections and deliveries could still be made by private carriers, it is likely that most traders would have preferred their parcels and small freight consignments to be dealt with by the railway's own lorry service and, for this reason, the goods yard at Bloxham was used mainly for coal and other wagon load traffic by the 1930s.

Bloxham gained considerable extra traffic during World War Two, when it became a convenient railhead for an RAF aerodrome that had been constructed at Barford St. John, about three quarters of a mile to the south-east of the station. This airfield was opened in June 1941 and was originally used as a Relief Landing

Another view of the station looking westwards from the road bridge, taken in the early spring of 1962. By this date, the landslip near Hook Norton Tunnel had curtailed the use of the line as a through route and goods services were operated from Banbury to Hook Norton and back. The station allotments are freshly turned and await their next planting, whilst a schoolboy football match is in progress on the pitch on the left. Most of them probably thought, if they considered it at all, that the station would always be there. In fact, it had only a little over eighteen months of life left, goods services being withdrawn in November 1963. *Joe Moss, courtesy Roger Carpenter*

Like many a small station, one of the mainstays of the goods traffic was domestic coal, along with agricultural produce and fertiliser. The 1960s was the decade in which many households began the switch to central heating, which saw much of this trade eroded away in any case over the next few years, so it would have been lost to the railways even without the closure of goods yards such as this. It was used over the years by at least two local merchants, Palmersons and Welfords. The signal box looks in smart condition and note the lads sitting on the roof of the platelayers' hut on the extreme right, no doubt watching the same football match, above, in progress.
Joe Moss, courtesy Roger Carpenter

The signal box, sited at the end of the Up platform, was an early 1890s replacement for one located opposite the goods shed, probably the original timber cabin supplied by the contractor. The standard Great Western design box is shown here in the early 1950s, with a corrugated-iron lamp hut to the left. The train staff changing apparatus was probably maintained in working order but little used by this date, the signalman no doubt preferring to leave his lonely vigil to catch a word with the locomotive crew on the once a day each way goods train. *Joe Moss, courtesy Roger Carpenter*

A view of the goods yard and the distinctive B&CDR design goods shed looking west towards Cheltenham in the early 1950s. The rather convoluted track layout will be noted, arranged once more so as to avoid facing points on the running line where possible. In later years, 'smalls' traffic was collected and delivered by BR road vehicles based at Banbury; the goods wagons standing in the yard would thus have been conveying full load traffic of some kind. *Joe Moss, courtesy Roger Carpenter*

Left: The view east towards Banbury in the early 1950s. The footbridge was erected at the behest of a local resident and landowner, Dr Hyde, in order that he could maintain his favourite walk after the railway had crossed his land. In the background is the bridge carrying the Adderbury road over the line.
Below: Looking back towards the station from the Adderbury road overbridge, with the Down Home signal just in front of Dr Hyde's bridge. The single line all the way from Adderbury to Kingham was surveyed for doubling in the 1920s but this may well have been with a thought to carrying out the work under a government job creation grant and the idea faded away as full employment slowly returned to the country.
Both Joe Moss, courtesy Roger Carpenter

Ground for RAF Kidlington. Its first aircraft were probably single-engined Harvards and twin-engined Airspeed Oxford trainers, though in January 1942, a number of Hotspur Gliders were assembled for use by the newly-formed 101 (Glider) Operational Training Unit.

In 1943 the airfield was used, albeit briefly, by the Gloster-Whittle E28 experimental jet aeroplane, which was then stationed at RAF Edge Hill. Barford St. John also became a test centre for the prototype F9/40 twin-jet Meteor aircraft, though by June 1944 it had become a Bomber Command training station, used by twin-engined aircraft such as Wellingtons and smaller training aircraft such as Miles Martinets. The airfield was ostensibly closed in November 1945, though it continued to play an active military role as a radio communications site during the Cold War period.

Like Hook Norton, Bloxham is full of attractive, brown stone houses and cottages but its greatest architectural glory is its Medieval church, with a slender 14th century tower and spire rising 198 feet above the village street. Nearby, All Saints' School, originally founded by the Reverend John Hewett in 1854, boasts some interesting Victorian gothic buildings, many of which were designed by the diocesan architect George Edmund Street – a pupil of Sir Gilbert Scott. In 1896, All Saints' Grammar School was conveyed to the Provost and Fellows of Lancing College and it was, thereafter, further developed as a private boarding school.

BLOXHAM IRONSTONE QUARRIES
(CLAY CROSS COMPANY)

Apart from coal and occasional consignments of sugar beet, the main form of bulk freight traffic handled at Bloxham was of course ironstone from the Clay Cross private siding. Ironstone working in the area to the north of the station had first been carried out by the Hook Norton Partnership but operations ceased following the liquidation of this concern. A revival took place in 1917 under the auspices of the Northampton Ironstone Company but this firm was itself in liquidation by 1925. Two years later, in 1927, the quarry was re-opened by the Clay Cross Company and this firm worked the site until February 1942, when it was closed on government orders.

It may seem odd that this action should have been taken at a time when iron ore was urgently needed for the war effort. On the other hand, the fact that a Q-site was being constructed in the vicinity of Lower Tadmarton offers a cogent explanation. Ironstone extraction was under way in and around Tadmarton by the early 1940s, and the railway siding from Bloxham station formed a useful link to the decoy factory and its 'dummy' marshalling yard. Moreover, the system of lights, metal tanks, troughs, trenches and other apparatus needed at a typical wartime Q-site could be conveniently hidden in the former quarry workings, thereby maintaining the necessary degree of secrecy from prying civilian eyes.

Bloxham quarry and its associated private siding was re-opened after World War Two and, in its final period of operation from 1948 until 1954, the quarry siding was worked by an 0-4-0 diesel shunter named *Amos*. This engine had formerly worked on the 3 foot gauge Ashover Railway, regauging being carried out when it was transferred to Oxfordshire. In earlier years, the quarry system had been worked by a Peckett 0-6-0 saddle tank, *Northfield*.

On leaving the goods yard, the Clay Cross siding immediately doubled to form two parallel sidings. These formed a headshunt and, by means of a reverse shunt, wagons could be propelled onto a further siding that extended westwards in the direction of Hook Norton. The branch to the quarry ran north-eastwards from the latter siding, curving north-westwards as it turned through ninety degrees to reach the workings near Tadmarton.

BLOXHAM QUARRIES
(BLOXHAM IRONSTONE COMPANY,
BLOXHAM & WHISTON IRONSTONE COMPANY)

Resuming their eastwards journey, Up workings dropped towards Adderbury. A little over one mile further on, trains passed the site of an abandoned ironstone siding on the Up side (40 miles 66 chains). This was used by the Bloxham Ironstone Company from early in 1917 until the closure of the site during the late 1920s. The facilities provided here included four parallel sidings for exchange traffic, together with a substantial brick engine shed for the quarry locomotives and the actual quarry branch. Between April 1918 and May 1919, the quarry employed about thirty German prisoners-of-war from a camp at nearby Banbury.

The sidings were sited on the Up side and controlled from a signal cabin opened in 1916 on the Down side of the running line. Three of the sidings were arranged as loops, with connections at each end, while the fourth was a dead-end road. The engine shed was situated at the end of a dead-end spur at the east end of the loops and this spur formed a headshunt for wagons entering or leaving the quarry branch. The signal cabin was closed around 1929 and the sidings were then worked from two ground frames.

The quarry system was normally worked by two locomotives, including the Peckett 0-6-0 saddle tanks *Margot* (Works No. 1456) and *Betty* (Works No. 1549), dating from 1918 and 1919 respectively. In its final years of operation, the quarry was worked by the Bloxham & Whiston Ironstone Company.

Unfortunately, the lines serving both of these quarries seem to have come and gone in between map revisions, whilst the Board of Trade surveys show only the point connections with the B&CDR line. Sketch plans can be found in *Track Layout Diagrams of the GWR Section 28* (R.A. Cooke).

The first trial load of ore was despatched from Bloxham Quarries in February 1917 but it was a full twelve months before regular production commenced. This Ministry of Munitions wagon was part of a large batch supplied by Gloucester RC&W Co. in July 1917, in anticipation of the new traffic starting. The Ministry in fact ordered huge numbers of wagons for use in various facets of the war effort, the vast majority of which quickly became available to private owner wagon users across the country with the cessation of hostilities in 1918.
Courtesy Gloucestershire Record Office

MILTON HALT

Continuing eastwards, Down workings soon reached the next stopping place at Milton Halt (41 miles 12 chains). This simple halt, opened on 1st January 1906, consisted of a short platform, 120 feet in length, on the Down side of the line, with a shelter for occasional travellers. The platform was of the usual sleeper-built construction, while the waiting shelter was another standard Great Western corrugated iron pagoda shed. At night, the platform was illuminated by oil lamps and a corrugated iron lamp hut was also provided for storage. For operational purposes, the halt was under the control of the Bloxham station master. The tiny hamlet of Milton, on the south side of the railway, had a population of just 169 at the time of the 1851 census.

The only known photograph of Milton Halt in operational days is this rather murky view looking east, which was probably taken in the 1930s. *Alan Brain collection*

Right: Milton Halt was situated on an embankment close to the village that it served. A path led up the side of the embankment to the halt from the lane in this photograph, which was taken on 7th October 1972, long after the track over the bridge had been lifted. *R.M. Casserley*

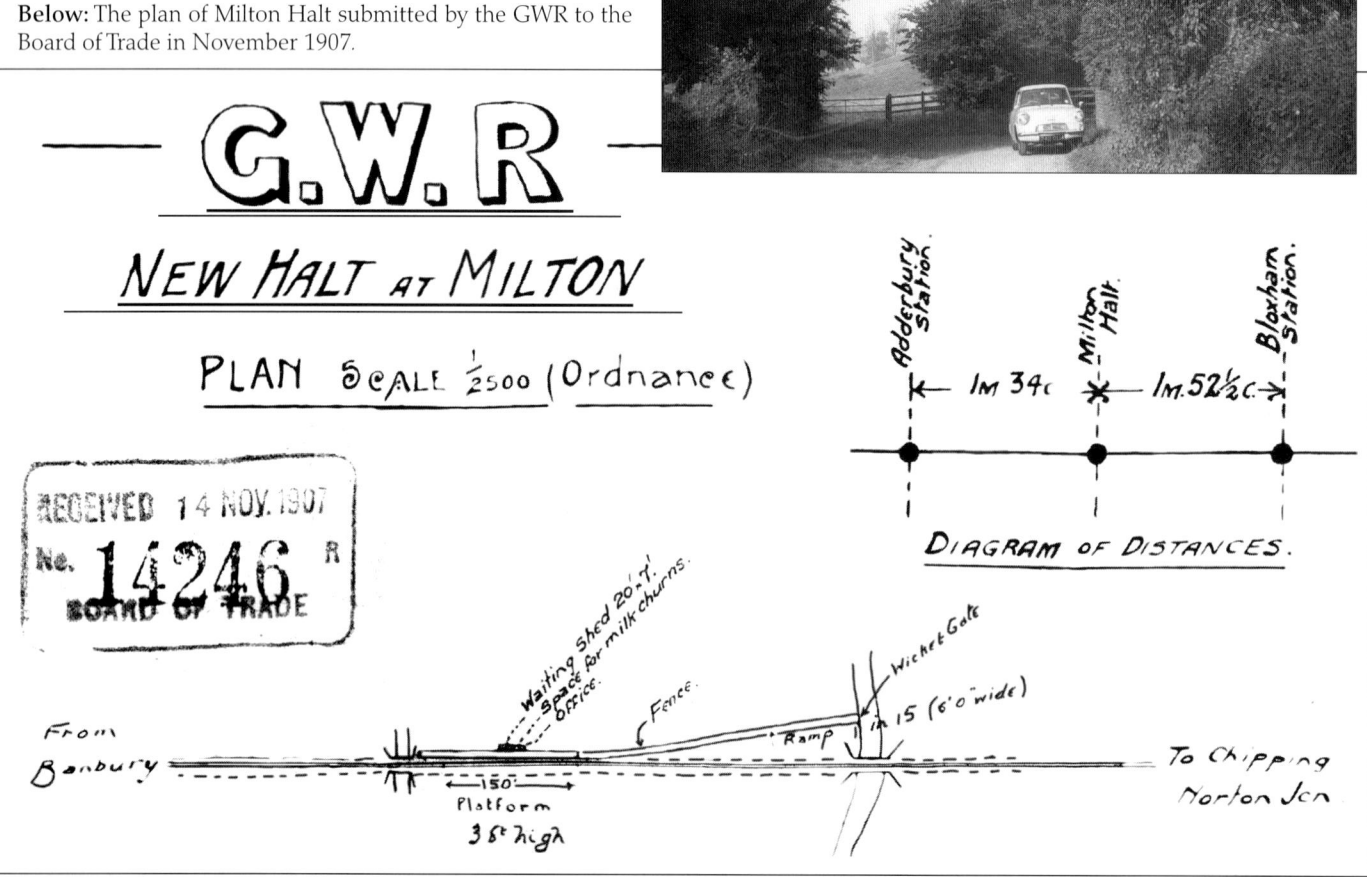

Below: The plan of Milton Halt submitted by the GWR to the Board of Trade in November 1907.

An unidentified 'Bulldog' Class outside-framed GWR 4-4-0 with the northbound 'Ports-to-Ports' Express near Milton Halt circa 1908. The train is comprised of the Great Western set of coaches, which at this period was made up of clerestory stock, whilst the roofboards denoting this express service can be clearly seen. *Courtesy Kidderminster Railway Museum*

ADDERBURY

Still heading eastwards, the route continued to Adderbury (42 miles 45 chains). This station was similar to the other intermediate stopping places between Kingham and King's Sutton, its brick station building and goods shed being more or less identical to those found at Hook Norton and Bloxham. Up and Down platforms were again provided, the main station building being on the Up side, while facilities on the Down platform were confined to a small waiting shelter of the now-familiar type. The platforms were linked by a barrow crossing and the A423 Oxford to Banbury road crossed the line on a single-arched brick bridge at the west end of the station.

The platforms were fenced with tubular metal railings and

The wide spaced centre of Adderbury village circa 1930, with a selection of architectural styles on view. A group of local children are resting on the grass verge and posing for photographer Frank Packer, as a Midland Red bus hurries through behind, raising a cloud of dust as it passes on its way to Banbury. *Oxfordshire County Council Photographic Archive*

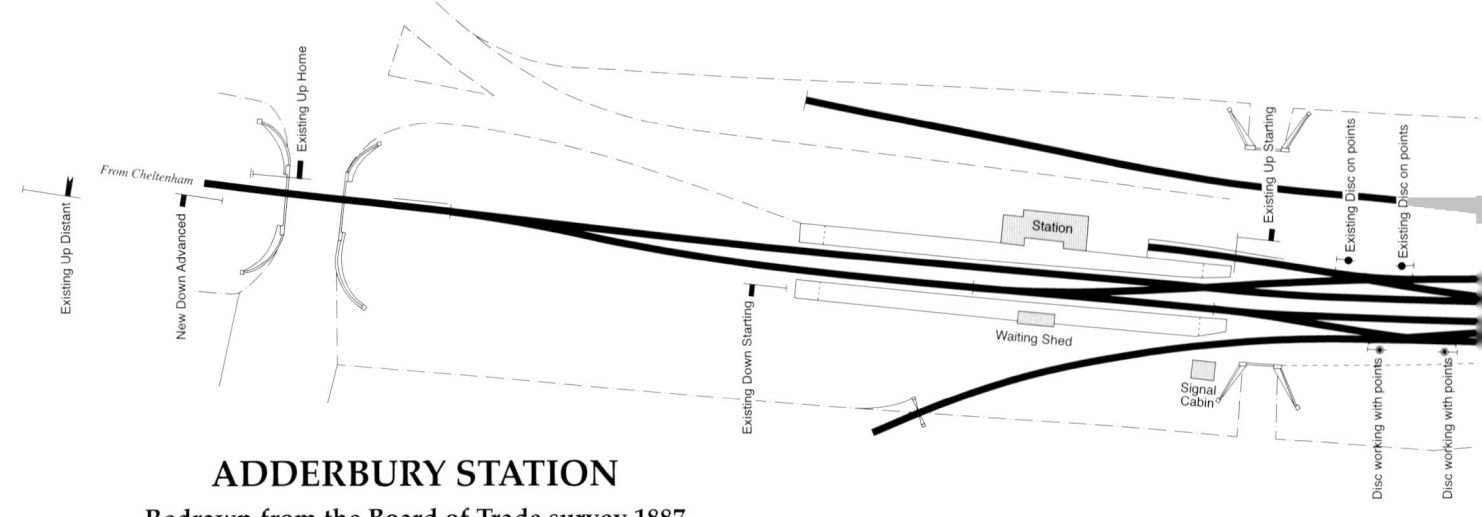

ADDERBURY STATION
Redrawn from the Board of Trade survey 1887

sheltered by rows of specially planted evergreens, while in summer time the station gardens provided some attractive floral displays. The station master's house was located behind the Down platform, near the A423 road bridge.

Adderbury's track layout incorporated a two-siding goods yard on the Up side, one of the sidings being the 'Goods Shed Road', while the other was a mileage siding for coal and other types of wagon load traffic. The goods yard was linked to the Up main line by two trailing connections and to the Down main line by means of a similar connection which crossed the Up main line on the level. A dead-end spur extended westwards from the Goods Shed Road to reach the cattle pens and an end-loading dock at the rear of the Up platform. The 5-ton yard crane originally provided here is presumed to have been sited east of the goods shed, in the fork of the two sidings. However, it had gone by 1912 and in its place, according to the *RCH Handbook*, was one of 1 ton 10 cwt. capacity, which does not appear in any of the photographs and thus is likely to have been the crane in the goods shed.

A long refuge siding on the Down side also served as a headshunt for a private siding connection to the Duffield Iron Corporation. This siding had first been laid around 1890, in connection with the Hook Norton Ironstone Partnership, connecting with their West Adderbury Quarries. However, as noted elsewhere, this undertaking had failed by 1903. In the January of the following year, the siding, the standard gauge tramway and the quarry were purchased by Cochrane & Co. (Woodside) Ltd, operators of Woodside Ironworks at Dudley. Although they signed the private siding agreement in January 1904, however, it appears that the quarries did not come back into production until around 1911. They had their own fleet of wagons for this traffic, which had instructions painted on for returning to Adderbury when empty. Cochrane's operation was busy throughout the war years but the postwar depression claimed Woodside Ironworks as a casualty and the quarry ceased working in 1922.

By the summer of 1925, the siding agreement was signed with T. Cashmore and others. Cashmores of Newport were scrap merchants and it is almost certainly the case that they were lifting the narrow gauge tramway which worked in the quarries and scrapping the other plant, which was then being removed by rail from Adderbury. However, just a couple of years later, a new concern appeared on the horizon, the Duffield Iron Corporation. Their interest lay in perfecting a new patented method of iron ore reduction using pulverised coal. It was not a success, although work continued on a small scale right up until World War Two. However, their entreaty to the War Department that their work was essential was not accepted and the site was requisitioned for use by the Northern Aluminium Company, as a recovery depot for salvaging materials from badly damaged aircraft.

In the post-war period, the former ironstone siding was used by Twyford's Seeds Ltd. and by the early 1960s it had been taken over by J. Bibby & Sons Ltd, a large firm with depots around the Midlands, dealing in agricultural feeds and produce. It was due to their extensive traffic that the line to Adderbury from King's Sutton remained in use until 1969, several years after the rest of the branch had closed.

In addition to private siding traffic, the station dealt with modest amounts of coal and general merchandise. The 1891 edition of *Kelly's Directory of Oxfordshire* shows just one coal dealer at Adderbury, this being J.B. Pritchard, who was both a coal merchant and a farmer. Later, domestic coal was distributed by Charles Wade, who used one or two coal wagons lettered 'CHARLES WADE COAL MERCHANT ADDERBURY'.

The layout at Adderbury station was slightly modified in connection with the doubling of the line between there and King's Sutton in 1906, although the general arrangement of the goods yard remained the same. Other modifications concerned the signalling, a new signal cabin of standard Great Western design being erected on the Down side in place of an earlier cabin. The replacement box was an all-timber structure, with a hipped slated roof and five-pane windows. The new signal box was on the approximate site of its immediate predecessor, to the east of the platforms of the Down platform. It is possible that the yard crane was also changed at the same time. A 5-ton crane similar to that at Bloxham was provided according to the 1904 *RCH*

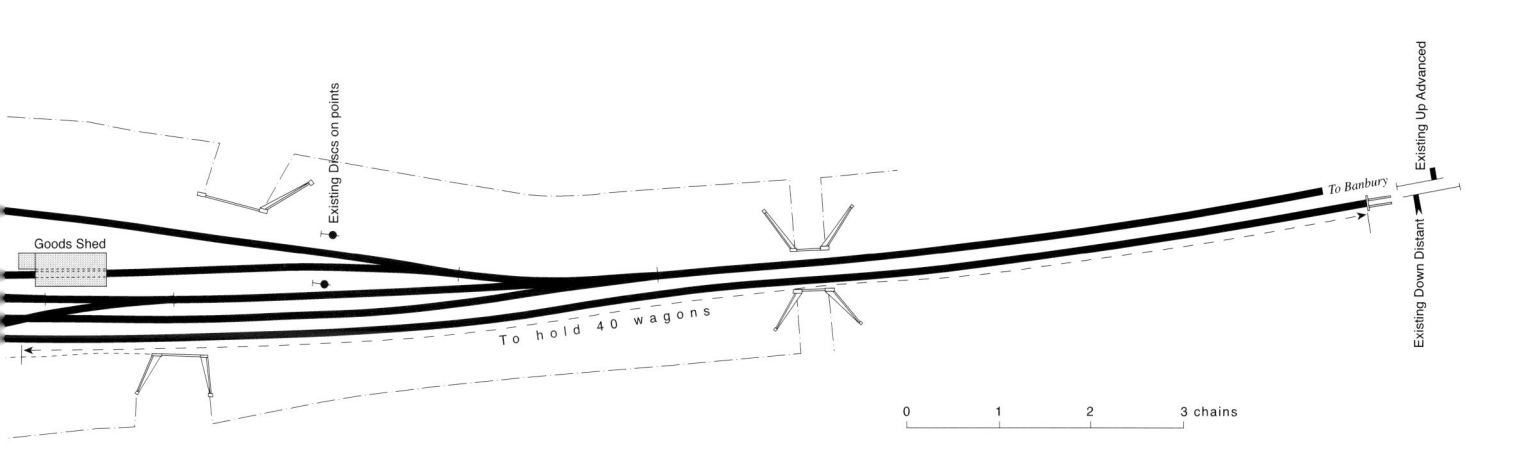

Handbook but the 1912 edition lists a crane of only one and a half tons capacity

Adderbury is divided into two parts by the Sor Brook, Adderbury East, to the north of the station, being the largest of the two settlements. The parish church of St. Mary rivals that at Bloxham in terms of architectural grandeur. A monument within the church commemorates the Reverend William Oldys, who was a staunch supporter of King Charles I during the Civil War and was apparently shot dead by one of his own parishioners in 1645.

This view of Adderbury was taken in early 1906, following completion of the doubling of the line between here and King's Sutton and showing the much altered station. Although the platforms have been described elsewhere as having been lengthened, it is obvious from these photographs that they were in fact totally completely rebuilt. The surface is all new, including the edging stones, whilst the brickwork of the supporting walls also all looks fresh. Likewise, the standard GWR iron spike platform fencing and the oil lamps are all new. The station buildings and goods shed were probably all that remained of the original B&CDR station. The ornamental flourishings on the lampposts are a delight.

Barry Davies collection

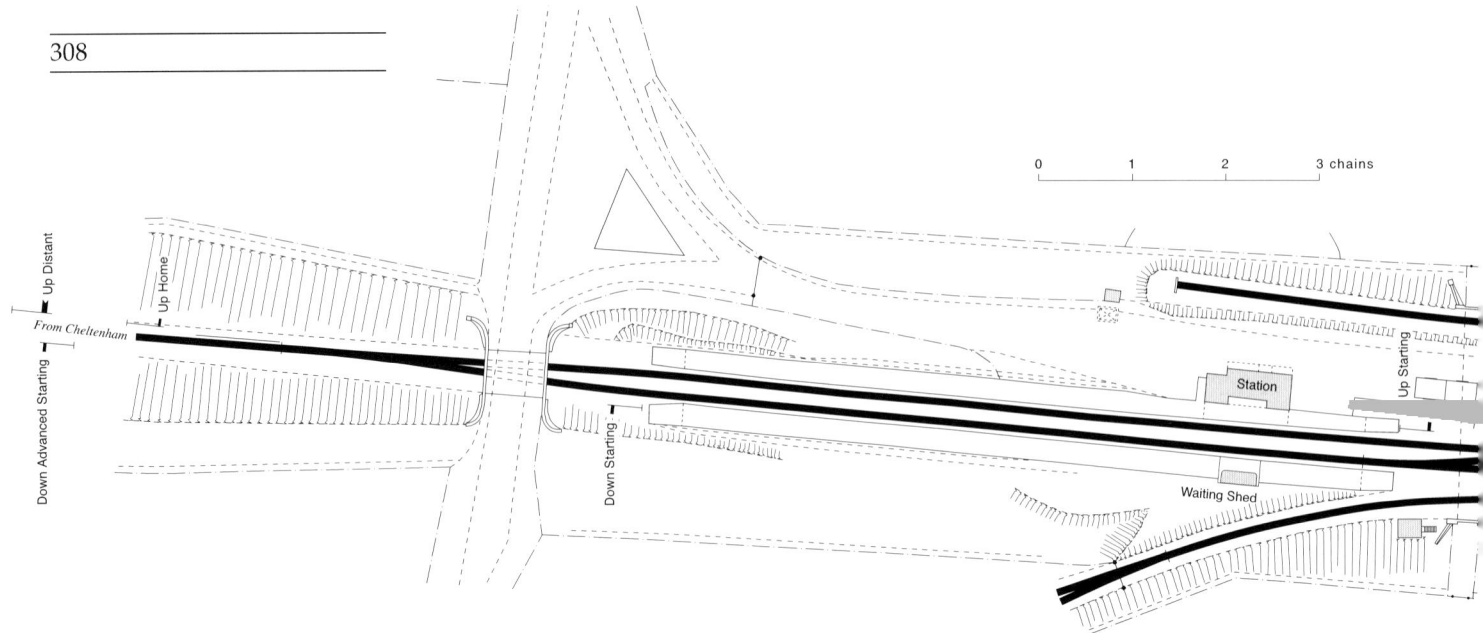

Up Distant | Up Home | From Cheltenham | Down Advanced Starting | Down Starting | Station | Waiting Shed | Up Starting

0　1　2　3 chains

ADDERBURY STATION
After doubling of the line from King's Sutton
Redrawn from the Board of Trade survey 1906

Below: Two examples of private owner wagons which operated from Adderbury. Cochrane's fleet were painted red, with white lettering shaded black and were lettered 'When empty to be returned to Adderbury'. Wagon No. 48 was delivered in January 1912. Charles Wade's wagons were in a similar livery although the red may have been somewhat darker. The variations in photographic emulsions, however, make it impossible to be sure. Wagon No. 11 was delivered in February 1915.

Gloucestershire Record Office

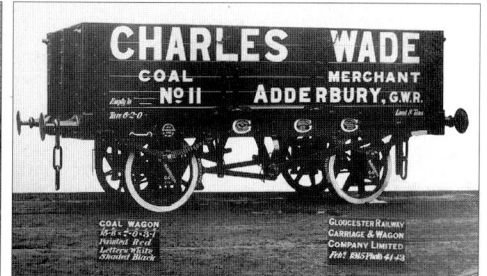

Left: The first signal box at Adderbury was opened with the line in 1887 but no photograph of it has yet been discovered. The replacement box, a standard GWR hipped roof, all timber structure, opened in December 1905. The line to Cochrane's quarries runs behind the box and the first cabin had stood immediately the other side of this. This photograph of the station, showing the new Adderbury Signal Box, was taken in early 1906, shortly after the work had been completed. Following his inspection in late 1905, Colonel Yorke of the Board of Trade wrote to the GWR sanctioning use of the double track formation and the associated changes to the siding connections. The signal box frame contained 35 levers and, subject to a minor modification with the interlocking, it too was passed for use. Note the cattle wagon standing on the short siding to the cattle pens on the extreme right. In the background is the Banbury-Oxford road bridge.

Barry Davies collection

This sylvan view of Adderbury station in one of the golden summers shortly before the First World War is taken from the A423 Banbury to Oxford road bridge, at the western end of the station and is thus looking towards Banbury. An unidentified 'Metro' tank has paused with its single auto-trailer, *en route* to Kingham. The station track layout was modified in 1906, in connection with the double tracking of the first section of the B&CDR line from King's Sutton, at which time a new signal box was also provided. It can be seen in the right background, with the private siding connecting to Cochrane's West Adderbury Quarries running off immediately behind. The first box was sited to the right of this siding. On the left, the long siding running along the back of the yard also tended to be used by Cochranes for wagon storage. The platforms were rebuilt and lengthened at the same time as the line doubling, which seems rather optimistic given that the single coach auto trains were always adequate for the passenger service on the eastern half of the route. However, it had been thought that much of the B&CDR line would be doubled and the route upgraded as part of a major East Midlands–South Wales link, so this may have been carried out with that in mind. In the event, their extended length must always have been something of an embarrassment. The neatly spaced oil lamps are also worthy of note.

Barry Davies collection

A '54XX' Class pannier (probably No. 5404 again) runs into the station with a Banbury to Kingham auto-train shortly before the service was withdrawn in June 1951. The signalman waits to greet the train with the single line staff for the section to Bloxham. Compare this picture with the view on page 307. The tree-lined platforms were typical of GWR practice at country stations and changed Adderbury's appearance quite dramatically. They are often the only survivor at the site of closed stations today. *Bob Brown collection*

A well known but delightful study of branch regular '54XX' Class 0-6-0PT No. 5404 at Adderbury with a Kingham-bound auto-service around 1950. The auto-trailer, which looks freshly painted, is W13. *Bob Brown collection*

Above: Collett '2251' Class 0-6-0 No. 2256 with a long train of sheeted open wagons at Adderbury on 3rd May 1960. The train may be westbound from here, to either Bloxham or Hook Norton but it is more likely that this is its destination. At a guess, the wagons contained a consignment bound for Twyford's Seeds and the locomotive had drawn forward into the station prior to shunting its train back into the yard. The train will then be split and the wagons shunted across into Twyford's private siding, off to the right. The station master's house is on the extreme right of the photograph.
C.H.A. Townley

Above: Looking west towards Cheltenham in 1962 with the signal box on the left and the Up Starting signal on the right. This latter was of a non-standard design, a miniature bracket signal in effect, so constructed for sighting purposes and because of the cramped location. The signal box was dismantled by volunteers from the Severn Valley Railway in the early 1970s, the intention being to rebuild it for use at Arley station. Whilst in storage there, however, it was found to be rotten beyond economic repair and was burnt instead. *Bob Brown collection*

Right: A slightly closer view of the Up platform and waiting shelter at Adderbury, again looking west towards Cheltenham.
The Lens of Sutton Collection

Looking towards Banbury in 1962, **above**, the reason for the Up Starting signal being located on a bracket in order to aid sighting by loco crews is obvious. The station building, **below**, was identical in design to those at Bloxham and Hook Norton but, unusually, was situated at the end of the platform furthest from the bridge due to the long sloping approach road. All the main buildings, including the signal box and goods shed, survived into the 1970s but the site is predictably now an industrial estate. *Joe Moss, courtesy Roger Carpenter*

Right: The smoke in the distance is from an unidentified '9F' Class 2-10-0, engaged in shunting its train of vans at Adderbury in February 1966. The array of vans includes representatives from all of the pre-1948 'Big Four' railway companies. The seed traffic to Bibby's mill was quite significant, with the goods yard, ironically, probably being as busy as it had ever been.

Below: The siding to Bibby's is seen running to the left behind the signal box. The hut on the left marks the site of the original cabin. Bibby's premises had seen a string of previous users, including the Northern Aluminium Co. They used the site for recycling the material from wrecked aircraft of both Allied and Axis forces during World War Two, which were brought in by train. *Both Roger Carpenter collection*

Below: The traffic for Bibby's Seed Company was the reason for the line remaining open as far as Adderbury until 5th April 1970. The characteristic B&CDR goods shed is seen along with rows of vans for the seed traffic. Note the pointwork, which was quite complicated for such a small station.
Joe Moss, courtesy Roger Carpenter

Above: A detailed view of the goods shed, taken in February 1966. The shed was not actually in use, the siding it stood on simply being used as one of the storage roads for the Bibby vans.
Roger Carpenter collection

Right: A nice study of the standard GWR signal box, circa 1960. At this date, the siding behind was serving Twyford's Seeds, Bibby's taking over the premises in 1963.
The Lens of Sutton Collection

Three photographs of the Duffield Iron Corporation Ltd's works at Adderbury, under construction in 1929. They had acquired the site in the October of the previous year, following dismantling of the remains of Cochrane's operation. The newly formed company was set up to investigate the viability of a new method of calcining iron ore using pulverised coal. The idea was to do away with the large calcining kilns such as those at Hook Norton, which were charged from the top and slow in operation. The use of pulverised coal was intended to speed up the process of calcination, as it would infiltrate the ore and burn more easily. The kiln built here was in fact hand-fed, although no doubt if production had ever got going on anything like a viable scale, something larger with a mechanical feed would have been put in place. Ore was once again mined from West Adderbury Quarry for use in the process, with the company purchasing a Hudson 'go-go' rail mounted tractor to haul the tram wagons to the works. Whether the company had to relay some tramway for this purpose or in fact not all of the track had been lifted is not known. Production continued on a small scale until 1940, when a delegation called on behalf of the Iron & Steel Controller – as a result of a request by the Duffield Corporation to the Ministry of Supply to support their efforts. Unfortunately for the company, the report was not in their favour and the site was instead requisitioned by the Ministry of Supply for the use of the Northern Aluminium Co. Much of the works was dismantled and new buildings erected which were taken over by Twyford's Seeds after the war.

All Neil Parkhouse collection

ADDERBURY & SYDENHAM IRONSTONE QUARRIES

From Adderbury, the route continued as a double track to its junction with the Oxford & Rugby main line at King's Sutton. Having left the station on a length of embankment, the railway entered a cutting with a length of about one third of a mile. Beyond, the route passed beneath the busy A41 road as it neared the Cherwell Valley; to the left, the remains of further ironstone workings could be seen. These were the former Adderbury and Sydenham quarries, which predated the Banbury & Cheltenham Direct line by several years.

Adderbury quarries were in operation by the end of the 1850s, ore being conveyed to King's Sutton station on a mile long narrow gauge tramway. The Adderbury workings were taken over by Alfred Hickman Ltd in 1889 and, in the following year, a private siding was provided on the recently opened B&CDR line to facilitate the transport of ore. The siding was situated about one mile to the east of Adderbury station, in convenient proximity to the quarries and the Oxford Canal. It was in use during the 1890s, the siding connections to what was, at that time, still a single line, being worked from a ground frame.

In his invaluable book *The Ironstone Quarries of the Midlands*, Eric Tonks suggests that ore from Adderbury Quarry may have been taken down the tramway to a wharf near King's Sutton and then transferred to narrow boats for the short trip along the Oxford Canal to Hickman's Wharf. There is, however, no clear evidence that this complicated method of transport was employed and one wonders what (if any) advantages it would have conferred, when a perfectly adequate transshipment point was available at nearby King's Sutton station. In any case, activities at Adderbury Quarry came to an end around 1900 and the siding was then closed.

Operations resumed on an adjacent site in 1914, the new workings being known as Sydenham Quarries because they were situated on land attached to Sydenham Farm. In connection with this revived activity, a new private siding agreement was made between Sir Alfred Hickman and the GWR, the resulting sidings being brought into use by the end of 1914. With World War One in progress, there was a pressing need for British iron ore and the reinstated facilities at Sydenham Quarries were laid out on a more expansive scale than their 19th century predecessors.

The layout consisted of a long reception line on the Up side of the main line, together with a number of exchange sidings and loading sidings. The reception line was linked to the Up running line by trailing connections at each end and to the Down line by a single facing connection. Incoming trains from the King's Sutton direction were able to run straight into the sidings, while Up workings from the Kingham direction were able to reverse into the sidings via the trailing connections. Access to the sidings was controlled

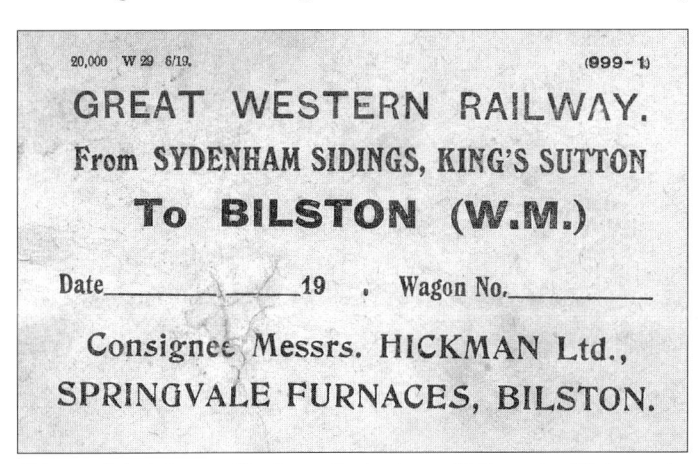

Wagon label for traffic from Sydenham Sidings to Hickman's Springvale Furnaces at Bilston, West Midlands. *S.C. Jenkins collection*

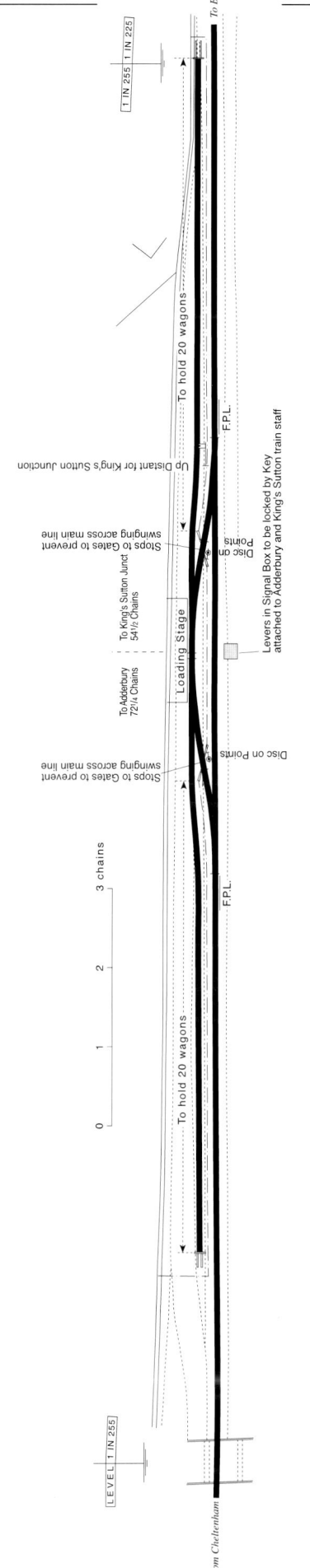

HICKMAN'S SIDINGS
Adderbury & Sydenham Ironstone Quarries
Redrawn from the Board of Trade survey 1890

from a signal cabin on the Down side of the running lines, that was in use from 1914 until 1929.

The exchange sidings were linked to the various quarries in the vicinity by a network of 2 foot gauge lines, by means of which iron ore was conveyed to a battery of five calcining kilns. Quarrying operations at Sydenham were run down after World War One but the infrastructure at Sydenham Sidings was left *in situ* for several years – presumably in anticipation of an upturn in the economy. In the event, the expected revival never materialised and the calcining kilns were finally dismantled in the early 1930s. In later years, the site was used by a firm known as Banbury Buildings Ltd.

The Sydenham quarry system was worked by a fleet of four narrow gauge locomotives, three of these being standard Andrew Barclay 0-6-0 side tanks, with 7 inch by 14 inch outside cylinders. These diminutive engines were known as *Winifred* (Works No. 1424), *Gertrude* (Works No. 1578) and *The Doll* (Works No. 1641), dating from 1915, 1918 and 1919 respectively.

The fourth locomotive at Sydenham quarries was *Margaret*, a standard Hunslet War Department 4-6-0T dating from 1918 (Works No. 1324), with $9^{1}/_{2}$ inch by 12 inch cylinders and 2 foot coupled wheels. This locomotive was very similar to the ex-WD locomotive nicknamed 'Black Bess', which had been obtained for service in the Brymbo quarries at Hook Norton. When not in use, the four Sydenham quarry locomotives were kept in a single road shed near the Great Western exchange sidings.

KING'S SUTTON

As Up workings neared the main line, they crossed the Oxford Canal and the River Cherwell in quick succession, the Cherwell marking the county boundary between Oxfordshire and Northamptonshire. A third bridge, on the far side of the river bridge, consisted of a series of underline culverts, by means of which winter flood water could pass beneath the line. For nearly the first two decades of the line's existence, there had been a signal box on the Up side of the branch, just before it reached the flood culverts. King's Sutton Branch Signal Box controlled the passage of trains through the short section of double track connecting with the main line. It was abolished in early 1906, with the double tracking of the section from King's Sutton to Adderbury.

Having joined the main line, branch workings continued northwards for a short distance before coming to a stand in the Down platform at King's Sutton station (43 miles 79 chains from Cheltenham and 82 miles 55 chains from Paddington).

It should, perhaps, be mentioned that on reaching the Oxford & Rugby main line, the putative direction of travel changed from 'Up' to 'Down'. As we have seen, eastbound Banbury & Cheltenham trains were regarded as Up workings in compliance with operating practice at Cheltenham St. James but at King's Sutton those same workings passed onto the Down main line and became 'Down' services for the remaining part of their journey to Banbury. In the westbound

Great Western 'Hall' Class 4-6-0 No. 4953 *Pitchford Hall* approaches the junction at King's Sutton circa 1932, with a northbound train of clerestory stock. The Banbury & Cheltenham Direct line curves away to the right. *Roger Carpenter collection*

An overall view of the junction on 19th May 1963, taken from an occupation overbridge sited just to the south of King's Sutton station. On the right is the end of the Down Refuge siding, whilst the line on the left is the Up Goods loop and exit from the tiny goods yard. In the right background can be seen the flood culverts for the River Cherwell and just beyond this, on the far (Up) side, until 8th January 1906 had stood King's Sutton Branch Signal Box. From that date, the double track was extended all the way to Adderbury and the box abolished. King's Sutton Signal Box, just out of the picture on the left, was renamed from King's Sutton Junction Signal Box at the same time. *Michael Hale*

direction, a similar situation obviously pertained in that Cheltenham trains followed the Up main line as far as King's Sutton and then diverged westwards onto the B&CDR route, thereby becoming Down trains for the rest of their journey.

King's Sutton, opened on 1st June 1872, was a two-platform station, with its main station building on the Up side. There was a small goods yard to the south of the Up platform, together with a goods refuge siding on the opposite side of the line. The Banbury & Cheltenham Direct route converged with the Up and Down main lines by means of a double track junction at the south end of the station. The Up and Down sides of the station were linked by a lattice girder footbridge, while the nearby goods yard was equipped with coal wharves, an end-loading dock, cattle pens and a 2-ton hand crane.

The most interesting feature at King's Sutton was perhaps its station building, which was similar in many ways to Hook Norton and the other Banbury & Cheltenham stations, albeit more ornate. The platform frontage was again recessed to form a small loggia and three tall chimney stacks punctuated the gabled roof. King's Sutton was, nevertheless, more attractive than its B&CDR counterparts in that the building was constructed of contrasting red and black brickwork, the vitrified black bricks being used as horizontal string courses to relieve the otherwise plain surfaces. There were, moreover, other refinements, notably Italianate details on the prominent chimney stacks, which formed a striking composition.

Amenities for waiting passengers on the Down platform were confined to a small, brick-built shelter with a single-pitched roof; like the main station building, this small structure resembled its counterparts on the Banbury & Cheltenham route. There was no goods shed, as such, at King's Sutton, although an arc-roofed corrugated iron shed served as lock-up for parcels and 'smalls' traffic. The last-mentioned structure was sited on the Up platform, beside the station building, in convenient proximity to the loading dock. At night, the platforms were illuminated by gas lamps.

The deposited plans of the Banbury & Cheltenham Direct Railway, dating from November 1872, reveal that there was, at that time, an ironstone loading siding on the Down side of the line, roughly on the site of the later refuge siding. Ironstone was brought from Adderbury Quarry (*qv*), on a narrow gauge tramway which crossed the Oxford Canal and the River Cherwell in order to reach the GWR main line. This method of transshipment persisted for several years, although the King's Sutton siding must have fallen out of favour following the opening of Sydenham Sidings, on the B&CDR route.

Whilst Banbury & Cheltenham line auto trains called at the

Quite a number of views exist in the LPC/L&GRP series of main line trains passing King's Sutton in the GWR era, of which two examples are shown here. **Above,** '43XX' Class mogul 2-6-0 No. 5399 clatters through the station with a lengthy goods train in September 1922. Note the siding behind the Down platform, which has obviously not been used for some time. **Left,** 'Badminton' Class 4-4-0 No. 4112 *Oxford* (originally numbered 3304 and to lose its name in May 1927) hurries by with a Newcastle-Bournemouth train comprised of Great Central and L&SWR stock. The first King's Sutton Signal Box (1873-87) stood where the ground signal can be seen on the left.
Above: Barry Davies collection
Left: R.M. Casserley collection

station, the goods yard was serviced mainly by pick-up freights on the main line, so strictly speaking does not concern us. However, a brief description would seem appropriate. On the Down side, a single siding ran behind the platform, which could only be accessed from the Down Refuge siding. Its purpose is not clear and it seems to have fallen out of use quite early on. It may have been a remnant of the ironstone loading siding mentioned previously.

On the Up side, the situation was rather more complex, as in order to avoid having a facing connection, trains had to shunt back into the yard. The tiny corrugated iron goods shed stood on the Up platform next to the station building, whilst there were two sidings in the yard. One formed a long loop with a short stub running off into a bay behind the Up platform, whilst the other ran the length of the rear of the yard. There was a weighbridge in the yard and for a short while a 1 ton crane was provided. It was not there in 1880 but is listed in the 1904 *RCH Handbook*, at which time the yard offered the full range of facilities. By 1912, however, the crane had gone, as had the facility to deal with general livestock, although horse boxes could still be catered for. A 2-ton crane had appeared by the 1930s, suggesting an upturn in traffic, possibly of agricultural goods.

The station was originally signalled from a signal box on the Down side but, in 1887, this earlier cabin was replaced by a new structure on the Up side of the running lines. The

King's Sutton station staff lined up for the photographer, probably sometime in the late 1920s. The view is looking north towards Banbury and it also shows the cast ironwork of the non-standard footbridge in good detail. Note the impressive floral display along the rear of the Down platform and no doubt there is a good reason for the chair on the platform. *Barry Davies collection*

Looking south along the Up platform towards the junction in the early 1960s, with just a glimpse of the signal box beyond the farm track over bridge in the distance. The goods yard weighbridge hut is behind the station building and note also the small nameboard mounted on the lamp in the left foreground. *The Lens of Sutton Collection*

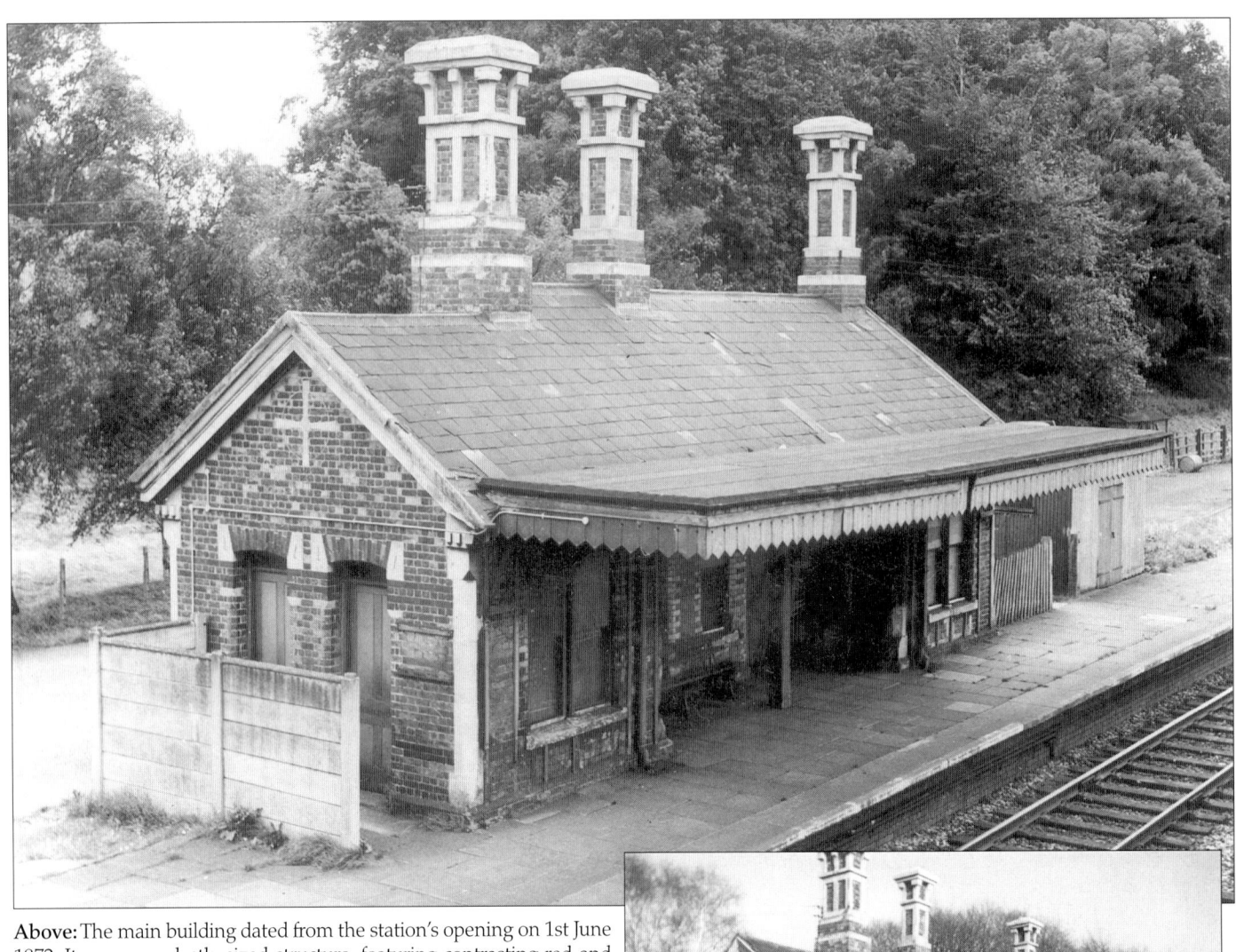

Above: The main building dated from the station's opening on 1st June 1872. It was a modestly sized structure, featuring contrasting red and black brickwork, with white stone quoins and other features, and with highly elaborate, if somewhat large, chimneys. The concrete modesty fence screening the doors to the Ladies and Gentlemen's conveniences was a later addition, quite possibly replacing a Victorian cast iron screen. The tiny corrugated iron hut which passed for the goods shed can also be seen at the other end of the building. *Bob Brown collection*

Right: This fine station building is seen here with windows boarded up, near the end of its existence on a Sunday evening in late summer; it was demolished around 1970. *Stanley C. Jenkins*

Left: A final view of the station, facing south towards the junction in 1962. King's Sutton became an unstaffed halt in 1951 but otherwise is still open today with the waiting shelter on the Down platform being the sole surviving example of the B&CDR type. The footbridge also still remains.
The Lens of Sutton Collection

Ex-LMS Stanier '8F' Class 2-8-0 No. 48137 ambles north along the main line towards Banbury with a long rake of empty mineral wagons on 21st August 1964. The train has just passed King's Sutton, the spire of the part 12th century church being visible in the centre distance, and is approaching the site of Astrop Sidings. *Neil Parkhouse collection*

replacement, of standard Great Western hipped-roof design, was sited some 14 chains to the south of the station, near the junction between the B&CDR and the main line, although this meant that the signalmen's view of the station was blocked by the bridge carrying a farm track across the line at this point. The track layout at the station and in the goods yard was substantially remodelled in 1910, at which time a new frame was also installed in the box.

King's Sutton was much busier than the intermediate stations on the Banbury & Cheltenham route. Its position on the busy main line between Oxford and Banbury, and convenient commuting distance between those two places, ensured that it always attracted relatively large numbers of passengers. Thus, in 1923, the station issued 27,290 tickets, the corresponding figures for 1930 and 1936 being 27,583 and 28,626 respectively. Season ticket sales varied between 37 and 134 a year during the 1930s, while freight traffic averaged around 2,800 tons per annum during that same decade.

King's Sutton, another typical Cotswold style village, was situated immediately to the east of the railway. Despite a destructive fire on 15th July 1785, which burned down over forty of the mainly thatched cottages, the village contained many attractive stone buildings, including another handsome church with a finely tapering spire, resembling those at Bloxham and Adderbury. The fact that these three churches were sited so close to each other, in a virtual straight line between King's Sutton and Bloxham, gave rise to a well-known rhyme, which contains the line: '*Bloxham for length, Adderbury for strength, but King's Sutton for beauty*'.

The village was situated within the ironstone producing district, the nearest workings being at Nell Bridge, about one mile to the south of the church. The Nell Bridge site was operative for a relatively short period during the 1870s, a siding being available at that time to facilitate the transport of ironstone between King's Sutton and the Midlands.

BANBURY

Leaving King's Sutton, trains maintained a north-north-easterly heading for a distance of about four miles as they followed the Cherwell Valley towards Banbury. To the left, observant travellers could clearly see the sinuous Oxford Canal, which followed a parallel course along the river valley towards Banbury. This 18th century waterway had been incorporated by Act of Parliament in 1769, and opened between Hawkesbury Junction and Banbury by 1778, the engineers being James Brindley and Samuel Simcock. The canal was extended southwards to Oxford in 1789-90, the extension being, in effect, an improved River Cherwell, the actual riverbed being utilised for several miles. Although rapidly eclipsed by the railway after 1850, the Oxford Canal continued to carry commercial traffic well into the 20th century, right into the 1950s in fact, with World War Two giving the waterway a new lease of life.

The earliest known view of Banbury GWR station is this engraving of circa 1854, which also shows the L&NWR station in the left background. The Brunelian train shed is seen in its original state and, with the exception of the porticoed entrance on the right of the shed, it is recognisable as the station which appears in the GWR official views over the next few pages. *Graham Kew collection*

Hurrying northwards along the Oxford & Rugby route, trains soon passed Astrop Sidings Signal Box, on the Down side of the line. This marked the approximate site of Astrop Quarry Sidings, which had served nearby ironstone workings until their closure around 1923. The original sidings on the Up side of the main line were subsequently lifted but Astrop Sidings Signal Box was retained in connection with long Up and Down running loops that had been completed in August 1908. Astrop Sidings Box was a typical Great Western hip-roofed cabin, which had replaced an earlier Victorian signal box on 5th April 1907.

Nearing Banbury, trains again crossed the county boundary between Northamptonshire and Oxfordshire, and with the former London & North Western line from Verney Junction now visible to the right, the 47 mile 40 chain cross-country journey from Cheltenham drew to a close. Passing Banbury Gas Works, trains finally came to a stand in Banbury Great Western station, which was later designated 'Banbury General', to distinguish it from the rival L&NWR establishment at Banbury Merton Street.

When opened to traffic on Monday 2nd September 1850, Banbury had been little more than a branch line terminus but when the Oxford & Rugby route was extended northwards to Birmingham in 1852, the Great Western station was elevated to main line status. Gardner's *History, Gazetteer & Directory of the County of Oxford*, published in 1852 before the completion of the GWR line to Birmingham, contained the following brief note on the railway facilities available at that early date:

There are two lines of railway here connecting Banbury with the Metropolis. The Great Western by Oxford and Didcot; and the London & North Western, via Bletchley. The stations of these rival lines are situated over Banbury bridge, just in the county of Northampton, and are close to each other. A new line is in course of formation for Warwick, etc., which will throw off the few remaining coaches upon that line of road.

The Directory lists Charles Bidden Fryer as the Great Western station master, while Edward Jakeman was in charge of the North Western terminus.

The evolution of Banbury station was a long and somewhat complex process. In its earlier guise, the station had featured a typical 'Brunelian' overall roof; the main station building was on the Down side, and the Up and Down platforms were linked by a lattice footbridge beneath the overall roof structure. The station was extensively remodelled at the end of the Victorian period, in order to deal with the additional traffic that was expected to flow to and from the Great Central system via the Banbury to Woodford line. These modifications were completed around 1903, by which time Banbury had gained two additional bay platforms on the Up side and another at the north end of the Down platform.

The overall roof was retained, although additional Up and Down lines for goods traffic were installed to the east of the wooden train shed. The enlarged station had five platforms, which were numbered from one to five. The Down main platform line was designated Platform One, while the terminal bay at its north end became Platform Two. Moving eastwards, Platform Three was the Up main platform, and Platforms Four and Five were the two Up side bays. These were situated at opposite ends of the main

With the timber train shed and buildings starting to look very tired, the GWR announced its plans to rebuild Banbury station in the mid 1930s. However, by the time that work had eventually begun, it was not long before it was interrupted by the outbreak of the Second World War and it was thus not until 1956, in BR days, that rebuilding recommenced. In the meantime, demolition of the rotting and heavily buttressed train shed was carried out in 1952. It is said that it shook alarmingly whenever a train thundered through. This photographic survey was commissioned in 1935 by the GWR, as it had with the B&CDR stations at Bourton and Stow, to record the old station prior to its demolition. The view, **above**, is looking north through the station, whilst the picture, **right**, shows the rear of the Up platform buildings and train shed, the higher portion of roof being the end of the footbridge. Rather like the Georgian terraces of Bath and Cheltenham, the front view is pleasing to the eye but the back certainly isn't! *Courtesy NRM*

Sunlight streams through the glassless roof into the gloom of the train shed, neatly picking out the platform furniture. Amongst the posters to be seen are examples for Palethorpes sausages, Bovril, Virol, P & O cruises, Hall's Distemper and Petter oil engines, as well as a GWR/SR joint timetable for through services to Brighton & Hastings, and an assortment of railway company posters. The footbridge is almost lost in the interior darkness. The ornate woodwork within the roof is also worthy of note. Both views are of the Up platform, looking north, **above**, and south, **left**. Platforms 4 and 5 were bays at either end of the station on the Up side. The B&CDR line auto-trains used Platform 4.

Courtesy National Railway Museum

Looking south through the train shed, in the direction of King's Sutton. The goods shed can be seen in the right hand distance, whilst the bay used by Bicester trains is to the left. The simple cast iron columns supporting the train shed certainly have a classical air to them.
Courtesy National Railway Museum

Left: The forecourt side of the main station building looking south, showing the original timber section to the right and the later brick-built refreshment rooms to the left (compare with the 1854 engraving on page 324). Note the posters for the GWR's centenary including, second from left, the famous '100 Years of Progress' with Sectretan's superb painting of an express on the sea wall at Dawlish. The timetable above the parked bicycle shows the LNER's services from Banbury over the former Great Central route.

Below: The clarity of these views alone justifies reproducing them in their entirety, as demonstrated by this superb interior study showing Wyman's bookstall on the Down platform, with a member of the station staff standing in front of the first class refreshment rooms – note the ornate glass. The *Times* offers the latest position on the Italian invasion of Abyssinia, the apathy surrounding which could be said to have been the slippery slope to the Second World War. *Courtesy NRM*

The Down platform looking northwards, showing the footbridge and roof trussing in more detail. Clearly things had been 'let go' somewhat, in anticipation of work starting on a new station. *Courtesy National Railway Museum*

The final view shows the station frontage looking northwards, with a solitary motor (taxi?) parked in front. Tired paintwork, corrugated iron on the roof and sagging timbers show how far the GWR had let the station slide. *Courtesy National Railway Museum*

'Hall' Class 4-6-0 No. 5947 *St. Benet's Hall* pauses at Banbury with the 2.38 pm Leamington Spa to Oxford train on 11th September 1937. The engine was just over two years old when this picture was taken and was one of two members of the class whose names were changed in May 1935 due to a grammatical error – the apostrophe had been missed out of the name. The other was No. 5912 *Queen's Hall*.   *H.C. Casserley*

Taken on the same day as the view above, GWR 'Saint' Class 4-6-0 No. 2914 *Saint Augustine* is seen coasting into Banbury with a northbound express. The joint LMS/GWR goods shed appears in the right background. No. 2914 dated from 1907 and was unusual in that it was fitted with a rocking fire grate for the first few months of its life. Withdrawn in 1946, it was one of a truly successful class, the design of which formed the basis for the 'Hall's.   *H.C. Casserley*

platform, Platform Four being at the south end, while Platform Five was to the north.

The Great Western rebuilt many of its larger stations during the 1930s, Taunton and Leamington Spa being two notable examples. The company intended to reconstruct several more of its main line stations, including both Oxford and Banbury but World War Two intervened before these ambitious plans could be put into effect. In the case of Banbury, the proposed rebuilding scheme was revived under the auspices of British Railways and in September 1955, the *Railway Magazine* reported that BR was about to start work on a new Banbury station, work being in full swing by the following year. In July 1957, it was reported that *'the new Banbury General station'* was nearing completion.

In connection with this scheme, an additional through track was laid along the west side of the main Down platform, which thereby became an island with platform faces on either side. Extensive new buildings were provided on the west side of the station, while new waiting shelters were erected on the Up and Down platforms. The main building

The rather basic canopies provided when the train shed was demolished were a temporary expedient and they did not last long, as the station was completely rebuilt in 1957. They are seen here in this north facing view taken on 27th October 1956. *R.M. Casserley*

was constructed of reinforced concrete with infilling of yellow brick and other materials, while the Up and Down sides of the station were physically connected by a massive, 40 foot wide overbridge with two spans, one of which was 30 feet wide, while the other had a width of 50 feet.

The main booking hall was situated on the Down side and a broad staircase gave access to the footbridge, which was large enough to contain waiting rooms and a refreshment room. The platforms were covered, for much of their length, by substantial pre-cast concrete canopies, supported on concrete beams placed at 20 foot intervals. The new station was, at the time of its completion, regarded as a startlingly modern edifice, although in retrospect it could be argued that the extensive use of brickwork means that this still-extant building now has a distinctly 'period' appearance.

Banbury's goods handling facilities were laid out on a lavish scale. The original goods yard, containing the usual goods shed for 'smalls' traffic, and mileage sidings for coal and other forms of wagon load traffic, were sited to the south of the passenger station, on the Up side of the running lines. There was a short, end-loading dock at the north end of the Down platform, while a number of additional goods loops and sidings were available on the Up side. The Up side facilities were considerably extended during the early 1900s when, as mentioned above, Up and Down goods lines were provided, together with two lengthy loop sidings and a number of dead-end sidings.

The original goods facilities were expanded at various times, notably during the early 1900s in connection with the Great Central line from Woodford & Hinton. The GCR line joined the Great Western route at a point known as Banbury Junction, 1 mile 14 chains to the north of the passenger station. A marshalling yard with seven (later eight) parallel sidings was installed alongside the GCR route at Banbury Junction and further sidings were sited on each side of the Great Western line. On 22nd July 1931, the GWR opened an additional marshalling yard on the Up side of the line between Banbury station and Banbury Junction, this new facility being known as Banbury Hump Yard.

Banbury's London & North Western Railway station was slightly older than its GWR neighbour, having been opened by the Buckinghamshire Railway on 1st May 1850. Although constructed and opened by a nominally-independent company, the Banbury Merton Street branch was in effect an integral part of the L&NWR system and, as such, it passed into LMS hands at the 1923 Grouping. The station featured two dead-end terminal roads on either side of a central 'island' platform. The north end of the platform was covered by an arc-roofed train shed, while the wooden station buildings were positioned at right angles to the terminal buffer stops.

The L&NWR goods facilities were spread out on both sides of the passenger station, the timber goods shed and loading area being to the west, while the station's extensive cattle sidings occupied a corresponding position on the eastern side of the line. Coal and other forms of bulk goods traffic was handled in two long sidings near the North Western goods shed, and there were additional facilities for the loading and unloading of vehicles or heavy machinery beside the cattle pens on the Up side of the line.

Left: A general view from the north end of the station facing Oxford on 27th October 1956, once again minus the train shed. On the right is the bay for trains using the ex-Great Central branch to Woodford & Hinton, with a service waiting to leave. Note also the cast iron letters forming 'General' have been removed from the station nameboard.
R.M. Casserley

Below: The 'Castle' Class 4-6-0s were a derivative of the 'Star' Class. No. 4000 *North Star*, seen here at a newly denuded Banbury station with the 1.20 pm all stations Birmingham-Paddington on 15th March 1952, was a 'Star' built in 1906 but was withdrawn and rebuilt as a 'Castle' in late 1929, keeping its name and number. It was finally withdrawn in May 1957.
H.C. Casserley

One of the Up side sidings continued south-eastwards, beyond the limits of Great Western property, to form a useful connection between the GWR and L&NWR stations, while another connecting line diverged from the Great Western station in order to serve the Banbury Gas Company. The latter siding formed an end-on juction with a corresponding L&NWR siding – although the resulting GWR-L&NWR link was hardly suitable for through running.

When traffic was exchanged between the GWR and LMS stations, wagons would normally be left on the connecting siding, from where they would be collected by a shunting engine. The story is told that, one night, an LMS signalman was telephoned by his Great Western counterpart, who asked if the LMS could receive a 'Paco'. The LMS employee did not have the slightest idea what a 'Paco' might be but he was reluctant to show his ignorance, and promptly accepted the proffered transfer. Shortly afterwards, an 0-6-0PT ventured along the transfer siding with a mysterious van and left it just inside LMS property in the usual way. The LMS signalman could just about discern the outline of the GWR vehicle on the sidings behind his box but he was still unsure what it might contain. After an hour or so, curiosity finally got the better of him, and he left the warmth of the signal box and crossed the intervening tracks

An auto service waits in the bay circa 1950. Trailer W81 is coupled to an unidentified '14XX' 0-4-2T, suggesting this may not be a B&CDR line train, as they were more usually handled by pannier tanks. This was, however, the bay used by the Banbury-Kingham autos. Note the crowd of schoolboy trainspotters at the end of the platform – happy days! *The Lens of Sutton Collection*

to obtain a better view of the 'Paco', which he could now see was a horse box. On discovering that the vehicle was unlocked, he entered the main compartment and could just make out a large wooden box; to his utter horror, this turned out to be a coffin containing the body of a dead airman, who had recently been killed in the war. Moreover, he later discovered that the deceased was one of his own relatives.

Although Banbury Merton Street was a comparatively large station (at least by branch line standards), the Great Western station was always regarded as a more important transport facility and when, in the 1930s, the Great Western decided to build a new station, it was suggested that Merton Street would be closed, enabling LMS passenger trains to be diverted into the GWR platforms. As we have seen, World War Two intervened before the rebuilding scheme could be put into effect and when British Railways opened a new Banbury General station in 1958, it was used only by Western Region services.

Banbury formerly boasted two engine sheds, the original Great Western shed being a modest single-road structure on the up side of the station, while the neighbouring L&NWR shed was a much larger, three-road structure. The opening of the Great Central line in 1900 led to a vast upsurge in activity at Banbury and it was therefore decided that the small shed on the Up side, would be replaced by a much larger depot on the opposite side of the running lines. Work on the new motive power depot commenced in 1907 and the shed was completed in the following year.

A report printed in the *Great Western Railway Magazine* stated that the new facilities were handed over to the Locomotive Department on 6th September 1908. The depot incorporated a standard Great Western straight road shed, measuring approximately 210 feet by 66 feet at ground level. The new building was of brick construction, with a double gabled roof that was swept down on its west side to cover a 210 foot range of offices. The shed contained four terminal roads, with the usual inspection pits, while the adjacent turntable was of 66 feet diameter.

Banbury engine shed was considerably enlarged during World War Two, when an additional coaling stage and several extra sidings were added to help deal with the demands of wartime operations. Plans to construct a four-road extension alongside the existing shed were not implemented, although two covered ash shelters were provided beside the enlarged coaling stage, to hide the glow of discarded firebox coal from enemy aircraft. Appropriately for wartime structures, the ash shelters were painted in a disruptive 'camouflage' livery scheme, similar to that applied to many other buildings during the 1939-45 conflict.

At the end of the war, Banbury shed had a large allocation, including numerous 4-6-0 mixed traffic engines and 2-8-0 heavy freight locomotives. On 31st December 1947, the allocation included twenty-two 'Hall' Class locomotives or other 4-6-0s, twenty-seven '28XX' or 'WD' 2-8-0s, ten moguls, four '2251' Class 0-6-0s, one '56XX' Class 0-6-2T, two '14XX' Class 0-4-2Ts and fifteen pannier tanks.

Banbury Great Western station was controlled from two standard hipped roof signal cabins, both of these being sited on the Down side of the running lines. They were known as Banbury South Box and Banbury North Box, and were

A general view of Banbury locomotive shed, BR code 84C, looking south and taken in the late 1940s. The repair shed, straight ahead, was added in 1944. Of corrugated iron construction, it carries wartime camouflage paint. The standard GWR brick-built four road shed on the right was completed in late 1908 and enough space was left on the eastern side to allow for future extension which, in the event, never took place. The building just left of centre was the sand store. The photograph was obviously taken during a quiet period, with only a handful of engines on view, including an unidentified mogul 2-6-0 on the right.

Stanley C. Jenkins collection

Two views of Banbury MPD taken in 1960, **above**, and 1964, **below**, with a selection of 4-6-0s, 2-6-0s and tank engines on view. The ramped coaling stage was situated behind the photographer. Note the encroaching weeds in the lower picture, as the end for steam neared. The shed closed two years after this view was taken.
Both Neil Parkhouse collection

If the GWR's plans for a new Banbury station had not been interrupted by the war, something in a similar style to Leamington Spa would no doubt have been built. By the time the whole scheme was resurrected by BR in the mid 1950s, new ideas in architectural design were in place, which saw an early incarnation of the British Railways 'modern image' concept built instead. Whilst not popular with many railway enthusiasts, the new station was undoubtedly a great improvement for passengers at the time, although these designs have dated quite heavily since they were built. The grimy steam locomotive sits a little uncomfortably with it also.
The Lens of Sutton Collection

sited at the south end and immediately to the north of the platforms respectively. Banbury Junction was controlled from a third cabin, Banbury Junction Box, just 1 mile 7 chains to the north of the station, while Banbury Merton Street station was controlled from an LMS type box.

With over 100,000 passenger bookings a year during the pre-Grouping period, Banbury was by any definition a very busy station. Sales of ordinary tickets averaged around 120,000 per annum during the 1930s, while at the same time season ticket sales reached 430 in 1936 and 561 by 1938. Goods traffic rose from 52,507 tons in 1903, to as much as 578,339 tons in 1929. Much of this traffic was in the form of ironstone and, as such, it was subject to severe fluctuations over the years. In 1935, for instance, the amount of goods traffic being dealt with had dropped to 90,172 tons, which was, however, still a very appreciable figure.

TRAFFIC DEALT WITH AT BANBURY

YEAR	STAFF	RECEIPTS (£)	TICKETS	PARCELS	GOODS (TONS)
1913	101	59,996	137,018	67,716	65,183
1930	176	187,764	148,196	95,496	519,690
1936	200	114,339	123,440	115,033	98,621
1937	210	119,318	120,044	120,814	97,461
1938	219	119,318	116,568	119,088	84,414

Banbury was, by any definition, an important railway junction, while for railway enthusiasts it had added significance in that locomotives and rolling stock from each of the 'Big Four' railway companies appeared on a regular basis. This diversity was alluded to in the *Railway Magazine* which, in December 1932, printed the following report from a correspondent:

Mr R.D. Canning writes to mention a cosmopolitan railway working he saw at Banbury on a recent Sunday, when the 9.15 am from Sheffield arrived at midday in charge of LNER 4-4-2 No. 4451, and consisted of four GWR and four Southern Railway coaches. It was taken forward by a GWR Mogul.

Mr Canning comments on the interests of Banbury in this respect as a railway centre. Through Banbury GWR station there are regular workings of LNER and SR stock, in addition to the owning company's coaches, and also regular LNE and GW locomotive duties, with occasional through SR locomotive workings to and from Birmingham at busy summer weekends. Next door is the LMSR Merton Street station, with the locomotive and coach workings of that company, so that all four groups are thus represented.

Banbury itself could be seen to the north and west of the railway stations but there was little for inquisitive visitors to see. Much of the town was of Victorian origin, including the famous 'Banbury Cross', which was erected in 1859 in imitation of an original Eleanor Cross that had been torn down in 1612. In earlier times, the town had boasted several interesting old buildings, including a castle and a Medieval parish church, but most of these historic structures were swept away during the 17th and 18th centuries. The castle was dismantled after the Civil War, whereas the church was blown up with gunpowder in 1790 to avoid the expense of restoring it.

Apart from its nursery rhyme cross, Banbury was famous for its 'Banbury Cakes', which were aptly described in F.G. Brabant's *Little Guide to Oxfordshire* (1906) as '*a sort of compromise between a tart and a mince-pie*'. These distinctive cakes were, according to the *Little Guide*, '*still industriously hawked at the neighbouring railway stations*' during the early years of the 20th century.

Chapter Eight

THE FINAL YEARS

A token exchange at Bourton-on-the-Water station, circa 1962. The fireman of this Cheltenham-bound service leans out of his cab to collect the single line token for the next section to Notgrove, although the signalman seems somewhat distracted. Note the presence of a second person in the box – shift changeover or perhaps just a visitor. *A.W.V. Mace collection, courtesy Milepost 92½*

The end of the war in Europe was followed, on 26th July 1945, by the election of a radical Labour government that had promised to nationalise rail transport, the coal industry and other major industries. Accordingly, at midnight on 31st December 1947, the Banbury & Cheltenham Direct line became part of the Western Region of British Railways. However, this momentous change of ownership made very little difference to the way in which the railway was operated, and the lines from Cheltenham to Kingham and from Kingham to Banbury continued to serve the public as they had done during the preceding Great Western era.

One obvious change carried out after 1948 concerned the liveries of engines and rolling stock. Up to Nationalisation, the locomotives seen on the Banbury to Cheltenham line had been painted in GWR green livery but in British Railways days the former Great Western engines seen on the route began to appear in unlined black. Local passenger vehicles were painted in an LMS style overall maroon livery, while freight rolling stock was turned out either in a reddish-brown 'bauxite' colour, or in light grey – bauxite being applied to fitted freight stock, whereas grey was reserved for unfitted, hand braked goods wagons.

LOCOMOTIVES & TRAIN SERVICES IN THE BR ERA

The route from Cheltenham to King's Sutton was still worked as two sections, with connections at Kingham. There was little attempt to provide through workings, though a few services from Cheltenham ran through to Chipping Norton for operational purposes. However, these always called at Kingham *en route*, where the locomotive ran round the train to continue on to Chipping Norton and,

Left: Collett '45XX' Class '4575' small prairie No. 5514 has just arrived at Kingham with the 5.50 pm from Cheltenham on 30th May 1958. In this instance, as can be seen, the train formation included a horse box and the locomotive is in fully lined BR passenger green livery. Driver and porter share a leisurely word as the fireman uncouples the train and the late evening sun casts shadows across the platform. *H.C. Casserley*

Below: Just four months before M&SWJR line passenger services were withdrawn completely, grimy ex-Southern Railway Maunsell 'U' Class mogul No. 31613 hurries through Charlton Kings with the 1.52 pm through service from Cheltenham St. James to Southampton Central in May 1961. *D.R. Lewis*

as a consequence, the direct line over the bridge quickly fell out of use after the war. There were six trains each way on the eastern section of line between Banbury and Kingham, together with a number of short-distance shuttle workings between Kingham and Chipping Norton.

The train service in operation on the Cheltenham to Kingham section continued to provide six passenger workings each way. In the Up direction, eastbound trains departed from Cheltenham St James at 6.36 am, 10.35 am, 12.10 pm, 2.45 pm, 5.45 pm and 7.10 pm, while Down services left Kingham at 7.53 am, 12.12 pm, 1.40 pm, 5.15 pm, 7.30 pm and 9.10 pm. The 2.45 pm early afternoon service from Cheltenham was an unadvertised through working, which arrived at Kingham at 3.30 pm and then operated the 4.00 pm service to Chipping Norton, returning to Kingham at 4.53 pm.

Freight traffic was conveyed by one pick-up working each way on both sections of the B&CDR route. On the eastern section, the daily freight train was scheduled to leave Banbury at 10.10 am and reach Kingham at 2.05 pm. The return working normally departed from Kingham at 6.05 pm. A similar service was provided on the western portion of the line, a daily pick-up freight service being scheduled to depart from Kingham at 10.15 am in the Down direction and reach Cheltenham St. James at 2.57 pm, having called *en route* at all of the intermediate stations.

An eastbound freight working left Cheltenham St James at 11.00 am and, after calling intermediately at Cheltenham South and Charlton Kings, it reached Andoversford at 11.53 am. Here, it passed the 10.15 am Down freight service from Kingham, before resuming its journey at 12.52 pm. Fifteen minutes were allowed for shunting at Notgrove and Stow-on-the-Wold but the train was scheduled to call at Bourton-on-the-Water from 1.41 pm until 2.10 pm, in order to attach or detach traffic; it also passed the 1.40 pm passenger service from Kingham to Cheltenham prior to resuming its journey to Kingham, where the scheduled arrival time was 2.44 pm.

As in pre-Nationalisation days, the basic train service between Cheltenham and Kingham was augmented by M&SWJR line services that ran over the B&CDR route between Lansdown Junction and Andoversford, *en route*

THE BANBURY & CHELTENHAM DIRECT RAILWAY

Right: Collett '45XX' Class 2-6-2T No. 5538 about to depart from Stow-on-the-Wold on the last leg of its journey to Kingham on 30th May 1958. *R.M. Casserley*

Below: Time for a brief conversation at Notgrove between signalman and station master, as one of the footplate crew examines the single line token before heading off to Andoversford and, ultimately, Cheltenham St. James.
Bob Brown collection

between Cheltenham and Southampton. In 1950, there were four M&SWJR workings each way, though by the mid-1950s the service had been reduced to three Up and three Down Southampton workings.

The decline in the fortunes of the M&SWJR line reached an even lower level on 30th June 1958, when reductions in the passenger service left only one through train each way on weekdays between Cheltenham and Andover, with a further two between Swindon and Andover. The link with the former Midland Railway at Cheltenham was severed on 3rd November 1958, when the surviving through service to and from Andover was diverted into the former Great Western terminus at Cheltenham St. James.

The branch passenger services between Cheltenham and Kingham were, in the British Railways era, usually worked by prairie tanks. Cheltenham Malvern Road Shed had an allocation of seven or eight '45XX' Class 2-6-2Ts during the later Great Western period and these 'small prairies'

Left: An unidentified BR standard Class '2MT' mogul waits at Chipping Norton sometime in the mid-1950s. These attractive and versatile engines appeared on the Chipping Norton branch from 1954, one of the class being sub-shedded at Kingham to cover the roster. They never succeeded in completely ousting the ex-GWR types, however, and the prairies seem to have pretty much taken over again by the time of closure. *Bob Brown collection*

Below: A very evocative view for many who lived in the popular 'pre-fabs' on this 1950s estate, when the railway was just part of the everyday scene. The photograph was taken from the remains of Gloucester Loop Junction Signal Box and depicts '45XX' Class 2-6-2T No. 4573 coasting down to Lansdown Junction with the 7.47 am Down service from Kingham on 27th May 1960. The locomotive is passing over the remains of the pointwork for the Hatherley Loop, which had been removed by this date. *D.R. Lewis*

continued to work on the B&CDR route during the 1940s and 1950s.

Collett '51XX' Class large prairie 2-6-2Ts also appeared and, by the 1960s, the latter engines had virtually assumed command of local passenger services between Cheltenham and Kingham. The 6100 number series locomotives of the '51XX' Class were used mainly in the London Division but a handful of these too worked on the B&CDR route, alongside the 4100s and 5100s. Numbers noted around 1960-2 included 4100, 4101, 4109, 4123, 4128, 4142, 5154, 5173, 5182, 6126 and 6137. On 17th July 1962, a member of the rarely-photographed 8100 number series was recorded on the line, the engine in question being No. 8106. The 8100s had been rebuilt with new boilers and smaller wheels but were still classified by the GWR as '51XX'. Many former GW prairie tanks had, by this time, been repainted in Great Western-style lined green livery, albeit with the British Railways rampant lion on their side tanks.

Most trains were composed of two non-corridor brake composites or brake thirds but corridor vehicles would sometimes appear and many services ran with fish vans or other fitted goods vehicles coupled at the rear. In the early 1960s, some trains were composed of British Railways Mk. 1 corridor stock in maroon or chocolate and cream livery – the latter colour scheme being a welcome revival of the traditional GWR livery, which looked particularly effective when the trains were headed by a prairie tank painted in Great Western-style green.

Push-pull working continued to be employed on the Banbury to Kingham line during the early British Railways period, with Collett '14XX' Class 0-4-2Ts or '54XX' Class 0-6-0PTs hauling the familiar ex-GWR auto-trailers. Goods services on the Banbury to Kingham line at this time were normally handled by '43XX' Class moguls, while those on the Cheltenham to Kingham section were often hauled by Collett '2251' Class 0-6-0s or Hawksworth '94XX' Class 0-6-0PTs.

Pannier tank classes had not been used to any great extent on either section of the B&CDR, tender engines or large tank locomotives being preferred for most duties, while four-coupled engines were predominant on the Banbury to Kingham auto-train service. Banbury shed had acquired a number of auto-fitted '54XX' Class 0-6-0PTs by the later GWR period but these seem to have been used principally on main line stopping services. Banbury's 0-6-0PTs nevertheless appeared on the Kingham route from time to time, some typical examples being Nos. 5404, 5407 and 5424.

Banbury shed also had a large allocation of Collett '57XX' 0-6-0PTs, some random examples being Nos. 3630, 3694, 3751, 4631, 4646, 5724, 7763, 8729, 8787 and 9782. These were occasionally used on Banbury to Kingham passenger services, presumably when '14XX' Class 0-4-2Ts or '54XX' Class 0-6-0PTs were not available. As the '57XX' Class locomotives were not auto-fitted, they had to run-round the

On 22nd September 1962, a rail tour from Paddington, organised by the Ian Allan publishing company, traversed the line from Cheltenham to Kingham on its return to London. The special was worked into Cheltenham St. James from the Gloucester direction behind No. 4992 *Crosby Hall*. With the Hall too large to turn on the turntable at St. James, ex-GWR '73XX' Class 2-6-0 No. 7335 was attached to the rear of the train in the station, to haul the tour forward from there. '51XX' Class large prairie No. 5154 was coupled to the mogul to assist on the steep climb up the Cotswold escarpment to Notgrove. No. 5154 is seen here leading No. 7335 and its train, bunker first, about a mile up the long climb from Andoversford. The prairie was detached at Notgrove. *D.R. Lewis*

single auto-coach at the end of each journey and, for this reason, they were hardly ideal replacements for the usual engines. In August 1961, Collett '57XX' Class 0-6-0PT No. 8743 was noted at the head of a Cheltenham to Kingham train, following the failure of a 2-6-2T prairie tank.

The only other 0-6-0PTs seen on the route in later years were the sturdy '94XX' Class 0-6-0PTs, which occasionally appeared at the head of local freight workings. The '94XX' Class panniers were designed by F.W. Hawksworth and introduced in 1947, at the very end of the Great Western period; they were notable in that they featured tapered boilers instead of the domed boilers carried by earlier GWR 0-6-0PTs. An example noted on the Banbury to Cheltenham route in the British Railways era was No. 8491, a long-standing resident of Gloucester shed.

The Midland & South Western Junction route was often worked by Southern Region 2-6-0s from Eastleigh during the British Railways era, and these engines continued to work through from Southampton to Cheltenham and back on certain services. For locomotive enthusiasts, the use of both Southern and Western Region motive power ensured that the section of line between Andoversford and Cheltenham remained a focus of interest and attention until the closures of the 1960s.

Locomotives seen on the route in the 1950s included SR 'U' Class moguls Nos. 31613, 31620, 31629, 31639, 31791 and

The Cheltenham to Kingham line was very occasionally used as a diversionary route, usually on a Sunday and sometimes because of the Severn Tunnel being closed for vital maintenance work. This train, headed by ex-GWR '43XX' Class 2-6-0 No. 6379 from Didcot shed, is believed to be an excursion from the London area destined for Porthcawl. It would have worked via Didcot, Oxford and Kingham. The train is seen approaching Hatherley Road bridge, on its way to Cheltenham St. James. Once there, the locomotive was turned and the train then proceeded towards Gloucester and the west. There was more to come, however, as a second part of this excursion, behind another ex-GWR mogul, followed 25 minutes later but the photographer, not expecting either train, had unfortunately run out of film by then! Both excursions retraced the route on their return and were seen leaving Cheltenham for Kingham and beyond at 9.25 pm and 10.00 pm that night. *D.R. Lewis*

31808, together with ex-GWR '43XX' Class 2-6-0s such as Nos. 6320, 6334 and 6372. Other Great Western classes remained hard at work on M&SWJR services and, in its last years of operation, lineside observers could see '55XX' Class prairie tanks, '57XX' pannier tanks and 'Manor' Class 4-6-0s on various parts of the M&SWJR route.

British Railways Standard locomotives never became fully established on the Banbury & Cheltenham Direct line, which was worked by former GWR locomotive classes until its demise. By January 1954, however, three British Railways standard class '2MT' 2-6-0s had been sent to Worcester for service on the Shipston-on-Stour branch, the new arrivals being Nos. 78004, 78008 and 78009. One of these BR Standard moguls was normally sub-shedded at Kingham, from where it worked both the Shipston-on-Stour and Chipping Norton branch services. Another example noted on these duties was sister engine No. 78001.

At the western end of the line, British Railways Standard classes also worked over the M&SWJR route on both passenger and freight duties. On 24th April 1958, for instance, Class '4MT' 2-6-0 No. 76086 was noted passing through Andoversford with a Down freight working, while on 12th May 1961, Class '4MT' 4-6-0 No. 75002 was seen at Cheltenham with a Midland & South Western Junction passenger working.

The B&CDR and M&SWJR routes were never dieselised and, in consequence, diesel locomotives or multiple units were rarely seen. One of the Chipping Norton branch services was nevertheless scheduled for diesel working during the late 1950s and early 1960s. The train in question left Oxford at 11.45 am and, having worked a local service on the OW&WR line, it became the 12.40 pm branch train to Chipping Norton. In the reverse direction, the balancing service returned from Chipping Norton at 1.00 pm.

In 1958, the single line sections between Adderbury and Andoversford were worked mainly by Electric Train Staff, although the Electric Train Token system had been installed throughout on the western section of the B&CDR route. The Train Staff sections were: Adderbury to Bloxham; Bloxham to Hook Norton; Hook Norton to Chipping Norton; and Chipping Norton to Kingham East Box. The Train Token sections were; Kingham West Box to Bourton-on-the-Water; Bourton-on-the-Water to Notgrove; and Notgrove to Andoversford Junction. Intermediate Token Instruments were provided at Stow-on-the-Wold.

CLOSURE BETWEEN KING'S SUTTON & CHIPPING NORTON

Sadly, the post-war years were a period of acute decline for rural railways such as the Banbury & Cheltenham Direct line. With the end of petrol rationing and the increasing use of private road transport, these lines began to lose what little passenger and freight still remained, and in these circumstances closures and retraction became inevitable. In the case of the eastern section of line between Kingham and King's Sutton, it was clear that very little passenger traffic was now being carried, and it was therefore decided that passenger services would be withdrawn

A Kingham to Banbury auto-service, headed by an unidentified '54XX' Class 0-6-0PT, approaches the southern entrance to the 418-yard long Hook Norton Tunnel around 1950. This cutting was susceptible to landslips over the years, and indeed still is. Bob Brown collection

between Chipping Norton and King's Sutton (exclusive), leaving the Kingham to Chipping Norton section as a dead-end branch.

The closure was carried out at short notice and with very little publicity, on Saturday 2nd June 1951. In announcing the closure, a British Railways spokesman claimed that there was *'a shortage of train crews at Banbury to work the summer holiday trains'* and this excuse was accepted by the travelling public without serious protest. The closure was, nevertheless, commemorated in appropriate fashion and numerous people turned out to witness the passage of the last regular passenger trains between Banbury, King's Sutton and Chipping Norton.

The last train was headed by '54XX' Class 0-6-0PT No. 5407 and it carried a special headboard bearing the legend '1887 LAST TRAIN 1951', together with a funereal wreath and the Union Flag. On leaving Chipping Norton, the single-coach auto-train set off a barrage of detonators, while at Bloxham the platform was thronged by a large crowd, including the Bloxham School Combined Cadet Force band. One of the passengers was George Manning, who, as a schoolboy, had purchased the first ticket from Bloxham station on 6th April 1887.

The cessation of regular passenger services did not entail the complete closure of the line, because goods services continued to run throughout from Banbury to Kingham. Freight train timings were little changed, with an outwards working from Banbury to Kingham at 10.10 am and a balancing return service from Kingham at 2.30 pm. The long term future of the Banbury to Kingham line, however, was inextricably linked to the fortunes of the ironstone industry. Unfortunately, the likely pattern of mineral extraction in north Oxfordshire was by no means clear.

Local government planners seemed confident that the local ironstone industry had a future and the *County of Oxford Development Plan*, published in 1952, anticipated that mineral extraction would continue to be an important activity. Working in the aftermath of World War Two, the county planners were still prepared to think strategically in terms of the long-term national interest and, in that sense, their recommendations now seem curiously dated:

> An extensive deposit of ironstone exists in the northern extremity of the County, and in fact covers the greater part of the Banbury Rural District. This ironstone has been substantially worked for many years, but owing to its fortunate situation comparatively near the surface, and the limited depth of the seam, a very considerable degree of restoration has been found possible. From the deliberations of the Ironstone Conference, it is obviously essential that the maximum reasonable use should be made of the country's resources in this connection consistent with the claims of other land users, notably agriculture, and with due regard to the limitation of serious desecration of the landscape.

A poor quality but rare view of the Banbury to Kingham auto train at Adderbury on the last day of operation, 2nd June 1951. For the final day's services, the auto-coach was adorned with a Union Flag and a wreath was added by a daily user of the line, together with a card reading *'In memory of an old friend'*. The view is looking west, with the train heading back to Banbury. *Bob Brown collection*

> The agricultural aspect has been largely met by the restoration referred to, and land has, therefore, been allocated in the Plan for further extraction of ironstone within the areas in the control of the Ironstone Industry, for which application has been made. With the co-operation of the Geological Survey it has also been possible to indicate the approximate limits of the known extent of the total ironstone field.
>
> It would not be appropriate to provide that the whole of this ironstone should necessarily be won, as the country's requirements cannot be sufficiently estimated over a very long period of the future. To meet this point, however, provision is hereby made whereby the existence of ironstone shall be taken into account before permission is granted for any other use of the surface which would preclude the ultimate winning of the mineral. By this method it is sought to husband the resources of the country, and yet at the same time keep the excavations under reasonable control.'

In the event, ironstone extraction in the area around Hook Norton had ceased by the mid-1950s. The once important Brymbo quarry was closed on 22nd June 1946, just one week's notice having been given to the unfortunate workers. The Brymbo Company had an interest in the Oxfordshire Ironstone Company at nearby Wroxton and as this was considered to be a more efficient undertaking, there seemed little justification for the continuance of work at Hook Norton. The abandoned facilities at Hook Norton were sold or scrapped in the next few months, some of the quarry railway equipment being sent overseas for further service on an industrial line in Tanganyika.

Four of the Hook Norton quarry locomotives were scrapped on site but *Russell* was eventually purchased by Messrs B. Fayle & Co. for use on their ball clay line on the Isle of Portland. The four calcining kilns were demolished, their remains being cut up for scrap, while the former quarries were returned to agriculture.

The demise of the Hook Norton quarry left just one

ironstone siding in operation on the Banbury & Cheltenham Direct line, the survivor being the Clay Cross Siding at Bloxham, which had re-opened in 1947. Sadly, the apparent reprieve was only temporary and this last quarry was finally closed in May 1954.

The Kingham to Banbury line was traversed by a special train, arranged by the Railway Enthusiasts' Club, on Sunday 24th April 1955. This working left Oxford at 11.55 am, and proceeded via Kingham, Chipping Norton and Banbury to Fenny Compton, where it joined the Stratford-upon-Avon & Midland Junction line. The tour continued via Broom Junction and Evesham, and having visited the freight-only Shipston-on-Stour branch, the special arrived back in Oxford at around 7.00 pm. The train, formed of five corridor coaches, was hauled over the Kingham to Banbury line by 'Dukedog' 4-4-0 No. 9015, although 'Dean Goods' 0-6-0 No. 2474 was employed on the Shipston-on-Stour line.

There were, in fact, several special workings over the Banbury & Cheltenham line during its final years of operation, including an Oxford University Railway Society brake van trip from Kingham to Banbury in the summer of 1957. A few months later, on Sunday 15th September 1957, a through diesel excursion ran from Windsor & Eton Central to Cheltenham St. James, in connection with a Railway Enthusiasts' Club tour of Gloucestershire lines. The diesel working ran outwards via Slough West Curve, High Wycombe, Oxford and Kingham, and returned from Severn Tunnel Junction direct to Reading and Paddington.

In August 1958, the B&CDR line was blocked by a land slide on the troublesome section between Hook Norton and Great Rollright Halt, and this effectively severed the route. British Railways considered that the little-used line was not worth repairing and, for the remaining part of its life, the Banbury to Kingham route was worked in two sections, between King's Sutton and Hook Norton, and from Kingham to Rollright Siding. Any traffic for Rollright was conveyed by the scheduled Chipping Norton goods services, which worked eastwards over the three mile Chipping Norton to Rollright section as and when required.

Curiously, the line was not immediately closed, and British Railways working notices referred to a blockage on the single line between King's Sutton and Kingham, which would continue *until further notice*. This suggests that, in the event of a sudden upturn in ironstone traffic, the slip would have been removed to allow a resumption of through

Top: An enthusiasts' brake van special traversed the line on 1st November 1956 from Kingham to Banbury. This is the view of Hook Norton station photographed from the rear of the train as it departed eastwards. Goods traffic was still healthy at this stage, as evidenced by the full sidings on the left. *R.M. Casserley*

Middle: Rollright Halt was also snapped as the train passed by. The waiting shelter was removed following the closure of the passenger service. *R.M. Casserley*

Bottom: Hook Norton No. 2 Viaduct circa 1960, with the surrounding vegetation starting to encroach. *Bob Brown collection*

Bloxham station slumbers in the warm summer of 1952, a year after the cessation of passenger services. The station gardens are still well tended and note the train staff changing apparatus alongside the Down line on the right. *Joe Moss, courtesy Roger Carpenter*

services. The line was actually blocked at a point 92 miles 58 chains from Paddington, just four chains to the west of Hook Norton Tunnel.

It was both sad and ironic that the Banbury to Kingham line should have been severed at a time when the Banbury & Cheltenham Direct was starting to gain favour as an excursion route. Excursion trains were, on the other hand, still able to run over the Cheltenham to Kingham section and in this context, the western half of the B&CDR line was traversed by an interesting special working on 5th July 1962; British Railways Standard '9F' Class 2-10-0 No. 92240 hauled a Womens' Institute excursion train from Somersham to Gloucester, outwards via Kingham and Cheltenham, and back via the same route later in the day.

CLOSURE OF THE CHELTENHAM TO KINGHAM LINE

The years immediately following World War Two were a time of rigid austerity, in which petrol and other commodities were strictly rationed and this ensured that the railway system remained busy. Moreover, the post-war Labour government was openly pro-rail in its transport policies and this factor seemed to guarantee that the railway system would have a secure future as part of a fully co-ordinated transport policy. In 1951, however, an incoming Conservative government initiated a reversal of policy and the railways were soon being portrayed as obsolete relics of the industrial revolution, that would have to be replaced by private road transport wherever possible.

The pace of closure and rationalisation increased after the October 1959 general election, when Ernest Marples was appointed Minister of Transport by Prime Minister Harold Macmillan. The new Transport Minister was the founder of a road-building firm, named Marples, Ridgway & Partners, and he was known to be in favour of a programme of grandiose motorway construction schemes as the answer to Britain's transport problems.

As we have seen, the first closure had taken place as early as 1951, with the withdrawal of passenger services between King's Sutton and Chipping Norton. A deletion of greater magnitude took place with effect from Monday 11th September 1961, when most of the former Midland & South Western Junction route was closed, leaving isolated sections in operation for local passenger and freight traffic. The section of line between Andoversford and Cirencester (Watermoor) was closed to all traffic, with a consequent reduction in the frequency of passenger services at the western end of the B&CDR route between Cheltenham and Andoversford.

The last trains between Andoversford and Cirencester ran on Sunday 10th September 1961, when two enthusiasts' specials visited the doomed section of line. One of these, arranged by the Stephenson Locomotive Society, left Birmingham Snow Hill at 9.40 am, and ran southwards via Cheltenham Malvern Road and Andoversford, returning from Andover Junction at 2.50 pm. Motive power was provided by 'Manor' Class 4-6-0 No. 7808 *Cookham Manor*.

Left: An unidentified Collett '51XX' Class 2-6-2T coasts into Malvern Road station with a Kingham-bound train in the late 1950s. Through the arch of the bridge, which carries the road from which the station took its name, Malvern Road East Signal Box can just be seen in the distance. It was actually situated to the north-east of the station. The box controlled movements at this end of Malvern Road, as well as the junction for St. James station.
Rev. J. Parker, courtesy Hugh Davies

Below: The bleak prospects for Cheltenham St. James station and the branch to Kingham are summed up in this circa 1962 photograph, on a wet and dismal day, looking along Platforms 1 and 2 from under the awning. St. James Station Signal Box can be seen in the right distance.
The Lens of Sutton Collection

The other special, organised by the Railway Correspondence & Travel Society, travelled southwards from Swindon to Andover behind '43XX' Class 2-6-0 No. 5306 and then proceeded northwards to Cheltenham, before returning to Swindon via Gloucester, Stonehouse and Stroud. These two workings were the last passenger trains to travel over the northern end of the Midland & South Western Junction line between Swindon and Andoversford.

In the meantime, the Cheltenham to Kingham line had continued to serve the public during the 1950s and early 1960s but, like other rural lines, its passenger traffic declined as local travellers turned to buses or private road transport in increasing numbers. By the early 1960s, some of the trains were running with virtually no passengers, while goods traffic had suffered such a steep decline that the daily pick-up service was replaced by a thrice-weekly goods trip from Gloucester. On the other hand, in January 1963 the *Railway Magazine* printed a letter from a correspondent who claimed that, based on daily observations from his study window over a four year period, *'on several trains there were enough people to warrant an extra coach'*. Indeed, the *'only service which was not patronised was the stopping train from Southampton'*, which had carried only *'five or six passengers a day during its final months of operation'*. However, this was in no small way due to BR's policy of strangulation of routes it wished to close and it was also noted in the railway press how M&SWJ line trains were re-timed into Cheltenham to miss vital connections in the last few years.

In common with many other rural lines throughout Britain, the Banbury & Cheltenham Direct line had never been regarded as a particularly remunerative route. This problem was compounded by a method of accounting adopted when dealing with branch lines, which treated them in isolation from the main line BR system and thereby ignored the 'network effect'. It was impossible to ascertain the true value of local lines and, as a result, the calculations of profit and loss were based purely upon the traffic receipts generated by the branch lines themselves.

Conversely, the cost of operating and maintaining these local lines was only too obvious and, viewed in this light, very few branch lines were really profitable. In the case of the Cheltenham to Kingham line, it was abundantly clear that the branch was carrying very few passengers and it therefore came as no real surprise when, in early 1962, it was announced that BR was seeking to withdraw passenger services from it and also from the Kingham to Chipping Norton branch.

In accordance with the normal closure procedures, the South West area of the Transport Users' Consultative

Above: '51XX' Class prairie No. 4142 from Gloucester (Horton Road) shed arrives at Malvern Road with a Kingham train in the last weeks of passenger services, on 25th September 1962. It is still possible to pass through the site of Malvern Road station as the trackbed is now a cycle path and walkway, and although the platform and associated buildings have gone, many of the slabs from the platform's surface were recovered for use on the Gloucester & Warwickshire Railway, which has re-opened part of the old Honeybourne line between Cheltenham Racecourse and Toddington stations.
R.K. Blencowe

Above and left: Two views of Cheltenham Leckhampton station taken shortly before closure in 1962, both looking east. By this date, the station was only visited by Kingham-line trains, the ex-M&SWJ route to Southampton having closed. The yard had also become overgrown following the withdrawal of goods services in the late 1950s, so the thrice weekly Gloucester-Kingham goods train did not stop here either. The new warehouse at the end of the yard, owned by Bloodworth's, local seed and fodder merchants, was built after closure of the yard. The fact all the signals are 'off' indicates that the box was also switched out when these views were taken.
The Lens of Sutton Collection

'5100' Class prairie tank No. 4106 arrives at Andoversford with a Cheltenham to Kingham train circa 1960. To the left of the locomotive's smokebox is the goods shed, which was to an identical design to that at Leckhampton. Note the 25 mph speed restriction sign between the tracks for Up trains. *Bob Brown collection*

Committee was asked to consider the proposed withdrawal of passenger services in the light of evidence produced by British Railways. On 16th January 1962, the *Gloucestershire Echo* reported that the closure proposal had been received by the TUCC, a Western Region spokesman being quoted as saying '*The line between Cheltenham and Kingham has been investigated, along with other branch lines in the region. On finishing the examination, it has been proved that it does not pay, and British Railways feel they have a case for closure*'.

On 30th January, the same newspaper reported that Cheltenham Borough Council was protesting against the closure in '*the strongest possible terms*', the protest being led by Councillor Arthur Dye, the then Deputy Mayor. The council argued that the proposed closure would result in a drastic reduction in travel opportunities, as well as bringing hardship upon the rural communities served by the threatened line. This argument was taken up, for obvious reasons, by Bourton-on-the-Water Parish Council, on the grounds that Bourton would be the hardest hit of all the communities along the route.

Many other letters were sent to the *Gloucestershire Echo* by irate or worried readers but these protests were all in vain. In practice, the powers of the Transport Users' Consultative Committees were severely limited. Their role was further curtailed by the Transport Act of 1962, which effectively transferred responsibility for decisions on opposed closure proposals from the TUCC and the Central Transport Consultative Committee to the Minister of Transport. As that Transport Minister was Ernest Marples – the chief architect of the mass closure programme – the future for loss-making rural lines such as the Cheltenham to Kingham route was bleak.

British Railways was under no obligation to publish any detailed financial information in support of its closure proposals and the Transport Users' Consultative Committees were not allowed to examine the question of freight train operation. The only defence that could be deployed against a threatened closure concerned the degree of 'hardship' that would result following the withdrawal of railway passenger services. The arguments therefore centred on the provision of alternative road transport services and when it became clear that a replacement bus service would be provided by Messrs Pulham & Sons, the fate of the Cheltenham to Kingham line was sealed.

A meeting of the TUCC held on 30th April 1962 supported the proposed closure, on the grounds that the replacement bus service would be '*reasonably adequate*'. Needless to say, Ernest Marples promptly accepted this recommendation, and, on 4th September, he formally ratified the closure decision. In commenting upon the closure announcement in its editorial on 5th September, the *Gloucestershire Echo* printed the headline '*End of a Farce*'.

Opposition to the proposed closure had been considerable but at a time in which the government of the day was making no secret of its desire to transfer as much traffic as possible from rail to road, the Tory Transport Minister's closure decision had been a foregone conclusion. It was decided that all railway passenger services between

The Notgrove signalman has time to shake out his mat in this bucolic early 1960s scene, whilst the little boy and his mother wait patiently for the next train to Bourton-on-the-Water. On the left, the charming little Down platform shelter was almost identical to that found at Andoversford. *Bob Brown collection*

The state of the trackbed in this view of Bourton-on-the-Water from Station Road bridge indicates that it is almost the end for passenger services, although the rest of the station was still in fine fettle in late 1962. A standard Western Region tubular post signal had replaced the old lattice post Down Starter. *Joe Moss, courtesy Roger Carpenter*

Left: With all the paraphernalia of a small station still adorning the platform, Stow-on-the-Wold bathes in sunlight whilst awaiting its fate in the summer of 1962. *Neil Parkhouse collection*

Below: Ex-GWR '51XX' Class 2-6-2T No. 4109 eases off after passing the 1 in 75 gradient post on its approach to Charlton Kings with the 8.50 am to Kingham on 13th October 1962, the last day of services. Note the horsebox marshalled behind the locomotive again, which seems rather odd in this context, unless it had been pressed into use for some other purpose. *D.R. Lewis*

Cheltenham and Kingham (exclusive) would be withdrawn, leaving a residual freight-only service at the eastern end of the route between Kingham and Bourton-on-the-Water. The Chipping Norton branch was also granted a reprieve, although in the event this would be only temporary.

The line was closed as planned, with effect from 15th October 1962 and, as this was a Monday, the last scheduled passenger trains ran on Saturday 13th October 1962. On that day, the stations and halts at Cheltenham South & Leckhampton, Charlton Kings, Andoversford Junction, Notgrove, Bourton-on-the-Water and Stow-on-the-Wold were deleted from the railway passenger network. It was expected that many people would wish to travel on the last scheduled trains and, in consequence, the normal two-coach branch train was replaced by a four-coach formation.

The 1.15 pm down service from Kingham to Cheltenham St. James, headed by 2-6-2 prairie tank No. 4161, was filmed at Kingham by a BBC film crew and interviews with last day passengers were broadcast in a local news programme on the following Monday. The 1.50 pm afternoon service from Cheltenham to Kingham was hauled by 2-6-2T No. 5173, while the final Up working left Cheltenham at 6.50 pm behind '41XX' Class 2-6-2T No. 4109. This service, which would form the very last Down working from Kingham, was made up of six coaches, and its departure from Cheltenham was accompanied by a barrage of detonators and music from the town band.

The final train left Kingham at 9.25 pm, with a large number of last-day travellers on board and, whistling frequently, it set off into the gloomy October night. Soon, the platform lamps at Kingham had been left far behind and the brightly lit train was running through open countryside. Little could be seen as the '41XX' laboured through pitch-black fields with its six packed coaches, though little groups of people had gathered on the bridges and stations to pay their last respects. All too soon, the last train arrived back in Cheltenham and an era of railway history was brought to a close.

This sequence of photographs depicts the 2.50 pm train from Cheltenham St. James to Kingham on the last day of operation, 13th October 1962. **Top left**, train engine '41XX' Class No. 4109 stands outside Malvern Road shed, adorned with the headboard that accompanied the various locomotives working the Kingham trains on the final day. Lettered 'Cheltenham–Kingham, the eleventh hour', it was made by photographer Ross Lewis and his friend Roger Bailey in their school metalwork class! **Top right**, the train waits to leave from Platform 2 at St. James. In the view, **centre**, the train is seen during a brief stop at Andoversford station and in the final picture, **right**, No. 4109 has just arrived in Platform 3 at Kingham. After the locomotive had run round, the train then formed the 4.00 pm service for Chipping Norton. *All photos D.R. Lewis*

With the trees and vegetation surrounding the stations on the line having matured over the years, it was an irony of timing that most of them looked at their best shortly before closure. Most had been given a lick of paint too, in order to force the balance sheet in favour of closure. Here looking quite delightful in its semi-rural setting, Chipping Norton basks in warm summer sunshine, as Collett '45XX' Class 2-6-2T No. 4573 sets out for Kingham in 1960. *P. J. Shoesmith*

CLOSURE OF THE CHIPPING NORTON BRANCH

The demise of the Cheltenham to Kingham line effectively turned the clock back 107 years, in that railway travellers had to use their nearest main line stations, or the still-extant branch line to Chipping Norton. The Bourton-on-the-Water branch also survived, albeit as a freight-only route, with a meagre service of three goods trains per week.

Although the Kingham to Chipping Norton line was still operative, British Railways made little or no effort to provide a useful service for local travellers. Indeed, in its last months of operation, the timetable was practically useless. There were just two trains each way, leaving Kingham at 7.10 am and 4.00 pm, and returning from Chipping Norton at 8.00 am and 4.53 pm respectively. These timings would have allowed commuters to reach Oxford or London in good time but there were no convenient trains back to Chipping Norton and, in these circumstances, it is hardly surprising that regular travellers utilised buses or private cars for their journeys to and from Oxford or other destinations.

In its final period of operation as a passenger route, the Chipping Norton branch was worked by a BR Standard Class '2MT' 2-6-0 stationed at Kingham. Hitherto, this locomotive had worked the morning passenger train as well as the branch goods service, the afternoon train being worked by the engine and stock of the 2.50 pm ex-Cheltenham. The cessation of services between Kingham and Cheltenham meant that this mode of operation was no longer feasible, and the Kingham-based engine was therefore employed to work the branch freight service and both passenger trips.

In November 1962, British Railways announced that the passenger service between Kingham and Chipping Norton would be discontinued with effect from Monday 3rd December. *'Alternative passenger road services'* would be provided by the City of Oxford Motor Services Ltd, although the existing arrangements for the collection and delivery of goods and parcels traffic in the area served by the railway would be maintained by British Railways road vehicles operating from Kingham and Chipping Norton stations. As there were no Sunday services, the last trains ran over the line on Saturday 1st December 1962.

The closure of the Kingham to Chipping Norton line was commemorated in the usual way and many people turned up to participate in the closure proceedings. Paradoxically, the doomed line was busier on its last day than it had been for many years and it was clearly a pity that those who travelled on the branch on this final day of operation could not have done so with greater regularity before the closure was announced!

The section of line between Chipping Norton and Rollright was also closed officially from 3rd December 1962 – although the last freight train had actually worked over the line on 30th November, when BR Standard class '2MT'

The 4.00 pm to Chipping Norton waits to leave from Platform 4 at Kingham on Saturday 22nd September 1962, having worked to here as the 2.50 pm ex-Cheltenham St. James. This was just three weeks before closure of the line from Cheltenham, whilst the Chipping Norton branch itself had just over two months to go. Although this was an ordinary service train, photographer Paul Strong managed to cab ride much of the journey of both lines. The group on the platform were not on this trip and were probably members of a railway club on a photographic sortie to Kingham and elsewhere.
Paul Strong

Left: '51XX' Class 2-6-2T No. 4101 pulls into Chipping Norton Down platform, with a three coach train making up the return service to Kingham on 6th October 1962.
Courtesy Kidderminster Railway Museum

Below: No. 4109 is here seen taking on water before departing with the 4.25 pm service to Kingham on 13th October 1962, still sporting the headboard seen previously, marking the final day of passenger services over the Cheltenham to Kingham section. *D.R. Lewis*

2-6-0 No. 78001 collected the last remaining wagons from Rollright Siding. Further goods closures followed at intervals, the lines from Kingham to Chipping Norton and Bourton-on-the-Water being closed to all traffic with effect from 7th September 1964. Track lifting had, meanwhile, started on the western section of the Banbury & Cheltenham route, '43XX' Class 2-6-0 No. 7319 being one of the engines used for this work.

Demolition started on the Chipping Norton branch in 1965 and soon the entire line had been destroyed between Kingham and Adderbury. Track lifting was carried out with the aid of a Class '08' 0-6-0 diesel shunter – perhaps the only time that one of these locomotives had been seen on the route. The work of destruction was accomplished by the summer of 1965, the remaining trackwork between Kingham and Bourton-on-the-Water being removed as part of the same demolition contract.

Further to the east, the section of line between Adderbury and Hook Norton was officially closed with effect from 4th November 1963 but Adderbury station remained in use as the western terminus of a goods-only branch from King's Sutton. The line was reduced to single track in December 1965 and finally closed to all traffic in August 1969, when private siding traffic finally ceased; the last customer had been Messrs J. Bibby & Sons. The line remained *in situ* for several months but it soon became clear that this residual section of the Banbury & Cheltenham Direct route would never be re-opened. The junction at King's Sutton and a short section of line was, however, retained until 1971.

In the meantime, the railway system around Cheltenham was also being subjected to an inevitable rationalisation programme, as a result of which all services were diverted into the former Midland station at Cheltenham Lansdown with effect from 3rd January 1966. Cheltenham St. James and Cheltenham Malvern Road were closed, and Cheltenham Lansdown thereby became the town's only remaining station.

At the eastern end of the erstwhile B&CDR route, King's Sutton was threatened with closure under the Beeching Plan, along with six other intermediate stations on the Oxford to Birmingham main line. Happily, King's Sutton was reprieved, although the other threatened stopping places were closed as planned with effect from Monday 2nd November 1964. Following these deletions, King's Sutton travellers were left with a limited train service between London, Oxford and Banbury, the station being served by five Up and seven Down trains by June 1965. Oddly, one of the Down workings commenced its journey at Bicester North but there was no corresponding Up service for returning travellers!

As the pace of closure and rationalisation gathered momentum throughout the 1960s, it became increasingly clear that every railway in the area was threatened with

Left: Two examples of unusual motive power at Adderbury in later years. Here, an unidentified '9F' Class 2-10-0 is engaged in shunting vans under the A423 bridge, whilst marshalling a train for Bibby's in February 1966. These locomotives were never seen beyond Adderbury but one did work over the western section of the line from Kingham, with a special from East Anglia to Cheltenham and Gloucester on 5th July 1962.
Roger Carpenter collection

Right: Introducing an even more discordant note to this rural backwater, an unidentified Class '47' type 4 Co-Co diesel stands at Adderbury in 1966, with a freight working which seems to include a road vehicle on a flat wagon. Station and signal box were by now looking very shabby, with peeling paint and weeds on the track bed. Bibby's mill can be seen in the left background, with the siding connection behind the box.
Courtesy Kidderminster Railway Museum

total extinction. The demise of the Chipping Norton branch left the Oxford, Worcester & Wolverhampton main line in splendid isolation as the only passenger line for miles round. Local travellers hoped that rationalisation had gone far enough but, in 1964, BR announced that most of the intermediate stopping places between Oxford and Worcester were also under threat.

The blow fell on Saturday 1st January 1966, on which day the OW&WR stations at Adlestrop, Blockley, Campden, Littleton & Badsey, Fladbury, Wyre Halt, Stoulton Halt and Norton Halt were closed completely. Fortunately, a number of other former OW&WR stations, including Handborough, Finstock Halt, Combe Halt, Ascott-under-Wychwood and Shipton for Burford were reprieved, while Evesham, Moreton-in-Marsh, Kingham and Charlbury became the designated 'park-and-drive' railheads for a large area of the Cotswolds.

Banbury, still a relatively busy station in terms of passenger traffic, lost its once-important freight traffic. The marshalling yards were closed from 4th May 1970, resulting in the loss of fifteen jobs and considerable local concern regarding the future of the station itself. Part of the former North End Yard was retained for a time in connection with what little freight traffic still remained, though in general the closure of the Great Central line in 1966, followed by the cessation of all ironstone traffic, dealt a body-blow to Banbury's railway freight business.

Local travellers began to suspect that just about every railway in the country had become target for the 'mad axemen' and in this climate of suspicion, newspapers such as the *Oxford Mail* frequently printed reports about renewed threats to the area's remaining rail links. In the case of Banbury, British Railways were able to refute the rumours of further retraction and the *Oxford Mail* was able to quote a railway spokesman who assured the public that there were '*no plans in the foreseeable future to carry out any major modifications at Banbury*'. He added that '*a glance at the graph of passenger receipts*' would show '*a very healthy position*' with traffic increasing '*week by week*'.

Dereliction setting in at Cheltenham Malvern Road in 1966. The shed and yard were out of use by this date and the station had been closed to passengers. The two tracks through the station were now used by Honeybourne line trains only, with Cheltenham St. James station having closed at the beginning of the year. The view is looking south west from Malvern Road bridge. Whilst the track bed through here is still accessible, industrial development has taken over the area to the right, although happily, the shed buildings still survive in use by local builders merchants Sharpe & Fisher.
The Lens of Sutton Collection

SOME POST CLOSURE DEVELOPMENTS ON THE B&CDR LINE

Chipping Norton goods yard was used as a coal yard by the Chipping Norton Co-operative Society for a few months after the final closure but, sadly, the station buildings and goods yard soon became a target for thieves and vandals. In April 1965, the *Oxford Mail* published an evocative photograph of the vandalised station building, framed by the lattice ironwork of the old footbridge. Under the headline *'Nostalgic Centenary'*, the paper pointed out that it was *'nearly 100 years to the day'* since the railway first reached Chipping Norton, although the centenary would be celebrated by ghosts in a derelict station:

The last goods train pulled out of Chipping Norton six months ago, and the last passenger train a year before that. Now even the rusting rails are gone. A demolition gang has started tearing up the four and a half miles of track that runs to Kingham … The booking office and waiting rooms are falling to pieces under the dual onslaught of weather and vandals. The brickwork is crumbling, gutters sag and most of the windows are shattered. An ancient GWR notice beside the weed-grown platform threatens trespassers with a forty shilling fine if they 'expose themselves to danger', but the only danger now is from falling tiles.

Amid the dust and debris of the signal box stands a tray of railway teacups that will never again steam with railway tea to relieve the tedium of a night shift. The tunnel that echoed to the whistle of the Hookey Flyer is now sealed. Birds sing in the tangle of evergreens on the down side platform, while not far off the traffic of a new transport age roars past.

A few months later, British Railways decided to demolish the station building, after two thieves were caught taking lead

An unusual view of the *porte cochere*, at the front of Cheltenham St. James station, looking northeast along St. James Square. Facing the camera, at the junction with Knapp Road, is the former Bethel Baptist Chapel (later the Christadelphian Hall). On the right can just be glimpsed St. Gregory's Roman Catholic church. The view was taken in the spring of 1966, after final closure to passenger services on 3rd January of that year. The station site, being so close to the town centre, was ripe for redevelopment and an office building, known as St. James House, now occupies this spot, with a supermarket and car park on much of the goods yard. *Bob Brown collection*

This view of the goods yard at St. James was also taken soon after closure. The view is looking west, along the goods yard with the rear of the large goods shed on the right and the smaller store beyond. Note the yard crane still in place, although track lifting has already started. *Bob Brown collection*

and other materials from the derelict structure. Every window in the goods office was soon broken, while the Co-operative Society's coal office was smashed up by intruders, who ripped out the telephone and stole weights and other equipment. Similar damage was inflicted on the weigh-house, while a former coal office that was being used as a sack store was virtually kicked into pieces by persistent vandals.

It was a similar story elsewhere on the Banbury to Kingham line as, with monotonous but perhaps inevitable regularity, the abandoned stations and other infrastructure was reduced to a state of ruin by the village idiots. At Bloxham, for instance, vandals smashed every window in the station building and signal box, while at neighbouring Hook Norton the parish council could hardly wait for their station to be removed in its entirety. When a gang of workmen turned up and started levelling the station site, the chairman of the parish council, Mr A.T. Williams, announced that he was *'delighted to see the demolition under way'*. The station, with its twenty foot deep cellar, was said to have become a danger to the public and Mr Williams added that the vice-chairman of the parish council had *'undertaken to get something done'*. There were plans for the station site to be used by a light engineering firm and although the final decision rested with the County Council, the parish council *'were very much in favour'* of the proposed industrial development, which would *'provide much needed light industry for Hook Norton'*.

Bloxham station also became the subject of a planning appeal after a road transport firm were refused permission to turn the site into a lorry depot. Oxfordshire County Council claimed that the proposed development would be detrimental to road safety. It was also pointed out that the use of the site as a depot would not improve the visual amenities of the area, while in 1965 British Railways had already stated that they would not object if part of the station site was used for residential development.

At Churchill Crossing, the level crossing became a subject of controversy in 1970, when local residents claimed that it was a 'hazard' for motorists speeding along the minor road from Churchill to Kingham. *'There is very strong local feeling about this; the crossing ought to have been taken away years ago when the railway was closed'*, asserted the chairman of Kingham Parish Council. In recent years traffic using the Churchill to Kingham road had increased tremendously, he added, and *'most members of the parish council'* shared his concern for the supposed rights of road users.

In many places, it seemed as if local residents wished to see all traces of the railway removed in their entirety, this feeling being particularly strong during the late 1960s, when the media invariably portrayed the railway system as nothing more than an antiquated relic of the Industrial Revolution. Attitudes to the abandoned viaducts at Hook Norton were, on the other hand, slightly less clear cut and there was genuine sadness when these once mighty structures were felled. The viaducts *'took two hundred men nearly two years to build and cost two men's lives'*, lamented the *Oxford Mail* but it took *'four Scotsmen just a few weeks'* to demolish them.

In fact, the demolition was only part completed, the object of the exercise being the recovery of hundreds of tons of

Above left: Some demolition occurred at Cheltenham prior to the complete closure of the line, with the Hatherley Loop being taken out of use. '45XX' Class 2-6-2T No. 4573 passes the part-dismantled Gloucester Loop Junction Signal Box with the 2.25 pm to Kingham in 1960. The truncated remains of the Hatherley Loop are in the foreground. Note the signal box nameboard is still in place.

Above right: Hawksworth Class '94XX' pannier tank No. 9471 cautiously backs a brake van down the remains of the Hatherley Loop on 19th April 1960. At this time preparations were in hand to remove the bridge girders which carried the loop over Hatherley Road, near Hatherley Junction.

Left: Track lifting on the B&CDR brought more strangers to the route. In March 1965, Austerity 2-8-0 No. 90276 trundles slowly past Bourneside Farm with a train of lifted rails from the Kingham line. On the right can just be glimpsed some back gardens from houses in Canterbury Walk, part of the then recent Warden Hill development.
All D. R. Lewis

scrap metal. The great stone pillars were left *in situ* and, as the *Oxford Times* remarked, they would remain *'as a tribute to the workmanship of the builders of eighty years ago'*.

The brick viaduct at the western end of the Banbury & Cheltenham Direct line at Dowdeswell was demolished by explosives shortly before 6.00 am on Sunday 30th April 1967, the act of destruction being witnessed by large crowds of people who took refuge on the surrounding hillsides. The demolition contractor reported that the viaduct was still structurally sound – the mortar had set as hard as the Victorian bricks that it bonded.

On a slightly happier note, Chipping Norton Tunnel eventually found a new role as a refuge for rare bats. On 1st October 1993, the *Oxford Times* reported that the Bat Conservation Trust, the Oxfordshire Bat Group and British Rail had fitted the tunnel with metal grills that kept out unauthorised visitors, while enabling the bats to enter or leave their place of refuge. A spokesperson from the Oxfordshire Bat Group explained that the site was used by at least five species of bats, which were able to live safely in ideal conditions within the tunnel.

THE RAILWAY TODAY

Today, numerous traces of the erstwhile Cheltenham to Banbury line can still be seen, although the three viaducts and many of the smaller bridges have been taken down. In places, entire embankments have been removed in connection with road improvements, while at Kingham the GWR station building was demolished in 1975, following the discovery of dry rot. Its replacement, comprising a modern ticket office and waiting room on the Down side, was officially opened on 27th November 1975. A fully glazed waiting shelter was erected on the Up platform but the GWR footbridge was retained as a link between the Up and Down sides, albeit without its roof covering.

Of the 48 miles of line between Banbury and Cheltenham, barely three and a half miles remain in use, these remnants being the still-extant line between Banbury and King's Sutton, together with very short sections of line at Kingham and Lansdown Junction. The only stations still open are those at Banbury, King's Sutton and Kingham, none of which were on the Banbury & Cheltenham Direct Railway (although King's Sutton could claim to have been a B&CDR station insofar as it

Right: In 1964, with Bourton-on-the-Water station still open for goods traffic, track lifting was progressed westwards from there to Cheltenham. For a time, Notgrove station was used as a railhead for materials recovered from the three mile section between there and Bourton. Here, in March 1964, the contractor's 0-4-0 diesel has arrived at Notgrove with a wagon load of lifted track panels for dismantling in the old goods yard. At the time this picture was taken, two or three BR trains per week would service the Notgrove railhead, to remove the loaded wagons. *D.R. Lewis*

Left: A final view of Notgrove looking west from the B4068 road bridge, on 8th May 1964. Another train load of materials has just arrived at the railhead, with one of Notgrove's distant signals being lifted off the recovery train by the contractor's crane. *B.J. Ashworth*

was opened in conjunction with the B&CDR scheme).

Much of the trackbed on the closed sections of line has survived, while at Bourton-on-the-Water at the start of the new millennium, the Cotswold stone station building was still standing, somewhat incongruously, by the side of a road leading to a small housing estate and various commercial premises. The building has been maintained by the County Council, who are to be commended for doing so, the interior apparently being little changed from the day the line closed.

However, in 2003, as this narrative was being completed, it was announced that the building was being donated to the Gloucestershire Warwickshire Railway for erection on their line. It is intended to site it at Broadway, on the line's northwards extension from Toddington, where all the original station buildings have been demolished although the goods shed still stands. Whilst it is a shame, perhaps, to see this last substantial remaining part of the B&CDR moved from its site, its new home will see the building in regular use again, doing what it was built for and close to part of the route it served. On a more serious note, however, part of the deal to move the building would see the valuable and original Cotswold stone roof tiles removed for re-use elsewhere, surely an act of architectural vandalism which cannot be countenanced, as it would destroy the station's

Right: The contractor's crane at rest at a point approximately one mile to the west of Notgrove in 1964. *D.R. Lewis*

Above: Ex-GWR '43XX' Class 2-6-0 No. 7319 has just come to a halt alongside Andoversford Junction Signal Box with a short train of recovered rail in 1964. The guard is about to open the box up in order to set the points for the Down road, so that the train could then proceed down to Cheltenham. The line up to Notgrove can be seen in the distance between the signal box and the locomotive. *D. R. Lewis*

Right: Having just left Sandywell Park Tunnel, mogul 2-6-0 No. 7319 drifts downhill towards Dowdeswell Viaduct on 3rd April 1964, with another light load of lifted rails recovered from the Kingham line. Colonel Yorke of the Board of Trade had sanctioned the use of this double track section on 29th March 1902, subject to a 20 mph speed restriction to allow consolidation of the formation. *D. R. Lewis*

historical integrity completely. It is to be hoped that good sense will eventually prevail but, at the time of writing, this is by no means certain.

Along the rest of the route, in truth very little remains in terms of structures bar a few bridges. Indeed, the route of the line through the southern outskirts of Cheltenham has been completely obliterated in many places by new house building. The first section of the line from Lansdown Junction to Leckhampton has suffered particularly badly in this respect. Cheltenham Leckhampton and Charlton Kings station sites are both occupied by industrial buildings, with the road bridges crossing the line at each being the only surviving original structures. Dowdeswell Viaduct was demolished with the use of explosives, in the late 1960s. Sandywell Park Tunnel is bricked up although both ends can be found, whilst at Andoversford the brick built goods shed survives in industrial use. Road widening and realignment has destroyed the site of the junction with the M&SWJR line and the bridge over the A40 with it. Nothing remains at Notgrove, although the lofty road bridge over the cutting was purportedly not demolished but filled in with spoil. Stow-on-the-Wold station building has been converted and enlarged as a private dwelling.

On the eastern section of the line, the situation is, if anything, worse. Nothing remains of the stations at Chipping Norton, Hook Norton, Bloxham or Adderbury, or at any of the halts. The viaduct piers still stand at Hook Norton and the tunnel entrances at Hook Norton and Chipping Norton can also be found, mostly with some difficulty. Looking for remains of the ironstone industry is also becoming increasingly difficult and very much a pursuit for the industrial archaeologist.

The wanton destruction of historic buildings, especially during the 1960s, must be condemned. Victorian railway buildings were substantially built and many of the structures along the Banbury & Cheltenham Direct line would have made attractive cottage-type properties if they had been converted into private dwellings. Even the goods sheds,

Right: A detailed view showing track lifting in progress near Charlton Kings on 5th December 1964. The photograph was taken from Little Herbert's Road bridge and is facing Andoversford. House building has today obliterated this view. The Up line is being lifted and the rails placed onto bolster wagons. The train engine for that day was prairie No. 6128 and the wagons were taken down to Malvern Road yard for further marshalling. *D.R. Lewis*

Left: The view the opposite way from Little Herbert's Road bridge a short while later, as large prairie No. 6128, one of the 6100 number series '51XX' Class 2-6-2Ts which were more usually to be found on London suburban passenger workings, gets under way with its load of recovered rail. The platforms of Charlton Kings station can be seen through the arch of Cirencester Road bridge in the distance. This record of the track lifting operations covered a number of angles and locations along the western section of the B&CDR, particularly through Cheltenham, which do not seem to have been well used by earlier generations of photographers. *D.R. Lewis*

Left: 'Manor' Class 4-6-0 No. 7808 *Cookham Manor* stands amid the debris in Leckhampton station on New Year's Day 1965, in readiness to push a rake of empty wagons up to Andoversford Junction for loading with recovered track materials. It was appropriate that this locomotive was used on such a duty, as it had been a regular over the ex-M&SWJR route in happier times. *D.R. Lewis*

Left below: Leckhampton Signal Box after the line's closure, having received attention from the local vandals. This box dated from the doubling of the line in 1902. The previous one had stood opposite the then single (later Up) platform. *M.P. Barnsley collection*

Below: Photographer Ross Lewis arrived at Leckhampton signal box one day in 1960 to find that one of the contractor's men was about to cut through the signal levers. The man cut the first lever off and presented it to him, after which he kept it for many years before donating it to the Gloucestershire & Warwickshire Railway at Toddington. *D.R. Lewis*

which often found an industrial use after closure, did not survive at any location along the route.

On the other hand, there was much greater interest in locomotive preservation following the end of steam operation and, in this context, some of the engines that once worked over the B&CDR route can now be seen on various preserved lines. Notable survivors include 'Manor' Class 4-6-0 No. 7808 *Cookham Manor*, '2251' Class 0-6-0 No. 3205 and '28XX' 2-8-0 No. 2818.

Some of the narrow gauge quarry locomotives have also survived, the most famous being the 2-6-2T *Russell*. After many setbacks, the locomotive returned to the Welsh Highland Railway, for which it was originally built, in September 2000. The engine worked on the line for several months but was taken out of traffic in 2003 for a major overhaul. At the time of writing, this historic locomotive is being rebuilt to its original condition with taller boiler mountings. *Russell* should be back in service on its native line by the spring of 2004.

Other survivors include *Gertrude* and *The Doll*, from the Sydenham quarry system. After further service with Stewarts & Lloyds at Bilston, *The Doll* was acquired in 1966 for use on the narrow gauge nursery railway at Bressingham in Norfolk. However, it was an inch too wide in gauge for this line and in 1969 was moved to the Leighton Buzzard Narrow Gauge Railway, where it still resides.

Above left: Looking towards Lansdown Junction in March 1965. The Down line has been lifted completely, whilst the Up line just manages to clear Hatherley Road bridge – the demolition contractor's job was nearly finished. Note the juxtaposition of crane jib and the spire of St. Mark's church, which almost resembles an Apollo rocket launch!

Above right: The girders from the Hatherley Road bridge are finally lowered onto one of Himpsold's lorries in 1966. There were actually two railway bridges in Hatherley Road within a short distance – the other carried the Hatherley Loop over the road just before it met the Birmingham to Bristol main line at Hatherley Junction.

Right: Two of the contractor's men take their rest whilst preparing Hatherley Road bridge for demolition in 1966. Note that the embankment towards Gloucester Loop Junction had been bulldozed away and metal plates placed in the road to protect the surface from the tracks of the plant manoeuvring around the site. This view was taken from the top of the Lansdown Junction Home signal, which had been relocated to the photographer's garden.
All D.R. Lewis

Right: The view from a sad windowless Bourton-on-the-Water Signal Box, looking out over a trackless goods yard in this sombre scene from 1965. Goods services had finally been withdrawn between here and Kingham in September 1964. *M.P. Barnsley collection*

Left: A weed-infested Bloxham station, looking east towards Hook Norton in 1963, following the final withdrawal of goods services west of Adderbury. The signal box, however, looks in tidy condition. *Bob Brown collection*

The remains of Adderbury station on 7th October 1972, following removal of the track. The view is facing east towards Banbury. *R.M. Casserley*

BIBLIOGRAPHY & FURTHER READING

At first glance, the following list would appear to contain ample material on the Banbury to Cheltenham line but, on closer examination, it will be seen that many of the listed books and articles relate to local history or locomotive matters, rather than railway history or infrastructure. In fact, little has ever been written on the history of this interesting cross-country route, although there has been a profusion of picture books and other peripheral material. The articles marked with an asterisk contain scale drawings which may be of interest to potential modellers of the B&CDR line.

Bagust, Harold, *Stow-on-the-Wold* (1979)
The Banbury Guardian, passim
Beckinsale, R.P., *Companion into Gloucestershire* (1948)
Brabant, F.G., *The Little Guide to Oxfordshire* (1906)
The British Railways Magazine, passim
Cannan, Joanna, *Oxfordshire* (1952)
Clifton, Michael, 'The Kingham Goods', *Great Western Railway Journal No. 23*, Summer 1997
Cooke, R.A., *Track Layout Diagrams of the G.W.R. and B.R. (W.R.): Section 27 Oxford* (1987)
Cooke, R.A., *Track Layout Diagrams of the G.W.R. and B.R. (W.R.): Section 28 Worcester-Oxford and Branches* (1997)
Copsey, John, 'Granges at Work', *Great Western Railway Journal, 27 & 28*, 1998
Copsey, John, 'The Aberdare 2-6-0s', *Great Western Railway Journal No. 21*, 1997
Cox, J. Charles, *The Little Guide to Gloucestershire* (1914)
Cummings, John, *Railway Motor Buses & Bus Services* (1980)
Dickens, Margaret, *A History of Hook Norton* (1928)
Fowler, William Warde, *Kingham Old & New* (1921)
Freezer, Cyril J., 'Locomotives of the GWR: The Aberdares', *Railway Modeller*, July 1969*
Freezer, Cyril J., 'Locomotives of the GWR: Granges & Manors', *Railway Modeller*, June 1968*
Freezer, Cyril J., 'Locomotives of the GWR: The 45XXs', *Railway Modeller*, January 1969*
Freezer, Cyril J., 'Locomotives of the GWR: The Smallest Prairies', *Railway Modeller*, December 1968*
Freezer, Cyril J., 'Locomotives of the GWR: The Final Prairies', *Railway Modeller*, December 1970*
Freezer, Cyril J., 'Locomotives of the GWR: The Big Prairies', *Railway Modeller*, October 1970*
Freezer, Cyril J., 'Locomotives of the GWR: The Moguls', *Railway Modeller*, August 1968*
Freezer, Cyril J., 'Locomotives of the GWR: The Ubiquitous Pannier', *Railway Modeller*, June 1967*
Gardner, Robert, *History, Gazetteer & Directory of the County of Oxford* (1852)
The Gloucestershire Echo, passim
Great Western Railway, *Traffic Dealt with at Stations & Goods Depots*, passim (PRO RAIL 253/45)
Great Western Railway, *Holiday Haunts*, passim
Great Western Railway, *Station Accounts Instruction Book*
Great Western Railway, *Towns, Villages, Outlying Works Etc* (1938)
Great Western Railway, *Working & Public Timetables*, passim
The Great Western Railway Magazine, passim
Heath, Christopher N., 'When Chippy Dick Chugged his way to Cheltenham', *Cotswold Life No. 68*, June 1974
Household, Humphrey, *Gloucestershire Railways in the Twenties* (1984)
Hurrell, Harold, *The Bliss Mill, Chipping Norton* (1996)
Iliffe Stokes, D.M. & G., 'A Rural Station & Platform Shelter', *Model Railway News*, May 1962*
Iliffe Stokes, Doris, 'Kingham Station', *Model Railway Constructor*, May 1961

Ingham, Paul, *Two Foot Gauge Rails to the Ironstone* (2000)
Jenkins, Stanley C. & Quayle, Howard I., *The Oxford Worcester & Wolverhampton Railway* (1977)
Jenkins, Stanley C., *The Fairford Branch* (1975)
Jenkins, Stanley C., *The Northampton & Banbury Junction Railway* (1990)
Jenkins, Stanley C., 'The Cheltenham to Kingham Line', *Steam Days No. 156*, August 2002
Jenkins, Stanley C., 'Life Before Preservation: The Gloucestershire Warwickshire Railway', *Steam Days No. 119*, July 1999
Kelly's Directory of Gloucestershire: various editions
Kelly's Directory of Oxfordshire: various editions
Lewis, June, 'Village Alphabet, Kingham', *Cotswold Life No. 61*, November 1973
MacDermot, E.T., *History of the Great Western Railway* (1927)
Meades, Eileen, *The History of Chipping Norton* (1949)
Mee, Arthur, *Oxfordshire* (1965)
The Oxford Chronicle, passim
The Oxford Mail, passim
The Oxford Times, passim
Potts, W., *A History of Banbury* (1958)
Pryer, D.A., 'Cheltenham St James', *The Railway Modeller*, April 1970*
The Railway Clearing House Handbook of Railway Stations, passim
The Railway Times, passim
Russell, J.H., 'Private Branch Line Closure', *Model Railway News*, June 1959
Russell, J.H., *The Banbury & Cheltenham Railway* (1977)
Sands, T.B., *The Midland & South Western Junction Railway* (1959)
Sands, T.B., 'The Passing of the Midland & South Western Junction Railway', *The Railway Magazine*, November 1961
Semmens, P.W.B., *The Heyday of GWR Train Services* (1990)
Sherwood, J. & Pevsner, N., *The Buildings of England: Oxfordshire* (1970)
Spencer Gilkes, J., 'The Banbury & Cheltenham Direct Railway', *The Railway Magazine*, August 1955
Thornton, E.C.B., 'Memories of Railways in the Cheltenham & Gloucester Area', *Railway World*, July-August 1963
Tonks, Eric, *The Ironstone Quarries of the Midlands II* (1988)
Turner, Chris, 'Chipping Norton', *Great Western Railway Journal No. 23*, Summer 1997
Turner, Chris, 'Kingham in the 1930s', *Great Western Railway Journal No. 34*, Spring 2000
Turner, Chris, 'Bourton-on-the-Water', *Great Western Railway Journal No. 40*, Autumn 2001
Verey, David & Brooks, Alan, *The Buildings of England: Gloucestershire* (1970)
Williams, Ethel Carleton, *Companion into Oxfordshire* (1935)
The Witney Express, passim
The Witney Gazette, passim
Wixey, K., 'Cheltenham & Gloucester Signalman', *Railway World*, April 1978
Woolley, Rob, 'Village Alphabet, Hook Norton', *Cotswold Life No. 85*, November 1975
Woolley, Rob, 'Hooky Ale', *Cotswold Life No. 93*, July 1976

366 THE BANBURY & CHELTENHAM DIRECT RAILWAY

INDEX

Accidents & incidents, 17-18, 95, 97, 103, 104, 118, 230, 245, 255
Adderbury & Sydenham Quarries, 88, 317-318, 319
Adderbury, 38, 39, 56, 59, 105, 112, 305-318, 343, 354, 364 *et passim.*
Adlestrop, 15, 17, 355
Air raids, 117, 297
Alfred the Great, King of Wessex, 11
Andoversford & Stratford-upon-Avon Railway, 62
Andoversford, 38, 48, 50, 61, 62, 100, 111, 112, 167-177, 348, 351, 360 *et passim.*
Astrop Sidings, 324
Badminton Hunt, the, 223-224
Banbury & Cheltenham Direct Railway, Origins of, 11-36
Banbury & Cheltenham Direct Railway, construction, 37-60, 64-67
Banbury & Cheltenham Direct Railway, opening of, 44-48, 52, 53, 56, 58
Banbury Cakes, 336
Banbury Cross, 336
Banbury Gas Works, 324, 332
Banbury General, 56, 63, 66, 111, 112, 323-336, 355, 358
Banbury Merton Street, 324, 331-333
Barford St. John Aerodrome, 116, 117, 299, 302
Baring-Young, Charles, 237
Barry Railway, 81
Betts, Edward Ladd (1815-72), contractor, 16
Birmingham & Gloucester Railway, 12, 13, 14
Birmingham & Midland Motor Omnibus Company, 109, 110, 305
Bliss Tweed Mill, 16, 17, 18, 20, 92, 87, 239, 242, 243, 244, 245, 261-4
Bliss, William (1810-83), Mill owner & promoter, 16, 17, 18, 20, 92, 261-64
Bloxham Ironstone Co, 303
Bloxham School, 302, 343
Bloxham, 38, 56, 59, 71, 112, 296-303, 345, 357, 364 *et passim.*
Bourton, Chipping Norton & Banbury Railway, 36, 37
Bourton-on-the-Water Railway, 9, 22-26, 29, 51, 189
Bourton-on-the-Water, 11, 25, 44, 48, 51, 52, 66, 71, 79, 89, 90, 111, 112, 114, 187-198, 337, 349, 359, 364 *et passim.*
Brecon & Merthyr Railway, 184
Brindley, James, canal engineer, 323
Bristol & Birmingham Railway, 14
Bristol & Gloucester Railway, 13, 14
Bristol Tramways & Carriage Company, 109, 110
Brunel, Isambard Kingdom (1806-59), GWR engineer, 12, 13, 17, 38, 39, 324
Brymbo Steel Company, 55, 94, 117, 118, 282, 290-295, 343
Burke, James, engineer, 29
Burlingham, Henry, coal merchant, 87, 89, 182
Camping coaches, 114, 188
Charlton Kings, 44, 49, 52, 66, 72, 84, 94, 101, 106, 107, 112, 152-163, 338 *et passim.*
Cheltenham & District Light Railway, 78, 119, 150
Cheltenham & Great Western Union Railway, 12, 13, 14, 27
Cheltenham & Oxford Union Railway, proposed, 27
Cheltenham Lansdown, 62, 120, 121, 354
Cheltenham Malvern Road, 128-133, 346, 347, 351, 354, 356
Cheltenham South & Leckhampton, 38, 44, 47, 49, 52, 72, 78, 80, 91, 147-151, 347, 362, 368
Cheltenham St James, 13, 38, 45, 46, 47, 69, 119-127, 346, 351, 354, 356, 357
Cheltenham tramway system, *see* 'Cheltenham & District Light Railway'
Cherwell, River, 11, 14, 38, 317, 318, 319, 323
Cheshire Lines Committee, 63
Chipping Norton Aerodrome, 116, 117
Chipping Norton Co-operative Society, 87, 94, 248, 250, 253, 356
Chipping Norton Gas Works, 87, 241, 242, 248
Chipping Norton Grammar School, 258
Chipping Norton Junction, 24, 25, 37, 38, 52, 57 (see also 'Kingham')
Chipping Norton Railway, 15-22, 26, 238, 248, 261, 264, 350
Chipping Norton,6, 12, 18, 19, 20, 21, 22, 78, 87, 92, 95, 97, 99, 108, 109, 110, 112, 116, 238-266, 340, 352, 353-354, 356-357, 358, 368 *et passim.*
Church of England, churches & chapels-of-ease, 37, 69, 122, 113, 127, 178, 198, 206, 255, 258, 267, 288, 296, 302, 307, 323, 336
Churchill Crossing, 231, 357
City of Oxford Motor Services, 108, 110, 229, 255, 353
Civil War, the, 12, 307, 336
Clarke, Seymour, B&CDR director, 39
Clay Cross Company, 299, 303
Clifford, George, coal merchant, 89, 190, 197, 252
Closures, 342-343, 344, 345-346, 348, 350-351, 353-354, 355
Cochrane & Co (Woodside) Ltd, 306, 309, 310
Collett & Sons, coal merchants, 94, 190, 197
Collister, John, engineer, 35
Cotswold Hunt, the, 112, 166
Courtney, Edward Baldwin (1836-91), 12th Earl of Devon, BC&DR director, 39
Coventry Collieries, 253
Crimean War, the, 20
Crook & Greenway, coal merchants, 135
Dale, Henry, 158, 161
Dalrymple, Hew, B&CDR director, 39
Dean Forest Coal Co, 253
Demolition, 356-364
Diesel power, 107, 342, 354, 355, 359
Dowdeswell Viaduct, 38, 44, 47-48, 61, 66, 67, 164-166, 358, 360
Duffield Iron Corporation, 306, 316
Dyer, Charles Kemp, B&CDR director, 58
Earl of Dudley's Siding, 55, 87, 274-275
Early, Charles (1824-1916), 28, 30
Early, John Vanner (1853-1920), 68
East Gloucestershire Railway, 9, 28, 29-34, 37, 38, 39-40, 47, 61, 152, 169, 177
East Suffolk Railway, 16, 22
Eastern Counties Railway, 16
Edgehill Aerodrome, 116, 302
Enstone Aerodrome, 117
Eugenie, Empress of France, 20
Evacuees, wartime, 116
Evans, Sir Arthur, archaeologist, 267
Eveson & Son, coal merchants, 252
Eynsham Hall, 224
Faringdon Railway, 29, 30, 31
Farrar, W.D., coal merchant, 149, 154
Fenton, William, OW&WR Chairman, 24
Finch & Son, coal merchants, 170
Fosse Way, the, 11, 187, 198, 206
Fowler, Sir John (1817-98), OW&WR engineer, 17, 20, 29, 36
Fowler, William Warde, 230
Fox, Sir Charles (1810-74), engineer, 28
Frost, Bernard T., coal merchant, 94, 248-9
GWR motor bus services, 108-110, 249, 255
Galton, Douglas (1822-92), Inspector of Railways, 33
General Strike, the, 213, 292
Gloucester & Cheltenham Tramroad, 12, 158
Great Central Railway, 62-63, 66, 80, 81, 82, 83, 84, 158, 324, 331, 333
Great North of Scotland Railway, 162
Great Northern Railway, 39
Great Western & Great Central Joint Railway, 27
Grouping, 1923, 72, 84, 184
Hastings, Warren (1732-1818), 235
Heythrop Hunt, the, 214, 223-224
Hickman, Alfred, 317
Hicks-Beach, Sir Michael, EGR director & President of Board of Trade, 29
Hitchman, William Simkins (1799-1881), promoter, 16, 17
Holst, Gustav, composer, 198
Hook Norton Brewery, 93, 286
Hook Norton Ironstone Partnership, 58, 88, 280, 281, 282, 285, 289-290, 306
Hook Norton Manor, 288
Hook Norton Tunnel, 53, 273, 274, 361
Hook Norton Viaducts, 53, 54, 55, 56, 58, 276-279, 282, 344, 357-358, 361
Hook Norton, 38, 54, 55, 58, 68, 76, 103, 109, 113, 275-295, 357 *et passim.*
Howell, Walter, B&CDR director, 38
Industrial locomotives, 158, 159, 161, 163, 281, 289, 292, 293-294, 295, 303, 318, 343, 362
Jessop's Pleasure Gardens, Cheltenham, 120

Kennedy, General Sir Michael, B&CDR Chairman, ... 58
King's Sutton, ... 37, 88, 113, 317, 318-323, 354, 358
Kingham Hill School, ... 113, 237
Kingham, ... 68, 72, 74, 75, 83, 85, 86, 98, 104, 113, 117,
.... 118, 207-230, 338, 351, 353, 358 et passim.
Langston, James, landowner & promoter, ... 16, 213, 235
Lansdown Junction, ... 133-145
Leckhampton Quarries, ... 73, 84, 157, 158-163
Leckhampton, see 'Cheltenham South & Leckhampton'
Lennox, Lord Alexander Gordon, B&CDR director, ... 39
Liddell, Charles, engineer, ... 30, 33, 35
Little Rissington Aerodrome, ... 116, 117, 209
Liveries, ... 26, 105, 186, 337
Locke, Joseph (1805-60), engineer, ... 63
Locomotive sheds, ... 19, 22, 43, 47, 128, 129, 131, 132, 133, 134,
.... 135, 137, 209, 213, 215, 218, 219, 227, 230, 238,
.... 244, 251, 254, 333-335, 339, 351, 356
London & Mid-Western Railway, proposed, ... 27
London & North Western Railway, ... 15, 24, 27, 29, 30, 34, 63
London & South Wales Railway, proposed, ... 63
London & South Western Railway, ... 27, 61
Looker, Richard B., ... 44, 45, 54, 58, 289
Lovatt, Henry, contractor & B&CDR director, ... 45, 58
Lucknow, siege of, ... 30
Manchester, Sheffield & Lincolnshire Railway, ... 62-63, 66
.... (see also 'Great Central Railway')
Marples, Ernest, Minister of Transport, ... 345, 348
Mason, Michael, GWR director, ... 234
Mercia, Kingdon of, ... 11
Midland & South Western Junction Railway, 50, 60, 61-62, 72, 88, 102, 105, 106,
.... 107, 121, 123, 133, 144, 146, 150, 167, 169,
.... 172, 176, 177, 338-339, 341, 342, 345, 346
Midland Counties & South Wales Railway, see Northampton & Banbury Junction
Railway
Midland Railway, ... 14, 27, 30, 31, 33, 62, 138, 339
Midland Red, see 'Birmingham & Midland Motor Omnibus Company'
Milton Halt, ... 113, 304
Moorsom, William Scarth (1804-63), engineer, ... 12
Moreton-in-Marsh Aerodrome, ... 116, 117
Motive power, ... 26, 70, 73, 74, 75, 76, 77, 80, 81, 83, 84, 85,
.... 90, 91, 94, 95, 96-107, 118, 133, 135, 137, 139, 142, 145,
.... 146, 273, 286, 296, 311, 318, 320, 323, 330, 332, 333-335,
.... 338, 339-342, 345, 348, 350, 351, 352, 353, 354, 355, 358, 360, 362
Napoleon III, Emperor of France, ... 264
Nationalisation, effects of, ... 337
Navvies, railway, ... 40-43, 53, 54
Newport, Abergavenny & Hereford Railway, ... 24
Nonconformity, religious, ... 30, 264, 356
Northampton & Banbury Junction Railway, ... 9, 34-36
Northern Aluminium Co, ... 314, 316
Notgrove, ... 39, 44, 48, 50, 52, 68, 70, 113, 115, 178-186, 339, 349, 359 et passim.
Ommanney, Octavius, B&CDR director, ... 38, 39
Overend, Gurney & Co, failure of, ... 34, 36
Oxford & Brentford Railway, proposed, ... 27
Oxford & Rugby Railway, ... 14, 15, 318, 324
Oxford Canal, the, ... 38, 58, 317, 318, 319, 323
Oxford, Witney, Cheltenham & Gloucester Railway, ... 27
Oxford, Worcester & Wolverhampton Railway, ... 9, 14-15, 16, 22, 24, 26, 27,
.... 28, 35, 193, 248, 275, 280, 342, 355
Oxfordshire Ironstone Co, ... 94, 117, 118, 343
Parnell, Charles Stewart (1846-91), at Chipping Norton, ... 258
Peto, Sir Samuel Morton (1809-89), contractor, ... 16, 17, 20, 22, 264
Piercy, Benjamin (1828-88), ... 290
Pole, Sir Felix, ... 213
Private owner wagons, ... 59, 80, 87, 94, 96, 131, 134, 135, 151, 154, 170,
.... 182, 190, 197, 202, 248-249, 250, 252, 253, 262,
.... 263, 295, 309 (see also 'Rolling stock')
Railway Mania, developments during, ... 13-15, 27, 28
Reed, George D., B&CDR director, ... 38
Rich, Francis H., Inspector of Railways, ... 25-26, 43-44, 53, 54, 56
Road feeder services, .. 108-114, 150, 169, 183-184, 193, 197, 229, 235, 255, 297, 299

Robertson, Henry (1816-88), ... 290
Rolling stock, freight, ... 59, 87-89, 91, 94, 95, 131, 134, 135, 151, 154, 162,
...... 170, 182, 190, 197, 215, 225, 248-249, 250, 252, 253, 262, 263, 295, 303, 309, 337
Rolling stock, passenger, ... 69, 74, 75, 77, 80, 81, 83, 84, 85, 102, 107,
.... 118, 180, 206, 212, 274, 333, 337, 340
Rollright Halt & Siding, ... 113, 267-272, 344, 354
Rollright Stone Circle, ... 267, 269
Roman occupation, the, ... 11, 54, 177, 178, 187, 296
Ross & Monmouth Railway, ... 36
Round Oak Steelworks, ... 275
Roy, Robert (1795-1873), ... 290
Royal trains, ... 118, 224-225
Rufford, Francis, OW&WR Chairman, ... 14
Russell, Sir William MP, EGR Chairman, ... 30, 31, 152
Salperton, ... 113, 178, 179
Sandywell Tunnel, ... 33, 38, 44, 48, 52-53, 60, 118, 164, 167, 360, 361
Sarsden Halt, ... 77, 107, 113, 232-237
Severn Junction Railway, ... 35
Signalling & signal cabins, ... 26, 44, 48, 52, 53, 68, 84, 70, 95, 106, 115, 120, 125,
..... 131, 134, 138-141, 143, 144, 147, 153, 154, 168, 169, 172, 174, 176, 177, 178, 180,
.... 181, 183, 185, 186, 199, 202, 207, 208, 213, 214, 215, 222, 226, 230, 233, 234, 235,
.... 236, 237, 239, 270, 283, 284, 285, 288, 289, 299, 301, 306, 308, 314, 315, 318,
.... 320, 324, 333, 337, 339, 342, 350, 354, 355, 358, 360, 362, 364 et passim.
Single line, operation of, ... 25, 26, 44, 52, 53, 68, 115, 176, 185, 196, 199,
.... 202, 208, 233, 342
Slaughters, Upper & Lower, ... 2, 113, 198
Smith, William (1769-1839), ... 235
South Wales & Cannock Chase Coal & Coke Co, ... 182
Stow Coal Company, ... 202
Stow-on-the-Wold, ... 23, 25, 26, 52, 53, 113, 198-206, 339, 350, 361 et passim.
Stratford-upon-Avon & Midland Junction Railway, ... 36, 344
Strickland, Walter, Witney Railway Chairman, ... 28, 30, 34
Swerford, ... 113, 273
Swindon & Cheltenham Extension Railway, ... 61
Swindon, Marlborough & Andover Railway, ... 61
Swinton & Knottingly Joint Railway, ... 81
Sydenham Sidings, ... 88, 317-318, 319
Syreford, ... 113, 177-178
Tadmarton, ... 113, 297, 299, 303
Tennyson, Alfred (1809-92), poet, ... 122
Toomer & Co, coal merchants, ... 232
Train services, ... 69, 71-72, 81-85, 87-88, 93, 94, 96, 103, 107-108, 337-339
Vernacular architecture, ... 187, 225, 288, 296, 302, 323
Vigoles, Charles Blacker (1793-1874), engineer, ... 63
Wade, Charles, coal merchant, ... 306, 309
Ward, William Humble (1867-1922), ... 274-275
Warwickshire Coal Co Ltd, ... 253
Watkin, Sir Edward (1819-1901), ... 63
Welsh Highland Railway, ... 293, 294, 362
Wessex, Kingdom of, ... 11, 206
West Midland Railway, ... 24-25, 28, 33, 187, 189, 193, 198-199
West of England textile industry, the, ... 12, 30, 261-264
Westfield, ... 113, 183
Wick Rissington, ... 113
Wilkinson, John, 1728-1808, ... 290
Wilkinson, Lt-Col J., B&CDR director, ... 39, 58
Wilson, Edward, B&CDR engineer, ... 36, 38
Wilson, John, B&CDR director, ... 58
Wilson, William, B&CDR engineer, ... 54, 56, 58
Windrush, River, ... 11, 79, 187, 193, 198, 264
Witley Court, ... 275
Witney Aerodrome, ... 116
Witney Railway, ... 28-29, 30
Witney, Burford & Andoversford Light Railway, ... 68
Woodhouse, George (1829-83), mill architect, ... 262
Worcester & Hereford Railway, ... 24
World War One, 75, ... 238, 247, 293-294, 303, 317
World War Two, ... 88, 115-117, 139, 141, 144, 145, 192, 193, 206, 209,
.... 256, 292, 297, 299, 302, 303, 314, 323, 325, 328, 330, 333, 343
Yolland, Colonel W., Inspector of Railways, ... 18
Yorke, Colonel H.A., Inspector of Railways, ... 178, 309

Cheltenham Leckhampton station in January 1965, looking west from under the Leckhampton Road bridge. *D.R. Lewis*

The car triumphant. Chipping Norton, 1970s. *The Lens of Sutton Collection*